Careful attention to Christian doctrine does not, in and of itself, produce deep devotion to our Lord Jesus, but such devotion can be expected to be served by a rich understanding of the universal scope of God's grace in Christ. With a view toward cultivating an ever- deepening love of God, daily devotional messages in book form have, in some measure, effectively served many individuals and families over the years.

In my humble opinion, though; in much such material, there has been an element of gospel distortion that can seriously mitigate the impact of the essential message that transforms human hearts and minds, namely, that God's love, and the purpose intrinsic to His love, will, without qualification, triumph over every enemy and all enmity until every knee bows in adoration before the Savior in Whom our Father has entrusted His eternal purpose.

Thomas Kissinger has been infused by the Spirit of God with a passion to make available a daily devotional that is free of those elements of contrariness to the true heart of the gospel of Christ that characterize much of conventional orthodoxy, and thereby free seeking hearts to know the God and Father of our Lord Jesus Christ as He really is. From this springs all true devotion to God and His cause. I am happy and honored to commend his labor of love to all my brethren in Christ looking for a book of daily devotionals as part of their spiritual discipline.

John R. Gavazzoni • Greater Emmanuel International Apostolic Team Ministries

This is a compelling work by Thomas Kissinger for whom I have tremendous respect. He understands that mankind needs inspiring words of Truth. This Daily Devotional will arrest your attention from the beginning. You cannot read it through one time and think you have it all figured out for underneath the top layer of truth are hidden more layers.

The author, with maturity beyond his years, has devoted himself to seeking out the best so the reader may have spiritual food every day.

*These pillars of **The Truth About God** will make you strong. I highly recommend everyone read what Thomas has for you each day.*

Dr. Harold Lovelace • Author, *Read And Search God's Plan*

The Glory Of God And The Honor Of Kings:
A Daily Devotional That Proclaims The Unlimited Love And Power Of God

Copyright © 2007 by Thomas M. Kissinger
Straightway Publishing Company

For further information, contact the author through Straightway Publishing Company

Published by:
Straightway Publishing Company
Post Office Box 45212 #261
Baton Rouge, LA. 70895
Email: tkissinger01@cox.net
(225) 766-0896

Book and cover design: Rich Baldwin

The Glory Of God And The Honor Of Kings:
A Daily Devotional That Proclaims The Unlimited Love And Power Of God
By Thomas M. Kissinger

1. Author 2. Title 3. Inspiration 4. Religion
Library of Congress Control Number: 2006904777
ISBN: 978-0-9785134-0-5 (Paperback)

Printed in the United States of America

THE GLORY OF GOD & THE HONOR OF KINGS

A DAILY DEVOTIONAL THAT PROCLAIMS
THE UNLIMITED LOVE AND POWER OF GOD

by

Thomas M. Kissinger

Straightway Publishing Company
Baton Rouge, Louisiana

To my wife Sarah, and our children Moriah, Makayla, and Micah. I love you all with all my heart!

To Dr. Harold Lovelace. Thank you for your stand for truth, and for inspiring me to put on paper the things that God has put in my heart!

To Louis Thompson. Your dedication to the things of the Lord has inspired me more than you will ever know. Thank you for teaching me of a position of testimony in Christ that will set the captive free. I hope to pass on God's divine nature and power to all I come in contact with!

To all those who have dared to seek for truth in a world darkened by the traditions and doctrines of men!

To Thomas St.Amant and Mary Cage. Thank you for your many hours of editing!

INCLUDING QUOTES AND EXCERPTS FROM THE FOLLOWING PEOPLE:

THOMAS ALLIN
GEORGE HAWTIN
J. PRESTON EBY
MARTIN ZENDER
RAY KNIGHT
LOUIS ABBOTT
A.P. ADAMS
GARY AMIRAULT
DR. ADAM CLARKE
A.C.THOMAS
DR. HAROLD LOVELACE
ORIGEN
CLEMENT OF ALEXANDRIA
GREGORY OF NYSSA
S. AMBROSE MILAN
NATHANIEL SCARLETT
BILL BRITTON
WILLIAM BARCLAY
ROBERT BURGESS
DR. LOYAL HURLEY
ABRAHAM LINCOLN
GEORGE ADDAIR
RAY PRINZING
J.W. HANSON
REV. DR. WHITBY
DR E.W. BULLINGER
DR. IVAN PANIN
HANNAH WHITALL SMITH
DR. STEPHEN JONES
JOHN GAVAZZONI
ALEXANDER POPE
KEN ECKERTY
JUDY VANDERBURG
JOSEPH ROTHERHAM
EMMET FOX
ELWIN R. ROACH
A.E. KNOCH
JOSEPH E. KIRK
KELLEY VARNER
DEREK CALDER
JOHN AYTO
MILES COVERDALE
MILLAR BURROWS
GEORGE MACDONALD
CHARLES PRIDGEON
ROBERT BEECHAM

UNIVERSALIST CHRISTIAN ASSOCIATION
KEITH NEWMAN
JIM RUTZ
BOB EVELY
DR. CHAPMAN
DR. ALLEN
DR. FIRBAIRN
EDWARD LEIGH
PROF. STUART
DR. THAYER
DR. CAMPBELL
LE CLERE
FLAVIUS JOSEPHUS
CANNON FARRAR
L. RAY SMITH
RANDY BONACORSO
ANDREW TELFORD
CHARLES SLAGLE
THOMAS B. THAYER
LLOYD ELLEFSON
OTIS SKINNER

SUGGESTED READING:

THE BIBLE, GOD

THE SECOND DEATH AND THE RESTITUTION OF ALL THINGS, ANDREW JUKES

THE BIBLE HELL, J.W. HANSON

THEOLOGY OF UNIVERSALISM, THOMAS B. THAYER

READ AND SEARCH GOD'S PLAN, DR. HAROLD LOVELACE

THE WRITINGS OF BILL BRITTON

THE WRITINGS OF J. PRESTON EBY

THE WRITINGS OF DR. STEPHEN JONES

THE WRITINGS OF RAY PRINZING

THE WRITINGS OF JOHN GAVAZZONI

THE WRITINGS OF A.P. ADAMS

THE WRITINGS OF GEORGE HAWTIN

THE WRITINGS OF RAY KNIGHT

THE WRITINGS OF CARLTON PEARSON

THE WRITINGS OF L. RAY SMITH

THE WRITINGS OF DR. E.W. BULLINGER

THE WRITINGS OF GARY AMIRAULT

THE WRITINGS OF ORIGEN

AN ANALYTICAL STUDY OF WORDS, LOUIS ABBOTT

CHRIST TRIUMPHANT, THOMAS ALLIN

THE WRITINGS OF CHARLES PRIDGEON

ABOUT THE AUTHOR

Thomas Kissinger came to Christ at age 20 on the night of May 7th, 1994. His conversion took place on the campus of Louisiana State University. It was on the corner of Chimes Street that he was approached by two men who handed him a piece of literature about God's love. Having already been drawn by the Lord a few days earlier to surrender his life, he sensed that this was no accident but a divine appointment to repent and believe on the Lord Jesus Christ. The next day he went to Family Worship Center in Baton Rouge, Louisiana. There he experienced for the first time in his life a delivering presence of God. Two weeks later he was baptized with the Holy Spirit and launched into a journey of seeking the One Who had sought and found him. He was ordained to the ministry on the 2nd day of July, 1997 and began the work of the ministry in the local prisons. In 2001 he had a dramatic revelation from the Lord concerning the reconciliation of all things. This glorious revelation did drastically change his life and ministry from that moment on.

GRAND STATEMENT

> *It is the Glory of God to conceal a thing:*
> *but the honor of kings is to search out a matter.*
>
> Proverbs 25:2

FOR ALL OF YOU WHO SEE YOURSELVES AS KINGS
AND PRIESTS UNTO GOD…

SEARCH OUT THE DEEP THINGS OF GOD.
SEARCH OUT THE TREASURE OF GOD'S TRUTH BURIED
UNDER THE RHETORIC OF MAN'S RELIGIONS.

SEEK AND YOU SHALL FIND!

INTRODUCTION

The spirit of prejudice stands in the way of all new views of truth. Prejudice has been defined as "a judgment or opinion formed without due examination of the facts or reasons that are essential to a just and impartial determination." It is prejudice that blinds the eye, stops the ear, misunderstands and misinterprets everything that comes its way. Its state of mind is not founded on facts but on some feeling of dislike or something of self-interest. There are those who will not accept any truth unless it is ministered in a certain conventional manner or supported by certain great names. Prejudice stands in the way of even a conservative and constructive advance. May God's Holy Spirit alone be our teacher.

Charles Pridgeon

January

February

March

April

May

June

1   THE LORD'S PRAYER - PART 6

2   THE LORD'S PRAYER - PART 7

3   THE LORD'S PRAYER - PART 8

4   THE LORD'S PRAYER - PART 9

5   THE LORD'S PRAYER - PART 10

6   READ ROMANS CHAPTER 5... I DARE YOU!

7   PHILIPPIANS CHAPTER 3 (THE PROCESS OF SALVATION)

8   ALL IN ALL POEM

9   PURE RELIGION

10   DAMN "<u>?</u>"

11   UNDERSTANDING SCRIPTURE

12   WHAT GOD HATES

13   NOTORIOUS SINNERS

14   UNBELIEF

15   PECULIAR PEOPLE

16   ARE YOU PREJUDICED?

17   DUNG

18   MATTHEW, MARK, LUKE, AND JOHN

19   WE THE FOLLOWING PROCLAIM

20   #1 GOD THE CREATOR LOVES

21   #2 JESUS CHRIST THE SON OF GOD

22   #3 THE TRUSTWORTHINESS OF THE BIBLE

23   #4 CERTAIN, JUST RETRIBUTION

24   #5 THE FINAL HARMONY OF ALL SOULS WITH GOD

25   THE MYSTERIES OF GOD

26   THE MYSTERY OF BABYLON

27   THE MYSTERY OF INIQUITY

28   THE MYSTERY OF GODLINESS

29   THE MYSTERY OF OUR CHANGE

30   THE MYSTERY OF HIS WILL

July

August

September

October

November

December

January 1

O WRETCHED MAN THAT I AM

Romans 7:18 gives us one of the most important revelations in the Bible. It states…For I know that in me (that is in my flesh,) dwells no good thing: for to will is present with me; but how to perform that which is good I find not…

What a statement! What an honest confession! What a revelation! In fact, this is the revelation of all revelations! This revelation tops the list!

Understanding this scripture is equivalent to the moment at which a pregnant mother's water breaks, for then she knows that the baby is on its way and sure to be born. After we come to an understanding that in our flesh dwells no good thing, we are surely on our way to delivering and birthing the very Christ-life. We must know what we are up against. We must identify our enemy. It is US!!! It is our flesh, our carnal mind, and the sin nature that we inherited from Adam. We inherited a corrupt nature that continually comes short of the glory of God. Realizing that our carnal mind is the enemy of God is probably about 98% of the battle (the other 2% being… realizing that God's divine nature is our power source, and learning to partake of His divine nature). Romans 8:6,7 states…For to be carnally minded IS DEATH; but to be spiritually minded is life and peace. Because the CARNAL MIND IS ENMITY AGAINST GOD: for it is not subject to the law of God, neither indeed can be…This revelation on the surface seems to be very discouraging and could leave us with no hope. It causes a person to say…O WRETCHED MAN THAT I AM! WHO SHALL DELIVER ME FROM THE BODY OF THIS DEATH? That is a good question that we must ask ourselves. We must then see ourselves as wretched outside of the life of God, but we are not left without hope. The apostle Paul said that we are to thank God through Jesus Christ our Lord. Thank Him for what?

Romans 8:1,2 states…There is therefore now no condemnation to them which are in Christ Jesus…vs. 2…For the law of the Spirit of life in Christ Jesus HAS MADE ME FREE FROM THE LAW OF SIN AND DEATH…We are to see ourselves as no longer under condemnation, IN CHRIST, walking after the Spirit, and FREE. Once you know the bad news, that there is no good thing in your flesh, you can have your eyes opened to the GOOD NEWS, which is IN CHRIST JESUS our Lord.

REJOICE AND BE THANKFUL!

January 2

REASON, THE EARLY CHURCH FATHERS, AND THE HOLY SCRIPTURES
(The above theme taken from: <u>Christ Triumphant</u>, Thomas Allin)

It is impossible to establish a system of beliefs without at least three very important things. These three things are:

1. Reason
2. The Early Church Fathers
3. The Holy Scriptures

Those who study the Bible will notice the harmony of these three things. Let us take a look at each one of the above mentioned aspects. This will enable us to properly formulate a sound system of beliefs in God.

1. As far as reason is concerned, Isaiah 1:18 states…Come now, and let us REASON together, says the Lord: though your sins be as scarlet, they shall be as white as snow; though they be red like crimson, they shall be as wool. The word "reason" means: to debate a case in court. The connotation of legal confrontation is clearly attached to this word. You must confront your beliefs and put them to the test! Don't just simply believe something because everyone else does! Find out the truth for yourself!

2. Let us take a look at what some of the most respected early church Fathers believed.

"We assert that the Word, Who is the wisdom of God, shall bring together all intelligent creatures, and convert them into His own perfection, through the instrumentality of their free will and of their own exertions. The Word is more powerful then all the diseases of the soul, and He applies His remedies to each one according to the pleasure of God - for the name of God is to be invoked by all, so that all shall serve Him with one consent." (Origen)

"The Son breaking in pieces His enemies is for the sake of remolding them." (Origen)

"All men are Christ's, some by knowing Him, the others not yet. He by the Father's will directs the salvation of all." (Clement of Alexandria)

"He saves all universally, but some are converted by punishment, others by voluntary submission." (Clement of Alexandria)

"Everything shall be subdued to Christ, and they shall be subdued by a full knowledge of Him and by a remodeling." (Gregory of Nyssa)

"All punishments are means of purification, ordained by divine love to purge rational beings from moral evil and to restore them back to communion with God…God would not have permitted the experience of hell unless He had foreseen through redemption, that all rational beings would, in the end, attain to the same blessed fellowship with Himself." (Gregory of Nyssa)

3. When a proper study is done of the Holy Scriptures, it will become undeniable that the truth of a universal salvation is taught and was purchased by the Lord Jesus Christ.

The scriptures speak of Jesus having saved:

All Men
Every Man

All Families
All Flesh
All Nations
All Things
The World
The Whole World
The Entire Creation

ENJOY YOUR SEARCH!

January 3

OVERCOMERS

He that has an ear to hear, let him hear what the Spirit says unto the churches; To him that overcomes will I...This statement is made several times in the book of Revelation. It can be found at: Revelation 2:7, 2:11, 2:17, 2:26, 3:5, 3:12, 3:21, and also in chapters 11, 12, 13, 17, 21. Obviously God wants us to be overcomers. The promises in the book of Revelation are made to the overcomers only. Don't you think that we should look into this overcomer thing?

Here is a series of scriptures that will shed some light on the idea of overcoming. Colossians 1:16 tells us that Jesus Christ created all things, including, thrones, dominions, principalities, and powers. Colossians 2:14 tells us that Jesus blotted out the handwriting of ordinances (the law) that was against us...nailing it to His cross; HAVING SPOILED PRINCIPALITIES AND POWERS, HE MADE A SHOW OF THEM OPENLY, TRIUMPHING OVER THEM IN IT. Ephesians 6:12 tells us that we wrestle not against flesh and blood, but against PRINCIPALITIES, AGAINST POWERS, AGAINST THE RULERS OF THE DARKNESS OF THIS WORLD, AGAINST SPIRITUAL WICKEDNESS IN HIGH PLACES...

I thought that Jesus defeated principalities (rulers) and powers (authorities)? HE DID! NOW IT IS YOUR TURN! Jesus created all things, overcame all things, and then left all things for us to have to overcome. How could we be overcomers if there was nothing to overcome?

This is the reason for God creating good and evil and subjecting the creation to it. This was done that we might learn to be overcomers. We must understand that overcoming is not an activity, but a position (spiritually speaking). THIS POSITION IS IN CHRIST! The next logical question would be...where is Christ? For we must see that we are positioned in Who Christ is and what He has accomplished. Ephesians 1:20,21 says that...the Christ is in heavenly places, far above all principality, and power, and might, and dominion, and every name that is named. Ephesians 2:6 says that...God has raised us up together, and MADE US SIT TOGETHER IN HEAVENLY PLACES IN CHRIST JESUS...

This heavenly place is not a physical location, but a place in the Spirit that gives us a heavenly mind, WHICH ENABLES US TO OVERCOME. How do we get to this place? SIMPLY BELIEVE! Believe what? Believe on the Lord Jesus Christ. That is what makes you a believer and an overcomer. Believe what the Bible says about you. You are dead to the old man and alive to the new creation man by FAITH IN CHRIST. This is the victory that OVERCOMES THE WORLD, EVEN OUR FAITH. WHO IS HE THAT OVERCOMES THE WORLD, BUT HE THAT BELIEVES THAT JESUS IS THE SON OF GOD (1ST John 5:4,5)?…Without faith it is impossible to please God (Hebrews 11:6). YOU ARE IN CHRIST! BELIEVE IT! YOU ARE AN OVERCOMER!

BELIEVE, RECEIVE, AND WALK IT!

January 4

MY TESTIMONY

Many people think of their testimony in terms of how many bad things they once did, comparing that to how many good things that they do now. God definitely uses that type of preaching, but that is not really our testimony. Revelation 12:11 states…and they overcame him (Satan) by the blood of the Lamb, and by the word of their testimony; and they loved not their lives unto the death…Revelation 1:2 also speaks of the testimony of Jesus Christ.

The word "testimony" means a witness or a martyr. Let us now formulate a proper understanding of what it is to have a testimony, or THE TESTIMONY OF JESUS CHRIST. It speaks of being a witness to the cleansing blood of Jesus. As well, it speaks of a laying down of one's life (a martyr, whether physically or spiritually). OUR TESTIMONY IS THAT WE IDENTIFY WITH CHRIST, BEING IN CHRIST AND HE IN US! WE ARE WITNESSES TO HIS LIFE-CHANGING POWER! Our testimony is clearly stated in Revelation 12:11. It is the blood of the Lamb and that we love not our lives unto the death of self. Doesn't that sound familiar?

How about:

… lose your life for His name's sake…
… lay down your life for your friends…
… make yourself of no reputation…

Our testimony is THE CHRIST-LIFE INSIDE OF US. IT IS CHRIST IN US THE HOPE OF GLORY! It is the death of self and the manifested life of Christ. Jesus, Who was God manifested in the flesh, was a witness to the Father, becoming a martyr for the sin of the world. We must drink of the same cup. We are witnesses for Jesus and His Kingdom. This causes us to become a martyr in the Spirit, loving not our lives unto the death. We are of course speaking of the death of the self-life. We are called to take on the same testimony that Jesus had. WE HAVE THE TESTIMONY OF JESUS CHRIST! Jesus overcame, causing us to be overcomers in Him. WHAT A TESTIMONY!

THIS IS THE WORD OF OUR TESTIMONY!

January 5

THE BATTLE AND THE FIGHT

It is interesting to note that the Bible makes a distinction between man finding himself in a battle and a fight. It is important to understand the nature of our battle and of our fight. Those who understand the difference between these two will continually find themselves walking in the Spirit. The opposite of walking in the Spirit is a life of continually frustrating the grace of God. 1st Samuel 17:47 states, concerning David's encounter with Goliath…And all this assembly shall know that the Lord saves not with sword and spear: FOR THE BATTLE IS THE LORD'S, and HE will give you into our hands…Now let us consider what the apostle Paul told Timothy concerning the fight in which mankind finds himself. 1st Timothy 6:12 states…FIGHT THE GOOD FIGHT OF FAITH, lay hold on eternal life (the life of the ages)…

We are here faced with two things:

1. THE BATTLE
2. THE FIGHT

We are told that the battle is the Lord's and that the good fight of faith is ours. So as we can see, God plays a part and we play a part. The purpose of the ages is one that involves God and man, or you could say that it is the purpose of God to be manifested in and through mankind (the human race). In order for this to take place, God must perform that which only He is capable of doing. We are then called upon to recognize and participate in what God has provided.

Here are three key ingredients to a victorious walk in God:

1. THE BATTLE IS THE LORD'S…
2. THE FIGHT IS OURS…
3. THE FAITH IS GOD'S GIFT TO US…
(… God has dealt to every man the measure of faith…Romans 12:3)

Here is a grand revelation that you should take to heart. It is worthy of much meditation. THE GOOD FIGHT OF FAITH, WHICH IS OURS, IS TO CONTINUALLY BELIEVE THAT THE BATTLE IS THE LORD'S!!! Let this thought become more than just mere words to you. Let it sink down deep into your spirit. It must become a way of life for you and a part of your thought process. This revelation allows you to rest, causing God to work on you, in you, and through you. This is what it means to labor (be diligent) to enter into His rest. Every thought, situation, trial, and tribulation must be diligently offered up to God in faith, believing that God will always fight your battles for you. THIS IS VICTORY AND PEACE IN THE MIDST OF THE STORM!

FIGHT THE GOOD FIGHT OF FAITH!

January 6

DESTRUCTION

1st Corinthians 3:17 states…if any man defile the temple of God, him shall God destroy; for the temple of God is holy, which temple you are…The word "destroy" means: to waste, ruin, shrivel, wither, defile, to reduce a thing to useless fragments, and to extinguish. Now let us seek to understand what is meant when the Bible speaks of destruction, for the real question is, what is it that is going to be destroyed (as far as man is concerned)?

You must put on the mind of Christ to be able to grasp Bible terminology. The destruction that is going to take place in man is to be understood in a spiritual sense. Here is a quote from S. Ambrose of Milan (390 A.D.) concerning the topic of destruction…"What then, hinders our believing that he who is beaten small as the dust is not annihilated, BUT IS CHANGED FOR THE BETTER: so that instead of an earthy man, he is made a spiritual man, and our believing that he who is destroyed, is so destroyed that ALL TAINT IS REMOVED, and there remains what is pure and clean." This topic of destruction is further clarified in 1st Corinthians 5:5 that states…to deliver such a one unto Satan FOR THE DESTRUCTION OF THE FLESH, THAT THE SPIRIT MAY BE SAVED IN THE DAY OF THE LORD…

Now we can see that God wants our flesh (carnality) to be destroyed. That which is to be destroyed is NOT THE PERSON, but the flesh, the carnal mind, and the sin nature which separates us from the knowledge of God. God destroys the propensity within the sinner to sin, but He does not destroy the person himself. He destroys the wickedness in the wicked person, which in turn destroys the wicked. You could also say that God destroys the desire of the wicked, which in turn destroys His enemies, not that they cease to exist, BUT THAT THEY CEASE TO BE HIS ENEMIES!!!

So what is the result of the destruction of the flesh? The result is THAT THE SPIRIT WILL BE SAVED IN THE DAY OF THE LORD! AWESOME!

We must ALL have the man of sin in us DESTROYED by the brightness of His coming (presence). God must destroy, burn up, and consume the wood, hay, and stubble within man. This causes the gold, silver, and precious stones of the Spirit of God to be PURIFIED within us, making us partakers of the divine nature. Thank God for the…

DESTRUCTION OF THE FLESH!

January 7

WHY THE NEED FOR OPPOSITES?
(This theme taken from: <u>Read and Search God's Plan</u>, Dr. Harold Lovelace)

It is important to realize and recognize THAT WE LEARN ABOUT SOMETHING FROM ITS OPPOSITE. That is why God created opposing forces. Isaiah 45:7 states…I (God) form the light, and create darkness: I make peace and create evil: I the Lord do all these things…YES…God is responsible for having created ALL things, including things that do oppose one another. Some others to consider are: bitter and sweet, sorrow and joy, darkness and light, good and evil, law and grace, natural things and spiritual things, death and life, and bondage and freedom. Why would God create such drastic opposing forces?

We must see that it was necessary for God to create these opposites in order to teach us of His ways. How could we know what good is if there were no such thing as evil? We must recognize God's ways, His dealings with the creation, and His process of revealing His nature in man. So many times we pray for God to do something in our lives and then fight against Him when He brings us what we prayed for. WHY? We do this because we don't understand His ways. We don't understand His use of opposites to teach us. If you ask God to make you a loving person, He will expose you to hate. He does this that you might see hate and love for what they are and what they produce, whether in your life or in the life of someone else. That is just one example. There are many others that will prove the same point, as you are well aware.

It is impossible to learn something in God without being aware of its opposite. Let us humble ourselves and become aware of God's ways, understanding His use of opposites to mold us and make us into His image.

WHAT A GREAT AND WISE GOD WE SERVE!

January 8

LET EVERYTHING THAT HAS BREATH PRAISE THE LORD!

This scripture (Psalm 150:6), like many others in the Bible, speaks of the whole creation praising and worshiping God its Creator. It points to a reconciliation and restoration of all things. Here is a quote from Gregory of Nyssa on this very topic…"Such is the meaning of this final Psalm, in which after the complete abolition of sin, praise shall be sung to God; which praise contain (implies) our being incapable of turning to sin, when every created being shall be harmonized into one choir, and when, like a cymbal, the reasonable creation, and that which is now severed by sin, shall pour forth a pleasing strain, due to mutual harmony. Then comes the praise of every spirit forever, abounding with increase unto eternity."

WOW! What an incredible statement! What an insight this man had into the purpose and plan of God! Let us catch the fire of his zeal and love for the whole creation! We must understand that God is interested in nothing less THAN THE DELIVERANCE OF THE ENTIRE CREATION. THIS WILL INCLUDE EVERY PERSON WHO HAS EVER LIVED OR WILL EVER LIVE. ALL SHALL PRAISE GOD!

Another scripture which testifies to this grand truth is Revelation 5:13, which states…And every creature which is in heaven, and on the earth, and such as are in the sea, and all that are in them, heard I saying, Blessing, and honor, and glory, and power, be unto Him that sits upon the throne, and unto the Lamb for ever and ever (unto the ages of the ages)…

ALL SHALL PRAISE HIS NAME!

January 9

I WILL ALSO ASK OF YOU ONE QUESTION

Mark 11:29 quotes Jesus as saying…I will also ask of you one question, and answer Me, and I will tell you by what authority I do these things…In verse 28 Jesus is asked a question by the chief priests, the scribes, and the elders. They were always trying to find a way to trap Jesus in His own words, even though they never did succeed. It is worth noting, however, that Jesus answered their many questions. MOST OF THE TIME JESUS ANSWERED THEIR QUESTIONS WITH A QUESTION. Why this method of answering a question with a question? That is a good question. This was done for one simple reason. GOD'S NUMBER ONE GOAL IS TO ENGAGE MAN INTO THE PROCESS OF THINKING OR MEDITATING UPON HIM. As long as we are talking and not listening, thinking, or meditating, we are not learning. It would have been useless to answer most of the silly questions that Jesus had been asked. He knew the answers but refused to answer them. His method of answering a question with a question pricked the hearts of His listeners, causing them to search their own hearts and motives. In many cases it exposed their wicked ways to them, causing them to humbly walk away and ponder things they had never previously thought of. INSTEAD OF TRAPPING JESUS, THEY WERE TRAPPED! Because of God's infinite love, grace, and mercy, HE LOVINGLY TRAPS ALL OF US INTO THINKING UPON HIM. He does this for He knows the outcome. He knows that as we think upon Him, that we shall know the truth, and the truth shall…

MAKE US FREE!

January 10

THINK IT NOT STRANGE

It is built into the Adamic Nature of man to think it is some strange thing every time he goes through a trial, whether it be mental, physical, social, or otherwise. That is why the Lord gave this awesome revelation to the apostle Peter, which states…Beloved, think it not strange concerning the fiery trial which is to try you, as though some strange thing happened to you: But rejoice, inasmuch as you are partakers of Christ's sufferings; that, when His glory shall be revealed, you may be glad also with exceeding joy (1st Peter 4:12)…WHAT A MUCH NEEDED WORD FROM GOD! Man in his carnal state needs to be assured that God loves him and is not mad at him. This passage of scripture gives us confidence in knowing that:

God is the One Who initiates our trials…

GOD IS THE FIRE that we go through…

God wants us to go through the fire…

Going through the CONSUMING FIRE OF GOD is the very thing that makes us into His image, for it is HIS FIRE that consumes our wood, hay, and stubble (carnal mind).

As a result of going through fiery trials, we become like Him, and do qualify to rule and reign with Him now and in the ages to come.

Here are some more scriptures that bring out this great truth…

Hebrews 12:6-7 states…whom the Lord loves He chastens, and scourges every son whom He receives. If you endure chastening, God deals with you as with sons…
(Read also Hebrews 12:6-13)

Hebrews 2:10 states…the captain of our salvation was made perfect through suffering..

Hebrews 5:8 states…Jesus learned obedience through the things He suffered…

2nd Timothy 2:12 states…If we suffer with Him, we shall also reign with Him…

James 1:2,3 states…count it ALL JOY when you fall into divers temptations…the trying of your faith works patience…

James 1:12 states…Blessed is the man that endures temptation: for when he is tried, he shall receive the crown of life, which the Lord has promised to them that love Him…

Romans 5:3 states…we glory in tribulations also: knowing that tribulation works patience; and patience experience; and experience, hope… (WHAT A REVELATION!)

COUNT IT ALL JOY!

January 11

WHAT IS DEATH?

Matthew 8:22 is perhaps one of the most informative, interesting, and profound statements that Jesus made. It states…But Jesus said unto him, follow me; and let the dead bury their dead…Have you ever really stopped and thought about what is being said here? The question that must be asked is, have you ever seen someone who is physically dead bury someone else who is physically dead? I DON'T THINK SO! So what was Jesus referring to in His statement? It becomes obvious that Jesus was referring to spiritual and physical death. We are now able to come to the conclusion that death is first and foremost something that is spiritual, which then leads to a death that is physical. But remember, IT IS FIRST AND FOREMOST A SPIRITUAL DEATH! We must understand that physical death is only a final manifestation of a spiritual condition in which man finds himself in. So…What is death?

The beautiful aspect of the Bible is that it interprets itself. So let us look to the Bible for the exact definition of what death is. Romans 8:6 states…FOR TO BE CARNALLY MINDED IS DEATH…In other words, they are one in the same thing. So what is the carnal mind? The carnal mind speaks of and means: the corrupt nature, the mind that we inherited from Adam, the Adamic Nature, the sin nature, or the flesh. We must remember that the Bible does refer to man as being DEAD IN SINS AND TRESPASSES. Understanding this will also help us to comprehend what it means to perish, or to be found in a perished condition. When scripture speaks of God, Who is not willing that any should perish, it is referring to this very thing (the carnal mind). It is stating that God is not willing for any one of us to remain in the perished condition in which we currently find ourselves. Once again, this perished condition in which man is born into (subjected to by God) is THE CARNAL MIND (DEATH). In essence, this is what we are BEING saved from. So what is it that saves us? THE LIFE OF JESUS CHRIST, OF COURSE! We are being saved through death to HIS LIFE. This is all made possible by the life, death, burial, and resurrection of the Lord Jesus Christ, FOR HE IS LIFE! IN HIM WE LIVE, AND MOVE, AND HAVE OUR BEING (Acts 17:28)…God is not willing that any of us should remain in the perished condition of death (the carnal mind), but that we would be AWAKENED to His ABUNDANT LIFE!

ARISE, OH CHILD OF GOD!

January 12

OVERCOMING EVIL WITH GOOD

Romans 12:21 states…Be not overcome of evil, but overcome evil with good…This all-important scripture, which speaks of the triumph of all that is good over all that is evil, gives us insight into the method of Almighty God. This method must also become our method. God must ultimately triumph over evil, or it must be said that evil has triumphed over God. PLEASE THINK ABOUT THIS! Here is a quote from <u>Christ Triumphant</u> (by Thomas Allin) to further establish this great point…"The question of universalism is usually argued on a basis altogether misleading, as though the point involved was chiefly, or wholly, man's endless suffering. Odious and repulsive to every moral instinct, as is that dogma, it is not the turning point of this controversy. The vital question is this, that the popular creed by teaching the perpetuity of evil, points to a victorious Devil, and to sin as finally triumphant over God. It makes the corrupt, nay, the bestial in our fallen nature to be eternal. It represents what is foulest and most loathsome in man, the most obstinate sin as being enduring as God Himself. It confers the dignity of immortal life on what is morally abominable. It teaches perpetual anarchy and a final chaos. It enthrones pandemonium as an eternal fact side by side with Paradise; and, gazing over its fetid and obscene abysses, it is not afraid to call this the triumph of Jesus Christ, this the realization of the promise that God shall be ALL IN ALL." (Thomas Allin)

If God is willing to cure all the evils of mankind, but is not able, this is an indictment against the power of God, and surely makes the thought of overcoming evil with good only wishful thinking at best. If God is able to cure all the evils of mankind, but is not willing, this is an indictment against the love of God, and surely makes Him out to be a cruel Creator and a hypocrite as well, FOR HE TOLD US TO LOVE OUR ENEMIES, BUT WILL TORTURE HIS ENEMIES FOREVER.

Let us shout from the mountaintops that GOD IS ABLE AND WILLING TO OVERCOME ALL EVIL WITH GOOD. To proclaim anything less than a salvation of all men, every man in his own order, is to declare Satan (the adversary) as King of Kings and Lord of Lords, making the cross (the atonement) of Jesus Christ a failed attempt to reconcile a lost world back to the Father again.

OUR GOD IS ABLE! OUR GOD IS WILLING!

January 13

THE PURPOSE (PLAN) OF THE AGES

Hebrews 1:2 states…God has in these last days spoken unto us by His Son, Whom He has appointed heir of all things, by Whom also He made the worlds…The English word "worlds" in this passage comes from the Greek word "aion" in its plural form, meaning AGES. This passage of scripture should have been properly translated…by Whom also He made the AGES…As we have just stated, the word "aion" means an age or ages, referring to a period or periods of TIME, whether short or long. The word "worlds" in this passage is a bad translation, not properly conveying or bringing out the correct meaning of the word "aion". With this in mind, let us now absorb what is being stated here in this passage.

This scripture states that Jesus Christ made the ages. We must understand that God's plan is a plan of ages which does have a beginning and an ending. Having an understanding of God's plan of the ages will set you free from the empty teachings of religion, which offers no explanation of God having any PURPOSE for the creation, whether it be past, present, or future. What is God's plan of the ages? Does He have a PURPOSE and a plan? Here is a quote from Nathaniel Scarlett which addresses this very subject…"There are dispensations of salvation and restoration - these should not be confounded together: the scripture distinguishes them. The saved are represented as that they shall not come into condemnation, shall have a part in the first resurrection, shall reign in life with Christ, shall be priests or communicators of divine grace to others, having received abundance of grace for that purpose: whereas the restored will be condemned, cast into the lake of fire and brimstone (a spiritual fire for the purpose of divine purification) in the future age of judgment, wherein they will receive many or few stripes (spiritually speaking) in proportion to their criminality, and until subdued they shall not see the light: thus God may truly be said to be THE RESTORER OF ALL MEN, ESPECIALLY OF THE FAITHFUL." (Nathaniel Scarlett)

Once you can grasp the concept of ages and dispensations, including those that are still yet to come (Ephesians 2:7), you will see that God's punishments, judgments, and wrath are for a period of time, but not forever. They are for the purpose of correction and are age-lasting, or it could be said that they are "of the ages" ("aionios"). GOD'S WRATH AND MAN'S TORMENT ARE NOT FOREVER, BUT AGE-LASTING!

WHAT A LOVING GOD!!!

His purpose of the ages begins with Adam and ends when HIS CONSUMING LAKE OF FIRE has burned up all the wood, hay, and stubble in every man, for this is the SECOND DEATH. The good news is that the LAST ENEMY THAT SHALL BE DESTROYED IS DEATH, INCLUDING THE SECOND DEATH, WHICH IS DEATH AND HELL CAST INTO THE LAKE OF FIRE. The lake of fire (God's consuming fire) is THE DEATH OF DEATH. It is the end of death and hell (the carnal mind and the triumph of the grave), SIGNIFYING THE TIME WHEN GOD SHALL BE ALL IN ALL!!!

Here is a list of the recognized DISPENSATIONS that are to be found contained within the AGES of time:

1. INNOCENCE
2. CONSCIENCE
3. HUMAN GOVERNMENT
4. PROMISE
5. LAW
6. GRACE (ALSO RECOGNIZED AS CHURCH)
7. KINGDOM (ALSO RECOGNIZED AS THE MILLENNIUM)
8. THE DISPENSATION OF THE FULLNESS OF TIMES (ALSO REFERRED TO AS THE AGE OF THE AGES)

Let God show you the awesomeness of HIS BEAUTIFUL PURPOSE! It consists of:

1. FORMER AGES (COLOSSIANS 1:26)
2. THE PRESENT AGE (MATTHEW 12:32)
3. THE APPROACHING AGE (MARK 10:30)

4. AGES TO COME (EPHESIANS 2:7)
5. THE END OF THE AGE (MATTHEW 28:20)
6. THE ENDS OF THE AGES (1ST CORINTHIANS 10:11)

HIS PURPOSE (PLAN) OF THE AGES IS BIGGER THAN YOU HAVE EVER IMAGINED!

January 14

THE LAW OF CIRCULARITY
(This theme and quotes taken from: The Law of Circularity, J. Preston Eby)

The following passages of scripture are key verses that unlock the idea or thought of the pre-existence of man. When we say pre-existence, we are of course meaning that man was first created in the spirit realm before being placed and subjected in and to the physical realm (notice Genesis 1:26-28 and Genesis 2:7). In essence, we were with God in the beginning, before our physical birth, coming out from Him. Please notice the following verses.

Psalm 90:1-3 states…Lord, You have been our dwelling place IN ALL GENERATIONS. BEFORE THE MOUNTAINS WERE BROUGHT FORTH, OR EVER YOU HAD FORMED THE EARTH AND THE WORLD, EVEN FROM EVERLASTING (AGE) TO EVERLASTING (AGE), YOU ARE GOD. You turn man to destruction; and say, RETURN, you children of men…

Romans 11:36 states…For OF Him, and THROUGH Him, and TO Him, are ALL THINGS…

Romans 11:36 (Amplified Version) states…For FROM Him and THROUGH Him and TO Him are ALL THINGS - for all things originate with Him and come from Him; all things live through Him, and all things center in and tend to consummate and to end in Him…

Let us now try to summarize what is being said from these scripture passages. These verses tell us that mankind has its origin in God, and that ALL came from God. He is the Father of us ALL! It shows us the pre-existence of man. We were with God in the beginning, before time began, before the purpose of the ages was put into motion. We are then to derive that mankind was subjected to vanity, not willingly (Romans 8:20), in order to go through the purpose of the ages, and to be made in the image of God (for this is to be seen as a process). And finally, mankind (including ALL THINGS) shall be reconciled unto God in the dispensation of the fullness of times, for God shall be ALL IN ALL (Colossians 1:20, Ephesians 1:10, 1st Corinthians 15:28).

Have you ever considered the following words that begin with the prefix "re": REturn, REstoration, REnew, REdemption, REconciliation, REsurrection, and REpent??? The prefix "re" means back again, or anew. It speaks of something that left its place of origin and has now made its circuit and come back to the point of its beginning.

According to J. Preston Eby: "The entire universe is an infinite sphere and each galaxy's solar system, star and planet within it moves continuously and harmoniously in circular motion, thus, all worlds and suns have circles for their pathway. This principle has been referred to by scientists as the "LAW OF CIRCULARITY." There is no such thing in the universe as an absolutely straight line of infinite length. All straight lines will be found to be portions of immense circles. Someone has said (a scientist) that if we were to build a telescope that could see into infinity, we would one day be looking at the back of our heads. We must see that this is also true of God's dealings with His whole creation. All that existed in Christ before the ages began, shall return into Him again that He may be the first and the last, the beginning and the end. All that came out of Him, lowered into the realm of the negative, completes its circuit and returns once more to its former estate - IN GOD! The first Adam had power to take ALL with Him into death, without their knowledge, or consent: therefore, the second Adam, the Lord from heaven, gathers up the same number in His redemptive work and man who came out of God shall return, that the circle may be unbroken." (The Law of Circularity, J. Preston Eby)

WE ARE ALL A PART OF THE CIRCLE OF GOD'S ETERNAL PURPOSE!

January 15

CREATION, REDEMPTION, AND COMPLETION

The following quote from A. P. Adams causes us to take a look at the true basis of man's creation, redemption, and completion…"The redemption of man is the completion of his creation, and depends for its final accomplishment on God and not on the individual." A statement such as this causes us to reflect on the GREATNESS OF ALMIGHTY GOD. It introduces us to the idea that our Heavenly Father is all-powerful and SOVEREIGN. This would then mean that God is in TOTAL CONTROL of the destiny of the human race. When we recognize THE SOVEREIGNTY OF GOD, we are set free from the foolish notion that we are responsible "to make" ourselves in the image of God. Many people do not recognize that God is responsible for their creation, redemption, and completion. The result of this is a life of condemnation, frustration, and failure. They place all the emphasis of their Christian walk on their "so-called" free will. In doing this, we absolutely strip God of His power and sovereignty, making His Spirit and His Word of none effect.

The scriptures are actually very plain concerning this subject. All we have to do is READ THEM AND BELIEVE THEM! Ephesians 1:11 tells us that God works ALL things after the counsel OF HIS OWN WILL…Ephesians 2:10 tells us that we are God's workmanship…HOW PLAIN CAN IT BE??? God is the One Who is working on us, FOR WE ARE HIS WORKMANSHIP! Philippians 1:6 tells us to be confident of this very thing, that He which has BEGUN a good work in you WILL PERFORM IT until the day of Jesus Christ …Who started the work? GOD! Who will finish the work? GOD! What work? YOU! YOU ARE GOD'S WORKMANSHIP!!! As well, Hebrews 12:2 states…looking unto Jesus the AUTHOR and FINISHER of our faith…Many people do not realize that it is God Who is responsible for authoring and finishing their faith. WHERE IS THERE ANY ROOM FOR MAN TO BOAST? HOW CAN WE TAKE ANY CREDIT FOR THE WORK THAT IS BEING ACCOMPLISHED IN US, FOR WE ARE GOD'S WORKMANSHIP?

It must become clear to us that GOD is responsible for, in charge of, and in total control of the creation, redemption, and completion of man (mankind, the entire human race). This will result in a race that has been totally and completely conformed to the image of its Creator. It will also result in man having DOMINION over all things (except for God of course), for this was the purpose of God from the very beginning (Genesis 1:26). It is God Who has purposed the creation, redemption, and completion of man, AND IT IS GOD WHO WILL BRING IT TO PASS! The only part we play is one of recognizing, believing, and submitting to the very Spirit of God. WE CANNOT DO THE WORK! If we were able to bring this to pass, then why would God have sent His Son to be the Savior of the world? But rest assured, for our final outcome of being made into the image of our Creator depends on God, not the individual. This is good news!

BE CONFIDENT OF THIS VERY THING!

January 16

WHAT CAUSES PERILOUS TIMES?

2ND Timothy 3:1 states…This know also, that in the last days perilous (dangerous) times shall come…The fact that perilous times are here is no big secret. Just listen to the nightly news, read the newspapers, or watch television. All you will hear is a report of increasingly perilous times. Since it is not a surprise that we are currently in perilous times, the more important question concerning this thought would be, WHAT CAUSES PERILOUS TIMES? Have you ever considered what actually brings on or causes these dangerous times in which we live? The key to answering this question is to be found in the very next verse. Vs. 2 states…MEN SHALL BE LOVERS OF THEIR OWN SELVES…So as we can see, the cause of perilous times is a LOVE OF SELF as opposed to a love of God! Let us now take a look at the UGLINESS of self and what it produces.

The love of self causes us to become:

1. Covetous
2. Boasters
3. Proud
4. Blasphemers
5. Disobedient
6. Unthankful

7. Unholy
8. Without Natural Affection
9. Truce Breakers
10. False Accusers
11. Incontinent
12. Fierce
13. Despisers Of Those That Are Good
14. Traitors
15. Heady
16. Highminded
17. Lovers Of Pleasures
18. Not A Lover Of God
19. A Form Of Godliness
20. One Who Denies The Power Of God

What an ugly list! Look at what the love of self produces. May we understand the disgusting results and fruit that the love of self produces. So what is the answer? The answer is the DEATH OF THE SELF-LIFE. This is obviously the opposite of the love of self. Bill Britton was a man with incredible insight into the things of God. Here is a quote from him concerning this very topic… "When you are forgotten, or neglected, or purposely set at naught, and you don't sting and hurt with the insult or the oversight, but your heart is happy, being counted worthy to suffer for Christ, THAT IS DYING TO SELF." (Bill Britton)

Let us realize that if the love of self produces perilous times, that the death of self will produce peaceful times. This is the very peace of God that the creation is longing for. Revelation 12:11 states…and they overcame him (Satan) by the blood of the Lamb, and by the word of their testimony; and they LOVED NOT THEIR LIVES UNTO THE DEATH…

LOSE YOUR LIFE FOR HIS NAME'S SAKE!

January 17

THE LAMB ON THE THRONE

As you read through the book of Revelation you will notice many startling things. It is interesting to note that Jesus, the Son of God, is portrayed as a LAMB Who sits on the throne. A LAMB ON A THRONE? Of all the symbols that could be used to typify a victorious king sitting on a throne, WHY A LAMB? Revelation 22:1 states…And he showed me a pure river of water of life, clear as crystal, proceeding out of the throne of God and of the Lamb…What comes to mind when you think of a throne? What comes to mind when you think of a lamb? Remember…The book of Revelation is the revelation of Jesus Christ. It is not something to be looked at in the natural or literal sense, but in the spiritual. This is not to say that the symbolism in this book will in no way be played out in the physical realm, but the true purpose of this book in the Bible is to REVEAL JESUS THE CHRIST, WHICH CONSISTS OF A MANY MEMBERED BODY OF BELIEVERS WITH THE LORD JESUS AS ITS HEAD! This book is one that must be unveiled or revealed to you by the Spirit of God. As a matter of fact, the entirety of the Bible must be unveiled to you by the Spirit of God. It can not be understood with raw intellect. The dead letters on the page must be quickened or made alive to you BY THE SPIRIT OF GOD! With this in mind, let us attempt to understand how that a LAMB, or becoming like a lamb, could result in sitting on a throne to rule and reign with all power.

1st Corinthians 15:42,43 states…So also is the resurrection of the dead. It is sown in corruption; it is raised in incorruption: It is sown in dishonor; it is raised in glory: it is sown in WEAKNESS; it is raised in POWER…If you were to categorize a lamb as weak or strong, which one would you choose? WEAK, OF COURSE! A lamb is weak, gentle, and characterized as not putting up a fight but being easily led in one direction or another. Acts 8:32 states…He (Jesus) was led as a sheep to the slaughter; and like a LAMB dumb before his shearer, so opened He not His mouth…vs. 33…and WHO SHALL DECLARE HIS GENERATION?…Now let us consider the word "throne". What does it speak of or signify? It speaks of dominion and rulership, of course. So we can see that God's power is manifested through weakness, as strange as that sounds. 2nd Corinthians 12:9 states…God's strength is made perfect in weakness…vs. 10…for when I am weak, then I am strong.

The death of Jesus, the LAMB of God, was in weakness, but He rose in power as the SAVIOR OF THE WORLD, HAVING FORGIVEN AND CLEANSED THE ENTIRE HUMAN RACE. NOW THAT IS POWER!!! THAT IS THE THRONE OF GOD! So the question still remains…Who shall declare His generation? The answer is…WE SHALL! We must see ourselves as part of the corporate LAMB that shall rule and reign with Jesus Christ. We must see ourselves as IN CHRIST, BEING SEATED ON THE THRONE OF GOD. Jesus is the head and we are His body…The LAMB slain from the foundation of the world. Remember…The MEEK (THOSE LIKE A LAMB) shall inherit the earth, ruling the nations with a rod of iron. He is bringing you from a LAMB to a LION, that you might possess the qualities of both, for meekness is not weakness BUT CONTROLLED STRENGTH. Every lion in God's Kingdom must start out as a lamb, FOR POWER WITHOUT HUMILITY IS A VERY DANGEROUS POSSESSION!!! Humble yourself in the sight of the Lord. In due season God will exalt you to the throne, for our God is…

THE LAMB AND THE LION!

January 18

TRINITY "?"

How are we to understand Father, Son, and Holy Spirit? Are there three Gods? Are there three separate beings that all make up one God? Is there a "so-called" trinity? Here is a big clue…THE WORD "TRINITY" IS NOT TO BE FOUND ANYWHERE IN THE CANON OF SCRIPTURE! As a matter of fact, it did not find a place formally in the theology of the church until the 4th century. The Encyclopedia of Religion and Ethics records: At first the Christian Faith was not Trinitarian… It was not so in the apostolic and sub-apostolic ages, as reflected in the New Testament and other early Christian writings. So where did it come from a why did it surface? THE TEACHING OF A "SO-CALLED" TRINITY WAS BIRTHED OUT OF THE CARNAL MINDS OF MEN, ATTEMPTING TO TAKE THINGS THAT ARE SPIRITUAL AND TO CONVERT THEM INTO THE REALM OF INTELLECT AND THEOLOGY! It is imperative that we understand that that which is spiritual CANNOT be converted into intellect. We must grasp the things of the Spirit in the Spirit and by the Spirit. Let us also remember that the NATURAL MAN cannot discern, understand, or perceive the spiritual things of the Kingdom of God, even though he thinks he does. Bible college and theology will not teach you about the true God. It will only teach you its watered down version of God, leaving you with many traditions and doctrines of men THAT MUST THEN BE UNLEARNED! So…Is there one God or three Gods? Let us look to the words of Jesus.

Mark 12:29 states…And Jesus answered him, The first of all the commandments is, Hear, O Israel; THE LORD THY GOD IS ONE LORD…Well…That did not take long. We are told straight from the lips of Jesus that God is ONE GOD! So how are we to understand the scriptures when they speak of this one God as a Father, a Son, and a Spirit? It is actually very simple. There is one God Who has manifested Himself as a Father, a Son, and a Spirit. He has manifested Himself in three ways, but that does not mean that this one God is made up of three separate beings. Father, Son, and Holy Spirit are not three separate beings Who all make up one God, but rather, they are three different manifestations of the same God.

To further clarify this simple point, think of your life and the different ways in which you are manifested to others.

Someone who is married and has children is a:

1. Father to their children
2. Son to their father
3. Husband to their wife

A person whose life is distributed in this manner is not made up of three different people, but is one person who is distributed in three different ways. In the same sense, God is to be seen as a Father, Who is a Spirit, and Who was manifested in the flesh. The true reality and identity of God is actually very simple, but has been greatly complicated by the traditions and doctrines of men. Let God reveal this simple truth to you. Remember when Philip asked Jesus about the Father? Jesus replied and said, "Have I been so long time with you, and yet you have not known Me, Philip? He that has SEEN ME HAS SEEN THE FATHER; and how do you say then, show us the Father? Do you not believe that I am in the Father, and the Father in Me? The words that I speak unto you I speak not of Myself: but the Father that DWELLS IN ME, HE DOES THE WORKS!!! (John 14:9,10)

HEAR, O CHILD OF GOD; THE LORD YOUR GOD IS ONE LORD!

January 19

THE AGE OF ACCOUNTABILITY "**?**"

Is there an age of accountability? What is the age? Is it the same for boys and girls? Does it come on your twelfth birthday? Does it come upon you right after you blow out the candles on your birthday cake (ha ha)? Let us look to the Bible to see if this teaching is of men or of God.

Well…GO FIGURE…THERE IS NOT ONE SCRIPTURE IN THE ENTIRE BIBLE TO SUPPORT SUCH AN IDIOTIC AND FOOLISH TEACHING SUCH AS THIS! So where did this teaching come from? Take a guess. How about…THE TRADITIONS AND DOCTRINES OF MEN! Of the teachings that belong to men, rather than to God, this particular one is quite fascinating, for it is totally and completely fabricated. In other words, it was invented, or simply made up, being grabbed out of the air to help proclaim the teaching of eternal torture, while trying to make God look not so bad in light of that false teaching. This "teaching", that an unbelieving child under the age of twelve, after dying, is declared righteous in the eyes of God due to it being under the age of twelve, has absolutely no scriptural evidence whatsoever. As man preached the false message of eternal torture down through the ages, he realized that according to this teaching it would mean that babies and young children would go to a hell and be tortured forever. In order to soften the blow of this horrific teaching while continuing to teach it, they simply MADE UP the idea of an age of accountability. This would in turn make God look good, and also would enable man to continue to preach his "so-called" good news of eternal torture. It is a "have your cake and eat it too" mentality. The question is then, does the Bible say anything about accountability? Well…Yes it does.

Romans 14:11,12 states…For it is written, As I live, says the Lord, EVERY KNEE SHALL BOW TO ME, AND EVERY TONGUE SHALL CONFESS TO GOD. SO THEN EVERY ONE OF US SHALL GIVE AN ACCOUNT OF HIMSELF TO GOD…Well…The scriptures have once again cleared up the confusing babble that is to be associated with the teachings of men. The truth of the matter is, WE ARE ALL ACCOUNTABLE TO GOD! Man's accountability to his Creator will ultimately have absolutely nothing to do with the age at which he dies. Those who die as babies, or those who die at a young age will of course be ushered into the loving arms of God, but this will have absolutely nothing to do with the age at which they died. IT HAS EVERYTHING TO DO WITH THE LOVE OF GOD, FOR GOD GIVES UP ON NO ONE! AS A MATTER OF FACT,

THERE IS NOTHING THAT CAN SEPARATE US FROM THE LOVE OF GOD, NOT EVEN DEATH (Romans 8:38)!

Many of God's people, due to their lack of study of the Bible, are not aware that the Bible speaks of future ages to come. Within these ages to come, God will deal with every person who has ever lived. All will come to know him as Lord and Savior, including those who died as babies and young children. All will confess with their mouths and believe in their hearts. All knees will bow to Him in worship and adoration. This is all because THE LAMB OF GOD TOOK AWAY THE SIN OF THE WORLD. We are all accountable to come to the saving knowledge of our salvation THAT WAS PURCHASED THROUGH THE CROSS OF THE LORD JESUS CHRIST. This has taken place, is taking place, and will continue to take place in the ages to come, until God is all in all. So then…

EVERY ONE OF US SHALL GIVE AN ACCOUNT OF HIMSELF TO GOD!

January 20

THE TITHE "?"

Is it correct to teach that the New Testament Church is bound to a tithe? Most preachers think so. It is taught every Sunday in churches all over the world that if you do not give a tithe (10% of your money) to your local church that you are cursed by God. These well-meaning ministers mean no harm, but they are misleading the people, and they are keeping the people under the legalistic letter of the law, rather than introducing them to the law of the Spirit of LIFE IN CHRIST JESUS!

Oh yes, the people are giving, but many are giving out of OBLIGATION rather than to prove the sincerity of their love toward God. Many are giving of their money because they are afraid of what God will do to them if they do not give. Let us now take a look at the TRUE BASIS FOR GIVING to God according to the NEW TESTAMENT.

THE APOSTLE PAUL DID NOT TEACH THE NEW TESTAMENT CHURCH TO PAY TITHES!!! He did however teach the church to give, and to give with a cheerful heart. 2nd Corinthians 9:6,7 states…But this I say, He which sows sparingly shall reap also sparingly; and he which sows bountifully shall reap also bountifully. Every man according as he purposes in his heart, so let him give; NOT GRUDGINGLY, OR OF NECESSITY: FOR GOD LOVES A CHEERFUL GIVER. In actuality, this scripture holds us to a much higher standard of giving than the Old Testament law of tithing. God wants you to DO THE BEST THAT YOU CAN! No percentage is mentioned here. If the best you can do is 5%, then give 5%. If you are able to give more, then give 10%, 20%, 30%, or 40%. If you are able to give it all, then give 100%. The most important point in giving is NOT THE AMOUNT, but that you do the best you can, and that you do not give grudgingly, or of necessity, but as a cheerful giver. IT IS TIME TO COME OUT OF THE LEGALISTIC MINDSET OF THE OLD TESTAMENT LAW OF THE TITHE. When ministers quote Malachi 3:8-11 as a means to put pressure on people to give, and as a means to teach them how to give, and as a means to make them feel guilty for not giving, THEY ARE OUT OF LINE, AND THEY ARE NOT RIGHTLY DIVIDING THE WORD OF TRUTH! This passage of scripture pertains to God's dealings with His people under the OLD COVENANT. WE MUST STOP TAKING PORTIONS OF THE OLD COVENANT THAT WE WANT TO INCORPORATE INTO THE NEW COVENANT, FOR IF YOU TRY TO KEEP ANY OR SOME OF THE OLD COVENANT YOU MUST KEEP IT ALL. IT IS ALL OR NOTHING!!!

According to Gary Amirault: "The apostle Paul did not quote a single tithing scripture to make people give, not one! The apostle Paul knew that only LEVITES could collect tithes. Paul introduced a new way of giving - OUT OF THE LOVE OF CHRIST IN YOUR HEART! When the writer of Hebrews used the word "tithe" in chapter seven, he was not dealing with tithing, but a higher priesthood than the Levitical Priesthood, that is, the priesthood after the order of Melchizedek. When Jesus spoke of tithing in Matthew and Luke, remember this: The New Covenant is not the set of books from Matthew to Revelation. The New Covenant was not ratified until Jesus offered up His blood in heaven which was after His resurrection. Prior to that, the Old Covenant, and the Levitical Priesthood was still in effect. Here is the conclusion of the matter: We should give, not from the letter of the law which kills, but from the Spirit Who prepares works for us to walk in. One comes from bondage to a set of laws, and the other comes from LOVE, which is the nature of God. The first usually produces pride and self-righteousness, and the latter produces joy. The higher ways of God are much better than the lower ways of the Old Covenant." (The Tithe Is Illegal, Gary Amirault)

GIVE BOUNTIFULLY WITH A CHEERFUL HEART!

January 21

ETERNAL TORTURE "?"
(This theme and quotes taken from: I Am A Convinced Universalist, William Barclay)

According to William Barclay: "When you think of God, what is the first thing that comes to mind? God is the Creator, Savior, Judge, King, Lord, and Supreme Sovereign Ruler of the universe. God is all these things, but above all, GOD IS LOVE! As well, God is our FATHER! So…GOD IS A LOVING FATHER! With that being said, let this statement sink down deep into your heart…No father could be happy while there were members of his family forever in agony. No father would count it a triumph to obliterate the disobedient members of his family. The only triumph a father can know is to have all his family back home. If one man remains outside of the love of God at the end of time, it means that that one man has defeated the love of God - AND THAT IS IMPOSSIBLE…!" (William Barclay)

Here is why we are obligated to condemn the teaching of eternal torture, which did come from the Catholic Church during the Dark Ages:

1. By believing it, we smear the character and nature of God, Who is our Father, Who is LOVE, Who is merciful, Who is FULL OF FORGIVENESS, and Who is GOOD.

2. By believing it, we must declare evil, Satan, and the will of man as STRONGER than God Who created all things.

3. As well, there are MANY mistranslations in the dearly beloved King James Version, which has been used to establish the doctrine of Evangelical Christianity. Of the MANY mistranslations to be found in the King James "VERSION" of the Bible, those that have done the most damage are the English words "eternal", "everlasting", "for ever", and "for ever and ever", which when researched will be found to be an INCORRECT TRANSLATION of the Hebrew and Greek words "OLAM", "AION", AND "AIONIOS", which do not refer to eternity, but rather to ages and time. The passages in the King James Bible that are translated to speak of eternal or everlasting punishment, in actuality do speak of AGE-LASTING PUNISHMENT (correction), or THE PUNISHMENT OF THE AGES. IT IS PUNISHMENT WITHIN THE AGES OF TIME FOR THE PURPOSE OF CORRECTION, BUT IT IS SURELY NOT ETERNAL TORTURE!!! We must also see that the purpose of punishment, judgment, vengeance, and the wrath of God is CORRECTION, NOT VINDICTIVE, ENDLESS, AND SENSELESS TORTURE. This type of punishment would have to be characterized as INSANE, and would serve no purpose.

4. The Bible is FULL of scriptures and passages that do declare the salvation of all men. This is taking place now and will continue in the ages to come.

Here are just a few:

Genesis 12:1-3
Psalm 22:27-29
Psalm 65:2
Psalm 66:3,4
Psalm 86:9
Isaiah 25:7,8
Isaiah 45:22-25
John 12:32
Romans 11:32
1st Corinthians 15:22-28
1st Timothy 2:4-6

(For a list of over 600 scriptures, refer to: Read And Search God's Plan, Dr. Harold Lovelace.)

The Bible clearly talks about the ultimate and complete triumph of God, when God will be everything to everyone (1st Corinthians 15:28). God is patient with His creation. He awaits the day when His love is answered by the return of love. The end result is this…

A UNIVERSE LOVED BY AND IN LOVE WITH GOD!

January 22

UNDERSTANDING GEHENNA

Matthew 18:8,9 states…Wherefore if your hand or your foot offend you, cut them off, and cast them from you: for it is better for you to enter into life halt or maimed, rather than having two hands or two feet to be cast into everlasting fire. And if your eye offend you, pluck it out, and cast it from you: it is better for you to enter into life with one eye, rather than having two eyes to be cast into hell fire…After studying the words "everlasting" and "hell" in the original Greek, this passage of scripture ceases to mean what many have tried to make it mean. For example, it does not mean that God is going to send people to a literal place called hell, and burn them there for ever and ever in literal fire. According to the King James "VERSION" this appears to be the case, but it is not so. LET US STUDY TO SHOW OURSELVES APPROVED!

The word "everlasting" in this passage comes from the Greek word "AIONIOS", which means age-lasting, or OF THE AGES. Instead of everlasting fire, it should be translated as THE FIRE OF THE AGES (Refer to the New Testament in Modern Speech). It means a period of time that BELONGS TO THE AGES, BUT IT CERTAINLY DOES NOT MEAN FOREVER OR EVERLASTING IN THE SENSE THAT WE THINK OF FOREVER AND EVERLASTING. To be blunt, IT IS A BAD TRANSLATION! The word "hell" in this passage comes from the Greek word "GEHENNA", which refers to the Valley of the Son of Hinnom (Ge - Hinnom) in the Old Testament. Jesus referred to this valley (the dump outside the city where garbage was burned day and night…because of the continual garbage being dumped into Gehenna, there was a continual fire burning to consume the garbage, and there were continual worms in the garbage) in His day to teach us something spiritual about God. He used Gehenna in a metaphoric way to describe what the fire of God was like. As well, when Jesus referred to cutting off our hands and feet and plucking out our eyes, He was OBVIOUSLY speaking in metaphoric and symbolic language, for He did not mean for us to literally do these things (Have you cut off any hands or feet, or plucked out any eyes lately?). This valley (Gehenna) that Jesus referred to symbolically spoke of the things in our lives that are fit for the spiritual garbage dump, such as wood, hay, and stubble (our carnality). Remember…GOD IS A CONSUMING FIRE. This statement is speaking of a SPIRITUAL FIRE, a fire that GOD IS, and a spiritual fire that does consume everything in us that is not pleasing to Him. As well, Gehenna was to be a fulfillment of Bible prophecy. This prophecy concerned the destruction of Jerusalem, which did take place in 70 A.D. - 73 A.D. This can be easily researched by studying the following scriptures: Jeremiah 7:30-34, Jeremiah 19:5-6, Jeremiah 32:35, Leviticus 18:21, Leviticus 20:2, Deuteronomy 18:10, 2nd Kings 16:1-3, 2nd Kings 21:6, 2nd Kings 23:10, Psalm 106:36-39, Matthew 23:33-36.

We now turn our attention to an in-depth explanation of Gehenna from: Hope For All Generations And Nations, by Gary Amirault…"Israel, during one part of its history began to mix the worship of Yahweh with some of the customs of the pagan nations around them. They molded a statue which was half man and half bull. They called this god MLK (The original Hebrew had no vowels). Molech meant King in Hebrew. Israel had made an image of Yahweh (their King) in the image of being half man and half animal. They felt this new practice was harmonious with the other religious traditions of the Hebrew faith. The Israelites took their own babies and placed them in the hands of this statue. Beneath the hands was a pot under which was a hot fire. The child would fall out of the hands of Molech into the burning pot. As the child screamed with pain, the adults would go into a sexual frenzy as the sounds of the burning children mixed with the beating of drums. Molech was a fertility god. These things were done in the VALLEY OF THE SON OF HINNOM (Referred to as Gehenna in the Greek). The Lord spoke through Jeremiah that He did not command Israel to do this, NOR DID IT COME INTO HIS MIND THAT THEY SHOULD DO THIS ABOMINATION, TO CAUSE ISRAEL TO SIN (Jeremiah 32:35). IT HAS NEVER EVEN ENTERED THE LORD'S MIND TO BURN PEOPLE IN LITERAL FIRE FOR THE PURPOSE OF TORMENTING THEM. THAT IS AN ABOMINATION TO HIM (Think about it!)! IF GOD PREPARED A PLACE IN WHICH HE WAS GOING TO TORTURE BILLIONS OF THE HUMAN BEINGS HE CREATED, HOW COULD HE SAY IT NEVER ENTERED HIS MIND? When Jesus used the word Gehenna, the place He was referring to was this valley in which Israel burned their own children, not God. The place called Gehenna (Translated hell) was the Greek form of the Hebrew Ge - Hinnom. This valley became a disgraceful reminder to Israel of what their forefathers did. It became the city dump. Jesus warned the very generation in which He lived (Matthew 23:33-36), that if they did not repent, they would find themselves thrown into this valley of garbage which burned day and night. To tell a Jew something like this was the absolute worst of insult. It meant that their lives were worthless. A Jew's honor was very important to him especially at his death. It was not uncommon to hire professional mourners at one's funeral. Imagine paying someone to cry tears at your funeral. This is an example of how vain God's people were during Jesus' physical presence on earth. Jesus told some of the most religious people of His day, their lives were only fit to be thrown in the city dump! WHAT AN INSULT! AND WHAT A PROPHECY! The very people who heard these words would find their bodies thrown over the Southwest wall of Jerusalem during the siege against the city in 70 A.D. Because they did not follow Christ and participated in His crucifixion, THEIR LIVES TRULY DID BECOME WORTHLESS!" (Gary Amirault)

Although Gehenna did refer to the destruction of Jerusalem, and does symbolically represent the fire of God burning the wood, hay, and stubble (our carnal minds) in our lives, IT SURELY DOES NOT MEAN OR SPEAK OF ETERNAL TORTURE. Gehenna is a place located ON THIS EARTH (The Valley of the Son of Hinnom). It is extremely important that we understand and teach its true literal and spiritual meaning, for in doing so we will be found rightly dividing the Word of truth. Having a proper understanding of Gehenna will set one free from the FALSE TEACHING of eternal torture. What a joy it is to know…

THE TRUTH ABOUT GEHENNA!

January 23

NOT FORSAKING THE ASSEMBLING OF OURSELVES

Hebrews 10:25 states…Not forsaking the assembling of ourselves together, as the manner of some is…The word "assembling" in this passage means: to gather together, collect, to gather together for corporate worship, our attachment to Jesus Christ and other believers, and not avoiding one's own responsibility as part of the body of Christ. As you can see, this passage of scripture speaks of more than just making sure that you do not miss a "church service", but rather, it speaks of THE BODY OF CHRIST. Many people who PRIDE THEMSELVES in the fact that they go to church every Sunday and Wednesday, and that they are there "every time the doors are opened", are not really assembling themselves together, but rather, they are just another warm body in the building. We must realize that what is being assembled is not a church service, BUT THE BODY OF CHRIST. It is not so much how many times that you "go to church", or where you "go to church", but it is recognizing that YOU ARE THE CHURCH, and that what is being assembled is the corporate BODY OF CHRIST. Many (especially preachers) use this scripture to load condemnation onto people if they miss a church service, not realizing that the assembling that God is talking about is not so much a physical meeting in a church building, but a spiritual assembling of the many membered BODY OF CHRIST.

So next time you "go to church", you must realize that you are being assembled together in the Spirit to become the BODY OF CHRIST. The mere act of you going to a building on a Sunday morning or a Wednesday night does not necessarily mean that you have assembled yourself together with Christ and His Body. It is the joining together of the BODY OF CHRIST, being in one mind and one accord with the MIND OF CHRIST, for the purpose of fellowship, worship, and teaching in the Lord. This can take place in a home, on the job, out in public, in a building, or ANYWHERE, FOR WE ARE THE CHURCH!!! We must STOP thinking that the mere act of going to a building twice a week or more is the only thing that constitutes the assembling of ourselves together with Christ and His Body. GO FORTH and attach (assemble) yourself to…

THE LORD JESUS AND HIS CHRIST (BODY)!

January 24

CHURCH

Ephesians 1:22,23 states…the church, which is His body, the fullness of Him that fills all in all…It is interesting to note that the Bible will always interpret itself. Ephesians 1:22,23 clearly defines what the church is. IT IS THE BODY OF CHRIST, THE FULLNESS OF GOD THAT FILLS ALL IN ALL!!!

Now that we know what the church is, let us talk about what it is not. It is not:

> Any particular denomination…
> A building made with hands…
> Any particular religion…
> A set of rules…
> Something that we go to on Sunday morning or Wednesday night…

THE CHURCH IS YOU! YOU ARE THE CHURCH! The word "church" comes from the Greek word "ekklesia", which means assembly, or a gathering of called out ones. We have become SO BUSY "going to church" that we have lost sight that WE ARE THE CHURCH, THE CALLED OUT ONES! IT IS TIME TO STOP HAVING CHURCH AND TO START BEING THE CHURCH! WE have perfected the art of "having church". We know when to clap, when to sing, when to pray, when to preach, when to cry, when to laugh, and when to go to the altar. We know how to fit it all in within two hours so that we can get to lunch on time. We have put God in our nice "churchy" box with a lid on top and wrapped Him all up with our pretty denominational wrapping paper. We must WAKE UP to the realization that church is not something that we go to, rather, it is who we are in Christ. YOU ARE THE CHURCH! YOU ARE THE BODY OF CHRIST! YOU ARE THE FULLNESS OF GOD!

BE THE CHURCH!

January 25

ALTAR CALLS "<u>?</u>"

The modern day church service goes something like this:

> The band leader starts up the music…
> The people begin to praise and worship the Lord for about thirty minutes…
> The preacher then exhorts the people for about fifteen minutes…

Someone sings a special song…

The collection plate is passed around to receive the offerings of the people…

The preacher preaches his message for the day (about thirty to forty-five minutes)…

Then the preacher PLEADS and BEGS the people to come to an altar where they can "get saved", healed, or delivered…Is begging the people to come to a man-made altar a scriptural thing to do? Let us look to the Bible.

How many "altar calls" do you find in the book of Acts-Revelation? Well…You guessed it. NONE! When the apostle Paul was asked by a man what must I do to be saved, what was his response? It was, BELIEVE ON THE LORD JESUS CHRIST! Where was the altar call? Did Paul forget to lead him in a "sinner's prayer"? As a matter of fact, the Bible speaks nothing about accepting the Lord at an altar. We are not told to accept the Lord, but rather, we are told to BELIEVE ON THE LORD JESUS CHRIST. In actuality, HE IS THE ONE WHO HAS ACCEPTED US IN CHRIST! As you can see, the apostles of the early church had revelation truth from God. They did not have to resort to the SILLY man-made tactics that the modern day church has resorted to. The altar call, as we know it, has its roots in the person and ministry of Charles Finney (1792-1875). Finney's meetings involved huge crowds and multiple conversions, and altar calls were used as a means to lead people to Christ. As long as an altar call is used to symbolize something that is already taking place in our hearts, it does not become a problem. The problem is though, THE CHURCH HAS MADE A GOD OUT OF GOING TO THE ALTAR. What was an altar used for in the Old Testament? It was used to offer up a sacrifice to God. The higher spiritual truth for us today under the New Testament is to be found in Romans 12:1. It states…present your bodies a LIVING SACRIFICE, holy, acceptable unto God, which is your reasonable service…We must understand that we are to BECOME AN ALTAR UNTO GOD, and that our life must become a sacrifice unto Him. It is not a matter of going to an altar as much as it is BECOMING AN ALTAR! We must STOP trying to force and manipulate people to come to a man-made altar, convincing them that walking an aisle is what saves them. Rather, we must help them to comprehend that GOD HAS ALREADY RECONCILED THEM TO HIMSELF THROUGH THE CROSS OF THE LORD JESUS CHRIST. As they are AWAKENED to this truth they will want to believe on the Lord Jesus Christ and be saved. When this takes place we BECOME AN ALTAR, and our lives BECOME A LIVING SACRIFICE unto God.

PRESENT YOURSELF AS A LIVING SACRIFICE UNTO GOD!

January 26

WE ARE THE OFFSPRING OF GOD

What does a dog give birth to?…A puppy, which turns into a dog of course. What does a cat give birth to?…A kitten, which turns into a cat of course. What does a cow give birth to?…A calf, which turns into a cow of course. What does (a) God give birth to?…A son, which turns into a god of course. WHAT?…YOU MIGHT ASK! Don't take my word for it. Look to the Bible for yourself.

Psalm 82:1,6 states…God stands in the congregation of the mighty; He judges among the gods…I have said, YOU ARE GODS; AND ALL OF YOU ARE CHILDREN OF THE MOST HIGH…Jesus also quoted this same verse in the book of John 10:34-36. Well…There you have it! WE ARE GODS! How can that be? Because WE ARE GOD'S OFFSPRING!

Acts 17:27,28 states…the Lord is not far from EVERY ONE OF US: for in Him we live, and move, and have our being; as certain also of your poets have said, FOR WE ARE HIS OFFSPRING…!!! The word "offspring" means: kind, race, nation, kindred, and stock. This describes who we are in relation to our Heavenly Father. Because we are ALL children of the Most High God, we are to see ourselves as His offspring, and destined to become like our Father, Who is God. What a beautiful truth! We are in the process of becoming GOD-LIKE (GODS). Everything that you go through is for this very reason and purpose.

Remember this:

1. WE ARE HIS CHILDREN!
2. WE ARE HIS OFFSPRING!
3. WE ARE GODS!

THIS IS OUR DESTINY!

January 27

RIGHTEOUSNESS

What is righteousness? Is it:

what kind of clothes you wear…?
how long a lady's dress is…?
what kind of haircut you have…?
how long your hair is…?
whether or not a lady wears jewelry or makeup…?
fasting…?
tithing…?
praying…?
reading the Bible…?
going to church…?
giving…?
trying as hard as you can to be good…?

The answer to all of these questions is…NO! It is none of these things. As a matter of fact, IT IS NOTHING EXTERNAL AT ALL. Here is the grand revelation of righteousness: RIGHTEOUSNESS IS NOT AN ACTIVITY, BUT IT IS A POSITION! It could also be said that it is a position of testimony. WHAT? Well…Let us take a look.

Philippians 3:9 states…and be found IN HIM (CHRIST), not having my own righteousness, which is of the law, but that which is through the faith of Christ, the righteousness WHICH IS OF GOD BY FAITH…

So there are two kinds of righteousness:

1. YOUR OWN RIGHTEOUSNESS
2. GOD'S RIGHTEOUSNESS (Read Luke 18:9-14)

The word "righteous" simply means that which is RIGHT. There is self-righteousness, which is one's own effort and trusting in yourself, and there is God's righteousness, which is faith in Christ, Who He is, and what He has accomplished. So righteousness is being IN CHRIST! IT IS A POSITION OF TESTIMONY IN CHRIST! It does not come from anything that you do. The things you do are a byproduct of your faith in Christ. Someone who is self-righteous is right in his own eyes. Someone who possesses the righteousness of God is righteous in the eyes of God, and to be right with God you must place your faith in the person and the work of the Lord Jesus Christ. Jesus the Christ is the only truly righteous one. You must see yourself as being IN HIM, FOR THAT IS HOW YOUR HEAVENLY FATHER SEES YOU. PLACE YOUR FAITH IN HOW HE SEES YOU, FOR THAT IS YOUR TRUE IDENTITY. This is the only righteousness that God honors. Our righteousness (self effort) STINKS IN HIS NOSTRILS! Genesis 15:6 states…Abraham BELIEVED in the Lord; and the Lord counted it to him for RIGHTEOUSNESS…Your righteousness is in Christ.

BELIEVE!

January 28

PEACE

What is peace? Is it never having a problem? Is it an absence of conflict? Is it smooth sailing at all times? Is it a life of total and complete perfection, never having a stressful moment? NO! The Bible speaks of two different kinds of peace.

They are:

1. PEACE WITH GOD
2. THE PEACE OF GOD

Romans 5:1 states…Therefore being justified by faith, we have PEACE WITH GOD through our Lord Jesus Christ…Philippians 4:7 states…And the PEACE OF GOD, which passes all understanding, shall keep your hearts and minds through Christ Jesus… Peace **with** God speaks of believing on the Lord Jesus Christ, which causes you to be justified (declared not guilty) in the sight of God. The peace **of** God speaks of being careful for nothing, but bringing everything to God in prayer with thanksgiving, which causes your heart and mind to be at rest, making you to feel and know that God is in control of everything, and that everything will work together for your good. This is what takes place as the believer goes through the process of sanctification. PEACE WITH GOD IS A JUSTIFYING PEACE. THE PEACE OF GOD IS A SANCTIFYING PEACE. A life without these two facets of the peace of God is hell indeed, for the true definition of hell (Hades) is UNPERCEPTION. A person who is not able to perceive (grasp) God's peace is surely a person who lives in constant inner turmoil. BUT REJOICE, FOR WE HAVE A LOVING FATHER WHO HAS EXTENDED TO US HIS JUSTIFYING AND SANCTIFYING PEACE. God's peace is the very thing that gives us confidence and assurance in the midst of the storms of this life. It does not make the storm go away, but it is THE VERY PRESENCE OF GOD THAT BRINGS US THROUGH THE STORM. PEACE…PEACE…WONDERFUL PEACE…COMING DOWN FROM THE FATHER ABOVE! PEACE…BE STILL!

HE IS OUR PEACE! (Ephesians 2:14)

January 29

JOY

What is joy? Is it being happy all the time? Is it always having a smile on your face? Is it trying to put on a good mood at all times? NO! It goes much deeper than that! IT IS YOUR STRENGTH! Nehemiah 8:10 states…for the joy of the Lord is your strength…Notice that joy produces strength, and that joy comes from the Lord. It is not your joy that produces strength, BUT IT IS THE JOY OF (BELONGING TO) THE LORD THAT PRODUCES STRENGTH. The word "joy" means: rejoicing and gladness. So what does the Lord rejoice over? What makes Him glad?

Hebrews 12:2 states…Looking unto Jesus…Who for the JOY that was set before Him endured the cross…How was there joy for Jesus in enduring the cross? Jesus found joy in enduring the cross because He knew what it would produce. It has produced, is producing, and will continue to produce a crop in His image. Jesus was one Son to bring many sons to glory. The joy of the Lord is YOU! He endured the cross for you. YOU ARE HIS JOY! The Lord rejoices and is glad in you, for He knows what you will become after being made conformable to His death, and apprehending His resurrection life. Your strength is that God rejoices in making you in His image.

LET HIM FILL YOU WITH GLADNESS AND REJOICING!

January 30

CAIN AND ABEL

Most people are familiar with the story of Cain and Abel. It is widely known and recognized, even among people who know very little or nothing at all about the Bible. Cain was a tiller of the ground. Abel was a keeper of sheep. Cain brought of the fruit of the ground an offering unto the Lord. Abel brought of the firstlings of his flock unto the Lord. The Lord had respect unto Abel and his offering: But unto Cain and his offering He had not respect. So Cain was filled with wrath, and rose up against his brother, and slew him. The question is, what does this story represent, and what spiritual meaning does it have for us today?

Cain represents: self-righteousness, the flesh, selfishness, the sin nature, man and his efforts, and that which kills or brings death. Abel represents: God's righteousness, the Spirit, selflessness, the divine nature, the Lamb and His sacrifice, and that which willingly lays down its life.

We must see and understand that Cain and Abel represent the spiritual conditions that we find ourselves in. You will either be found trusting in your own efforts, or you will trust in the sacrifice of the Lamb of God. Remember…Cain slew his brother Abel. The flesh (man's carnal efforts) will ALWAYS seek to kill the operation of the Spirit (the force of God), whether in your life, or the lives of others. As we LAY DOWN OUR LIVES by trusting in the sacrifice of the Lamb of God, we receive the greatest honor of all. GOD DECLARES US AS RIGHTEOUS. WE ARE JUSTIFIED IN HIS SIGHT! Hebrews 11:4 states…By FAITH Abel offered unto God a more excellent sacrifice than Cain, by which he obtained witness that he was righteous, God testifying of his gifts: and by it he being dead yet speaks…

Jesus was the SUPREME SACRIFICE, and we are to offer ourselves as a living sacrifice. By putting our faith in the slain Lamb, and by laying down our lives in EXCHANGE for His life, we obtain witness that we are righteous. Let us leave the ways of Cain, choosing rather to join the ways of Abel. In Christ…

WE ARE RIGHTEOUS!

January 31

PROGRESSIVE REVELATION

Is there such a thing as progressive revelation? If so, what is it? Let us first establish that there is such a thing as REVELATION, and then establish what it is, and that it is progressive.

2nd Corinthians 12:1 states…I will come to visions and revelations of the Lord…Galatians 1:12 states…For I neither received it (the gospel) of man, neither was I taught it, but by the revelation of Jesus Christ…Ephesians 1:17 states…the Father of glory may give unto you THE SPIRIT OF WISDOM AND REVELATION in the knowledge of Him…the eyes of your understanding being enlightened…

The word "revelation" means: to uncover or unveil, to make manifest that which was previously hidden, secret, or unknown. To see that God's revelation (unveiling of His purpose and plan to the creation) is progressive, we need only to look at the history of the Bible. God created Adam, who existed in innocence until his fall, which brought him into conscience, which led man into human government, and then to the promise to Abraham, and then to the law of Moses, and then to the grace or church age of Jesus Christ, which will culminate with the ages to come (the Millennium and the Age of the Ages), which will bring about the dispensation of the fullness of times, in which ALL will be gathered together in Christ. IS THIS NOT PROGRESSIVE? OF COURSE IT IS!!! God's great and mighty purpose of the ages is being unveiled step by step to the creation in a progressive way. This means that we must not camp out on past and present knowledge of God, but remain open to His progressive revelation, which will always line up with the Holy Scriptures when they are studied. Many people remain as IMMATURE CHRISTIANS because they refuse to keep an open mind to the progressive revelation of God. THEY THINK THEY KNOW IT ALL. Remember…God gives grace to the humble, BUT HE RESISTS THE PROUD. Humble yourself and ask God to open up to you the mysteries of His Kingdom. Ask Him to reveal to you the purpose of the ages. He wants you to understand and to be a part of His…

PROGRESSIVE REVELATION!

February 1

THE 42ND GENERATION

The 42nd Generation! What in the world is it? Get out your Bible and turn to Matthew 1:1-16. Notice that there are 42 generations listed, but that the 41st generation is Jesus, the son of Joseph. So who is the 42nd Generation? The key is to be found in vs. 17, which states…all the generations from Abraham to David are fourteen generations; and from David until the carrying away into Babylon are fourteen generations; and from the carrying away into Babylon unto CHRIST are fourteen generations…So the answer to our question is CHRIST. CHRIST is the 42nd Generation. Is there a difference between Jesus and Christ? That is a very good question! Who or what is (the) Christ?

1st Corinthians 12:12 states…for as the body is one, and has many members, and all the members of that one body, being many, are one body: SO ALSO IS CHRIST…Do you see it? Do you grasp what was just said? Christ is to be seen as a many membered body with Jesus as its head. The Christ is made up of more than just one man. IT IS A CORPORATE MAN! IT IS A MANY MEMBERED MAN. It could be said that Jesus is THE CHRIST (Anointed), and that we are HIS CHRIST (Anointed).

According to Bill Britton: "The 42ⁿᵈ Generation referred to as "Christ" in Matthew 1:17 refers to the Christ in 1ˢᵗ Corinthians 12:12,27. The 42ⁿᵈ GENERATION IS NOT JESUS ALONE, BUT IT IS HIS SON, THE OVERCOMER OF REVELATION 21:7." (<u>The 42ⁿᵈ Generation</u>, Bill Britton)

The 42ⁿᵈ Generation is Jesus and YOU! It speaks of those that are called out of all ages as the true seed of Abraham to rule and reign with Jesus now and in the ages to come. This will culminate in, and bring about what the apostle Paul referred to as the MANIFESTATION OF THE SONS OF GOD. WHAT A GENERATION! WHAT A PROMISE! WHAT A HOPE! WHAT A DELIVERANCE FOR THE ENTIRE CREATION! Revelation 21:7 states…He that overcomes shall inherit all things; and I will be His God, and he shall be My son…IT IS YOU…#42 (6 X 7…6=MAN, 7=THE PERFECTION OF GOD…HENCE, THE PERFECTION OF GOD MANIFESTED THROUGH MAN).

WE ARE CALLED TO BE THE 42ⁿᵈ GENERATION!

February 2

HEAVEN

According to J. Preston Eby: "The English word "heaven" is derived from the old Anglo-Saxon term "heave-on," meaning to be lifted up, up-lifted. It means to be "heaved-up" or "heav-en." In the scriptures, heaven is used to describe three rather distinct and different realms. It refers to the earth's atmosphere, outer space, and finally, it speaks of where God dwells. Not only is God our Father, but He is our Father in heaven. By saying God is in heaven (as Jesus did say), Jesus did not mean to localize or locate God. He was not telling us of a place where God is and where God lives apart from any other place in the universe. Those who think of heaven as a place, usually think of Him as being very distant. Somehow we have gotten the idea that heaven is a long way off. This error has crept into many songs sung by the church world such as: "When We All Get To Heaven" and "Won't It Be Wonderful There" (just to name a few). Where did we get this conception of heaven from? Certainly not from Jesus or the apostles! When Jesus was talking to Nicodemus, He said, "No man has ascended up into heaven, but He that came down from heaven, even the Son of man WHICH IS IN HEAVEN" (John 3:13). That is, Jesus claimed that while He was sitting and talking to this rabbi, He Himself was actually in heaven. This means of course, that heaven is here and now. Heaven for the child of God is not a future hope. It is a present reality. Jesus the Christ, when a man on earth, was at the same time in heaven. And so also are we who are "as He is" (1ˢᵗ John 4:17). Our Lord was in heaven; He came down from heaven, and still was in heaven; and this heaven is, in the Greek, OURANOS. It is something a person can be in, can descend from, and still possess. And the meaning of the word is "elevation, height, exaltation." (<u>Our Father Which Art In Heaven</u>, J. Preston Eby)

Ephesians 2:6 states…God has raised us up together, and made us to sit together IN HEAVENLY PLACES IN CHRIST JESUS…We are here told that the location of heaven, or the heavenly place that we desire is to be found IN CHRIST! This is not a physical location, but a spiritual position of being IN CHRIST! We must STOP thinking of heaven, or the heavenly place of God, as something that is "UP THERE, AND WE ARE DOWN HERE." We must come to the realization that heaven is where we are IN CHRIST!!! We must see heaven as a state of being that is available to us in the here-and-now. It is the very ABUNDANT LIFE OF THE LORD JESUS CHRIST! Many remain in hell (Hades, unperception, the carnal mind, separation from God in their mind), thinking that one day in the sweet by-and-by they will finally get their mansion in the sky and be able to experience God. Let us AWAKEN TO THE LIFE OF GOD IN CHRIST that is available to us now. Heaven is available to us now…

IN CHRIST!

February 3

CHRIST IN YOU

What is the hope of creation? Who is the hope of creation? Where is the hope of creation? Colossians 1:26,27 states…Even the mystery which has been hid from ages and from generations, but now is made manifest to His saints, to whom God would make known what is the riches of the glory of this mystery among the Gentiles, which is CHRIST IN YOU, the hope of glory…We can now see that the hope of creation is the revealing of the mystery of God, which has been hid for ages. As well, CHRIST IS THAT HOPE, AND CHRIST IS IN US!

With this in mind, we are able to come to these conclusions:

Christ is a mystery that must be revealed by God.
Christ is to be revealed throughout the ages of time.
The mystery of Christ is to be revealed in us.
This unfolding mystery of the ages is the hope of the entire creation.
Christ in us is the blessed hope.

Please take note of this very important point: IT IS NOT CHRIST IN HEAVEN THE HOPE OF GLORY, BUT IT IS CHRIST IN YOU THE HOPE OF GLORY!!! The only hope of God ever being glorified in the earth is that Christ would be revealed TO YOU, IN YOU, AND THROUGH YOU for the world to see. The only way that anyone will ever see Jesus, hear about Jesus, or learn about Jesus is THROUGH YOU! You are a vessel of God's glory.
Galatians 4:19 states…My little children, of whom I travail in birth again until CHRIST BE FORMED IN YOU…Galatians 1:15,16 states…But when it pleased God, Who separated me from

my mother's womb, and called me by His grace, TO REVEAL HIS SON IN ME…The hope of the whole creation is being formed inside of YOU. REJOICE!

WHAT A HOPE!

February 4

SODOM AND GOMORRAH

What about Sodom and Gomorrah? Has God doomed these sinners forever? The story of Sodom and its exceeding wickedness is known to every Bible reader (Genesis 19). Its awful destruction is still remembered and spoken of by many people today. Nevertheless, many people have never noticed the wonderful prophecy of future restoration and blessing for Sodom. FUTURE RESTORATION OF SODOM? BLESSINGS OF GOD UPON SODOM? WHAT?

Ezekiel 16:55 states…When your sisters, Sodom and her daughters, SHALL RETURN TO THEIR FORMER ESTATE, and Samaria and her daughters shall return to their former estate… Matthew 10:15 states…It shall be MORE TOLERABLE for the land of Sodom and Gomorrah in the day of judgment, than for that city…

Many people are not aware that the Bible declares that Sodom and Gomorrah shall be raised up again in the day of judgment to be corrected and finally restored TO THEIR FORMER ESTATE. WHAT A MERCIFUL AND LOVING GOD!!! Please note that many cities will be dealt with MORE SEVERELY than Sodom and Gomorrah. SO DON'T BE TOO HARD ON SODOM AND GOMORRAH! As far as the destruction of the city is concerned, it was necessary, and part of the purpose of God to bring about His progressive revelation in the earth. But we must keep in mind that just because God pours out judgment and wrath on people, does not mean that He has cast them off forever. His judgments and His wrath do not last forever. They are temporary and for the purpose of correction. OH THAT CHRISTIANS WOULD BE ABLE TO UNDERSTAND THIS ABOUT THEIR HEAVENLY FATHER!!! God does not condone wickedness of any kind. But God is able to correct the sinner and restore him to his former estate. Remember…GOD IS LOVE! Remember…LOVE NEVER FAILS! IT IS IMPOSSIBLE FOR GOD TO GIVE UP ON SODOM AND GOMORRAH, FOR HE LOVES THEM, AND HIS LOVE WILL NEVER FAIL THEM!

Isaiah 57:16 states…For I (God) will not contend for ever, neither will I be always wroth (Old Testament word for wrath): for the spirit should fail before me, and the souls which I have made…Lamentations 3:31,32 states…For the Lord will not cast off for ever: But though He cause grief, yet will He have compassion according to the multitudes of His mercies…Let God show you His GREAT compassion and mercy for all.

GOD LOVES ALL, EVEN SODOM AND GOMORRAH!

February 5

LET THIS CUP PASS

Matthew 26:39 states...and Jesus fell on His face, and prayed, saying, O My Father, if it be possible, let this cup pass from Me: nevertheless not as I will, but as You will...As we take into consideration that Jesus was God manifested in the flesh, we are then in position to understand this statement that He makes. He was a representation of God and man. He was referred to as the Son of man AND the Son of God. As the Son of man, Jesus was identifying with man (mankind) when He prayed, saying, LET THIS CUP PASS FROM ME. This "cup" that He spoke of was referring to His death on the cross. This statement seems to be out of character for Jesus. WHY THIS STATEMENT?

As Jesus suffered in the Garden of Gethsemane, and did sweat great drops of blood, He made this statement to identify with man in the agony of the death of the self-life. The cup represents the death of self. It is the death of our ways and the life of His ways. This is the cup that Jesus drank for us as a man, and this is the cup that we must also drink of. It is a bitter cup with a bitter taste, but it has a sweet aftertaste, for it results in resurrection life. It initially speaks of death, but after it has done its work it will yield the fruit of righteousness, peace, and joy in the Holy Spirit. Man is ever trying to get out of drinking the cup of the death of self. When we do not drink of the cup we miss the opportunity to partake of resurrection life, for life can only come out of death. THE DEATH OF SELF IS THE KEY TO THE RESURRECTION LIFE AND POWER OF GOD!

As the Son of God, Jesus identified with God when He also said, YOUR WILL BE DONE! Jesus typified man and God, FOR HIS LIFE WAS A REPRESENTATION OF BOTH. He was the MEDIATOR between man and God. As the Son of man He identified with man (let this cup pass), and as the Son of God He identified with God (Your will be done). JESUS DRANK THE CUP! We are now able, through Jesus, to drink the cup that represents the death of self, and to enter into His resurrection life. THANK YOU LORD FOR DRINKING THE CUP!

YOUR WILL BE DONE!

February 6

WHO, WHAT, WHERE IS SATAN?

Is Satan a literal angelic being with a pitchfork, horns, wings, a tail, and a red suit? With just a little bit of research and some common sense, it will become clear that our understanding of Satan is based primarily on the traditions and doctrines of men, rather than what the Bible actually teaches. As Gary Amirault has stated, we will come to find out that..."FIRE AND TORMENT WITH MUCH SUPERSTITION WAS ADDED TO GREEK MYTHOLOGY AND FICTION.

THE GODDESS OF HEL FROM NORSE MYTHOLOGY BECAME SATAN, HERO OF MOST ESCHATOLOGY." To be blunt, the Christian explanation of Satan IS NOT CORRECT!

The word "Satan" means ADVERSARY. This speaks of someone or something that opposes or attacks. This is WHO Satan is. He is the adversary. Ephesians 2:2 sheds a tremendous amount of light on understanding Satan. It states…Wherein in time past you walked according to the course of this world, according to the PRINCE OF THE POWER OF THE AIR, THE SPIRIT THAT NOW WORKS IN THE CHILDREN OF DISOBEDIENCE…So…Satan, who is here referred to as the prince of the power of the air, IS A SPIRIT, AND IS IN US. This spirit is said to be at work in the children of disobedience.

After having stated these things, we are now able to come to these conclusions:

SATAN IS THE ADVERSARY (THIS IS WHO HE IS)

SATAN IS A SPIRIT (THIS IS WHAT HE IS)

SATAN OPERATES IN MAN, ESPECIALLY IN AND
THROUGH THE CHILDREN OF DISOBEDIENCE (THIS IS WHERE HE IS)

Do you remember when Jesus referred to Peter as Satan (GET THEE BEHIND ME SATAN)? Do you remember when the scriptures stated that SATAN ENTERED JUDAS? How can Satan be a literal being if Jesus referred to Peter as Satan, and it is said that Satan ENTERED Judas? When Jesus referred to Peter as Satan, He was recognizing the prince of the power of the air, the satanic spirit that was at work in Peter. This was due to the fact that Peter was being used by that spirit to discourage Jesus from fulfilling His mission, in telling Jesus that He did not have to die for the sin of the world, and be raised again the third day. As far as Judas is concerned, how could a literal being enter him (THINK ABOUT IT)? This is OBVIOUSLY referring to the SPIRIT OF SATAN entering him.

As was previously discussed, this SPIRIT looks to make its home in THE CHILDREN OF DISOBEDIENCE. WHY IS THIS SO HARD FOR CHRISTIANS TO UNDERSTAND??? GOD IS A SPIRIT, AND LOOKS TO MAKE HIS HOME IN THE CHILDREN OF OBEDIENCE. Why should we find it strange that Satan would be a spirit and operate in the same manner? Once again, many have been SEDUCED BY THE TRADITIONS AND DOCTRINES OF MEN, RATHER THAN STUDYING AND PRAYING FOR THEMSELVES. They would rather have their pastor tell them about God (whether it is right or not) than to know Him for themselves. Let us turn away from the traditions and MYTHS of men to our Heavenly Father's…

SPIRIT AND TRUTH!

February 7

GOD GIVES THE INCREASE

1ST Corinthians 3:6,7 states…I have planted, Apollos watered; but God gave the increase. So then neither is he that plants any thing, neither he that waters; but God that gives the increase… This scripture gives us insight into the WAYS of God. It speaks of how we are to minister to people, not getting upset with them when they do not understand what it is that they are being taught. ONLY GOD CAN AND WILL GIVE THE INCREASE! This means that it takes the Spirit of God to reveal (unveil) spiritual things to man. You may minister to someone on a certain subject and they will not understand it. Someone else may minister to them on the same subject, and then God will give the increase. DO NOT BE UPSET WITH THIS! Remember…IT TAKES GOD TO GIVE THE INCREASE. God may use you to plant and someone else to water, or He may use someone else to plant and you to water; but only God can give the increase. We must recognize that it takes people quite a long time to grasp spiritual things.

The seed of the Word of God must be planted in the heart of a person, then it must be watered, and then it must have time to grow. Finally, God will cause that seed to bring forth the fruit of wisdom and revelation in the knowledge of Him. He uses man to plant and to water, but He is the only One Who can give the increase (to make something come alive, or be quickened in a person's heart). We must be aware of, recognize, and understand that there is a process to man coming out of his carnality. It is:

1. PLANTING
2. WATERING
3. AND GOD GIVING THE INCREASE

ASK FOR HIS INCREASE TODAY!

February 8

OFF THE DEEP END?

Have you gone off the deep end? I SURE HOPE SO! The next time someone tells you that you have gone off the deep end concerning the things of God, you can tell them…THANK YOU! OF COURSE I HAVE!

Psalm 42:7,8 states…DEEP CALLS UNTO DEEP at the noise of Your waterspouts…Yet the Lord will command His lovingkindness in the daytime, and in the night His song shall be with me, and my prayer unto the God of my life…Daniel 2:22 states…He reveals THE DEEP THINGS; He knows what is in the darkness, and the light dwells with Him…1st Corinthians 2:10 states…But

God has revealed them (the things that He has prepared for us) unto us by His Spirit: for the Spirit searches all things, yea, THE DEEP THINGS OF GOD...

Many are not aware that there is a DEEP in man that calls out to the DEEP in God. There is a longing in us to know the deep things of God, which includes the MYSTERIES of His Kingdom. WE MUST FIRST RECOGNIZE THAT THERE ARE DEEP SECRETS AND MYSTERIES THAT ARE HIDDEN BY GOD, AND THEN ASK GOD TO REVEAL THESE DEEP THINGS TO US. It is time to come out of the SHALLOW END of the traditions and doctrines (teachings) of men, and to come into the DEEP RICHES of the knowledge of Christ! Most Christians love to remain in SHALLOW RELIGIOUS WATERS, never maturing in God, and remain as babes on the milk of the Word. They refuse to let go of their spiritual sugar tit.

IT IS TIME TO LAUNCH OUT INTO THE DEEP, O CHILD OF GOD! Ask God to reveal to you His mysteries and secrets. He is the One that placed the DEEP in you that longs for the DEEP in Him.

CALL UNTO THE DEEP IN GOD!

February 9

LOST YOUR MIND?

Have you lost your mind? I SURE HOPE SO! The next time someone tells you that you have lost your mind concerning the things of God, you can tell them...THANK YOU! OF COURSE I HAVE!

Romans 12:2 states...And be not conformed to this world (age): but be TRANSFORMED BY THE RENEWING OF YOUR MIND...2nd Corinthians 3:14 states...But their minds were blinded: for until this day remains the same veil untaken away in the reading of the Old Testament; which veil is done away in Christ...2nd Corinthians 4:4 states...the god of this world (age) has blinded the minds of them which believe not...Philippians 2:5 states...Let this mind be in you, which was also in Christ Jesus...Hebrews 8:10 states...I will put My laws into their mind, and write them in their hearts...1st Corinthians 2:16 states...But we have the mind of Christ...

Due to the fact that our minds are blinded by the god of this age, our minds need to be transformed and renewed. We are then told that we need the same mind in us that was in Christ, and that the laws of God must be put in our mind, giving us the MIND OF CHRIST. In actuality, WE MUST LOSE OUR MINDS!!! We must lose the carnal mind, which is death, having it transformed and renewed into the mind of Christ, which is life. LOSING YOUR MIND IS A GOOD THING!

WE HAVE THE MIND OF CHRIST!

February 10

KEEP YOURSELVES FROM IDOLS

According to Dr. Loyal Hurley: "1ˢᵀ John 5:21 states…Little children , keep yourselves (guard against) from idols. Amen…The most important thinking in the world is the thinking that men (mankind) do about God. True ideas of God lead to nobility of life; false ideas of God lead to the opposite." (<u>The Outcome Of Infinite Grace</u>, Dr. Loyal Hurley)

The word "idol" speaks of false gods, or FALSE IDEAS OF THE TRUE GOD. The religions of men have created many idols (false ideas) in our hearts. These idols are preconceived ideas about God that are not true. Two of the most damaging idols that have been produced by the teachings of men are:

1. Eternal Torture
2. Annihilation

We say that God is ALL-POWERFUL, and then turn around and deny it! As well, we say that God is ALL-LOVING, and turn around and deny it! The two most popular thoughts about God's dealings with the wicked, is that He will either torture them forever, or that He will exterminate (annihilate) them. In neither of these two sets of beliefs could God be ALL-POWERFUL AND ALL-LOVING! According to the teaching of eternal torture and annihilation, God either can not correct the wicked, or He does not want to correct the wicked. EITHER WAY, YOU HAVE A LIMITED GOD!!!

With a little bit of study, prayer, and meditation, we can see that the teachings of eternal torture and annihilation are IDOLS that have been set up in the hearts of men by organized religion. Either God is ALL-POWERFUL, or He is not. Either God is ALL-LOVING, or He is not. KEEP YOURSELVES FROM FALSE IDEAS OF GOD! Anything short of ALL REALMS of intelligence being ultimately brought under the sway of the power and the love of Christ is IDOLATRY!

GUARD AGAINST THESE FALSE IDEAS OF GOD!

February 11

HE SHALL BE SATISFIED

Do you think that God, Who is love, would be satisfied with just a portion of the creation being saved? If you had bought one hundred acres of land, would you be satisfied with receiving only one acre? I DON'T THINK SO! Neither will God be satisfied until THE ENTIRE CREATION IS RESTORED BACK UNTO HIM! It was for this very reason that God was manifested in the flesh and came to this earth. He came to be the SAVIOR OF THE WORLD. He did not come to be the potential savior, that is, He will be your savior if you do everything just right. NO! He came to be the ACTUAL SAVIOR OF THE WORLD! He is the Lamb of God that TAKES AWAY THE SIN OF THE WORLD!

Remember…YOU ARE NOT YOUR OWN! YOU ARE BOUGHT WITH A PRICE! YOU BELONG TO GOD! The reason that we belong to God is that HE PAID FOR US, AND THAT HE PURCHASED US THROUGH THE DEATH OF THE LORD JESUS CHRIST! HE HAS (PAST TENSE) FORGIVEN YOU OF ALL YOUR SINS!!! JESUS PAID IT ALL! IN FULL! No matter what organized Christianity says, HE IS GOING TO GO AFTER THE ENTIRE AMOUNT OF HIS PURCHASED POSSESSION!

Isaiah 53:11 states…He shall see the travail of His soul, AND SHALL BE SATISFIED…Our Heavenly Father will be satisfied with nothing less than ALL OF HIS PURCHASED POSSESSION! 1ST John 2:2 states…And He (Jesus) is the propitiation (atonement) for our sins: AND NOT FOR OUR SINS ONLY, BUT ALSO FOR THE SINS OF THE WHOLE WORLD…

HE SHALL BE SATISFIED!

February 12

ABRAHAM LINCOLN

How fitting it is to talk about Abraham Lincoln today. It is his birthday. Happy Birthday, Abe! Abraham Lincoln, the 16th President of the United States of America, was a believer, and accepted the Holy Scriptures as inspired by God Himself. But there is one point that is not often found in popular writings about him. ABRAHAM LINCOLN BELIEVED IN THE ULTIMATE SALVATION OF ALL MEN! (You can research this at www.savior-of-all.com.)

He took the passage, "As in Adam all die, even so in Christ shall all be made alive," and followed up with the proposition that Adam's transgression was totally and completely reversed, and was made just and right by the atonement of Christ. Abraham Lincoln understood punishment for sin to be a Bible doctrine, but also understood that it must cease when justice is satisfied. He knew that all that were lost by the fall were made good by the sacrifice of the Son of God, EVERY MAN IN HIS OWN ORDER.

Lincoln often referred to 1st Corinthians 15 to support his view of the salvation of all men. He very clearly was a believer, and knew the Bible better than any other President, especially in his understanding of the restitution of all things. What a man! What a President! What a servant of God! HAPPY BIRTHDAY, ABE! Your message of truth is marching on.

IN CHRIST SHALL ALL BE MADE ALIVE!

February 13

FIRSTFRUITS

James 1:18 states…Of His own will begat He us with the word of truth, that we should be a kind of firstfruits of His creatures…The word "firstfruits" speaks of the beginning of something, or the first of the ripe fruits. The word "firstfruits" would then signify to us that that which is considered a firstfruit is not the full harvest, but it does point to the fact that there is more fruit to come. The firstfruits is not the end of the harvest, but it is just the beginning of GOD'S GREAT HARVEST!

The Jewish people of the Old Testament had three great feasts in a one year period. They were:

1. THE FEAST OF UNLEAVENED BREAD
2. THE FEAST OF WEEKS
3. THE FEAST OF INGATHERING

These three great feasts go hand in hand with three harvests:

1. BARLEY HARVEST
2. WHEAT HARVEST
3. GRAPE HARVEST

These three major feasts are also known as:

1. PASSOVER
2. PENTECOST
3. TABERNACLES

They do correspond to our:

1. APRIL
2. JUNE
3. OCTOBER

These three harvests do spiritually represent the way in which God is reconciling all things unto Himself. They represent:

1. REMNANT
2. NATIONS
3. WORLD (THE ENTIRE CREATION)

This great harvest of mankind is being gathered unto God now, and will continue in the ages to come. It is to take place in:

1. THIS PRESENT AGE
2. THE MILLENNIUM
3. THE AGE OF THE AGES (DISPENSATION OF THE FULLNESS OF TIMES)

This present age in which we find ourselves is the age in which God is gathering in a REMNANT, or FIRSTFRUITS. This remnant is then to be used in the coming Age to be the very manifested sons of God, which will result in all nations coming to the knowledge of the Lord. (Read Isaiah 2:1-4.) This remnant is to be used as well in the Age of the Ages, playing a part in the final phase of God's great harvest, which will result in the gathering of ALL REMAINING THINGS IN CHRIST (Ephesians 1:9-11, Colossians 1:20). This will be the consummation and completion of God's great harvest, which will result in Him being ALL IN ALL (EVERYTHING TO EVERYONE).

According to Ray Knight: "We must realize that the firstfruits is not the end of God's dealings with man, but just the beginning. According to God's pattern given in the Old Testament, there must come forth a firstfruits company that is separated away first from the whole just as the sheaf of firstfruits was waved as the evidence that the whole harvest would follow (<u>Firstfruits</u>, Ray Knight)." REJOICE! You are the firstfruits of God. Your very salvation GUARANTEES the rest of the harvest to come.

READ EPHESIANS 2:7!

February 14

GOLD, SILVER, PRECIOUS STONES, WOOD, HAY, STUBBLE

1st Corinthians 3:12,13 states…Now if any man build upon this foundation (Jesus Christ) gold, silver, precious stones, wood, hay, stubble; every man's work shall be made manifest: for the day shall declare it, because it shall be revealed by fire; and the fire shall try every man's work of what sort it is…

What an interesting scripture! This scripture passage gives us insight into the ways of God and man, and how that God deals with man. Notice the particulars in these two verses of scripture. They are:

      1. THE FOUNDATION
      2. BUILDING ON THE FOUNDATION
      3. GOLD, SILVER, PRECIOUS STONES
      4. WOOD, HAY, STUBBLE
      5. FIRE

Are these things to be understood literally or spiritually? Well…SPIRITUALLY OF COURSE! We do so much damage to the scriptures when we literalize things that are to be understood spiritually. There is also much damage done to the scriptures when we spiritualize something that is not to be spiritualized, but that is another issue, and another topic for another day. In this particular case, we are to understand this passage in a spiritual sense.

1. There is only one foundation that can be built on, and that foundation is the Lord Jesus Christ (Who He is, and what He accomplished).

2. We are called upon to recognize this foundation, and then to build upon it.

3. That which man builds upon this foundation, which is to be recognized by God as fruitful, is characterized as gold, silver, and precious stones. (These represent divinity.)

4. That which man builds upon this foundation, which is to be recognized by God as unfruitful, is to be characterized as wood, hay, and stubble. (These represent carnality.)

5. We are to see GOD AS A CONSUMING FIRE! His fire does try the believer's work, which in turn does consume his wood, hay, and stubble (carnality), and does purify his gold, silver, and precious stones (his potential for divinity).

Wood, hay, and stubble represent carnality, self, the sin nature, or the Adamic Nature that we inherited from Adam. Gold, silver, and precious stones represent divinity - and/or the divine nature that is hidden in man, buried under wood, hay, and stubble.

So then the goal of God, WHO IS A CONSUMING FIRE, is to burn up the carnal mind (the corrupt nature within man), and to purify man, depositing His very divine nature within him. This is brought about by the FIERY TRIALS of God in and through our wilderness experiences. As we come to understand this process, we will learn to burn without complaining (Well...At least we will not complain quite as much). Let us boldly enter into the fire of God, NOT FIGHTING FIRE WITH FIRE, BUT YIELDING TO HIS FIRE WITH SUBMISSION!

GOD IS A CONSUMING FIRE!

February 15

THE RESTITUTION OF ALL THINGS

Acts 3:20,21 states...Jesus Christ, Which before was preached unto you: Whom the heavens must receive until the times of restitution of all things, which God has spoken by the mouth of all His holy prophets since the world began...What an unbelievable statement! What does it mean? Let us find out.

"Restitution" means: the act of restoring something that has been taken away or lost; the act of making good or rendering an equivalent as for loss or injury. It means restoration. Now let us look at the grammatical construction of this sentence and what it declares.

Notice that there is a comma after the word things. This means that what follows the word things refers back to the original statement. With this in mind, it is now easy to see that all the prophets from the beginning of the world had prophesied that there would be a restoration of all things, and that the restoration would indeed be universal, and would include all things. The reason that so many Christians fail to see this great truth is due to the fact that they have little or no knowledge of what the Bible teaches about the AGES TO COME. Not being aware of these ages to come greatly hinders our understanding of the purpose and plan of God, and blocks us from being able to understand the restitution of all things.

Go back to the LAW, the PSALMS, and the PROPHETS. You will see the COUNTLESS prophecies which declare the restitution of all things. IT IS TRUTH! IT IS MARVELOUS! IT IS BIGGER THAN YOU COULD EVER IMAGINE! IT IS UNDENIABLE! There shall be a restitution of all things!

IT SHALL COME TO PASS!

February 16

METAPHORS IN SCRIPTURE

According to Webster, a "metaphor" is: the application of a word or phrase to an object or concept IT DOES NOT LITERALLY DENOTE, suggesting comparison to that object or concept, as in "A mighty fortress is our God." A metaphor is a comparison to a literal object or concept, but it is actually not the literal thing that it is being compared to. We must realize that the Bible is full of metaphors, symbols, parables, types, and shadows. The most deadly thing you can do is to try to interpret the Bible with your intellect, which is the natural (carnal) mind. God uses metaphors to speak to us, because the ways of the Spirit are so much higher than the ways of man. His use of metaphors helps us to understand the higher ways of the Spirit. A problem arises though, when we take the metaphor or parable literally. It is to be seen as a comparison of something literal, to convey a spiritual concept of God, but not to be taken literally.

Here are a few metaphors to consider:

A mighty FORTRESS is our God…
God is a consuming FIRE…
The LAMB of God that takes away the sin of the world…
I am the DOOR…
If your hand offends you CUT IT OFF…
If your eye offends you PLUCK IT OUT…
My SHEEP hear my voice…
I am the good SHEPHERD…
Behold, He comes with CLOUDS…
Caught up in the CLOUDS to meet the Lord in the AIR…
His eyes were as a FLAME OF FIRE…
His feet like BRASS…His voice as the sound of many WATERS…
THE LAKE OF FIRE…
From your belly shall flow RIVERS OF LIVING WATER…
A Lamb having SEVEN HORNS, SEVEN EYES…THE SEVEN SPIRITS OF GOD…

As well, the entire book of revelation is a metaphor, which gives to us the unveiling of Jesus Christ.

There are obviously many other metaphors in the Bible, many of which are not understood by the casual reader of scripture. If a person is willing to HUMBLE HIMSELF, diligently read, study, and pray, the mysterious metaphors of the Bible will become very simple, and easy to understand. Understanding metaphors in the Bible, and God's use of them, will enable you to grasp the SPIRIT OF THE WORD, rather than just the letter of the Word. Remember…The letter kills…

BUT THE SPIRIT BRINGS LIFE!

February 17

WHAT IS CHRISTIANITY?

Acts 11:26 states…And the disciples were called Christians first in Antioch…The word "Christian" means: one who believes in, follows, and demonstrates the life and teachings of Jesus Christ. Without the Lord Jesus Christ there would be no such thing as a Christian or Christianity. In essence then, Christianity revolves around a person, and in fact IS A PERSON. This person, is of course, the Lord Himself. Christianity is NOT:

A SET OF DOCTRINAL BELIEFS…
A DENOMINATION…
A RELIGION…
A BUILDING MADE WITH HANDS…

A knowledge of the scriptures alone does not a Christian make. It is WHO the scriptures speak of that makes Christianity what it is. Remember…Eternal life (the life of the ages) is to know God, and Jesus Christ Whom He has sent (John 17:3)…Being a true Christian is not so much what we do, as much as it is Who we know. The doing of Christianity will become a byproduct of the One that we are in relationship with. The One that we speak of, is of course, THE RISEN CHRIST!

According to William Barclay: "There was one mistake into which the early church was never in any danger of falling. In those early days men never thought of Jesus Christ as a figure in a book. They never thought of Him as someone Who had lived and died, and Whose story was told and passed down in history, as the story of someone Who had lived and Whose life had ended. They did not think of Him as someone Who had been but as someone Who is. They did not think of Jesus Christ as someone Whose teaching must be discussed and debated and argued about; they thought of Him as someone Whose presence could be enjoyed and Whose constant fellowship could be experienced. Their faith was not founded on a book; their faith was founded on a person." (William Barclay)

LOOK UNTO JESUS!

February 18

THE JUDGMENT SEAT OF CHRIST

Romans 14:10 states…But why do you judge your brother? Or why do you set at nought your brother? For we shall all stand before the judgment seat of Christ…As well, 1ˢᵗ Peter 4:17 states… For the time is come that judgment must begin at the house of God…The word "judgment" means a separating. This judgment must begin AT THE HOUSE OF GOD. So where is the house of God? Is it in the sweet by-and-by? Is it a mansion in the sky? NO! YOU ARE THE HOUSE OF GOD (1ˢᵗ Peter 2:5)!

As a believer, judgment has already begun in our lives, for we are the house of God. In essence, WE ARE AT THE JUDGMENT SEAT OF CHRIST NOW! In addition to seeing this, we must also come to realize that JUDGMENT IS NOT A BAD THING, BUT A GOOD THING. IT IS A VERY GOOD THING! Isaiah 26:9 states…WHEN GOD'S JUDGMENTS ARE IN THE EARTH, THE INHABITANTS OF THE WORLD WILL LEARN RIGHTEOUSNESS…

Our life, our ways, our thoughts, and our deeds are being judged and separated by God NOW! We are being separated FROM SELF, AND UNTO OUR FATHER. We are being transformed into the image of God. God is bringing us through His judgments. For what purpose?

1ˢᵗ Corinthians 6:2 states…Do you not know that the SAINTS SHALL JUDGE THE WORLD… THE WORLD SHALL BE JUDGED BY YOU…We are being judged now that we might judge the world in the ages to come. We must allow God to correct us now that we might be instruments of His correction to the remainder of the creation. God's dealings with us at His judgment seat are to qualify us to be judges now and in the ages to come.

WE SHALL JUDGE THE WORLD! (Read Obadiah 1:21)

February 19

THE CHASTENING OF THE LORD
(Hebrews 12:5-11)

Hebrews 12:5,6 states…My son, despise not the chastening of the Lord, nor faint when you art rebuked of Him: For whom the Lord loves He chastens, and scourges every son whom He receives…The word "chastening" means: tutorage, education, training, correction, instruction, and nurture. We must see that God chastens us to tutor us, educate us, train us, correct us, instruct us, and to nurture us. We must grasp this great truth about God, for those who fail to understand the chastening of the Lord will have a miserable Christian experience. They will always be under the impression that God is mad at them, not understanding His ways, and not understanding the nature of their Father.

All of God's dealings with man are for the purpose of CORRECTION. Just as a natural father would chasten his son to correct him, in the same sense, OUR HEAVENLY FATHER CHASTENS US TO CORRECT US. As well, all judgment, punishment, wrath, vengeance, and chastening from the Lord is for our good, and is for the purpose of correction, and does result in our being reconciled unto Him. We must STOP thinking of God as some angry monster that is foaming at the mouth, just waiting to vindictively, senselessly, and endlessly torment and torture all who do not get right. HE KNOWS THAT WE ARE NOT RIGHT (RIGHTEOUS)! THIS IS THE VERY REASON THAT HE CHASTENS US!!! So what is the outcome of His chastening?

God's chastening brings about the peaceable fruit of righteousness. So whether it be His judgment, punishment, wrath, vengeance, or His chastening, the end result will be a person in love with and loved by God, having been corrected by their Heavenly Father. OUR GOD IS ABLE AND WILLING TO…

CHASTEN US ALL!

February 20

TOP 25

Here is a list of what I consider to be twenty-five of the most powerful passages of scripture in the Bible. These are key verses that UNLOCK the mysteries and secrets of the purpose and plan of God. Ask God to give you the spirit of wisdom and revelation in the knowledge of Him concerning these scriptures. ENJOY YOUR SEARCH!

1. Colossians 1:16…Jesus Christ created ALL THINGS (including principalities and powers)…

2. Isaiah 45:7…God created good AND EVIL…

3. Isaiah 14:12 & Ezekiel 28:13,15…These passages of scripture describe who Lucifer is. Here are some hints: Who was the Garden of Eden made for? Who was in the Garden, and was perfect UNTIL iniquity was found in him? You also need to do a word study on the name Lucifer.

4. Isaiah 54:16…God created the waster to destroy…

5. Psalm 90:1-3…We were with the Lord before the earth was formed…God put us in destruction…He says return…

6. Romans 8:20…The creation was made subject to vanity (futility or failure), not willingly (not of its own choice, but by the will of Him Who so subjected it)…

7. Ephesians 1:17-19…The spirit of wisdom and revelation in the knowledge of Him…

8. Proverbs 25:2…God conceals or hides the truth…We are to search it out…

9. Colossians 1:26,27…God is a mystery that has been hid for ages…It is now made manifest…IT IS CHRIST IN YOU…

10. 1st Corinthians 12:12…CHRIST is a many membered body (man)…

11. Luke 17:20,21…The kingdom of God is WITHIN YOU…(AWESOME)…

12. Hebrews 1:2…God made the AGES (worlds is a mistranslation)…

13. Genesis 12:3…ALL families of the earth shall be blessed…

14. Psalm 22:27…ALL the ends of the world shall REMEMBER and turn unto the Lord (WOW!)…

15. Psalm 65:2…ALL flesh will come to God…

16. Psalm 72:11…ALL kings and nations shall serve Him…

17. Acts 3:21…The restitution (restoration) of ALL things…

18. 1st Corinthians 15:22-28…This is probably one of the most powerful portions of scripture in the entire Bible. It outlines the entire purpose of God. It starts with Adam and ends with God being ALL IN ALL…

19. Ephesians 1:9-11…The dispensation of the fullness of times…ALL THINGS gathered into Christ…This is referred to as God's SACRED SECRET…

20. Colossians 1:20…God will reconcile ALL THINGS unto Himself…

21. Philippians 2:10,11…EVERY KNEE SHALL BOW (this refers to a worshipful bow)… EVERY TONGUE CONFESS JESUS CHRIST AS LORD (as well, read Romans 10:9,10 and 1st Corinthians 12:3)…

22. Philippians 3:21…God will subdue ALL THINGS unto Himself…

23. 1st Timothy 2:4-6…God will have ALL MEN to be saved…A ransom for ALL… Testified in DUE TIME…

24. 1ST Timothy 4:10…GOD IS THE SAVIOR OF ALL MEN…

25. Romans 11:36…OF Him, THROUGH Him, and TO Him are ALL things…

This is just a drop in the bucket of key verses in the Bible that UNLOCK His purpose and plan for the entire creation. For over 600 key verses, read: <u>Read And Search God's Plan</u>, by Dr. Harold Lovelace.

ENJOY YOUR SEARCH!

February 21

THE SOVEREIGNTY OF GOD

According to George Addair: "By the sovereignty of God, we mean the supremacy of God. We mean His Kingship and Headship. It literally means , "the Godhood of God." To declare that God is sovereign is to declare that He is God. It is to declare "that He is the most high, doing according to His will IN THE ARMY OF HEAVEN AND AMONG THE INHABITANTS OF THE EARTH, so that none can stay His hand or say unto Him, What have You done?" Daniel 4:35." (The Absolute Sovereignty Of God, George Addair)

Either God is sovereign or He is not. If He is not sovereign, then He is limited in some way, and that makes Him like us. If God is sovereign, then that means He is responsible for all of the creation. He is the author and finisher of everything. HE IS IN CHARGE OF EVERYTHING!

God is responsible for:

> CREATING EVERYTHING
> GOOD AND EVIL
> THE FALL OF MAN
> THE CREATION MADE SUBJECT TO VANITY
> PUTTING MAN INTO DESTRUCTION
> THE CRUCIFYING OF THE LORD JESUS
> ULTIMATELY RESTORING EVERYTHING BACK TO HIMSELF

Understanding the sovereignty of God will SET YOU FREE from the silly things that people preach and teach about God, claiming that He is fighting against the Devil and the powers of darkness, trying to do the best He can, but will ultimately lose the vast majority of His creation. THAT IS SILLY AND OUTRIGHT RIDICULOUS! Here are some scriptures that clearly declare the ABSOLUTE SOVEREIGNTY OF GOD:

> Isaiah 46:10
> Daniel 4:35
> Psalm 37:23
> Psalm 33:15
> Psalm 115:3
> Acts 15:18
> Romans 9:11-24
> Romans 11:25-36
> Ephesians 1:11
> 1st Timothy 6:15
> Revelation 4:11

RELAX!!! GOD IS IN TOTAL AND COMPLETE CONTROL OF EVERYTHING! HE IS...

SOVEREIGN ALMIGHTY GOD!

February 22

THE "SECOND" COMING "?"

According to J. Preston Eby: "It may surprise many people to learn that the Bible nowhere speaks of the "second coming" of Christ. We must purge our conversation, purify our terminology, and remove from our consciousness the multitude of non-scriptural and extra biblical expressions carried over from Mystery Babylon." (Looking For His Appearing, J. Preston Eby)

We have been taught by man to think in terms of the first and second coming of Christ, rather than looking to the Bible which speaks of the progressive revelation of Jesus Christ, and of His progressive comings. This thought is brought out in Micah 5:2.

Micah 5:2 states…Who is to be ruler in Israel, Whose GOINGS FORTH have been of old, from everlasting…(Notice GOINGS is plural) Let us now arrive at the mature understanding of the GOINGS FORTH of the Lord, for the Bible speaks of many comings of the Lord.

The Lord comes:

WITH CLOUDS
AS LIGHTNING
AS A THIEF
AS THE BRIDEGROOM
AS THE MORNING STAR
AS THE SON OF RIGHTEOUSNESS ARISING
IN RESURRECTION POWER
IN FLAMING FIRE
AS REFINER'S FIRE AND FULLERS' SOAP
IN THE AIR
AS THE RAIN
ON A WHITE HORSE
AS KING
AS THE CHIEF SHEPHERD
WITH HIS ANGELS
WITH HIS SAINTS
TO HIS SAINTS
IN HIS SAINTS
IN JUDGMENT
WITH REWARDS
WITH A SHOUT
WITH THE VOICE OF THE ARCHANGEL
WITH THE TRUMP OF GOD
TO THE MOUNT OF OLIVES
TO HIS TEMPLE
IN GLORY
AS LORD

IN HIS KINGDOM
AS SEASONS OF REFRESHING
ETC.
ETC.

Are you getting the point yet? We have limited Jesus Christ to a first and second coming (which words are not even found in the Bible), and we have totally missed the point of HIS PROGRESSIVE REVELATION TO MANKIND. THESE COMINGS OF THE LORD ARE TO BE CHARACTERIZED AS HIS GOINGS FORTH.

The Greek word "parousia", which occurs twenty-four times in the New Testament, comes from the verb "paremi", which means at hand, or to be present. "Parousia" denotes the presence of one who has already arrived. THE COMING OF THE LORD IS ACTUALLY HIS PRESENCE. James 5:7 states…Be patient unto the coming (presence) of the Lord…

HIS GOINGS FORTH HAVE BEEN OF OLD, FROM EVERLASTING!

February 23

AN EXCELLENT SPIRIT

Proverbs 17:27,28 states…He that has knowledge spares his words: And a man of understanding is of an excellent spirit. Even a fool, when he holds his peace, is counted wise: And he that shuts his lips is esteemed a man of understanding…If there were ever a scripture verse that needed to be applied to our lives, this is definitely one of them. A sure sign of a fool is one who has diarrhea of the mouth. Let us now notice a few of the words in this passage and their meanings.

The word "understanding" in verse 27 means discerning. The word "excellent" in verse 27 means quiet, and the word "understanding" in verse 28 means wisdom, or a wise man. We can now conclude that a discerning person is of a quiet spirit, and he that shuts his lips is a wise man.

Remember the story of Joseph? Joseph proved in the end to be a man with a quiet spirit, one who was discerning, and one who was wise. What was it that he discerned? GOD'S WAYS! Joseph came to realize that what his brothers meant for evil, God meant it unto good, to save much people alive. Joseph told his brothers to…be not grieved, nor angry with yourselves, that you sold me: for God did send me before you to preserve your life. WHAT AN EXAMPLE OF A DISCERNING WISE MAN WITH AN EXCELLENT SPIRIT! Joseph entered into Egypt as a slave, and then became the most powerful man in all of Egypt under Pharaoh! Joseph understood that YOUR ATTITUDE DETERMINES YOUR ALTITUDE!!! If you humble yourself under the mighty hand of God, He will exalt you in due season. May we learn to discern GOD'S WAYS, having an excellent spirit, and may we grow into men and women of wisdom.

BE OF AN EXCELLENT SPIRIT!

February 24

GOING BACK TO THE BASICS "**?**"

Have you ever heard someone tell you that they were "going back to the basics"? It is quite a common statement among Christians. It sounds really holy, doesn't it? It has a good ring to it, don't you think? The question is then, should we go back to the basics? NO!

That has got to be the biggest "cop out" statement of all time!!! The words "cop out" mean to avoid a responsibility. What is it that we are avoiding by going back to the basics in God? We are avoiding and refusing to GROW UP IN GOD.

God never told us to go back to the basics. He did however tell us to BUILD UPON THE BASICS. We must have the basic (elementary) knowledge of the gospel written on our hearts, and then we are to GROW IN GRACE AND IN THE KNOWLEDGE OF THE LORD. When people are challenged to learn something about God that is new to them, they throw up their hands and say…I am going back to the basics. What they are really saying is this: "I do not want to be moved out of my comfort zone. I already have all my ducks in a row. Please do not trouble me with any other knowledge about God. I would rather camp out and remain as a babe in Christ." In essence, THEY ARE SCARED TO GROW UP IN GOD!

You can assure yourself of this: TO GO BACK TO THE BASICS IN GOD IS TO GO BACKWARDS IN GOD! We must understand that God's revelation to man is a PROGRESSIVE REVELATION. We must always be ready to move in God, having our spiritual ear tuned in to His voice. Listen to the apostle Paul's frustration in dealing with people who wanted to stay as babes, or go back to the basics. 1st Corinthians 3:1-3 states…And I, brethren, could not speak unto you as unto spiritual, but as unto carnal, even as unto babes in Christ. I have fed you with milk, and not with meat: for hitherto you were not able to bear it, neither yet now are you able. For you are yet carnal…Hebrews 5:13 states…For every one that uses milk is unskillful in the word of righteousness: for he is a babe. But strong meat belongs to them that are of full age…

Please understand that the basics (the milk of the word) are very important. We should spend time drinking of the milk of the word, for there is nothing wrong with being a babe in Christ. But there comes a day that every baby must GROW UP! As we begin to grow in God, we are then able to take the solid foundation (the basics) of simple faith in Jesus Christ, and begin to build on top of it. DO NOT continually go back to the basics. To go back to the basics in God would be the same as a grown man continually seeking to lay in his mother's arms and drink a bottle. The church is full of people who do not want to grow up in God.

We must go forward in God, not backward in fear and pride. It is time to graduate to the strong meat of the word, becoming teachers, rather than having to be taught over and over again, while remaining as a bottle-fed babe in Christ.

MAY WE GROW IN GRACE AND IN THE KNOWLEDGE OF THE LORD!

February 25

THERE SHALL BE A RESURRECTION

Acts 24:14-16 records the apostle Paul giving an explanation of his hope toward God. He states…THERE SHALL BE A RESURRECTION OF THE DEAD, BOTH OF THE JUST AND UNJUST…This statement was also made by Jesus in John 5:28,29, which states…Marvel not at this: for the hour is coming, in which all that are in the graves shall hear his voice, And shall come forth; they that have done good, unto the resurrection of life; and they that have done evil, unto the resurrection of damnation (judgment)…These passages do speak of the general or second resurrection, in which ALL THOSE THAT ARE IN THE GRAVES SHALL COME FORTH. This resurrection does include just and unjust people. As well, Daniel spoke of this in Daniel 12:2, which states…And many of them that sleep in the dust of the earth shall awake, some to everlasting life, and some to shame and everlasting contempt (the correct translation actually speaks of age-abiding life and age-abiding abhorrence…The Emphasized Bible).

In the book of Revelation, John spoke of a FIRST RESURRECTION that would include only overcomers (those that did overcome the beast nature and the carnal mind…Revelation 20:4-6). It then goes on to state that THE REST OF THE DEAD LIVED NOT AGAIN UNTIL THE THOUSAND YEARS WERE FINISHED…This is obviously a BETTER RESURRECTION. The apostle Paul referred to this resurrection in Hebrews 11:35, which states…Women received their dead raised to life again: and others were tortured, not accepting deliverance; THAT THEY MIGHT OBTAIN A BETTER RESURRECTION…Those that are privileged to be a part of the BETTER RESURRECTION will be those that do play a part in ruling the nations with a rod of iron (Revelation 2:26,27). THEY SHALL HAVE POWER OVER THE NATIONS! THESE ARE THE OVERCOMERS!!! This company shall consist of overcomers from all ages that did qualify to be a part of the first resurrection. They shall be the very extension of the manifestation of God to all the earth. They shall be used of God to bring ALL NATIONS UNTO THE FATHER (Read Psalm 2:8-10).

It is very important that we understand, recognize, and teach the resurrection of the dead. There are some that say that the resurrection has already taken place. This is error, and is a result of not rightly dividing the Word of truth. The apostle Paul dealt with this in 2nd Timothy 2:17,18, which states…Who concerning the truth have ERRED, SAYING THAT THE RESURRECTION IS PAST ALREADY; AND OVERTHROW THE FAITH OF SOME (this was spoken in reference to Hymenaeus and Philetus)…As well, there are those that deny bodily resurrection altogether. This is a result of spiritualizing scriptures that are not to be spiritualized. The people that teach this, whether they realize it or not, are following in the footsteps of the Sadducees. Matthew 22:23 states…The same day came to Him the SADDUCEES, WHICH SAY THAT THERE IS NO RESURRECTION…Jesus rebuked them for their incorrect teaching, and told them that THEY DID ERR, NOT KNOWING THE SCRIPTURES, NOR THE POWER OF GOD (Matthew 22:29)…In addition to all of this evidence, the apostle Paul covered the topic of resurrection in 1st Corinthians chapter 15. The entire chapter is devoted to this topic. This is how a portion of it reads from The New Testament In Modern Speech:

15:1 But let me recall to you, brethren, the Good News which I brought you, which you accepted, and on which you are standing,

15:2 through which also you are obtaining <u>salvation</u>, if you bear in <u>mind</u> the words in which I proclaimed it--unless indeed your <u>faith</u> has been unreal from the very first.

15:3 For I repeated to you the all-important fact which also I had been taught, that <u>Christ</u> <u>died</u> for our <u>sins</u> in accordance with the Scriptures;

15:4 that He was buried; that He rose to <u>life</u> again on the third day in accordance with the Scriptures,

15:5 and was seen by Peter, and then by the Twelve.

15:6 Afterwards He was seen by more than five <u>hundred</u> <u>brethren</u> at once, most of whom are still alive, although some of them have now fallen <u>asleep</u>.

15:7 Afterwards He was seen by James, and then by all the <u>Apostles</u>.

15:8 And last of all, as to one of untimely <u>birth</u>, He appeared to me also.

15:9 For I am the least of the <u>Apostles</u>, and am not fit to be called an <u>Apostle</u>--because I <u>persecuted</u> the <u>Church</u> of <u>God</u>.

15:10 But what I am I am by the <u>grace</u> of <u>God</u>, and His <u>grace</u> bestowed upon me did not <u>prove</u> ineffectual. But I <u>labored</u> more strenuously than all the <u>rest</u>--yet it was not I, but <u>God</u>'s <u>grace</u> working with me.

15:11 But whether it is I or they, this is the way we <u>preach</u> and the way that you came to believe.

15:12 But if <u>Christ</u> is <u>preached</u> as having risen from the dead, how is it that some of you say that there is no such thing as a resurrection of the dead?

15:13 If there is no such thing as a resurrection of the dead, then <u>Christ</u> Himself has not risen to <u>life</u>.

15:14 And if <u>Christ</u> has not risen, it follows that what we <u>preach</u> is a delusion, and that your <u>faith</u> also is a delusion.

15:15 Nay more, we are actually being <u>discovered</u> to be bearing false witness about <u>God</u>, because we have testified that <u>God</u> <u>raised</u> <u>Christ</u> to <u>life</u>, whom He did not raise, if in reality none of the dead are <u>raised</u>.

15:16 For if none of the dead are <u>raised</u> to <u>life</u>, then <u>Christ</u> has not risen;

15:17 and if <u>Christ</u> has not risen, your <u>faith</u> is a <u>vain</u> thing--you are still in your <u>sins</u>.

15:18 It follows also that those who have fallen <u>asleep</u> in <u>Christ</u> have <u>perished</u>.

15:19 If in this present <u>life</u> we have a *<u>hope</u>* resting on <u>Christ</u>, and nothing more, we are more to be pitied than all the <u>rest</u> of the <u>world</u>.

15:20 But, in reality, <u>Christ</u> *has* risen from among the dead, being the first to do so of those who are <u>asleep</u>.

15:21 For seeing that <u>death</u> came through man, through man comes also the resurrection of the dead.

15:22 For just as through <u>Adam</u> all <u>die</u>, so also through <u>Christ</u> all will be made alive again.

15:23 But this will happen to each in the right order--<u>Christ</u> having been the first to rise, and afterwards <u>Christ</u>'s people rising at His return.

15:24 Later on, comes the End, when He is to surrender the Kingship to <u>God</u>, the <u>Father</u>, when He shall have <u>overthrown</u> all other <u>government</u> and all other <u>authority</u> and <u>power</u>.

15:25 For He must continue King until He shall have put all His <u>enemies</u> under His <u>feet</u>.

15:26 The last <u>enemy</u> that is to be <u>overthrown</u> is <u>Death</u>;

15:27 for He will have put all things in subjection under His feet. And when He shall have declared that "All things are in subjection," it will be with the manifest exception of Him who has reduced them all to subjection to Him.

15:28 But when the whole universe has been made subject to Him, then the Son Himself will also become subject to Him who has made the universe subject to Him, in order that GOD may be all in all.

Here are some more thoughts on the resurrection from Dr. Stephen Jones: "Paul makes it clear that the resurrection of Jesus Christ is the pattern for our own resurrection as well. The only reason we shall be raised from the dead is because Christ was raised as the Pattern Son.

Paul's argument shows the inherent contradiction of this Sadducee doctrine. If there is no such thing as resurrection, but that man simply goes to heaven when he dies, then Jesus was not raised. But if Jesus was not raised, then we are yet in our sins, because he "*was raised again for our justification*" (Rom. 4:25). So the only way we attain the promise of God is if Jesus was raised from the dead. But if He was, it is the pattern of our own resurrection as well. That is the path of Paul's logic.

Most Christians today do not hold the Sadducee position which denies the resurrection of the dead. Yet there are teachers today, claiming to be Christians, who do deny this. Like the Sadducees, they do not comprehend the importance of "*the redemption of our body*" (Rom. 8:23). Paul calls it "the adoption" and the great "hope" of the Christian (Rom. 8:24). Without this "hope," death is the end, and we are of all men most to be pitied. Some believe that the first resurrection is merely the life that a Christian receives when he is justified by faith. To support this view, they cite scriptures exhorting us to "die daily" and be raised in newness of life. This view attempts to deny the bodily resurrection of the dead in favor of a more spiritualized view. This was the view of the Sadducees who denied the resurrection altogether (Matt. 22:23; Acts 4:1, 2).

A variation of this view teaches that the first resurrection is spiritual, but the second is physical. This variation does not actually deny the resurrection of the dead, but these do not understand that there are two bodily resurrections that are yet future. I believe that when the full picture is known, as revealed in the rest of this booklet, it will be apparent that neither of the spiritualized views above are accurate. On the individual, personal level we are indeed to "die daily" and be raised with Christ daily. But this is only a type and shadow of resurrection. Our justification by faith is not resurrection itself.

The spiritualizing of resurrection has its roots in the Greek world view; the idea of the bodily resurrection has its roots in the Hebrew world view. I believe that if we go back to the beginning and study the foundations of these views, we can come to the truth of the matter." (The Purpose Of Resurrection, Dr. Stephen Jones http://www.gods-kingdom.org/Resurrection/PurposeResurrection.html)

IN LIGHT OF ALL THIS, WE HAVE HOPE TOWARD GOD!

February 26

THE PURPOSE OF GOD

What is the purpose of God? Does God have a purpose? Why do we serve God? What is this Christian walk all about? These are questions that you must ask yourself. Most people spend a lifetime of "going to church" and never stop once to ponder these thoughts.

Most people are content to know that:

> They are a sinner…
> They need Jesus…
> They have believed on Him…
> They will die one day and go to be with the Lord…

If this is all that God wanted us to know about His purpose, then why did He go to such great lengths to send His only begotten Son to lay down His life for the world, and to be a pattern for us to follow after? Surely there is a purpose for all the things that we go through in this life!

According to Bill Britton, "The life of Jesus, in His humanity here on this earth, was a DIVINE PATTERN FOR THE PERFECT END-TIME BODY OF CHRIST." In essence, we are to be patterned after the very life of the Son of God. Jesus is the PATTERN SON!

Romans 8:28,29 states…them who are called according to His PURPOSE. For whom he did foreknow, He also did predestinate TO BE CONFORMED TO THE IMAGE OF HIS SON, that He might be the firstborn among many brethren…The word "purpose" means: a setting forth, setting up, resolve, and design. God has set forth, set up, resolved, and designed for us to be made in the image of His Son. This has always been His purpose, for He did state this from the very beginning…LET US MAKE MAN IN OUR IMAGE (Genesis 1:26)…THIS IS THE PURPOSE OF GOD! We are to be made in His image, that we might have dominion over all things (except God Himself). Once again, God's purpose in man is that he (man) should have dominion over all of God's creation. We need only to look at the life of Jesus to see a picture of this dominion. Jesus demonstrated GOD'S DIVINE NATURE, AND MANIFESTED GOD'S DIVINE POWER. As we submit to the process of sonship, we too shall be partakers of His divine nature, and shall become a vessel for His divine power. We are in the process of being made in His image.

WE ARE CALLED ACCORDING TO HIS PURPOSE!

February 27

THE WORD OF GOD

What is the Word of God? More importantly, WHO is the Word of God? Is the Bible the Word of God? If it is, which one (Bible) is correct, for there are many translations? Is the King James Version the Word of God, or is it another version or translation that is the Word of God? Sounds confusing…Huh? Let us see if there are some statements in the Bible that answer this all-important question. What or Who is the Word of God?

John 1:1 states…In the beginning was the WORD, and the WORD was with God, and the WORD was God…John 1:14 states…And the WORD was made flesh, and dwelled among us… Revelation 19:3 states…And He (Jesus) was clothed in a vesture dipped in blood: AND HIS NAME IS CALLED THE WORD OF GOD…Well…There you have it! The WORD of God is a person. It is the Lord Jesus Christ!

The Amplified Bible reads as follows (John 1:1)…In the beginning (before all time) was the Word (Christ), and the Word was with God, and the Word was God Himself…The Word of God that is spoken of in this passage is the Logos (the spoken Word of God). No wonder that Jesus said…I come (in the volume of the book it is written of ME,) to do Your will, O God…The Lord Jesus Christ is the personification, and manifestation in the flesh, of the SPOKEN WORD (Logos) of God. He is the living Word of God! We must understand that the Bible is very important, but what is more important, is WHO the Bible speaks of. It speaks of…

JESUS, THE CHRIST (ANOINTED), THE WORD OF GOD!

February 28

SPIRIT, SOUL, BODY

1st Thessalonians 5:23 states…And the very God of peace sanctify you wholly; and I pray your whole spirit, soul, and body be preserved blameless unto the coming of our Lord Jesus Christ… What an informative scripture! This verse tells us that man is a three-part being.

He is made up of:

    1. SPIRIT
    2. SOUL
    3. BODY

The word "spirit" comes from the Greek word "pneuma", which refers to the breath of God. This breath (Spirit) of God is what enables man to become a living soul. The word "soul" comes from the Greek word "psuche", which refers to our mind, will, and emotions. We obviously know what our body is. It is the physical part of man that houses his spirit and soul. With this in mind, let us now attempt to understand the PROCESS of our salvation.

Our spirit is saved as we believe on the Lord Jesus Christ. This is referred to as JUSTIFICATION. Our soul is being saved through the transforming power of God's divine nature. This is referred to as SANCTIFICATION. Our bodies are yet to be saved at the last trump. This is referred to as GLORIFICATION. In essence, WE ARE SAVED, WE ARE BEING SAVED, AND WE SHALL BE SAVED! The next time someone asks you if you are saved, tell them NO! Tell them that you are in the process of God's salvation, which is the salvation of your spirit, soul, and body.

This is to be seen as well in symbolic form in the Old Testament. As we study the three main feasts of the Jewish people (PASSOVER, PENTECOST, AND TABERNACLES), WE WILL FIND THAT THEY DO REPRESENT THE SALVATION OF OUR SPIRIT, SOUL, AND BODY. Can we be honest enough to admit that we are God's workmanship? Can we be honest enough to admit that we are a work in progress? We have not yet attained to our FULL SALVATION, but we are in the PROCESS of being made in His image. Thank God for the cross and the blood of Jesus Christ, which is saving us…

SPIRIT, SOUL, AND BODY!

March 1

THE CORRECTIVE JUDGMENTS OF GOD

According to Ray Prinzing: "Man has long viewed God's judgments as a vindictive action prompted by a motive for revenge and supported by a tumultuous wrath that must be pacified. NOT SO! Such is a gross caricature of our God! His mercy and grace are superabundant, and though He finds it necessary to chasten, His wisdom and righteousness produce a just and pure chastisement conditioned to correct the situation, and thus bring forth a creature improved by the process." (Redemption, Ray Prinzing)

We must understand that all of God's judgments ARE CORRECTIVE IN NATURE! Hear it again! GOD'S JUDGMENTS ARE FOR THE PURPOSE OF CORRECTION! Jeremiah 10:24 states…O Lord, CORRECT ME, BUT WITH JUDGMENT; not in Your anger, lest You bring me to nothing (lest You diminish me)…As you can see, judgment brings about correction, and correction is the result of judgment. They go hand in hand. The Hebrew word for correct is "yasar", and has also been translated as - to instruct, to chasten, be taught, and be reformed. The Greek word is "paideuo", and includes the thought of child-training, involving the whole process of discipline which girds us up to the right way.

The purpose of God's judgments, which are corrective, must always be seen in this light. If they were corrective in the past, and are corrective now, then they will be corrective in the ages to come. Remember…When God's judgments are in the earth, the inhabitants of the world will learn righteousness (Isaiah 26:9)…Read 1st Chronicles 16:13-36 and Psalm 72. These passages of scripture declare that the whole creation is longing for the judgment of God. Let the heavens be glad, And let the earth rejoice: And let men say among the nations, The Lord reigns…

HIS JUDGMENTS ARE IN ALL THE EARTH!

March 2

VENGEANCE

Romans 12:19 states…Dearly beloved, avenge not yourselves, but rather give place unto wrath: for it is written, Vengeance is Mine; I will repay, says the Lord…Sounds pretty bad, huh? All judgment, punishment, wrath, fire, and vengeance scriptures sound bad to the carnal mind. When we think of these terms, we think of God inflicting punishment, pain, injury, suffering, and loss for the purpose of vindication, satisfaction, and malicious retaliation. THIS TYPE OF THINKING IS NOT CORRECT! THIS IS THE WAY THAT THE CARNAL MIND PERCEIVES GOD AND HIS DEALINGS WITH MAN. COME OUT from this Babylonian mindset that paints a picture of God as an angry torture-hungry monster. GOD IS OUR FATHER! HE LOVES US! THAT IS WHY VENGEANCE BELONGS ONLY UNTO HIM! HE IS THE ONLY ONE WHO KNOWS HOW TO ADMINISTER IT IN A JUST WAY!

If vengeance was left up to man, we would all be in BIG TROUBLE. We are mean, vindictive, malicious, and always on the lookout for retaliation. God, Who is our Father, is not like that. **According to Ray Prinzing:** "The word "vengeance" literally speaks of that action which is out of righteousness, out of that which is just, and for the purpose of bringing everything else into alignment with that which is just. Only a just action can produce justice. Two wrongs never make a right." (Redemption, Ray Prinzing)

VENGEANCE IS A GOOD THING! IT IS A VERY GOOD THING! Only God has the power, wisdom, and love to bring it about in a just way. The Lord, through the manifested sons of God, shall declare the DAY OF THE VENGEANCE OF OUR GOD; to comfort all that mourn (Isaiah 61:2)…Our God, Who is just, will not fail to repay every wrong, and to reward every right, while at the same time correcting, chastening, and restoring ALL THINGS AND ALL PEOPLE UNTO HIMSELF!

VENGEANCE IS HIS…THANK GOD!

March 3

IT'S ALL GOOD

According to Dr. Harold Lovelace, "The Good News is: The Bad News is also Good News!" This is quite a statement! Do we believe it? Do we understand it? Much of Christianity teaches us that God is fighting against evil, principalities, powers, and Satan. THIS IS NOT WHAT THE BIBLE TEACHES!

The Bible states that:

> GOD CREATED GOOD AND EVIL…(Isaiah 45:7)
>
> GOD CREATED PRINCIPALITIES AND POWERS (RULERS AND AUTHORITIES)… (Colossians 1:16)
>
> GOD CREATED THE WASTER TO DESTROY… (Isaiah 54:16)
>
> ALL POWER IS OF GOD…(Romans 13:1)
>
> ALL THINGS ARE OF GOD…(2ND Corinthians 5:18)

Well…That settles it! God is in charge of and responsible for everything (the good and the bad)! Romans 8:28 states…And we know that ALL THINGS work together for GOOD to them that love God, to them who are the called according to His purpose…

Can we GROW UP in God? Can we be mature enough to see God's hand in ALL THINGS? God is not fighting against evil, but has created it to be a tool in His hand. He uses it to show us how to overcome evil with good. How could we know what good was if there were no such thing as evil (THINK ABOUT IT)? Bad news is actually good news in disguise. I know it is easy to say that, but tough to always believe it. Nevertheless, it is true!

Remember…ALL THINGS ARE OF GOD (Romans 11:36, 1st Corinthians 8:6, 1st Corinthians 11:12, 2nd Corinthians 5:18, Ephesians 1:11, Hebrews 2:10)! There is nothing that has ever happened, is happening, or ever will happen that God is not able to work together for our good.

WOW!

So…"The Good News is: The Bad News is also Good News!" Do you believe that God is that BIG of a God? Do you really believe He is SOVEREIGN?…ALMIGHTY?…ALL-POWERFUL?… ALL-KNOWING?…ALL-PRESENT?…ALL-LOVING? Let us not limit God!

ALL THINGS ARE OF GOD!

March 4

ISOLATION

Matthew 5:14-16 states…You are the light of the world. A city that is set on a hill can not be hid. Neither do men light a candle, and put it under a bushel, but on a candlestick; and it gives light unto all that are in the house. Let your light so shine before men, that they may see your good works, and glorify your Father which is in heaven…Surely you have heard the statement…NO MAN IS AN ISLAND! Well…It is true. If we are a light in the midst of darkness, then we are not to hide or isolate ourselves. We are to see ourselves as vessels, called to shine forth the light of the Father. If we isolate ourselves from people, then we are headed for disaster.

As we charge ahead into the deep things of God, we must guard against this very thing. Isolation is a side road that will lead you to destruction. On this road there is a ditch on either side called PRIDE AND BITTERNESS. Many people become prideful because they know something about God that others do not. As well, many people become bitter because they can not convince others to see what they see (perceive) in God. STAY AWAY FROM THIS ROAD! DO NOT ISOLATE YOURSELF FROM FELLOWSHIP WITH PEOPLE! ISOLATION IS A RECIPE FOR RUIN AND HEARTACHE! DO NOT FORSAKE THE ASSEMBLING OF YOURSELF TOGETHER WITH OTHER BELIEVERS, AND EVEN ALL TYPES OF PEOPLE!

We must learn to be all things to all men, that we might by all means save some (1st Corinthians 9:22)…In actuality, we need fellowship as much as others need our fellowship. God will not share His glory with any one person alone, but He will share it with His body (the body of Christ). This body must be willing to come together in one mind and one accord. This is obviously the opposite of isolation.

LET YOUR LIGHT SHINE!

March 5

I WILL MAKE A NEW COVENANT

Jeremiah 31:31-33 states…Behold, the days come, says the Lord, THAT I WILL MAKE A NEW COVENANT with the house of Israel, and with the house of Judah: Not according to the covenant that I made with their fathers in the day that I took them by the hand to bring them out of the land of Egypt; which My covenant THEY BRAKE, although I was a husband unto them, says the Lord: But this shall be the covenant that I WILL MAKE with the house of Israel; After those days, says the Lord, I WILL PUT MY LAW IN THEIR INWARD PARTS, and write it in their hearts; and will be their God, and they shall be My people…WHAT A BEAUTIFUL AND UNCONDITIONAL PROMISE!

This promise is to be performed by the Lord and not man. THIS IS THE NEW COVENANT! This passage of scripture speaks of the difference between the LAW OF MOSES and THE LAW OF THE SPIRIT OF LIFE IN CHRIST JESUS. So many Christians are still trying to live under the Old Covenant. They are bound by a legalistic way of thinking and living, which leads to a self-righteousness in their lives that stinks to the high heavens. Man can do nothing with the Old Covenant, BUT BREAK IT!

Under the New Covenant, God will write His laws in our inward parts and in our hearts. Notice this: The Old Covenant was based upon man's performance. The result was (and always is) FAILURE. The New Covenant is based on God's performance. As we learn to place our faith in God's performance (Christ and Him crucified), the result will always be VICTORY! Remember… We are God's workmanship.

The New Covenant is a work of the Spirit, whereas the Old Covenant was a work of the flesh. The New Covenant is based upon us BELIEVING AND PLACING OUR FAITH in God's performance. The Old Covenant was based upon man's ability to perform God's law. God gave man the law to show him that he (man) was not able to keep it in and of himself. It was a schoolmaster (a tutor or guardian of boys) to lead us to Christ, for only God (by His Spirit) can write His laws on our heart, and in our inward parts (our minds).

We must realize the difference between the letter of the law and the spirit of the law. The letter of the law was written upon tables of stone, but the spirit of the law is to be written upon the tables of our hearts and minds. In essence, Jesus did not come to destroy the law, BUT TO FULFILL IT. He blotted out the handwriting of ordinances that was against us (the letter of the law), which was contrary to us, and took it out of the way, NAILING IT TO HIS CROSS; (Colossians 2:14)…He paved a NEW AND LIVING WAY FOR US! By nailing the letter of the law to His cross, He opened the door for the spirit of the law to be written upon our hearts. The apostle Peter said it like this…WE HAVE BEEN MADE PARTAKERS OF THE DIVINE NATURE (2nd Peter 1:4)…

Partaking of God's divine nature is not to be seen as something that is complicated, but in actuality, it is to be seen as something simple. It simply means to participate and operate in what God has already provided and accomplished for us. IT CAUSES US TO REST FROM THE WORKS OF THE FLESH, WHICH DO PROFIT NOTHING! Along with God's divine nature comes HIS DIVINE POWER, which becomes our power source. This new power source enables us to overcome the flesh (the carnal mind or corrupt nature of Adam). As we go through this process, GOD IS ACTUALLY WRITING HIS LAWS UPON OUR HEARTS.

The Old Covenant showed man that he did continually miss the mark of God (sin). The New Covenant shows man the ability of God to perform a life-changing work in our hearts and lives. There is so much more to be said on this beautiful subject, for this is the very heart of the GOOD NEWS. How sweet it is to trust in the performance of our Lord and Savior Jesus Christ, rather than having to rely on our own pitiful efforts.

THIS IS GOD'S NEW COVENANT!

March 6

I WILL NEVER LEAVE YOU

There have been times in all of our lives when we have denied, rejected, and not believed in God. The atheist, when questioned about God, with a sarcastic shrug of the shoulders, will surely say that he or she does not believe in God. The answer to mankind, whether a weak Christian, or an atheist is: IT DOES NOT MATTER IF YOU DO NOT BELIEVE IN GOD RIGHT NOW. HE BELIEVES IN YOU!!! Hear it again. HE BELIEVES IN YOU, CARES FOR YOU, HAS CREATED YOU, AND WILL NEVER LEAVE OR FORSAKE YOU!

God has formed you in your mother's womb, and has a purpose for you. He is the potter and we are the clay. He knows what is in the heart of man. He knows it is hard for us to believe in Him at times, for many times we walk by sight and not by faith. Remember Peter? He denied even knowing Jesus, but the Lord knew he would do that, and had already prayed for and forgiven Peter in advance. JESUS BELIEVED IN PETER, EVEN THOUGH AT ONE TIME PETER FOUND IT DIFFICULT TO BELIEVE IN JESUS. Luke 22:31,32 states…And the Lord said, Simon (Peter), Simon, behold Satan has desired to have you, that he may sift you as wheat: But I have prayed for you, that your faith fail not: and when you are converted, strengthen your brethren…WOW!

Jesus looked beyond Peter's failures to the potential that was in Peter down the road. Remember Hebrews 13:5? It states…For He has said, I WILL NEVER LEAVE YOU, NOR FORSAKE YOU… STOP basing your experience with God on your performance. He said that He would NEVER LEAVE US. This sounds like someone Who is committed, does it not? He knows that there are going to be times when we operate in unbelief, and struggle to believe Him and in Him. But rest assured. HE BELIEVES IN US (or you could say that He believes in His ability to bring us through every situation).

The Lord loves you, believes in you, has forgiven you, has prayed for you that your faith fail not, will convert you, AND WILL NEVER LEAVE OR FORSAKE YOU. HE IS WITH YOU…

ALWAYS!

March 7

UNDERSTANDING THE PURPOSE OF THE AGES (OLAM, AION, AIONIOS)

Ephesians 3:11 states…According to the eternal purpose which He purposed in Christ Jesus our Lord…The words "eternal purpose", when looked up in the original Greek, should literally read…THE PURPOSE OF THE AGES. This is one of the many mistakes made by the King James Version. This version is consistently WRONG when it comes to its handling of the Greek word "aion", which means an age or period of time.

Here are some quotes from: The Outcome Of Infinite Grace, by Dr. Loyal Hurley, to help clear up the misunderstanding and mistranslation of the words "olam", "aion", and "aionios", which all refer to time, and are not endless in their meanings as we have been incorrectly taught.

"The Hebrew word "olam" and the Greek word "aion" both mean "age" or "eon". For evidence of this refer to Young's Analytical Concordance. Incidentally, Robert Young in his "Literal Translation of the Bible" always translates these word by "age" and never once as "ever", "everlasting", or "eternal". The Hebrew word "olam" comes from a root meaning hidden. The word therefore means a period of time, but a period of unknown or hidden length. The word was often used to mean a man's lifetime because it was an unknown period. The adjective "aionios" is often translated "age-lasting" or "age-during", but would be more properly translated "pertaining to the ages", that is, something that occurs within the ages, but not necessarily lasting even through one entire age."

"Many things in your Bible will continue to be confusing, and apparently contradictory, until you see this truth of the scriptures (about ages)."

"There are so many Biblical statements that become clear when one grasps the truth of the ages."

"Only as one sees the plan of the ages does he see the beauty of God's program for the redemption of the race. (1st Corinthians 15:22-28)"

"The scriptures speak often of this present age. Again they speak of ages past, and ages to come. (Ephesians 2:7 speaks of the ages to come)"

We can now clearly see that all of God's dealings with man are confined to the ages of time (the purpose of the ages). The life of God would be more properly stated as "the life of the ages", or God's life inserted into the ages of time. The punishment, wrath, judgment, vengeance, and consuming fire of God are all also to be seen as "of the ages", and for the purpose of correction. Matthew 25:46, according to the King James Version, speaks of everlasting punishment. This is once again an incorrect translation of the Greek word "aionios", which should be translated "the punishment of the ages". In actuality, the word "punishment" should be translated as CORRECTION, for it does come from the Greek word "kolasis", which means a punishment (correction) for the BETTERING of the offender.

As we mentioned earlier, Ephesians 2:7 speaks of at least two ages to come. These ages are referred to as the Millennium and the Age of the Ages. When speaking of both of these ages at the same time, the Bible (in the original Greek) refers to these ages as THE AGES OF THE AGES. This means that there have been ages, but these two ages are of greater significance than all of the previous ages that have gone before them. When the Bible (in the original Greek) speaks of the final age, it refers to it as THE AGE OF THE AGES. This means that the final age (also referred to as the dispensation of the fullness of times) IS THE GREATEST AGE OF ALL!!! The purpose of the Millennium is to gather ALL NATIONS unto the Father. The Age of the Ages, which is the final age, and the greatest age of all, is for the purpose of gathering ALL THINGS INTO CHRIST (Colossians 1:20) that have not been previously gathered into Him. This age will bring about the end of death and hell (Hades, the grave).

The study of ages will set you free from the traditional teaching of the church, which has led us to believe that God will lose the vast majority of His creation to eternal torments forever. This is not the God of the Bible. For our God will be…

ALL IN ALL!

March 8

THE APOSTLE PAUL'S MESSAGE

What was the apostle Paul's message? Do you know? Are you sure? Before we talk about what his message was, we need to talk about what his message was not. PAUL DID NOT TEACH A SALVATION FROM EVERLASTING TORTURE IN HELL! Check his writings for yourself. How many times does the word "hell" appear in his writings (keep in mind that he wrote about ¾ of the New Testament)? What is the answer? How about…ZERO!!!…WHAT?

Paul did use the word "Hades", that could have been translated "hell", and was translated "hell" in other places, but the King James Version did not translate it "hell" in this case. 1st Corinthians 15:55 states…O death, where is your sting? O grave ("Hades", or "hell"), WHERE IS YOUR VICTORY?…WHAT?

The English word "grave" in this passage comes from the Greek word "Hades". This same word ("Hades") was translated "hell" in many other spots, including the PARABLE of Lazarus and the Rich Man. Why did they not translate it as "hell" here? The reason it was not translated "hell" here, was due to the fact that it would have made their eternal torture and hell-fire doctrine fall to the ground, and become of no consequence. O HELL, WHERE IS YOUR VICTORY?

"Grave" is actually the correct translation, but the point is…THE KING JAMES TRANSLATORS PICKED AND CHOSE HOW THEY WANTED TO TRANSLATE A WORD IN ORDER TO MAKE IT FIT THEIR TEACHINGS. YOU CAN NOT DO THAT! YOU MUST MAKE YOUR TEACHINGS TO CONFORM TO THE BIBLE, AND WHAT THE WORDS MEAN IN THE ORIGINAL LANGUAGES (Hebrew and Greek).

Most church leaders teach a salvation from everlasting torture in a literal fire. Where do they get that from? Surely they do not get it from the apostle Paul, for he did not teach it.

They get it from:

1. THE CARNAL MIND…
2. THE DARK AGES (AUGUSTINE)…
3. THE TRADITIONS AND DOCTRINES OF MEN…
4. THE MISTRANSLATION OF THE WORDS "OLAM", "AION", AND "AIONIOS"
5. THE MISTRANSLATION OF THE WORDS "SHEOL", "HADES", "GEHENNA", AND "TARTAROO"…

So…What was the apostle Paul's message? Paul spoke of:

THE MINISTRY OF RECONCILIATION…
THE IN-GATHERING OF ALL THINGS UNDER THE HEADSHIP OF JESUS CHRIST…
GOD HAVING MERCY ON ALL…
ALL DYING IN ADAM…
ALL BEING MADE ALIVE IN CHRIST, EVERY MAN IN HIS OWN ORDER…
GOD BEING ALL IN ALL (EVERYTHING TO EVERYONE)…

JUDGMENT, PUNISHMENT, WRATH, AND VENGEANCE FOR THE PURPOSE
    OF CORRECTION…
EVERY KNEE BOWING (A WORSHIPFUL BOW)…
EVERY TONGUE CONFESSING JESUS CHRIST AS LORD…

This is quite different from the everlasting torture and hell-fire gospel ("so-called") of the modern day church. Paul's message was TRUTH. Today's message is TRADITION. Why don't you check out Paul's writings for yourself. I would rather know the truth.

HOW ABOUT YOU?

March 9

ORIGEN'S GRAND STATEMENT

Here is what J. W. Hanson said about Origen: "This greatest of all Christian apologists and exegetes, and the first man in Christendom since Paul, was a distinctive Universalist. He could not have misunderstood or misrepresented the teachings of His Master. The language of the New Testament was his mother tongue. He delivered the teachings of Christ from Christ Himself in a direct line through his teacher Clement; and he placed the defense of Christianity on Universalistic grounds. When Celsus, in his "True Discourse," the first great assault on Christianity, objected to Christianity on the ground that it taught punishment by fire, Origen replied that the threatened fire possessed a disciplinary, purifying quality that will consume in the sinner whatever evil material it can find to consume."

In 249 A.D., Origen was arrested, tortured and died in 251 A.D. Most honest Christian writers consider him one of the greatest Christian leaders ever. Origen was responsible for composing the first system of Christian theology in the year 230 A.D., of which a fundamental and essential element was the doctrine of the universal restoration of all fallen beings to their original holiness and union with God. In the year 544 A.D., this doctrine was for the first time condemned and anathematized as heretical. From and after this point (A.D. 553) the doctrine of eternal punishment reigned with undisputed sway during the Middle Ages that preceded the Reformation. With man having painted a picture of God as the Eternal Tormentor, NO WONDER THE WORLD WENT INTO THE DARK AGES! THAT FALSE MESSAGE BRINGS WITH IT A DARKNESS THAT SWALLOWS UP THE LIGHT OF THE TRUE GOSPEL! With this in mind, let us now turn our attention back to Origen and his GRAND STATEMENT.

Here is Origen's GRAND STATEMENT…"with God the one fixed point is the end, when God shall be all in all. All intelligent work has a perfect end of Colossians 1:20 and Hebrews 2:19, he says: Christ is the Great High Priest, not only for man but for every rational creature. In his Homilies on Ezekiel, he says: If it had not been conductive to the conversation of sinners to employ suffering, never would a compassionate and benevolent God have inflicted punishment. Love, which never fails, will preserve the whole creation from all possibility of further fall; and God will be all in all forever."

Do you believe God is compassionate? Do you believe God is love? Do you believe His love will never fail? Let us join the ranks of this great theologian, and declare our God as merciful and compassionate. Let us declare THAT GOD IS LOVE, AND THAT HE IS A LOVE THAT WILL NEVER FAIL!!!

HIS LOVE WILL NEVER FAIL!

March 10

EARS TO HEAR

HE THAT HAS EARS TO HEAR, LET HIM HEAR!

According to Dr. E. W. Bullinger: "These words were never used by mortal man. They were heard only from the lips of Him Who spoke with Divine authority (Matthew 7:29); and on earth only on seven distinct occasions, in order to emphasize and call attention to the utterance He (Jesus Christ) had just made." (Dr. E. W. Bullinger)

The seven occasions are found in:
1. MATTHEW 11:15
2. MATTHEW 13:9
3. MATTHEW 13:43
4. MARK 4:23
5. MARK 7:16
6. LUKE 8:8
7. LUKE 14:35

For the eight occasions after the ascension of Christ, see: Revelation 2: 7, 11, 17, 29; 3: 6, 13, 22; 13:9

Let us now turn our attention to the book of Revelation, and that this phrase is uttered SEVEN TIMES IN TWO CHAPTERS. Do you think these words are important, or what? Let us stop and think for a minute! What is the book of Revelation? IT IS THE REVELATION OF JESUS CHRIST! It is the unveiling of the Christ. So...It takes ears to hear to receive the revelation of Jesus Christ. What does this phrase mean? It means to perceive or understand something with the mind.

Remember the parable of the sower? Jesus said…he that received seed into the good ground is he that hears the word and UNDERSTANDS it…This brings forth fruit, some hundredfold, some sixty, some thirty…

Having ears to hear is equivalent to:

RECEIVING REVELATION FROM GOD…
UNDERSTANDING HIS WORD…
SEEING, HEARING, AND UNDERSTANDING SPIRITUAL THINGS…
PERCEPTION OF GOD…
SEEING THE KINGDOM OF GOD…

How do we acquire ears to hear? ASK, SEEK, KNOCK! We must humble ourselves and DILIGENTLY ask, seek, and knock. Jesus said…I will open My mouth in parables; I will utter things which have been kept secret from the foundation of the world…

WOW!

We must understand that the understanding of God is LOCKED UP in parables, secrets, and in mysteries. What unlocks the parables, secrets, and mysteries of God? THE VERY SPIRIT OF GOD UNLOCKS THEM TO US. He does it by giving us ears to hear.

So let us ask, seek, and knock for ears to hears. Without ears to hear, we are seeing, but we see not, and we are hearing, but we hear not, NEITHER DO WE UNDERSTAND! Thank God for ears to hear. Blessed are your eyes, for they see: and your ears, for they hear.

O FATHER…GIVE US EARS TO HEAR!

March 11

COME OUT OF HER

Revelation 18:4 states…And I heard another voice from heaven saying, Come out of her, MY PEOPLE, that you be not partakers of her sins, and that you receive not of her plagues…Revelation 17:5 states…And upon her forehead was a name written, MYSTERY, BABYLON THE GREAT, THE MOTHER OF HARLOTS AND ABOMINATIONS OF THE EARTH…

According to Dr. E. W. Bullinger: "Babylon, which means CONFUSION, is the fountainhead of all idolatry and systems of false worship. This is the mystery of iniquity (2nd Thessalonians 2:7) seen in all the great religions of the world. All alike substitute another god for the God of the Bible; a god made either with hands or with the imagination, but equally made; a religion constituting of human merit and endeavor." (Dr. E. W. Bullinger)

So as we can see, Babylon is the confusion of man-made religion of any kind, including the governmental and economic systems of man as well. Babylon is that spirit of confusion in man that permeates his mind, producing false and idolatrous ideas about God. This is BABYLON THE GREAT, THE MOTHER OF HARLOTS AND ABOMINATIONS OF THE EARTH! IT IS CONFUSION! Those who are captivated by her (Babylon) are wooed into an idolatrous relationship, in which they do fornicate with a false god, or false ideas of the true God. In essence, it is the religious, governmental, and economic ideas of MAN. IT IS THAT WHICH MAN PRODUCES, WHICH DOES COME OUT OF HIS BEAST NATURE, AND IS THE VERY SPIRIT OF ANTI-CHRIST (that which is against or instead of Christ)!

The good news is that there is another city that is spoken of in the book of Revelation. This city is the city of God. It is JERUSALEM! This city represents the true God, along with HIS GOVERNMENT, AND HIS TRUE PLAN OF ECONOMICS FOR THE HUMAN RACE. This government is now available to the sons of God through faith in Jesus Christ. IT IS THE GOVERNMENT OF GOD! It is that government which is currently being set up in the body of Christ, and will continue into the ages to come, until the creation is set free. The question is…How much of the creation will be set free? If we are to truly believe what the Bible teaches, then we must admit that the government of God, which is to be manifested through the sons of God, will result in the deliverance of the entire creation (EVERY PERSON WHO HAS EVER LIVED, OR WILL LIVE)!

Notice who is told to come out of Babylon in Revelation 18:4. IT IS GOD'S PEOPLE!

WHAT?

YES…God's people are presently in confusion. They are confused about the purpose and plan of God. Many do not yet understand the hope of their calling, which is: TO JUDGE THE WORLD IN RIGHTEOUSNESS, AND TO SET THE CREATION FREE! O CHILD OF GOD…COME OUT OF HER (BABYLON, CONFUSION)! BE SET FREE, TO SET THE CREATION FREE! Free from what? FREE FROM CONFUSION ABOUT OUR GOD!!! We must learn that our Father is LOVE! He is a love that NEVER FAILS!

God wants to give you:

1. POWER
2. LOVE
3. A SOUND MIND

Babylon is:

1. WEAKNESS
2. HATE
3. CONFUSION

COME OUT OF HER, GOD'S PEOPLE!

March 12

FROM DELUSION TO DUNAMIS

The church is pictured in the book of Acts as full of power (dunamis, Acts 1:8), and turning the world upside down (Acts 17:6). The church is presently in a state of STRONG DELUSION (2nd Thessalonians 2:11), and says that it is rich, and increased with goods, and has need of nothing; not knowing that it is wretched, and miserable, and poor, and blind, and naked (Revelation 3:17). WOW! WHAT HAPPENED?

The apostle Paul prophesied in 2nd Thessalonians 2:3 that there would come a falling away. This falling away began in about the year 313 A.D. with the entrance of a man named Constantine. He was responsible for the legalization of Christianity. This resulted in the secularization of the church. Christianity became a matter of fashion. Many heathen customs and usages, under altered names, crept into the worship of God and the life of the Christian people. This resulted in the people of Christianity forsaking the truth in exchange for the traditions and doctrines of men. So…GOD SENT THEM STRONG DELUSION, THAT THEY SHOULD BELIEVE A LIE! Naturally, the downward spiral of the church continued.

According to Dr. Harold Lovelace: "The great truth of the salvation of all creation by God was denounced by the Fifth General Council of the Catholic Church held in Constantinople from May 4, A.D. 553 until June 2, A.D. 553. The dark ages came upon the world for about 1,000 years, and this great truth was hidden." (Read And Search God's Plan, Dr. Harold Lovelace)

The first sign of hope was in 1517 A.D., when Martin Luther broke away from the Catholic Church, by stating…THE JUST SHALL LIVE BY FAITH! We must realize this: Martin Luther came out of the Dark Ages, but he brought some of the Dark Age teaching with him, ESPECIALLY THE TEACHING OF ETERNAL TORTURE.

The church has been gaining some ground ever since. BUT THE CHURCH IS STILL WEAK! WHERE IS THE POWER (DUNAMIS) OF THE BOOK OF ACTS? Many people are in bondage to a LIE. The Bible states that you shall know the truth, and the truth shall make you free. If the body of Christ is not free, then it does not know the truth.

The early apostles had the power (dunamis) of the Spirit of God, which led them into REVELATION TRUTH OF THE PURPOSE AND PLAN OF GOD. If it is true that the same baptism with the Holy Spirit is available to us today, which it is (and many have received the baptism with the Holy Spirit), then what is it that we are missing, and why is there no power in the body of Christ? The only logical conclusion is that we are missing revelation truth concerning the purpose and plan of God. Remember…IT TAKES SPIRIT AND TRUTH TO BE A TRUE WORSHIPPER OF GOD! As we take our position in Christ, preaching the true gospel under the inspiration and anointing of the Holy Spirit, we will once again see the power (dunamis) of God. THE REASON THE CHURCH IS WEAK AND LIMITED, IS DUE TO THE FACT THAT IT IS BELIEVING AND PREACHING A LIE!!! IT PREACHES A GOD WHO IS WEAK AND LIMITED, AND WHO DOES NOT CARE ABOUT HIS CREATION, BUT WILL ETERNALLY TORTURE WELL OVER 95% OF ALL THE PEOPLE WHO HAVE EVER BEEN BORN. IT PREACHES A WEAK, LIMITED, AND UNMERCIFUL GOD, WHICH IN TURN CAUSES THE BODY OF CHRIST TO BE WEAK, LIMITED, AND UNMERCIFUL (you are what you eat)!

Oddly enough, this falling away was DESIGNED BY GOD HIMSELF, to separate truth lovers from lovers of injustice. Remember…It is the glory of God to conceal a thing: but the honor of kings is to search out a matter (Proverbs 25:2)…Let us line up with God's truth. He is bringing us from…

DELUSION TO DUNAMIS (POWER)!

March 13

HOLY SPIRIT BAPTISM

Have you received the Holy Spirit since you believed? In Acts 19:1-7, we find the apostle Paul coming into Ephesus and addressing this very situation. He simply asks the disciples there…HAVE YOU RECEIVED THE HOLY SPIRIT SINCE YOU BELIEVED? They did not even know what he was talking about.

Many today in Christendom do not know what Paul was talking about either. They reject the baptism with the Holy Spirit, saying…it passed away with the early apostles, or they say that you are automatically baptized with the Holy Spirit at the moment you believe on the Lord Jesus Christ. In addition to this, they are strongly against the idea of speaking in tongues, for they say that this too did pass away with the early apostles.   SAD…ISN'T IT?

The very Holy Spirit of the living God is available to us, and many either reject it (because of their denominational beliefs), or they find some way to explain it away. Well…Such is the story of the Gentile Church.

The baptism with the Holy Spirit is clearly a separate experience after believing on the Lord Jesus Christ. Paul cleared this issue up for all to see. Paul asked the question…Have you received the Holy Spirit SINCE YOU BELIEVED? Paul was obviously making a distinction between believing on the Lord Jesus Christ, and then receiving the baptism with the Holy Spirit, which is then evidenced by speaking with tongues. Acts 19:6 states…And when Paul had laid his hands upon them, THE HOLY SPIRIT CAME ON THEM; AND THEY SPOKE WITH TONGUES AND PROPHESIED…

For those who say that this experience has passed away with the early apostles, FOR THEM IT HAS! But for those who believe the Bible, IT HAS NOT PASSED AWAY, FOR WE KNOW BY EXPERIENCE THAT IT IS STILL REAL TODAY!

Read also:

Acts chapter 2…
The entire book of Acts…
Paul's comments on speaking in tongues in his epistles…

Mark 16:17 states…And these signs shall follow them that believe; In My name shall they cast out devils; THEY SHALL SPEAK WITH NEW TONGUES…

Are you a believer in the Lord Jesus Christ? Have you received the Holy Spirit since you believed? Seek God for what He wants to give you! As well, keep in mind that it is not just a one time experience (read Acts 4:29-31). The Holy Spirit of God was over His people in the Old Testament (a cloud by day and a fire by night). The Holy Spirit of God was with His people as He came to be manifested in the flesh (Jesus…Emmanuel…God with us). And finally, the Holy Spirit of God is IN US, and shall come forth out of us as rivers of living water.

Even the Spirit of truth; Whom the world cannot receive, because it sees Him not, neither knows Him; for He dwells with you, AND SHALL BE IN YOU (John 14:17)…

HAVE YOU RECEIVED THE HOLY SPIRIT SINCE YOU BELIEVED?

March 14

WHAT IS GOD'S NAME?

There is much controversy over the question of God's name. Many try to determine God's name by looking to the Old Testament alone. This can not be done, for the New Testament is the fulfillment of the Old Testament. The Old Testament sheds some light on this question, so we will start there.

In the Old Testament, God's name is represented by the tetragrammaton (four letters) Yod He Waw He, transliterated into the Roman script YHWH. Because it was considered blasphemous to utter the name of God it was only written and never spoken. This resulted in the original pronunciation being lost. The name may have originally been derived from the old Semitic root (hwy) meaning "to be" or "to become".

According to Dr. Stephen Jones: "*Adonai Yahweh* is one of the prophet Ezekiel's favorite terms for Yahweh. He uses the term 214 times—for example, Ezekiel 2:4. It is translated "The Lord God" in the KJV. Personally, I would prefer NOT to translate the term at all, but simply leave it as it reads in the Hebrew: *Adonai Yahweh*. However, if men insist on translating it, the term could more accurately read, "Lord Yahweh." (Putting The Sacred Names In Perspective, Dr. Stephen Jones)

The name Yahweh (YHWH) comes from a verb which means "to exist, be". This, plus its usage, shows that this name stresses God as the independent and self-existent God of revelation and redemption (Genesis 4:3, Exodus 6:3). The name Yahweh tells us much about the character and nature of God.

It tells us that He is:

SELF-EXISTENT
THE GREAT I AM

I AM THAT I AM
INDEPENDENT
SELF-SUFFICIENT

As well, there are many who claim that the name of God is Jehovah (Form of <u>YAHWEH</u> used in older translations of the Bible, produced by blending the letters of the tetragrammaton with the vowels from <u>ADONAI</u>.).

While the name Yahweh tells us much about God, it still leaves us with just a general picture of God, and a longing for a greater, more specific name that defines Who and what He is. Let us now look to the New Testament to know beyond a shadow of a doubt what God's name is.

John 17:6 states…(Jesus is speaking) I HAVE MANIFESTED YOUR NAME unto the men which You gave Me out of the world…John 17:26 states…(Jesus is speaking) And I have declared unto them YOUR NAME, and will declare it…John 8:58 states…Jesus said unto them, Verily, verily, I say unto you, Before Abraham was, I AM (Sound familiar?…How about…I AM THAT I AM!)…Revelation 1:8 states…(Jesus is speaking) I AM Alpha and Omega, the beginning and the ending, says the Lord, Which is, and Which was, and Which is to come, THE ALMIGHTY… John 14:7 states…   (Jesus is speaking)…IF YOU HAD KNOWN ME, YOU SHOULD HAVE KNOWN MY FATHER ALSO: AND FROM HENCEFORTH YOU KNOW HIM, AND HAVE SEEN HIM…Finally, Jesus states in John 5:43…I AM COME IN MY FATHER'S NAME!!!… Well…What name did He come with? YES…YOU GUESSED IT! The name He came with was… J E S U S! **According to Dr. Stephen Jones:** "(The Greek name itself is spelled *Iesous* or *Iesus* and is translated into English as Jesus. Of course, the "J" in the English language did not come into usage until about 200 years ago, so prior to this time it was spelled with an "I"." [<u>Putting The Sacred Names In Perspective</u>, Dr. Stephen Jones])!

The name Jesus is the English form of *Iesous*, which was the Greek form of the Aramaic name *Yeshua*. *Yeshua* is itself a contracted form of *Yehoshua* (see <u>JOSHUA</u>). It means SAVIOR (YAHWEH SAVES)!

Well…There you have it! It is undeniable! We have our answer!

GOD'S NAME IS JESUS!

March 15

PROVE ALL THINGS

1ST Thessalonians 5:21 states…Prove all things; hold fast to that which is good…The word "prove" in this passage means: to test, try, approve, or to examine. The apostle Paul is here telling us to test, try, approve, and to examine ALL THINGS. Did he say to prove some things? NO! HE SAID TO PROVE **ALL** THINGS!

Why is it then, that so many Christians are afraid to, do not want to, or will not test, try, approve, or examine their beliefs in God?

Here are the two main reasons:

1. They already have a belief system about God, and they refuse to stay open minded, afraid that they will come across something in their studies that will either confuse them, or show they have been believing something about God that is incorrect. They are not willing to go against the traditions and doctrines of men. In other words, they have all their "ducks in a row", have put God in a box, and already have their mind made up about God. THEY REFUSE TO STUDY OR EVEN CONSIDER ANYTHING CONTRARY TO WHAT THEY HAVE ALREADY BEEN TAUGHT. THIS IS DECEPTION, AND STRONG DELUSION!

2. They are LAZY! They do not want to take the time to prove (examine) or think through their beliefs. This is also part of DECEPTION, AND STRONG DELUSION!

We must test all of our beliefs with the Holy Scriptures. The object of our study must be to arrive at TRUTH! WHAT IS THE TRUTH? This is what the goal of examining all things is… THAT WE SHALL KNOW THE TRUTH, AND THE TRUTH SHALL MAKE US FREE!

According to Dr. Harold Lovelace: "Many people are satisfied with the status quo. They just accept what has been told to them for the truth and never question it. The truth is so important, and it is the truth that will make us free. If we receive less than the full amount of truth, we are denying ourselves of God's blessings. Everything you hold to be true should be tested, doubted, searched, and researched again against all reasonable standards to see if it is in fact truth. You see, all truth, as far as teachings, doctrines, etc. about the Lord God and His Word will in ALL CASES GLORIFY HIM. If it does not, discard it. Many of man's own ideas, those passed down to him or those popular, are accepted without question. Accepting these ideas without researching them is not wise. After all, when you question, doubt, or search thoroughly as the Bereans to see if those teachings are so, you will NOT DO ANY DAMAGE TO THE TEACHINGS WHICH YOU ARE RESEARCHING. Again, if the idea or dogma can't stand the test TO GLORIFY GOD, it should be discarded anyway. In other words, know WHY you believe what you believe." (Read And Search God's Plan, Dr. Harold Lovelace)

PROVE ALL THINGS!

March 16

THE YEAR OF JUBILEE

Leviticus 25:8-10 states…And you shall number seven Sabbaths of years unto you, seven times seven years; and the space of the seven Sabbaths of years shall be unto you forty and nine years.

Then shall you cause the trumpet of the Jubilee to sound on the tenth day of the seventh month, in the Day of Atonement shall you make the trumpet sound throughout all your land. And you shall hallow the fiftieth year, and proclaim liberty throughout all the land unto all the inhabitants thereof; it shall be a Jubilee unto you; AND YOU SHALL RETURN EVERY MAN UNTO HIS POSSESSION, and you shall return every man unto his family...

According to Bill Britton: "In basic terms, every fifty years a great change took place in Israel. Everything was to be restored just as it was when the tribes originally inherited the land. If a man waxed poor and sold his land and became a slave or servant to others, this continued only until the year of Jubilee. At that time all slaves were set free, and every man returned to his original inheritance. I HOPE YOU CAN SEE WHAT THIS MEANS TO THE HUMAN RACE! It has a spiritual meaning, and held out a hope to humanity that God had set a day when all bondage would cease and everything that God had given to mankind in the beginning would be restored." (The Year Of Jubilee, Bill Britton)

When we look at the law of Jubilee in the Old Testament as it pertained to natural Israel, we can then see what this law means spiritually to the entire creation. Remember...All the things that happened to natural Israel, happened unto them for examples: and they were written for our admonition, upon whom the ends of the ages are come.

We must see that the Year of Jubilee in the natural represents something that will take place in the Spirit. Because Jesus died on the cross, He has GUARANTEED A JUBILEE FOR THE ENTIRE CREATION, every man in his own order. Jesus purchased the entire creation by laying down His life, shedding His blood, AND TAKING AWAY THE SIN OF THE WORLD. JESUS IS THE JUBILEE!

Because there was a manifestation of the Son of God, there shall be a manifestation of the sons of God, which will result in the creation being set free and restored to the Father (Romans 8:19-22). How much of the creation do you think that the sons of God will set free? How about...ALL OF THE CREATION! Sounds like Jubilee, doesn't it? YOU BETTER BELIEVE IT!

The ages to come (the Millennium and the Age of the Ages) will prove to be a Jubilee for ALL NATIONS, ALL PEOPLE, AND ALL THINGS!

EVERY MAN SHALL RETURN UNTO HIS POSSESSION!

March 17

RECONCILING THE WORLD UNTO HIMSELF

2nd Corinthians 5:18-19 states...And all things are of God, Who HAS RECONCILED us to Himself by Jesus Christ, and HAS GIVEN to us the ministry of reconciliation; To wit, that GOD WAS IN CHRIST RECONCILING THE WORLD UNTO HIMSELF, not imputing their trespasses unto them, and HAS COMMITTED unto us the word of reconciliation…Let us take note of the terminology in this passage of scripture…

HAS RECONCILED…
HAS GIVEN…
GOD WAS IN CHRIST…RECONCILING THE WORLD UNTO HIMSELF…
HAS COMMITTED…

These words speak of something that is past tense, already accomplished, done, completed, and finished. What a GRAND DAY it is when it becomes a revelation to you that God has (past tense) reconciled you unto Himself. He reconciled you unto Himself before you even knew that you needed to be reconciled. He reconciled you when you were yet His enemy.

The word "reconcile" means: to change, exchange, as coins for others of equivalent value, return to favor with, to receive one into favor, and to make friendly. It is IMPERATIVE that we understand that GOD WAS NOT RECONCILED TO US, BUT WE WERE RECONCILED UNTO HIM! Well…What about repentance? We must understand that when a person repents, this is not what reconciles them to God. When a person repents, IT IS BECAUSE THEY HAVE BEEN AWAKENED TO THE FACT THAT GOD HAS ALREADY RECONCILED THEM UNTO HIMSELF!!!

According to A. P. Adams: "The sinner is not redeemed because he repents, BUT IS CALLED UPON TO REPENT BECAUSE HE HAS BEEN REDEEMED." (The Atonement, A. P. Adams)

This means…THE ENTIRE CREATION (ALL OF MANKIND) HAS BEEN RECONCILED TO GOD THROUGH JESUS CHRIST. IT HAS BEEN ACCOMPLISHED! So…What next?

The scriptures tell us that the message of reconciliation is to come to every man in his own order. They testify to the fact that ALL WILL BE MADE ALIVE IN CHRIST! What remains is for man to go through the process of salvation, which includes: JUSTIFICATION, SANCTIFICATION, AND GLORIFICATION! But remember…This process of salvation is made possible only because GOD WAS IN CHRIST RECONCILING THE WORLD UNTO HIMSELF. In the mind of God we are already reconciled to Him. The sin debt has been paid in full by the PRECIOUS BLOOD OF THE LORD JESUS CHRIST! What remains is for us to BECOME WHAT GOD HAS DECLARED US TO BE! He has imputed (to attribute or ascribe) to us His righteousness. In essence, He has given us His righteousness on credit, and based on our faith in the Son of God. As we go through the process of SONSHIP (the salvation process of being made into a fully mature son of God), and as God writes His laws on our hearts, WE ARE BECOMING RIGHTEOUS! NO…we are not earning righteousness, but rather we are God's workmanship, and what is taking place is a work of the Spirit, in which God is bringing our condition up to the level of our position, and bringing our state (of being) up to the level of our standing in Him!

2nd Corinthians 5:20-21 states…Now then we are ambassadors for Christ, as though God did beseech you by us: we pray in Christ's stead, BE RECONCILED TO GOD. For He has made Him to be sin for us, Who knew no sin; that we might be made the righteousness of God in Him…

BE RECONCILED TO GOD!

March 18

THE FATHER

There is no story in the Bible quite like the story of the Prodigal Son. It is actually about TWO LOST SONS who both need the forgiveness of their father. Notice the character of the father in the story. Notice that his character and nature never changes. He is one of wisdom, compassion, and love. The father in this story has not a vindictive or vicious bone in his body. He was willing to give his younger son his inheritance, watch him go waste it, wait and watch for him to come to himself, and come home. And finally, to rejoice when he did come home. NOW THAT IS A LOVING FATHER!

We must understand that this story portrays the never-failing love of our Heavenly Father. Our Father, Who is all-powerful and all-loving, WILL NEVER GIVE UP ON HIS CREATION UNTIL ALL HIS LOST SONS COME HOME, whether now or in the ages to come. NOW THAT IS A GOOD DAD!

The father in this story had every right to be angry with his younger son. He could have refused to forgive him by not letting him come back home again. But the father said to his servants…Bring forth the best robe, and put it on him; and put a ring on his hand, and shoes on his feet: And bring here the fatted calf, and kill it; and let us eat, and be merry: FOR THIS MY SON WAS DEAD, AND IS ALIVE AGAIN; HE WAS LOST, AND IS FOUND (Luke 15:22-24)…

Let us also remember… that the father saw him (his son) when he was a great way off, and had compassion, and RAN, and fell on his neck, and kissed him (Luke 15:20)…

The father was SO LOVING that he even forgave his other SELF-RIGHTEOUS, MEAN, AND ANGRY SON, who refused to rejoice over his brother's homecoming. WHAT A LOVING FATHER!!! He forgives riotous living and self-righteousness.

Let us once and for all see our Heavenly Father as the COMPASSIONATE, LOVING, AND MERCIFUL GOD THAT HE IS! YES…There is a consequence for sin! But our Father is powerful enough and loving enough to cause us to come to ourselves, and to bring us back…

HOME AGAIN!

March 19

THE JUSTICE OF GOD

Exodus 22:5 states…If a man shall cause a field or a vineyard to be eaten, and shall put in his beast, and shall feed in another man's field; of the best of his own field, and of the best of his own vineyard, SHALL HE MAKE RESTITUTION…

Let us consider this portion of the Old Covenant, taking into account the spiritual implications of this law, and how that it applies to God and His dealings with the creation in our day and age, and for all of time for that matter.

Jesus told us in Matthew 13:38…that THE FIELD IS THE WORLD…This would obviously represent the entire human race. Remember…GOD SO LOVED THE WORLD (ALL)! We are told in Genesis 3:1… that the serpent was more subtle than any BEAST OF THE FIELD, WHICH THE LORD GOD HAD MADE…Revelation 20:2 states…that the SERPENT IS THE DEVIL (SATAN)…So it would have to be said that God created Satan (the spirit that now works in the children of disobedience). So…What is being said here? Let us put all these thoughts together.

GOD put HIS BEAST (THE SERPENT, SATAN) in the FIELD (THE GARDEN OF EDEN, WHICH GARDEN WE ARE, THE WORLD), and he (THE BEAST) devoured, and did eat the life of Adam (the human race). SO…GOD WAS RESPONSIBLE TO SEND THE BEST (JESUS CHRIST) OF HIS FIELD TO MAKE RESTITUTION! DO YOU SEE IT??? DO YOU UNDERSTAND???

God was responsible for the fall of Adam (subjecting the creation to vanity, NOT WILLINGLY)! This was the purpose of the ages. It was all, and is all a SCHOOLMASTER to bring us to CHRIST! If Adam would have never fallen (sinned, transgressed), THEN JESUS WOULD HAVE NEVER COME. If Jesus would have never come, then we would have never KNOWN the Father, for Jesus said…If you have seen Me, then you have seen the Father…Jesus was the most perfect revelation of the Father. He was God manifested in the flesh!

According to A. P. Adams: So…Here is the point: "THE JUSTICE OF GOD IS NOT **AGAINST** THE SINNER, DEMANDING HIS CONDEMNATION, BUT **FOR** HIM, INSURING HIS SALVATION!" (The Atonement, A. P. Adams)

The word "justice" means: the quality of being just; righteousness, equitableness, or moral rightness, the quality of being true or correct. So…In order for God to be JUST, RIGHTEOUS, RIGHT, TRUE, AND CORRECT, HE WAS RESPONSIBLE TO SEND HIS BEST (JESUS CHRIST) TO MAKE RESTITUTION!

WHY?

Because He (God):

> PUT HIS BEAST (SATAN) IN THE FIELD (THE WORLD)…
> PUT MAN INTO DESTRUCTION (PSALM 90:1-3)…
> SUBJECTED THE CREATION TO VANITY, NOT WILLINGLY(ROMANS 8:20)…

What a restitution it will be! There shall be a restitution of all things, which God has spoken by the mouth of all His Holy Prophets since the world began (Acts 3:21)…

JUSTICE AND RESTITUTION FOR ALL!

March 20

GO AND LEARN WHAT THAT MEANS

Matthew 9:12,13 states…Jesus said unto them (the Pharisees), They that be whole need not a physician, but they that are sick. But go and learn what that means, I will have mercy, and not sacrifice: for I am come not to call the righteous, but sinners to repentance…

In these verses of scripture, we find Jesus in one of His many disputes with the Pharisees. They were always ready to argue and to point the finger at the publicans and the sinners. So…How did Jesus respond? What did He do?

Jesus exposed the Pharisees for what and who they were. They were, and are, and do represent: Someone who has a knowledge of the scriptures, BUT DOES NOT KNOW OR UNDERSTAND WHAT THEY MEAN. The Pharisee spirit claims to know God, but DOES NOT KNOW GOD. It is one of intellect and self-righteousness, which depends totally on the carnal mind for its interpretation of scripture. Many people live in a world of quoting scriptures, BUT THEY DO NOT KNOW WHAT THE SCRIPTURES MEAN. The Pharisees were masters at quoting the scriptures, but they were babes in their understanding of them.

Let us HUMBLE OURSELVES in asking God to show us what the Holy Scriptures mean. For without the spirit of wisdom and revelation in the knowledge of Him (God), we can only hope to become a fine tuned and polished PHARISEE! ARE YOU WILLING TO GO ON A JOURNEY TO FIND OUT WHAT THE WORDS OF THE BIBLE REALLY MEAN? It is important to know the words of the Lord, BUT IT IS MORE IMPORTANT TO KNOW WHAT THEY MEAN!

GO AND LEARN WHAT THEY MEAN!

March 21

SINNERS IN THE HANDS OF A LOVING GOD

According to Gary Amirault: IS GOD LOVE?…OR…IS GOD ANGER? WHICH ONE IS HE? "According to Jonathan Edwards, God is an angry God. Jonathan Edwards has come down to us in history as one of the all-time great men of the Protestant mold. His sermon, "Sinners in the Hands of an Angry God," is considered to be an all-time classic. He was a leading player in what came to be known as the "Great Awakening," an American Revival of the 18th century. It is reported that after he dangled huge audiences over the lake of fire with his polished and extreme language, PEOPLE WOULD GO HOME AND COMMIT SUICIDE. Jonathan Edward's God was an angry God. He followed the footsteps of his apostle in the faith, John Calvin. John Calvin did not bring people to their own self-destruction. HE BURNED THEM HIMSELF! (He had Michael Servetus, one of his theological enemies, burned to death in green slow-burning wood.) John Calvin followed after his apostle in the faith - Augustine. Augustine was perhaps the most influential early church leader in bringing the doctrine of eternal punishment from paganism into Christianity. Prior to Augustine, there were FEW who held such teaching." (<u>Sinners In The Hands Of An Angry God</u>, Gary Amirault)

Let us look at the fruit of Augustine's students:

JOHN CALVIN BURNS PEOPLE TO DEATH OVER THEOLOGICAL MATTERS...

PEOPLE LEAVE JONATHAN EDWARD'S SERMONS TO GO HOME
AND COMMIT SUICIDE...

Last time I checked, neither burning people to death, nor committing suicide were to be found as fruits of the Spirit. These people (Augustine, John Calvin, and Jonathan Edwards) are the Fathers of the false message of eternal torture. They held to a VERY DARK PICTURE OF OUR GOD. Their ideas about God have infiltrated the minds of many, many people. To this day, Evangelical Christianity preaches its message of eternal torture without even considering that it could be incorrect. It has found itself locked into the same DARK PICTURE OF GOD. Christians have come to accept this WARPED VIEW of their Heavenly Father. They are somehow able to accept that GOD IS LOVE, AND THAT GOD IS ALSO THE ETERNAL TORMENTOR AT THE SAME TIME. I guess you could say...THEY BELIEVE IT IS LOVE TO TORTURE SOMEONE FOREVER. WHAT A WARPED VIEW OF OUR HEAVENLY FATHER!!! Have you ever thought through that belief? Can you imagine someone being tortured forever in literal fire (so they say)? THAT IS SICK! Would you take one of your children and torture them forever? Would you torture them even for one moment, with no purpose of correction in mind? ANY SANE PERSON WOULD SAY...NO! Well... Are we more loving than God? Do we have more power to correct than God? Is God that shallow of a being, that the only method that He has to deal with His enemies is to torture them forever? WHAT KIND OF GOD IS THAT? DO WE WANT TO SERVE A GOD LIKE THAT? THAT SOUNDS MORE CRUEL THAN HITLER!!! IF SO, WE SHOULD BEGIN TORTURING OUR ENEMIES JUST LIKE OUR HEAVENLY FATHER DOES HIS! DON'T WE WANT TO BE LIKE OUR GOD? So...What are we to do?
WE ARE TO TEACH AND PREACH THE TRUTH! GOD IS LOVE! WE ARE SINNERS IN THE HANDS OF A LOVING GOD!!! YES...Our Heavenly Father does punish, but it is for the purpose of CORRECTION.
According to Gary Amirault: "Punish He will, for our Father is just. In age-long correction, you can surely trust. On vindictive torment our Father's not bent. MERCY WILL, YES! TRIUMPH OVER JUDGMENT." (<u>What The Hell Is Hell</u>?, Gary Amirault)

WE ARE IN THE HANDS OF A LOVING GOD!

March 22

A QUOTE FROM GEORGE HAWTIN

The following words by George Hawtin are most challenging: "The established visible church has preached its multiplied sermons seeking to prove its tradition that the vast majority of God's human creation will be LOST, finally, irrevocably, and eternally, and not only will they be lost to God forever and ever, but they will be given up to the most sadistic, inhuman, ungodly torments that could be devised by the vilest fiends. According to the tradition of the church this hellish torment is to fall upon all who do not believe. It matters not a whit whether they had opportunity to believe or not. It matters not at all if they were born in the darkest jungles of Africa, the swamps of Borneo, or the deserts of India or China. The fact that they never heard there was a God will be no excuse whatever. The fact that they never heard that God had a Son will not impede their dreadful destruction. Heathen who never heard that God had a Son are, according to this teaching, faced with the same dreadful doom as men who heard the gospel from their birth and yet rejected it. To add to the stupidity of their teaching they make pitiful attempts to prove that this is the justice of God and that God is manifesting His love in the punishment of sin. The doctrine of eternal punishment is based on a literal interpretation of some of the metaphors of scripture, to the complete neglect of many other scriptures. No doctrine has ever been propounded with more confidence and greater bitterness nor with a grossness and coarseness more hideous and repugnant, and, in the face of the love and kindness of God, more inconceivable and incredible" -end quote. (George Hawtin)

think about it!

Think About It!!

THINK ABOUT IT!!!

March 23

THE SPIRIT OF GOD MOVED

Genesis 1:1-3 states…In the beginning God created the heaven and the earth. And the earth was without form, and void; and darkness was upon the face of the deep. AND THE SPIRIT OF GOD MOVED upon the face of the waters. And God said, Let there be light : and there was light…John 3:5,6 states…Jesus answered, Verily, verily, I say unto you, Except a man be born of WATER and of the SPIRIT, he cannot enter into the kingdom of God…

Can you see the similarities between these two passages of scripture? They both speak of water and Spirit. We must see that the water represents the first act of creation. It represents the natural man, and the natural birth. When a woman gives birth to her child, first her water breaks, and then the baby comes forth. This of course is our natural birth. The natural man in scripture is many times represented by the word EARTH, or something similar. Remember…We have a treasure hidden in EARTHEN VESSELS.

It takes the Spirit (Breath) of God to make something alive. Remember…The Spirit quickens (makes alive). Genesis 2:7 states…And the Lord God formed man of the dust of the ground, and breathed into his nostrils the breath of life; and man became a living soul…

We must understand that life, light, love, and all things that pertain to these three are ONLY FOUND IN THE SPIRIT OF GOD! Outside the Spirit of God is death, darkness, and hate, which man produces as a result of his carnal mind, which is the corrupt nature of Adam (the sin nature).

Remember…The natural man can not discern the things of the Spirit of God. THEY ARE SPIRITUALLY DISCERNED! Let us ask the Father to move by His Spirit on the waters of our carnality. Then, and only then, will we be enlightened to understand our Father and His purpose of the ages. We shall then go from darkness to light.

LET THERE BE LIGHT!

March 24

IN MY NAME

John 14:13 states…And whatsoever you shall ask in My name, that will I do, that the Father may be glorified in the Son…What does it mean to ask for something in the NAME of Jesus? What does it mean when we say, IN THE NAME OF JESUS? Well…The answer is in the meaning of the word "name". The word "name" means: character or nature. So…to ask for something in the name of Jesus, is to ask in the NATURE AND CHARACTER OF JESUS.

What is the nature and character of Jesus? Remember…Jesus said…for I do always those things that please Him (the Father, John 8:29)…The character and nature of Jesus is one that seeks to please the Father, to do His will, and to be a vessel through which the Father may be glorified. Many people USE the name of Jesus, but do not ask in the NAME (nature) of Jesus. THERE IS A DIFFERENCE! Remember…TO ASK IN HIS NAME, IS TO ASK IN HIS NATURE AND CHARACTER.

As we pray in His name (nature), we will only pray for and ask for what will please the Father. Many people suppose that material gain is godliness, and they are greedy of filthy lucre (greedy for money). As they quench their thirst for things, they use the name of Jesus to acquire it. They are using and speaking the name of Jesus, but what they are doing is NOT IN THE NAME (NATURE) AND CHARACTER OF JESUS! It is in the name of SELF-PROMOTION. Remember…THE LOVE OF MONEY IS A ROOT OF ALL EVIL (1st Timothy 6:10)…

We must realize that the name of Jesus is NOT A MAGIC WORD TO GET THINGS, BUT THAT IT IS THE NATURE AND CHARACTER OF GOD. This very nature is to be manifested in and through us. Let us not use the name (nature) of Jesus to quench our thirst for material possessions. This will cause us to err from the faith, and to pierce ourselves through with many sorrows. But let us grow IN THE NAME (NATURE) OF JESUS! This will enable the...

FATHER TO BE GLORIFIED IN HIS SONS!

March 25

THE LOST SHEEP OF THE HOUSE OF ISRAEL

It is important for us to rightly divide the Holy Scriptures. Many people open the Bible and begin to quote scriptures without even considering who is speaking, who is being spoken to, the setting, circumstance, and situation of the day in which it was spoken.

According to Miles Coverdale: "It shall greatly help you to understand scripture if you mark--not only what is spoken and written, but of whom, and to whom, with what words, at what time, where, to what intent, with what circumstances, considering what goes before and what follows after." (Miles Coverdale)

Matthew 10:5,6 states...These twelve Jesus sent forth, and commanded them, saying, GO NOT INTO THE WAY OF THE GENTILES, AND INTO ANY CITY OF THE SAMARITANS ENTER NOT: BUT GO RATHER TO THE LOST SHEEP OF THE HOUSE OF ISRAEL... Matthew 15:24,26 states...Jesus said, I am not sent but unto THE LOST SHEEP OF THE HOUSE OF ISRAEL...It is not profitable to take the CHILDREN'S (Israel's) bread, and to cast it to the DOGS (the Gentiles)...

As we can see, Jesus came to speak first, foremost, and directly to the JEWS ONLY! His primary mission was to convince the Jews that He was the Messiah, and to convince them to repent and believe on Him as the Savior of the world. Jesus, the KING OF THE JEWS, knew that HIS OWN PEOPLE would reject Him as Messiah, but to fulfill all things, He went to them first with the message of the Kingdom of God.

Here are some scriptures that show this very thing:

Matthew 8:12 states...But the children of the kingdom (the Jews) shall be cast into outer darkness: there shall be weeping and gnashing of teeth (their current day situation in which they find themselves in, for they are blinded to the fact that their Messiah has already come)...Matthew 21:43 states...Therefore say I unto you, The kingdom of God shall be taken from you (the Jews), and given to a nation (the Gentiles) bringing forth the fruits thereof...Acts 18:6 states...And when they (the Jews) opposed themselves, and blasphemed, he (Paul) shook his raiment, and said unto them, Your blood be upon your own heads; I am clean: from henceforth I will go unto the Gentiles...

We can clearly see that Jesus went to the Jews, and that the apostle Paul went to the Gentiles. Jesus warned the Jews that if they did not repent, the Kingdom would be taken from them and given to the Gentiles. In essence, THE RICH MAN (the Jews) did not repent, and the Kingdom was given to LAZARUS (the Gentiles). THE "PARABLE" OF THE RICH MAN AND LAZARUS IS ABOUT THIS VERY THING!

As we know, the Kingdom was indeed taken from the Jews and given to the Gentiles. But Israel is not left without hope! Romans 11:25 states…For I would not, brethren, that you should be ignorant of this MYSTERY, lest you should be wise in your own conceits; THAT BLINDNESS IN PART IS HAPPENED TO ISRAEL, UNTIL THE FULLNESS OF THE GENTILES BE COME IN…Paul then goes on to tell us the GOOD NEWS, which is that…

ALL ISRAEL SHALL BE SAVED!

March 26

THE AGES OF THE AGES

Daniel 7:18 states…But the saints of the MOST HIGH shall take the kingdom, and possess the kingdom for ever, even for ever and ever. Have you ever considered what for ever and ever means? Does it mean eternity and eternity? THAT WOULD BE RIDICULOUS! How could you add an eternity on top of eternity? (Think about it!)

These words ("for ever", "even for ever and ever"), when looked up in the original Hebrew, should be translated: UNTO THE AGE, EVEN UNTO THE AGE OF THE AGES. We are now able to see that there are two ages represented in this verse.

They are:

1. THE AGE (THE MILLENNIUM)
2. THE AGE OF THE AGES (THE DISPENSATION OF THE FULLNESS OF TIMES)

These two ages are referred to in the original languages of the Bible as… THE AGES OF THE AGES. This means: There have been ages, but these two ages are the ages of all ages. They are the two greatest ages of all the previous ages. THEY ARE THE AGES OF THE AGES!

Remember…"Aion", which means an age, has many compounds. They are:

1. AGE
2. AGES
3. UNTO THE AGES OF THE AGES
4. UNTO THE AGE OF THE AGE
5. UNTO THE AGE OF THE AGES

The Age of the Ages (also referred to as the Age of the Age) is the greatest age of all, and the Ages of the Ages refers to the two greatest ages of all. The apostle Paul spoke of the ages to come in Ephesians 2:7. These ages that he referred to are THE AGES OF THE AGES. Paul went on to tell us that these ages to come would contain THE EXCEEDING RICHES OF THE GRACE OF GOD IN HIS KINDNESS TOWARD US THROUGH CHRIST JESUS! -WOW!-

The question is then, what are we going to do with His exceeding riches, grace, and kindness? Well…We are going to set the creation free! IT IS CALLED THE MANIFESTATION OF THE SONS OF GOD!!! Thank God for the ages to come, for they are…

THE AGES OF THE AGES!

March 27

THE FAITH

2ND Corinthians 13:5 states…Examine yourselves, whether you be in the faith…Notice what is being said here. We are to examine (try) whether or not we are IN THE FAITH! It does not say, examine yourselves whether or not you have faith, but rather, examine yourselves whether you be IN THE FAITH! So…What is THE FAITH?

The words "THE FAITH" speak of faith in a specific person, and a specific work. The person and the work are: The Lord Jesus Christ, His cross, and His resurrection. We must then come to the conclusion that, THE FAITH is…Jesus Christ as the crucified and risen Lord! It is not faith to get things, but faith in Jesus Christ as the crucified and risen Lord of all!

The majority of preaching on faith, is a faith to get material things, rather than faith in the person and work of the Lord Jesus Christ. The word "faith" in 2nd Corinthians 13:5 means and refers to the doctrine of faith, or of the gospel promising justification and salvation in Christ.

So…If THE FAITH refers to the person and work of the Lord Jesus Christ, and we are to examine ourselves whether we are in THE FAITH, then we are to examine ourselves to see whether or not we are IN CHRIST (Who He is, and what He has accomplished). Sound familiar? Galatians 2:20 states…I am crucified with Christ: nevertheless I live; yet not I, but Christ lives in me: and the life which I now live in the flesh I live by THE FAITH of the Son of God, Who loved me, and gave Himself for me…

WOW!

EXAMINE YOURSELF!

March 28

NUMBERS IN SCRIPTURE

According to Ray Knight:

"Dr. E. W. Bullinger was a direct descendant of the Bullinger of the Swiss Reformation. He lived from 1837-1913 and was a mighty spiritual man as well deep into the Word of God. He discovered numerical patterns in scripture and creation which led him to believe that His God had purposely placed it there for a reason. His insight to creation and the numerical patterns in God's Word are especially precious."

"Dr. Ivan Panin, a converted Russian Nihilist, later a Harvard Scholar, professor, and mathematician…he once tutored Albert Einstein…learned Greek and Hebrew in four years. He then added Aramaic to his skills. He, quite separately from Bullinger, discovered the mathematical construction of scripture as seen in the two languages used…Hebrew and Greek."

"These two men of God spent many years recording their works and we have access to their findings today and are sincerely blessed by the insight that they have shown us. The "seal of sevens" on all scripture of our Bible was mind boggling…Panin and his assistant WERE CONVERTED THROUGH THEIR DISCOVERY! Panin died in 1942 after spending the remainder of his life in the Word unveiling its mighty treasures." (The above information is from: Bible Numbers Are Mighty, Ray Knight)

Each number has a spiritual meaning:

1 = unity, union, oneness
2 = witness, double portion
3 = completeness, divine perfection
4 = world, creation, earth
5 = grace, God's goodness
6 = carnal man, flesh
7 = spiritual perfection
8 = new beginning
9 = finality
10 = trial, testing
11 = disorder, chaos
12 = divine government
13 = sin, rebellion, satan
14 = salvation, generations
15 = spiritual rest
16 = love
17 = victory
18 = bondage
19 = faith
20 = redemption

21 = degradation of sin
22 = light
23 = death
24 = priesthood
25 = forgiveness
26 = the gospel of Christ
28 = eternal life
29 = departure
30 = maturity
31 = increase
32 = covenant
33 = promise
34 = the naming of a son
35 = hope
36 = fully man
37 = the Word of God
38 = slavery to the flesh
39 = disease, weakness
40 = probation, proving
42 = achievement
45 = preservation
46 = temple devoid of spirit
49 = Jubilee announced
50 = Pentecost, Jubilee year
60 = God's vessel before judgment
70 = God's vessel after judgment
100 = liberty, deliverance
120 = the end of all flesh, the full anointing
144 = the spirit filled life, first resurrection
153 = the sons of God
200 = what man has without God
276 = carnal man devoid of spirit, Babylon
300 = complete deliverance
490 = blessed time
600 = warfare
666 = the beast nature
888 = Jesus, fullness of Christ's body
1000 = the glory of God

COUNT NUMBERS, FOR NUMBERS COUNT!

March 29

THE DESIRES OF YOUR HEART

Psalm 37:4 states…Delight yourself also in the Lord; and He shall give you the desires of your heart…Let us take note of what is actually being said here. The scripture plainly states, THAT GOD WILL GIVE YOU THE DESIRES OF YOUR HEART! It does not say that we will have desires in our heart, and that God will grant these desires to us, but rather, it states that the very desires that you have in your heart WILL BE GIVEN TO YOU AND PLACED THERE BY GOD HIMSELF!

Many people think that these types of scriptures mean that THEY can just dream up anything they want in their heart, and then God will give it to them. THIS IS NOT SO, AND THIS IS NOT WHAT IS BEING SAID! Many preachers take these types of scriptures out of context, and then use them to justify their lust for material gain. LET US STOP THAT FOOLISHNESS !

As we delight in the Lord, abide in Him, and ask in His name (nature), He will give to us His desires. We will then find ourselves asking for the very same things that He desires. In essence, HIS DESIRES BECOME OUR DESIRES!!!

DELIGHT YOURSELF IN THE LORD!

March 30

THE TESTIMONY OF HANNAH WHITALL SMITH

The following excerpt is from Hannah Whitall Smith's autobiography <u>The Unselfishness of God and How I Discovered It</u>. She was perhaps one of the greatest women evangelists of all time. She is the author of <u>The Christian's Secret of a Happy Life</u>. Millions of copies of this book have been sold, and many Christians of all denominations have been blessed by her writings. This excerpt was originally published in her autobiography. However, after her death, the publishing company decided to totally eliminate three chapters from her book which describe her belief in the universal reconciliation of mankind. We pray that this excerpt will bless you as it has blessed us.

"One day I was riding on a tram-car along Market Street, Philadelphia, when I saw two men come in and seat themselves opposite to me. I saw them dimly through the veil, but congratulated myself that it was only dimly, as I was thus spared the wave of anguish that had so often swept over me at the full sight of a strange face. The conductor came for his fare, and I was obliged to raise my veil in order to count it out. As I raised it I got a sight of the faces of those two men, and with an overwhelming flood of anguish, I seemed to catch a fresh and clearer revelation of the depth of the misery that had been caused to human beings by sin. It was more than I could bear. I clenched my hands and cried out in my soul, "O, God, how canst thou bear it? Thou mightest have prevented it, but didst not. Thou mightest even now change it, but Thou dost not. I do not see how Thou canst go on living, and endure it." I upbraided God. And I felt I was justified in doing so. Then suddenly God seemed to answer me. *An inward voice said, in tones of infinite love and tenderness, "He shall see the travail of His soul and be satisfied."*

"Satisfied!" I cried in my heart, "Christ is to be satisfied! He will be able to look at the world's misery, and then at the travail through which He has passed because of it, and will be satisfied with the result; If I were Christ, nothing could satisfy me but that every human being should in the end be saved, and therefore I am sure that nothing less will satisfy Him." And with this a veil seemed to be withdrawn from before the plans of the universe, and I saw that it was true, as the Bible says, that "as in Adam all die -even so in Christ should all be made alive." As was the first, even so was the second. The "all" in one case could not in fairness mean less than the "all" in the other. *I saw therefore that the remedy must necessarily be equal to the disease, the salvation must be universal.*

I saw all this that day on the tram-car on Market street, Philadelphia--not only thought it, or hoped it, or even believed it--but knew it. It was a Divine fact. And from that moment I have never had one questioning thought as to the final destiny of the human race. God is the Creator of every human being, therefore He is the Father of each one, and they are all His children; and Christ died for every one, and is declared to be "the propitiation not for our sins only, but also for the sins of the whole world" (1 John 2:2). However great the ignorance therefore, or however grievous the sin, the promise of salvation is positive and without limitations. If it is true that "by the offense of one judgment came upon all men to condemnation," it is equally true that "by the righteousness of one the free gift came upon all men unto justification of life." To limit the last "all men" is also to limit the first. The salvation is absolutely equal to the fall. There is to be a final "restitution of all things", when "at the name of Jesus every knee shall bow, of things in heaven, and things on earth, and things under the earth, and every tongue shall confess that Jesus Christ is Lord to the glory of God the Father." Every knee, every tongue-words could not be more embracing. The how and the when I could not see; but the one essential fact was all I needed-somewhere and somehow *God was going to make every thing right for all the creatures He had created. My heart was at rest about it forever.*

I hurried home to get hold of my Bible, to see if the magnificent fact I had discovered could possibly have been all this time in the Bible, and I had not seen it; and the moment I entered the house, I did not wait to take off my bonnet, but rushed at once to the table where I always kept my Bible and Concordance ready for use, and began my search. Immediately the whole Book seemed to be illuminated. On every page the truth concerning the "times of restitution of all things" of which the Apostle Peter says "God Hath spoken by the mouth of all His holy prophets since the world began," shone forth, and no room was left for questioning. I turned greedily from page to page of my Bible, fairly laughing aloud for joy at the blaze of light that illuminated it all. It became a new book. Another skin seemed to have been peeled off every text, and my Bible fairly shone with a new meaning. I do not say with a different meaning, for in no sense did the new meaning contradict the old, but a deeper meaning, the true meaning, hidden behind the outward form of words. The words did not need to be changed, they only needed to be understood; and now at last I began to understand them."

WHAT A TESTIMONY!

March 31

GOD IS RESPONSIBLE / MAN IS ACCOUNTABLE

Although the words responsible and accountable appear to mean the same thing, they do have different meanings, and do portray two different ideas or thoughts. "Responsible" means: chargeable, with being the source or occasion of something. "Accountable" means: answerable, having to answer for your actions. So...What is God responsible for? What is man accountable for?

God is responsible (the source of) for:

ALL THINGS...

CREATING ALL THINGS...

CREATING LIGHT, DARKNESS, GOOD, EVIL, THRONES, DOMINIONS,
    PRINCIPALITIES, AND POWERS...

CREATING SATAN (the Prince of the Power of the Air, the SPIRIT that now works
    in the children of disobedience)...

SUBJECTING THE CREATION TO VANITY (futility, failure),
    <u>NOT WILLINGLY</u> PUTTING MAN INTO DESTRUCTION...

THE TREE OF THE KNOWLEDGE OF GOOD AND EVIL...

These statements can be supported by researching the following scriptures:
2nd Corinthians 5:18, Colossians 1:16, Isaiah 45:7, Genesis 3:1, Isaiah 54:16, Ephesians 2:2, Romans 8:20, Psalm 90:1-3, Genesis 3:6. So...As we stated earlier, GOD IS RESPONSIBLE FOR EVERYTHING, OR YOU COULD SAY THAT ALL THINGS ARE OF GOD!!! HEAR IT AGAIN! GOD IS RESPONSIBLE FOR, AND THE CAUSE OF...<u>E V E R Y T H I N G</u>! Remember...ALL POWER IS OF GOD (Romans 13:1)!

Now...What is man accountable for?

Romans 14:2 states...that every one of us shall give an account of himself to God. Ephesians 6:12 states...that we wrestle against principalities, powers, the rulers of the darkness of this world, and spiritual wickedness in high places...Remember...God created all this (Colossians 1:16)! This would then mean that man is ACCOUNTABLE to learn how to overcome these things. Romans 12:21 states...overcome evil with good...This would also tell us that we are accountable to learn how to overcome evil with good. BUT HOW???

Colossians 2:14,15 tells us...that Jesus, through His cross, spoiled principalities and powers, making a show of them openly, triumphing over them in it...

We are now able to conclude that Jesus created all things, overcame all things, and now holds us accountable to overcome all things. BUT HOW???

We overcome by placing our faith in the person and the work of the Lord Jesus Christ. We are ACCOUNTABLE to SUBMIT to God and His redemption plan. 2nd Corinthians 5:19 tells us that

God was in Christ reconciling the world unto Himself…be reconciled to God…In essence, God was responsible to reconcile the world unto Himself, and man is accountable to recognize that reconciliation, and to be reconciled to God. It is important that we do not think that just because God is responsible for everything, that man is not held accountable to God for his actions. The part that we play is one of submission to the sovereignty of God, for in doing this, we do show that we UNDERSTAND that…

GOD IS RESPONSIBLE…AND MAN IS ACCOUNTABLE!

April 1

AS THE WATERS COVER THE SEA

Habakkuk 2:14 states…For the earth shall be filled with the knowledge of the glory of the Lord, as the waters cover the sea…WHAT AN AWESOME STATEMENT! The latter end of the statement explains the first part of the statement. The latter part explains how much of the earth will be filled with the knowledge of the glory of the Lord. The question is, HOW MUCH OF THE SEA IS COVERED BY WATER? Well…You guessed it. ALL OF IT! This would then tell us that ALL OF THE EARTH shall be covered and filled with the knowledge of the glory of the Lord.

Hebrews 8:10,11 states…For this is the covenant THAT I WILL MAKE with the house of Israel after those days says the Lord; I WILL PUT My laws into their minds, and write them in their hearts: I WILL BE TO THEM a God, and they shall be to Me a people: And they shall not teach every man his neighbor, and every man his brother, saying, know the Lord: FOR ALL SHALL KNOW ME, from the least to the greatest…

WHAT A PROMISE!

These scriptures, which are to be seen as sovereign declarations and unconditional promises, testify that all nations and all people will come to know the Lord in the ages to come. They are promises from God with no exceptions and no conditions! CAN YOU BELIEVE THEM? DO YOU BELIEVE THEM? WILL YOU BELIEVE THEM?

We must begin to see how BIG of a God that we serve. His purpose for the entire creation is much bigger than we have ever imagined. It includes the whole earth, every man, and all things!

ALL SHALL KNOW HIM!

April 2

MATTHEW 25:46

According to Louis Abbott: "Matthew 25:31-46 concerns the judgment of NATIONS, not individuals. It is to be distinguished from other judgments mentioned in scripture, such as the judgment of the saints (2 Cor. 5:10-11); the second resurrection, and the great white throne judgment (Rev. 20:11-15). The judgment of the nations is based upon their treatment of the Lord's brethren (verse 40). No resurrection of the dead is here, just nations living at the time. To apply verses 41 and 46 to mankind as a whole is an error. Perhaps it should be pointed out at this time that the Fundamentalist Evangelical community at large has made the error of gathering many scriptures which speak of various judgments which will occur in different ages and assigning them all to "Great White Throne" judgment. This is a serious mistake. Matthew 25:46 speaks nothing of "grace through faith." We will leave it up to the reader to decide who the "Lord's brethren" are, but final judgment based upon the receiving of the Life of Christ is not the subject matter of Matthew 25:46 and should not be interjected here. Even if it were, the penalty is "age-during correction" and not "everlasting punishment." (An argument was introduced by Augustine, and since his day incessantly repeated, that if *aionios kolasis* does not mean "endless punishment," then there is no security for the believer that *aionios zoe* means "endless life," and that he will enjoy the promise of endless happiness. But Matt. 25:46 shows the "eonian chastisement" and "eonian life" are of the same duration-lasting during the eons, and when the eons end, as scripture states they will (1 Cor. 10:11; Heb. 9:26), the time called "eonian" is past and the life called "eonian" is finished, but life continues beyond the eons, as Paul teaches at 1 Cor. 15:26: "The last enemy that shall be destroyed is death." That is, the last, the final one in order. How will it be destroyed? First Corinthians 15:22 gives the answer: "For as IN ADAM ALL are dying, even so IN CHRIST ALL shall be made alive." Death is destroyed when ALL have been vivified, or made alive, IN CHRIST. There will then be no more death. Just as life is destroyed by death, so death is destroyed by life. Our present bodies are mortal and corruptible (1 Cor. 15:44-55), but when mankind is made alive IN CHRIST they will be raised immortal and incorruptible.)" (<u>An Analytical Study Of Words</u>, Louis Abbott)

As we can see, what is presented in Matthew 25:46 is:

1. Aionios Zoe
2. Aionios Kolasis

These are :

1. The life of the ages
2. The correction of the ages

According to A. P. Adams: -"THE WORD "KOLASIS", WHICH IS HERE RENDERED "PUNISHMENT", SIGNIFIES A <u>PUNISHMENT FOR THE CORRECTION AND BETTERING OF THE INDIVIDUAL</u>, HENCE IT COULD NOT BE ENDLESS." (<u>Matthew 25:46</u>, A. P. Adams)

WHAT A LOVING GOD! WHAT AN AWESOME FATHER! God is able and willing to save and CORRECT to the uttermost. HE DOES NOT NEED TO, NOR DOES HE WANT TO, NOR COULD IT EVER SERVE ANY PURPOSE TO TORTURE SOMEONE FOREVER!

GOD IS LOVE!

April 3

JOHN 3:16

The most quoted verse in all of the Bible is John 3:16, which states…For God so loved the world, that He gave His only begotten Son, that whosoever believes in Him should not perish, but have everlasting life…The Young's Literal Translation reads as follows - For God did so love the world, that His Son - the only begotten - He gave, that every one who is believing in Him may not perish, but may have life age-during (the life of the ages)…The Concordant Literal New Testament reads as follows - For thus God loves the world, so that He gives His only begotten Son, that every one who is believing in Him should not be perishing, but may be having life eonian (the life of the ages)…

Notice how that the Young's Literal and the Concordant Literal use the words…IS BELIEVING and BE PERISHING. We must understand what it means to perish and to believe. We must see and understand that we are born in a perished condition. Perishing is not so much something that is going to happen to you if you do not believe on the Lord Jesus Christ, as much as it is something that has already happened, and IS HAPPENING TO YOU BECAUSE OF THE NATURE THAT YOU WERE BORN WITH, A NATURE THAT YOU INHERITED FROM ADAM!

So…God is not willing that any should perish, but that all should come to repentance   (2nd Peter 3:9). In other words, God is not willing that you BE PERISHING, or that you remain in your perished condition. Remember…TO BE CARNALLY MINDED IS DEATH! It is important for us to see that perishing and death are first and foremost SPIRITUAL CONDITIONS that men find themselves in at birth. This condition continues on UNTIL they believe on the Lord Jesus Christ.

Remember…Jesus said…LET THE DEAD BURY THEIR DEAD…He was referring to:

1. SPIRITUAL DEATH
2. PHYSICAL DEATH

He that IS BELIEVING has entered into the life of the ages. We have passed, and are passing from death to life. This refers to God's life inserted into the ages of time. We are being brought from the carnal mind (to perish, death) to the mind of Christ (to be spiritually minded, the life of the ages).

In conclusion, we see that Jesus came to save us out of, and through A DEATH (the carnal mind) IN WHICH WE WERE ALREADY INVOLVED! The scriptures tell us to believe on the

Lord Jesus Christ, and so we should, for in doing this we are BEING SAVED from sin (missing the mark of God's nature) and death (the carnal mind). WHAT A SAVIOR! Believe, and enter into...

THE LIFE OF THE AGES!

April 4

JOHN 3:17

As we discussed previously, John 3:16 is the most quoted verse in all of the Bible. Many do not understand what "to perish" or "to die" means, for they are spiritual concepts that refer to the carnal mind. Many as well, do not go on to the next verse and read it. It contains a beautiful truth that is waiting to be discovered. Let us venture on to verse 17 and be liberated from the traditions and doctrines of men.

John 3:17 states...For God sent not His Son into the world to condemn the world; but that the world through Him might be saved...So...DID HE DO IT? DO WHAT? Well...DID HE SAVE THE WORLD? The answer is...YES!!!

1ST John 4:14 states...And we have seen and do testify that the Father sent the Son TO BE THE SAVIOR OF THE WORLD...Well...Did Jesus succeed or fail? 1st Timothy 2:4 states...God will have ALL MEN TO BE SAVED, and to come to the knowledge of the truth. For there is one God, and one mediator between God and men, the man Christ Jesus, WHO GAVE HIMSELF A RANSOM FOR ALL, TO BE TESTIFIED IN DUE TIME...Romans 5:10 states...For if when we WERE enemies, WE WERE reconciled to God, by the death of His Son...

Let us summarize the matter:

1. God sent His Son NOT TO CONDEMN, but to SAVE THE WORLD...
2. The Father sent the Son to be the Savior of the world...
3. God will have all men to be saved...
4. Jesus Christ is a ransom for all, which will be fully testified IN DUE TIME...
5. We WERE (past tense) reconciled to God when we WERE (past tense) enemies...

So...Is the world already reconciled to God? YES! They just don't know it yet! God is in the process of awakening ALL MEN TO WHAT HAS ALREADY BEEN ACCOMPLISHED IN AND THROUGH THE CROSS OF JESUS CHRIST. As they are awakened, they will repent and exercise faith in the person and work of the Lord Jesus Christ. This awakening process is to take place on the individual level, and is to take place in the entire human race as well. On the individual level, we are to experience the salvation of our spirit, soul, and body. This is referred to as justification, sanctification, and glorification, and is to be seen as a PROCESS, in which we are saved, we are being saved, and we shall be saved.

On the corporate level (speaking of the entire human race), mankind is being brought to the saving knowledge of the Lord Jesus Christ in…

THREE GREAT HARVESTS:

REMNANT (THIS PRESENT AGE)

NATIONS (THE AGE TO COME , THE MILLENNIUM)

WORLD, OR ALL THINGS (THE AGE OF THE AGES, THE DISPENSATION
OF THE FULLNESS OF TIMES)

Remember…These three great harvests are seen in type and shadow in Israel's…

THREE GREAT FEASTS:

1. PASSOVER (BARLEY HARVEST)
2. PENTECOST (WHEAT HARVEST)
3. TABERNACLES (GRAPE HARVEST)

As we have stated, Passover, Pentecost, and Tabernacles are to be experienced (spiritually speaking) by all men on the individual and corporate levels of humanity. It will result in the salvation of all men (spirit, soul, and body), and will also culminate with a universal and triumphant declaration, in which GOD SHALL BE ALL IN ALL (everything to everyone, 1st Corinthians 15:28), having brought the entire creation unto Himself, in the order of REMNANT, NATIONS, AND WORLD (ALL THINGS, Colossians 1:20)!!!

Jesus did not come to condemn, so why does the church continually preach condemnation? Many do not understand what Christ HAS ACCOMPLISHED. They think that THEY had something to do with their salvation. Remember…For by GRACE are you saved through faith; and that NOT OF YOURSELVES: IT IS THE GIFT OF GOD: NOT OF WORKS, LEST ANY MAN SHOULD BOAST (Ephesians 2:8,9)…

YES…You must have faith! But faith is not what saves you. THE GRACE OF GOD HAS ALREADY SAVED YOU! The faith that we exhibit in the Lord Jesus Christ is nothing more than proof that God has awakened us, the fruit of that awakening, and that which GIVES US ACCESS to what CHRIST HAS ALREADY ACCOMPLISHED!!! In essence, the very faith that we have to believe in God is also a GIFT FROM HIM, for God has dealt to every man the measure of faith.

AMEN!

April 5

FORGIVENESS

Luke 23:34 states…Then said Jesus, "Father forgive them for they know not what they do.".…

WOW!!!

THERE IS NO OTHER STATEMENT IN THE BIBLE MORE POWERFUL THAN THIS STATEMENT! The only other statements in the Bible that could even be considered in the same class are…GOD IS LOVE…and…LOVE YOUR ENEMIES!
FATHER <u>FORGIVE</u> THEM FOR THEY KNOW NOT WHAT THEY DO!

WHAT A STATEMENT!

As Jesus was being crucified to take away the sin of the world, HE MANIFESTED THE LOVE OF GOD as He saved us from sin and death, by saying…FATHER FORGIVE THEM FOR THEY KNOW NOT WHAT THEY DO…Not only did Jesus forgive those who were actually crucifying Him, but He also forgave the whole world (all who have ever lived, or will live).

WHAT A SAVIOR!

By forgiving us, Jesus paved the way and left us THE EXAMPLE of what the Father is like. Matthew 6:12 states…And forgive us our debts, as we forgive our debtors…We must have a revelation of God's forgiveness, and then extend that same forgiveness to all men (even our enemies)! Remember what Stephen did in the book of Acts? As they stoned Stephen to death, he said…"Lord, LAY NOT THIS SIN TO THEIR CHARGE.".…

WOW!

Stephen had a revelation of the forgiveness and love of God. May we press in to know the true God of the Bible, WHO IS LOVE, AND HAS FORGIVEN TO THE UTTERMOST! We must see that Jesus is our Jubilee. He has released the entire creation from its sin debt, EVERY MAN IN HIS OWN ORDER!
According to Dr. Stephen Jones: "Even as Jesus Christ is the central Person of all history, the law of Jubilee is the most fundamental law of all creation. The law of Jubilee is the basis of <u>FORGIVENESS</u> and grace. It is the purpose and goal of the law itself. It compels a climax of earth history and a full end of the dominion of darkness and sin. The basic law of Jubilee is recorded in Leviticus 25:8-13." (<u>The Law Of Jubilee</u>, Dr. Stephen Jones)

PRAISE GOD! WE ARE FORGIVEN! NOW…LET US FORGIVE ALL!

April 6

AWAKE

1ST Corinthians 15:34 states…Awake to righteousness, and sin not; for some have not the knowledge of God: I speak this to your shame…What an interesting choice of words. This is what must take place in your heart and life. It needs to continually take place. As we can clearly see, MAN MUST BE AWAKENED! Awakened to what?

God awakens us to:

1. WHO HE IS
2. WHAT HE HAS ACCOMPLISHED

The word "awake" in this passage means: to return to sobriety of mind. Notice that this passage does not say, be righteous, but rather, AWAKE to righteousness. Whose righteousness? GOD'S RIGHTEOUSNESS!

2ND Corinthians 5:18-21 states…All things are of God, Who has (past tense) reconciled us to Himself by Jesus Christ, and has (past tense) given to us the ministry of reconciliation; to wit, that God was (past tense) in Christ, reconciling the world unto Himself, not imputing their trespasses unto them, and has (past tense) committed unto us the word of reconciliation. Now then we are (already to be taking place) ambassadors for Christ, as though God did beseech you by us: we pray you in Christ's stead, be reconciled to God. For He has (past tense) made Him to be sin for us, Who knew no sin; that we might be made the righteousness of God in Him…

So…Who is God? THE SAVIOR! What has He accomplished? HE HAS RECONCILED US! Now…Let us awaken to His salvation, for we have already been reconciled, and we are now called to be reconcilers. We have been justified by faith, and are now to enter into His sanctification PROCESS, which is: THAT WE MIGHT BE MADE THE RIGHTEOUSNESS OF GOD IN HIM.

We have been justified (declared righteous) by faith, and we are now being sanctified (made righteous) by faith. We have been, and are being, AWAKENED to God's righteousness by the SOVEREIGN DRAWING (DRAGGING) of the Spirit of the living God.

AWAKEN US, O MIGHTY GOD!

April 7

RECONCILIATION IN THE HEAVENS

Read Colossians 1:16-20. This is one of the most powerful passages of scripture in the Bible.

It states that:

1. ALL THINGS WERE CREATED BY JESUS CHRIST...
2. ALL THINGS WILL BE RECONCILED UNTO JESUS CHRIST...

The word "reconciliation" means: to bring back together again, to make friendly. Think of what is being said. God created ALL things by Jesus Christ, and God will reconcile ALL things unto Himself by and through the blood of His cross, whether in EARTH, or in the HEAVENS. Is there anything left out? Is there anything or anyone that will not be reconciled unto God? HE WILL RECONCILE ALL THINGS UNTO HIMSELF! WHAT A POWERFUL GOD! WHAT A LOVING FATHER! WHAT A POWERFUL AND ALL-INCLUSIVE CROSS!

According to J. Preston Eby: "Oh, what a vast and all-inclusive statement that is (Colossians 1:20)! All the principalities and powers in heaven and earth are included in the reconciliation effected by the blood of His cross. Oh, what a mighty redemption! Oh, what a universal reconciliation!" (Reconciliation In The Heavens, J. Preston Eby)

We must understand that Jesus will not only reconcile all people unto Himself, but also ALL THINGS! Redemption is not for humanity alone, BUT FOR THE WHOLE CREATION! The question of questions is this: What about principalities, powers, rulers of the darkness of this world, spiritual wickedness in high places, demons, wicked and foul spirits, and even the satanic spirit that now works in the children of disobedience (the prince of the power of the air)??? Will these things be reconciled to God?

YES!

Don't be offended. Remember that Jesus said...And blessed is he, whosoever shall not be offended in Me (Matthew 11:6)...If God chooses to create **all things**, including evil, and then to reconcile **the same all things**, including evil, unto Himself, why should we be offended by that? Evil is simply a tool in God's hands to teach the creation, and to bring the human race to a place where its latter end is GREATER (MORE BLESSED) than its beginning. This can be seen from a careful study of the book of Job. Job 42:11 tells us that all of Job's friends bemoaned him, and comforted him OVER ALL THE EVIL THAT THE LORD HAD BROUGHT UPON HIM...The Lord gave Job twice as much as he had before. In essence, Job was better off for having been exposed to the powers of darkness. He had heard of God, but now he UNDERSTOOD God, and was brought to a place of humility and repentance. And so shall it be with the entire human race, for the story of Job does represent God's dealings with all of mankind.

Revelation 4:11 states...You are worthy, O Lord, to receive glory and honor and power: FOR YOU HAVE CREATED <u>ALL THINGS</u>, AND FOR YOUR PLEASURE THEY ARE AND WERE CREATED...

It is not about us. IT IS ABOUT HIM! His purpose of the ages is to reconcile all things unto Himself. Philippians 3:21 states...HE IS ABLE EVEN TO SUBDUE ALL THINGS UNTO HIMSELF...

ALL THINGS!

April 8

SEARED WITH A HOT IRON

1ST Timothy 4:1 states...Now the Spirit speaks expressly, that in the latter times some shall depart from the faith, giving heed to seducing spirits, and doctrines of demons; speaking lies in hypocrisy; having their conscience seared with a hot iron...Here is this same verse as it reads from Today's English Version...The Spirit says clearly that some people will abandon the faith in latter times; they will obey lying spirits and follow the teachings of demons. Such teachings are spread by deceitful liars, whose consciences are dead, as if burnt with a hot iron...

2nd Peter 2:1 says it this way...False prophets appeared in the past among the people, and in the same way false teachers will appear among you. They will bring in destructive UNTRUE DOCTRINES, and will deny the Master Who redeemed them, and so they will bring upon themselves sudden destruction...(Today's English Version)

It is interesting to take note of 1st John 2:18, which states...Little children, IT IS THE LAST TIME...In essence, John was saying that the latter times had already begun, even in his day. This would then tell us, that those who are spoken of in 1st Timothy 4:1 have already surfaced, and have already caused MANY to depart from "THE FAITH", giving heed to seducing spirits, and doctrines of demons; speaking lies in hypocrisy; having their conscience seared with a hot iron...It is sad to say that the church is always waiting for something to happen THAT HAS ALREADY HAPPENED. They are so very careful to watch for deception, and a great falling away, but it has already taken place about 1,700 years ago with the entrance of a man by the name of Constantine.

Prior to Augustine in the 5th Century, the vast majority of Christians, including the leadership, believed in the salvation of all mankind through Jesus Christ. They understood that punishment in the ages to come was for the purpose of purification and correction. Of the six theological schools known to the early church, four taught the salvation of all, one taught annihilation, and only one taught eternal torment.

So...What are seducing spirits, doctrines of demons, and speaking lies in hypocrisy? They are thoughts of STRONG DELUSION sent by God into the minds of men who received not the love of the truth. These thoughts brought in UNTRUE DOCTRINES, OR DAMNABLE HERESIES, WHICH RESULTED IN THE TEACHING OF "ETERNAL TORTURE", and many other things that are nothing more than the traditions of men. This untrue doctrine (eternal torture) has made the Word of God of none effect in the lives of MANY people.

The downward spiral which led up to this false doctrine began with Constantine (313 A.D.) and the legalization of Christianity, and culminated with Augustine, WHOSE CONSCIENCE WAS SEARED WITH A HOT IRON. He was instrumental in arguing (400-430 A.D.) that the Greek word "aionios" signified endless and eternal torment, which in fact IT DOES NOT, but does only refer to punishment within the ages of time. Augustine's conscience was dead (burnt, seared) to the love of God. He, along with many others after him, believed that God would be glorified in tormenting people forever. NOW THAT IS A CONSCIENCE SEARED WITH A HOT IRON!!! Slowly the corruption spread, and little by little the pagan dogma gained upon the Christian doctrine, till the primitive teaching on this point was condemned in a church council held A.D. 553; and the doctrine of endless punishment sanctified as a fundamental article of Christian faith.

According to Dr. Harold Lovelace: "The Dark Ages, as they are known, came upon the world for about 1,000 years, AND THIS GREAT TRUTH WAS HIDDEN." (Read And Search God's Plan, Dr. Harold Lovelace)

What do you think made the Dark Ages so dark? Well…How about the DAMNABLE HERESY (UNTRUE DOCTRINE) of the teaching of eternal torture? WHAT A DARK PICTURE OF GOD! Let us come out of darkness into His marvelous light. God is able to take a conscience that has been seared with a hot iron, and to turn it into the mind of Christ!

THANK GOD!

April 9

O LOVE OF GOD

The love of God is greater far
Than tongue or pen can ever tell;
It goes beyond the highest star,
And reaches to the lowest hell;
The guilty pair, bowed down with care,
God gave His Son to win;
His erring child He reconciled,
And pardoned from his sin.

Refrain

O love of God, how rich and pure!
How measureless and strong!
It shall forevermore endure
The saints' and angels' song.

When years of time shall pass away,
And earthly thrones and kingdoms fall,
When men, who here refuse to pray,
On rocks and hills and mountains call,
God's love so sure, shall still endure,
All measureless and strong;
Redeeming grace to Adam's race—
The saints' and angels' song.

Refrain

Could we with ink the ocean fill,
And were the skies of parchment made,
Were every stalk on earth a quill,
And every man a scribe by trade,
To write the love of God above,
Would drain the ocean dry.
Nor could the scroll contain the whole,
Though stretched from sky to sky.

Words: Frederick M. Lehman: he wrote this song in 1917 in Pasadena, California, and it was published in *Songs That Are Different*, Volume 2, 1919. The lyrics are based on the Jewish poem Haddamut, written in Aramaic in 1050 by Meir Ben Isaac Nehorai, a cantor in Worms, Germany; they have been translated into at least 18 languages.

One day, during short intervals of inattention to our work, we picked up a scrap of paper and, seated upon an empty lemon box pushed against the wall, with a stub pencil, added the (first) two stanzas and chorus of the song…Since the lines (3rd stanza from the Jewish poem) had been found penciled on the wall of a patient's room in an insane asylum after he had been carried to his grave, the general opinion was that this inmate had written the epic in moments of sanity. Frederick M. Lehman, "History of the Song, *The Love of God*," 1948

The Lord Jesus Christ has written these words on the walls of our hearts. They are there to be discovered, and to be awakened to, FOR GOD IS LOVE! He has indeed extended redeeming grace to Adam's race, and His love does indeed reach to THE LOWEST HELL!

WHO SHALL SEPARATE US FROM THE LOVE OF CHRIST?

April 10

MAN'S "FREE WILL?" VS. GOD'S SOVEREIGN LOVE

According to John Gavazzoni: "Everything that occurs, occurs within the sovereign will of God. Nothing is accidental. All has been foreseen by Him because **all things come to pass by His decision,** so that everything has occurred by Him, **either doing something to make it come to pass, or by deliberately refusing to act so as, by that absence of His action, to trigger certain consequential results. The truth is that the only One in the universe who has true free will is God Himself.** As is true of every good thing, free will is something found in God's very nature and **we can only experience freedom of will by God causing us to participate in His freedom by causing us to become** *"partakers of the divine nature"* (II Pet. 1:4); and that is His choice not ours." (Free Will, John Gavazzoni)

So…Is man able to make choices? OF COURSE HE IS! But that does not mean that they are totally free choices. To say that we have a totally free will means that we are always able to make UNCAUSED CHOICES, and that is just not the case!

Take for example:

1. Jonah: Now the Lord had prepared a great fish to swallow up Jonah. And Jonah was in the belly of the fish three days and three nights. THEN JONAH PRAYED…(Jonah 1:17-2:1)

2. Paul: But the Lord said unto him (Ananias), Go your way: for he (Paul) is a CHOSEN VESSEL unto Me, to bear My name…(Acts 9:15)

3. Pharaoh: Even for this same purpose have I (GOD) RAISED THEE UP (Pharaoh), that I (God) might show My power in you (Pharaoh)…and whom He (God) will HE (GOD) HARDENS…(Romans 9:17,18)

4. Esau: Jacob have I (God) loved, but Esau have I hated…THE CHILDREN BEING NOT BORN YET…ACCORDING TO THE ELECTION…(Romans 9:11,13)

5. Israel: GOD HAS GIVEN THEM THE SPIRIT OF SLUMBER, eyes that they should not see, and ears that they should not hear…(Romans 11:8)

6. The Twelve Apostles: (Jesus speaking) You have not chosen Me, BUT I HAVE CHOSE YOU… (John 15:16)

7. The Gentiles: But Isaiah is very bold, and says, I was found of them THAT SOUGHT ME NOT (speaking of the Gentiles); I was made manifest unto them THAT ASKED NOT AFTER ME…(Romans 10:20)

8. All Men: (Jesus speaking) And I, if I be lifted up from the earth, WILL DRAW (DRAG) ALL MEN UNTO ME…(John 12:32)

Well…That about covers it! SO MUCH FOR FREE WILL! Yes…We are able to make choices, but we must understand that our choices in some way or another are INFLUENCED BY GOD! They are choices WITHIN THE SOVEREIGNTY OF GOD!

So…Is man a robot? NO!

According to John Gavazzoni: "Now some, completely indoctrinated by the dumbed-down notion of free will, upon being confronted with what I've just shared, without any depth of thought at all, **would accuse me of making man out to be a mere robot.** But, I ask, if God has a free will, and brings man into participation with that will, how can freedom be defined as robotic? Freedom by definition, involves not being controlled by another. **The relationship of God's will to us, is not one of making us do something against our will, but by bringing our will into union with His. This is not coercion, this is causation,** and it is causation by the force of love which ultimately **worked by God leaving us to ourselves to do what we would do left to ourselves; which was to crucify His Son, and then to love such enemies back to Himself by the power of forgiving love."** (Free Will, John Gavazzoni)

WHAT A SOVEREIGN AND LOVING FATHER!

April 11

THE GARDEN OF EDEN

Let us take a fresh look at the Garden of Eden and its spiritual implications for us today. The Garden of Eden is much more than a literal garden in which two literal people existed. It has a deep and spiritual meaning that unlocks the purpose and plan of God in our lives.

Genesis 2:7 states…And the Lord God formed man of the dust of the ground, and breathed into his nostrils the breath of life; and man became a living soul…Let us consider the physical Garden of Eden, what was in it, and what those things do represent spiritually.

The Garden of Eden contained:

    1. MAN (ADAM)
    2. THE TREE OF LIFE
    3. THE TREE OF THE KNOWLEDGE OF GOOD AND EVIL
    4. A RIVER (SPLIT INTO FOUR HEADS)
    5. EVE (A HELPMATE, WOMAN)
    6. THE SERPENT (DECEPTION)
    7. GOD

Now let us consider the deeper and spiritual meaning of this Garden of Eden. 1st Corinthians 15:45-47 states…And so it is written, The first man Adam was made a living soul; the last Adam was made a quickening spirit. Howbeit that was not first which is spiritual, but that which is natural; and afterward that which is spiritual. The first man is of the earth, earthy: the second man is the Lord from heaven…Can you see that there are ONLY TWO MEN?…

1. THE FIRST MAN…ADAM
2. THE SECOND MAN…CHRIST

We are either in Adam or in Christ! So…Let us get spiritual for a minute.

SPIRITUALLY SPEAKING, YOU MUST SEE YOURSELF AS THE GARDEN OF EDEN! IN ESSENCE, YOU ARE THE GARDEN OF EDEN!

This would then mean that all men have within themselves:

ADAM = DEATH, EARTHY, EARTHBOUND, THE EARTHLY REALM

THE TREE OF LIFE = CHRIST IN YOU THE HOPE OF GLORY, THE HEAVENLY REALM

THE TREE OF THE KNOWLEDGE OF GOOD AND EVIL = SELF, APPROACHING GOD THROUGH THE FLESH

A RIVER = RIVERS OF LIVING WATER, THE SPIRIT OF GOD THAT IS MANIFESTED IN FOUR WAYS (KING, SERVANT, MAN, GOD…HENCE: MATTHEW, MARK, LUKE, JOHN)

EVE = OUR TENDENCY TO BE LED AWAY AND DECEIVED, THE SOUL OF MAN (AS WELL…ADAM REPRESENTS THE SPIRIT OF MAN, FOR OUR SPIRIT IS TO BE SEEN AS MASCULINE, AND OUR SOUL IS TO BE SEEN AS FEMININE)

THE SERPENT = THE BEAST NATURE, THE MARK OF THE BEAST, THE CARNAL MIND

GOD = THE POTENTIAL FOR GODLINESS IN MAN, FOR WE ARE THE OFFSPRING OF GOD, WE HAVE BEEN MADE PARTAKERS OF THE DIVINE NATURE

As stated earlier, Adam and Eve do also represent our spirit and soul, for our spirit is masculine, and our soul is feminine. As we learn to partake of the Tree of Life (Christ), we shall experience His life. If we continue to partake of the Tree of the Knowledge of Good and Evil (the carnal mind, that which is antichrist), we shall continue to experience death. Please meditate on this garden, FOR IT IS YOU! The "Garden of Eden" means to be hedged about or protected in pleasure and delight. This is, of course, only an introduction to understanding the spirituality of the Garden of Eden. May we see the importance of this garden within, for God is bringing us from death to…

DELIGHT!

April 12

BECOMING A CREDITOR

Do we really want to become like our Lord and Savior Jesus Christ? Then we must learn THE POWER OF FORGIVENESS! It has been said, "To err is human, but to forgive is Divine." (Alexander Pope)

To live your life on this earth, and not learn the Divine Principle of FORGIVENESS, is to miss everything that Jesus Christ taught and performed. To read the Bible, and not grasp the ultimate theme of God's love and forgiveness, is to miss the very meaning of the Book. OUR READING IS IN VAIN if we do not come away from the Bible with the very nature of God, WHICH IS LOVE AND FORGIVENESS! So...let us plunge into the depths of God's love and forgiveness!

According to Dr. Stephen Jones: "All victims of injustice are creditors and have certain rights before the law of God. Most men become angry and often quite bitter over these injustices. Those who know the heart of God have learned to forgive those who wrong them and to rejoice when men persecute them. The overcomers are men and women that God intends to put into positions of rulership in His Kingdom. The overcomers have a heart to declare the Jubilee in the earth, which will set the nations free in the coming Age of Tabernacles. As creditors, they and they alone retain the lawful right to forgive the debt owed to them--and actually have the heart to do so. These are overcomers. The primary qualification of an overcomer--one who aspires to attain to the Feast of Tabernacles--is to be a forgiver. WE MUST UNDERSTAND THAT THE POWER OF FORGIVENESS AND LOVE TRANSCENDS THE POWER OF THE GRUDGE AND THE POWER OF SIN!" (<u>The Laws Of The Second Coming</u>, Dr. Stephen Jones)

Where do we get this power to forgive and to love? Well...From God, of course! 1st John 4:19 states...WE LOVE HIM (AND OTHERS), BECAUSE HE FIRST LOVED US...As well, we forgive others, because God through Christ forgave us.

Let us begin to enter into the Feast of Tabernacles (spiritually speaking) as we demonstrate THE DIVINE NATURE OF OUR FATHER, BY LOVING AND FORGIVING THE WHOLE WORLD (for they know not what they do), which makes us a creditor, and qualifies us for the coming Age of Tabernacles!

FORGIVE!

April 13

ENTER IN AT THE STRAIT GATE

Matthew 7:13,14 states...Enter in at the strait gate: for wide is the gate, and broad is the way, that leads to destruction, and many there be which go in thereat: Because strait is the gait, and narrow is the way, which leads unto life, and few there be that find it…We have just quoted one of the most popular verses in the Bible. Now…Let us talk about what it means. Let us rightly divide this all-important passage of scripture.

This passage of scripture refers to the REMNANT (the overcomers, the firstfruits company, the body of Christ, the barley company).

It would do us well to remember, and to take note of, that there are scriptures that refer to:

1. THE REMNANT
2. THE NATIONS
3. THE ENTIRE CREATION

This happens to be a passage that talks about the remnant (the few there be that find life in this present age). The subject matter of this passage is not, "flying off to heaven, or busting hell wide open after you die". As a matter of fact, Jesus spent very little time talking about what happens to man after physical death. His subject matter was always pertaining to THE KINGDOM OF GOD, WHICH HE DID SPEAK OF AS A PRESENT DAY REALITY, WAITING TO BE EXPERIENCED BY THOSE WHO WERE HUNGRY FOR GOD. Remember…

The Kingdom of God is not a physical location that we are going to fly away to in the sweet by-and-by, but is defined as:

1. RIGHTEOUSNESS
2. PEACE
3. JOY…IN THE HOLY SPIRIT

This means that there are few who understand the Kingdom of God in this present age. There are few who SEE (PERCEIVE) the Kingdom of God. There are few who enter into this narrow way of the life of Christ, WHICH ENTAILS HAVING YOUR FLESH (YOUR CORRUPT NATURE, CARNAL MIND, WOOD, HAY, AND STUBBLE) DEALT WITH BY THE CONSUMING FIRE OF GOD! YES…IT IS A NARROW WAY, AND FEW THERE BE THAT FIND IT!

There is only a remnant of people being dealt with in this present age, but the GOOD NEWS is, that there are at least two more ages to come, which will include the gathering in of ALL NATIONS, AND ALL THINGS! (Read Ephesians 2:7.) Those who do not enter into this narrow way now are headed for destruction. The question is then, WHAT IS IT THAT IS GOING TO BE DESTROYED?

The Bible speaks of the destruction of the flesh (the carnal mind, or nature of man that is contrary to the Spirit of God), that the spirit may be saved in the day of the Lord (1st Corinthians 5:5). This speaks of the destruction of the carnal (corrupt) mind (nature) of man. Those who are in the narrow way now have already entered the PROCESS of the destruction of the flesh. In essence, the destruction of the flesh is a good thing. With that being said though, IT IS BETTER to enter into the narrow way NOW, than having to suffer loss, being saved; yet so as by fire (1st Corinthians 3:15). As well, the unbeliever must go through the purifying fire of God, for our Father will leave nothing undone. For those who have the ears to hear, the Spirit calls for you to come into the narrow way of the Lord Jesus Christ NOW! But let us rest assured that ALL WILL EVENTUALLY COME TO THE FATHER, FOR JESUS ASSURED US THAT HE WOULD DRAW (DRAG) ALL MEN UNTO HIMSELF!

PRAISE GOD FOR THE NARROW WAY!

April 14

EYE HAS NOT SEEN

1ST Corinthians 2:9 states…But as it is written, Eye has not seen, nor ear heard, neither has it entered into the heart of man, the things which God has prepared for them that love Him. But God has revealed them unto us by His Spirit: for the Spirit searches all things, yes, the deep things of God…As well, Ephesians 2:6,7 states…God has raised us up together, and made us sit together in heavenly places in Christ Jesus: THAT IN THE AGES TO COME HE MIGHT SHOW THE EXCEEDING RICHES OF HIS GRACE IN HIS KINDNESS TOWARD US THROUGH CHRIST JESUS…1ST Corinthians 6:2,3 states…Do you not know that the saints SHALL JUDGE THE WORLD?…Know you not that we shall judge angels?…Obadiah 1:21 states…and SAVIORS (Deliverers) shall come up on mount Zion TO JUDGE the mount of Esau; and the kingdom shall be the Lord's…Isaiah 2:3,4 states…for out of Zion (the overcomers) shall go forth the law, and the Word of the Lord from Jerusalem. And He shall judge among the nations, and shall rebuke many people: and they shall beat their swords into plowshares, and their spears into pruning hooks: NATION SHALL NOT LIFT UP SWORD AGAINST NATION, NEITHER SHALL THEY LEARN WAR ANY MORE…Romans 8:19,21 states…For the earnest expectation of the creature (creation) waits for the manifestation of the sons of God…Because the creature (creation) itself shall also be delivered from the bondage of corruption into the glorious liberty of the children of God…

Are you beginning to see a picture of the ages to come yet? CAN YOU SEE? CAN YOU HEAR? IS IT ENTERING INTO YOUR HEART? God is revealing it unto us by His Spirit! ARE THE EYES OF YOUR UNDERSTANDING BEING ENLIGHTENED? DO YOU KNOW WHAT IS THE HOPE OF YOUR CALLING?

We are called out of darkness into His marvelous light to SHOW FORTH the praises of God NOW AND IN THE AGES TO COME! God is qualifying you to be a:

1. DEMONSTRATION OF HIS GRACE
2. SAVIOR (DELIVERER)
3. PEACEMAKER (BRINGING WAR TO AN END)
4. MANIFESTATION OF THE SON OF GOD
5. JUDGE

HALLELUJAH!

April 15

WHY?

Why? Why what? Why is it so hard for people to believe the simple declarations of scripture that declare that Jesus Christ is the SAVIOR OF THE WORLD? The Bible very clearly speaks of the salvation of ALL MEN! So…Why?

Let us consider these things:

People are vengeful.

Many Bibles have been tainted with the PAGAN DOCTRINE of the Dark Ages (eternal torture).

Mankind has a natural tendency to stay with what we are most familiar with, EVEN IF IT IS UNTRUE…Remember…The traditions and doctrines of men make the Word of God of none effect.

Political, religious, and economic powers have found "fear of hell" to be an extremely effective power to keep the masses in subjection.

We do not understand God's sovereignty, foreknowledge, power, omniscience, purpose of creation, and His unconditional love.

We fail to believe DIRECT STATEMENTS OF SCRIPTURE declaring the ultimate salvation of all through the saving work of Jesus Christ (the atonement).

We fail to understand the purpose of God's: judgment, punishment, wrath, vengeance, and fire, for they are all for the purpose of correction and purification.

We can either humble ourselves and fall on the rock (Christ), receiving this beautiful revelation now, or we can have the rock fall on us in correction in the ages to come. But make no mistake about it, ALL WILL EVENTUALLY COME TO THE SAVING KNOWLEDGE OF THE LORD JESUS CHRIST!

1ST Timothy 2:3-6 states…For this is good and acceptable in the sight of God our Savior; Who will have all men to be saved, and to come unto the knowledge of the truth. For there is one God, and one Mediator between God and men, the Man Christ Jesus, Who gave Himself a ransom for all, to be testified in due time…

So…Why not? Why not believe the truth of the glorious gospel of Jesus Christ? All we have to lose is our ignorance, pride, and self-righteousness. How could we not believe that a God Who is all-powerful and all-loving will save all men from sin and death?

(This theme and quotes taken from: <u>What Pleases Our Father</u>, Gary Amirault)

WHY NOT BELIEVE IN HIS UNLIMITED POWER AND LOVE?

April 16

THE GREATEST LIE EVER TOLD

According to Ken Eckerty: "You have all heard preachers and evangelists speak of the "Greatest Story Ever Told." It is a story of love, of sacrifice, and of "everlasting mercy." It is a story that has been told for over two thousand years with great passion and tears, and one that has changed the lives of countless millions all over the world. This story, of course, is none other than the story of the life and ministry of Jesus Christ. On this website (www.savior-of-all.com), you will hear of that story, but you are also going to hear (maybe for the first time) another story. This story, like the other, is told with equal passion—perhaps even more. This story, unlike the other, is a lie. It is the "Greatest Lie Ever Told" to man, and you might be very surprised to find out where this lie comes from. It does not come from those we would consider heathen; nor does it come from atheists, or even those who are violently opposed to God and religion. No, this lie does not come from those we would expect. The greatest lie the world has ever heard comes straight from the very people who love and follow Jesus Christ. It comes from our pulpits, it is taught in our Sunday school classes, it is broadcast all over the world through our television ministries, and it is preached by the missionaries who are in the remotest places of the world.

Have I gotten your attention yet? OK, so what is this lie? It is the lie that says that God will eternally torment most of His creatures; it is the lie that says that Jesus Christ cannot save most men; it is the lie that says that death will continue to exist forever, and it is the lie that says there will come a time when God will never be able to show mercy and love to the majority of those He created. Yes, this is the lie of religion and it is one that has all but consumed Evangelical Christianity, so much so that the Church's message has become one of fear rather than one of love and victory. It has taken the beautiful judgments of God and turned them into a sadistic torture chamber, and worse than this, it has made a miserable failure of the work of Jesus Christ in that only a small minority of the billions of people who have ever lived will ever see heaven. This website's purpose (www.savior-of-all.com) is two fold: 1) to proclaim the victory and power of the cross of our Lord Jesus, and 2) to expose the false doctrine of "eternal" punishment (as it is taught by orthodox Christianity).

Why is it important that we study the issue of the final destiny of man? Some people have told me that this issue is not really pertinent to them because it focuses on future things and our concern should be with the "here-and-now." I absolutely agree that our focus should be on the "here-and-now", which is why we need to seek out the heart of God on this matter. However, I disagree that our conclusion on this matter in no way affects the way we live. Understanding this issue is extremely important because it will significantly affect how we respond to those around us (both toward Christians and non-Christians alike), and how we deal with adversity in our lives. Also, in order to be able to effectively minister to the world with the gospel, we must know both the beginning and <u>the end</u> of God's plan for man." (<u>Exposing The Greatest Lie Ever Told</u>, Ken Eckerty)

Remember…In Adam all die, even so in Christ shall all be made alive. But every man in his own order…If all die in Adam, but all will not be made alive in Christ, THEN THE CROSS OF CHRIST HAS FAILED, AND ADAM WAS MORE POWERFUL THAN JESUS CHRIST! When we preach the message of eternal torture, that is what we are saying. THINK ABOUT IT! That, my friend, is the…

GREATEST LIE EVER TOLD!

April 17

A FORM OF GODLINESS

The greatest single cause of atheism in the world today is Christianity. Most Christians acknowledge Jesus with their lips, and then walk out the door and deny Him with their lifestyle. That is what an unbelieving world simply finds unbelievable.

We must realize that the world can see right through all of our religious games. They know that the message of fear, hate, and confusion (which Evangelical Christianity preaches) is nothing more than SOUNDING BRASS AND A TINKLING CYMBAL! In simple terms, the church is making a lot of noise, and is a FORM OF GODLINESS WHICH DENIES THE POWER OF GOD!

This means that most of Christianity is an external form of the Christian life with NO INNER POWER! Let us turn away from this external facade of self-righteousness that STINKS to the high heavens!

Our problem is not the:

MUSLIMS
MASONS
HOMOSEXUALS
CATHOLICS (or any other religion, cult, or denomination)
GOVERNMENT (who is in office)
MIDDLE EAST
TEN COMMANDMENTS (whether or not they are hanging on the walls in public places)
RIGHT TO PRAY IN SCHOOLS OR PUBLIC PLACES

Our problem is THAT WE (the church) ARE A FORM (mere appearance) OF GODLINESS WITH NO POWER! So…What is the answer?

2nd Timothy 1:7 states…For God has not given us the spirit of fear; but of POWER, AND OF LOVE, AND OF A SOUND MIND…We have forsaken the power of God for the spirit of fear. We must STOP preaching a "gospel of fear", and start preaching the GOOD NEWS! What good news? The good news that GOD WAS IN CHRIST RECONCILING THE WORLD UNTO HIMSELF!

As we line up with God's truth, we will once again be a church of power, love, and of a sound mind. Then, and only then, will the world be interested in this God that we are interested in. Instead of being just a form…

LET US BE TRANSFORMED!

April 18

WHAT IS THE PURPOSE OF RULING AND REIGNING?

1ST Corinthians 15:25-27,28 states…For He must reign <u>UNTIL</u> He has put all enemies under His feet. The last enemy that shall be destroyed is death. For He has put all things under His feet…AND WHEN ALL THINGS SHALL BE SUBDUED UNTO HIM, then shall the Son also Himself be subject unto Him That put ALL THINGS UNDER HIM, THAT GOD MAY BE ALL IN ALL…

So…How long will Jesus reign? UNTIL He has put all enemies under His feet, destroyed death (including the second death), and until He has subdued all things unto the Father. This will cause God to be ALL IN ALL (EVERYTHING TO EVERYONE)! The question is though, what is the purpose of ruling and reigning?

Ruling and reigning is for the purpose of:

1. DEALING WITH AND CORRECTING REBELLION
2. CAUSING THE ENEMIES OF GOD TO SUBMIT TO HIM
3. DESTROYING DEATH (its physical and spiritual aspects)
4. PUTTING ALL THINGS UNDER GOD'S FEET
5. THAT GOD MAY BE ALL IN ALL

How is it that God will accomplish this task? He is going to bring this about through THE OVERCOMERS! Revelation 2:26,27 states…And he that OVERCOMES, and keeps my works unto the end, TO HIM WILL I GIVE POWER OVER THE NATIONS: AND HE SHALL RULE THEM WITH A ROD OF IRON; as the vessels of a potter shall they be broken to shivers: even as I received of my Father…Psalm 66:3,4 states…Through the greatness of Your power shall Your enemies SUBMIT THEMSELVES UNTO YOU. ALL THE EARTH shall worship You, and shall sing unto You…

CAN YOU SEE? The whole idea of ruling and reigning is for the purpose of SUBDUING ALL THINGS UNTO THE FATHER! When all things are subdued unto the Father, Jesus Christ will no longer need to rule and reign, for it will not be necessary. GOD WILL THEN BE EVERYTHING TO EVERYONE!

In the meantime, let us seek first the Kingdom of God that we might be a part of Revelation 2:26 (the overcomers that will set the creation free). For He must reign…

UNTIL HE HAS PUT ALL ENEMIES UNDER HIS FEET!

April 19

THE MINISTER OF GOD

Mark 10:43-45 states…whosoever will be great among you, shall be your minister: And whosoever of you will be the chiefest, shall be servant of all. For even the Son of man came not to be ministered unto, but to minister, and to give His life a ransom for many…

The word "minister" means: A SERVANT, TO SERVE. We have developed a modern day idea of a minister that goes something like this…We must find the smartest person we can find, vote that person into position, pay that person a big salary, and believe and hang on every word that he says. This person must also wear the finest clothes, drive the finest car, live in the finest home, and be in luxury every moment of every day. This person must be the only one to teach and preach, while all others must keep their mouths shut and listen. HAVE WE MISSED IT, OR WHAT? Remember…The word "minister" means to BE A SERVANT.

In essence, Jesus was telling us that the definition of greatness is SERVANTHOOD (to serve others with a servant heart and attitude). According to Jesus, those who are servants are GREATEST in the Kingdom of God. Do you want to be great in the Kingdom of God? BE A SERVANT! HAVE A SERVANT HEART! SEEK NOT TO BE SERVED, BUT TO SERVE! For even the Son of man came not to be served, but to serve, and to give His life a ransom for many. This is what it means to be a true…

MINISTER (SERVANT) OF GOD!

April 20

IT IS TIME TO SOAR

(Taken from the song: <u>Eagle Saints Begin To Fly</u>, Judy Vanderburg)

Naked I stood a fallen man, through no fault of my own
My inheritance…forgotten
No memory of who I was born to be, but still I knew deep inside of me
I had a higher purpose, there was a greater plan

I was born to live in Your presence, I was meant to soar in the heavens
No longer marred by the mark of man, no longer clothed in the rags of sin

In Your righteousness I now stand, a new creation
A brand new man…accepted
With eyes wide open, I now see, Your Kingdom Lord, for You live in me
No longer rejected, I'm Your beloved son

Eagle saints begin to fly…Eagle saints begin to fly
Eagle saints begin to fly…Eagle saints begin to fly

Do you hear the call? Do you have ears to hear? IT IS TIME TO ARISE IN CHRIST AND SOAR IN THE HEAVENS! Isaiah 40:31 states…But they that wait upon the Lord shall renew their strength; THEY SHALL MOUNT UP WITH WINGS AS EAGLES; they shall run, and not be weary; and they shall walk, and not faint…

What comes to mind when you think of an eagle soaring? HOW ABOUT FREEDOM! An eagle flies high above a storm in the heavens. It is totally free from the damaging effects of the storm. John 8:32 states…And you shall know the truth, AND THE TRUTH SHALL MAKE YOU FREE…

Let us consider that:

1. If we are not soaring in the heavens (seated in heavenly places in Christ), then we are not free.
2. If we are not free (free from bondage, sin, and self), then we do not have the truth.
3. If we do not have the truth, then we are embracing a lie (deception).
4. If we are embracing a lie, then we are a form of godliness, denying the power of God.

As we come to the knowledge of the truth concerning our TRUE IDENTITY IN CHRIST, we are then able to shed our Adamic Nature. As we do this, we begin to soar in the heavens (spiritually speaking), and we find ourselves flying high above the storms of life. Let us mount up with WINGS AS EAGLES! DO YOU HEAR THE CALL?

EAGLE SAINTS BEGIN TO FLY!

April 21

FLESH AND BLOOD

1ST Corinthians 15:50 states…Now this I say, brethren, that flesh and blood cannot inherit the kingdom of God; neither does corruption inherit incorruption…

Here is the same verse as it reads from the New Testament In Modern Speech…But this I tell you, brethren: our mortal bodies cannot inherit the kingdom of God, nor will what is perishable inherit what is imperishable…

Let us now attempt to discuss the nuts and bolts of this scripture verse. We will focus our attention on:

1. FLESH AND BLOOD
2. THE KINGDOM OF GOD
3. INHERITING THE KINGDOM OF GOD

To put this scripture into its proper context we must first see what the apostle Paul is talking about in this chapter (1st Corinthians chapter 15). The theme of this chapter is the resurrection of the dead. The resurrection that Paul is speaking of is not a spiritual resurrection, but rather a bodily resurrection. The chapter starts out with Paul speaking of the death, burial, and resurrection of the Lord Jesus Christ, and that He was seen by Peter, and then by the twelve. It goes on to say that afterwards He was seen by more than five hundred brethren at once. As well, He was seen by James, and then by all the apostles. Paul then states that Jesus appeared unto him. After establishing the resurrection of the Lord Jesus Christ, Paul then deals with those who deny the possibility of the bodily resurrection of the rest of the dead. He further states, that if there is no such thing as a resurrection of the dead, THEN CHRIST HIMSELF HAS NOT RISEN FROM THE DEAD! Please keep in mind that Paul is not referring to a spiritual resurrection, but rather to the actual bodily resurrection of the Lord Jesus Christ, which is then to become the PATTERN for our own resurrection as well. The resurrection of the Lord Jesus Christ then becomes the pattern and guarantee for the resurrection of the entire creation. The key to understanding this is to be found in the statement…But this will happen to each man in the right order (1st Corinthians 15:23)…

The order is simply this:

    1. CHRIST
    2. CHRIST'S PEOPLE (THE REMNANT, OR FIRSTFRUITS OF CHRIST)
    3. THE REST OF THE DEAD

To understand what the resurrection will be like, read the rest of the chapter. As well, take into consideration the verses that speak of Jesus after His bodily resurrection. Remember…JESUS IS THE PATTERN!

The words "flesh and blood" do speak of the corrupt nature of man. As well, they speak of our corrupt (mortal) body. Both our corrupt nature and body are subject to sin and death (whether spiritual or physical death). This is saying that our corrupt nature and mortal body cannot inherit the Kingdom of God, whether now or in the ages to come. This means that we need a NEW NATURE AND A NEW BODY. Jesus demonstrated this by His resurrection, for He had all power in HEAVEN AND IN EARTH. He was unlimited in the spirit realm, AND He was unlimited in the physical realm due to His glorified body. When Jesus appeared to His disciples after His resurrection, He assured them that He was not a spirit. He said…BEHOLD MY HANDS AND MY FEET, THAT IT IS I MYSELF: HANDLE ME, AND SEE; FOR A SPIRIT HAS NOT <u>FLESH AND BONES</u>, AS YOU SEE ME HAVE…This is the pattern for our resurrection! Notice that Jesus said that He had flesh and bone, but mentions nothing about blood. Please keep in mind that this flesh and bone body that Jesus spoke of was not the same type of body that went into the tomb. IT WAS A GLORIFIED (SPIRITUAL) BODY (1st Corinthians 15:42-49)!

According to Dr. Stephen Jones: "Men have long speculated on the ages to come. What will happen, when, and in what order? What will the condition of men be when they are raised (1 Cor. 15:35)? What is the purpose of the reign of Christ in the age to come, known to the Hebrews and early Christians as the Kingdom Age, or the Messianic Age? How does it differ from the age that follows it, described as "the new heaven and the new earth" having a "new Jerusalem"? The key to understanding the Kingdom of God is to view it in its three stages of development, rather than pitting one view against another. Some say the Kingdom is NOW, and they are certainly correct. Others say the Kingdom is FUTURE, and they are correct as well. A few even say that the Kingdom of God began with Moses, and they too are correct. The Kingdom of God did indeed begin in the time of Moses when God first organized Israel into a Kingdom at Horeb. But the Kingdom of God was manifested in a greater manner under a Pentecostal anointing in the second chapter of Acts. But the Kingdom of God is also yet future as of this writing. We await the outpouring of the Spirit under the Feast of Tabernacles, which will manifest the Kingdom of God in its highest form on the earth. Only this view is large enough to encompass both those who believe the "Kingdom Now" idea, as well as the "Future Kingdom" viewpoint. We believe that the term "resurrection" is never used in the Bible for anything but a physical raising from the dead. We certainly understand that the believer is given life at his justification, but this does not negate the need for resurrection. Paul made it plain in 1 Corinthians 15 that the resurrection of Jesus Christ was the pattern and basis of our own resurrection. Jesus took time to carefully explain to His disciples that He had been raised in a physical body, though He was certainly not subject to the limitations of our present flesh. (See Luke 24:36-43.) In other words, when a man is justified by faith in the blood of the Lamb, he receives a Passover anointing from God, but this does not bring him personally into the fullness of the Spirit. When a man receives the Spirit of God through the anointing of Pentecost, he receives a fresh anointing, but it is only an earnest, and he is still left with imperfections by which he falls short of the glory of God. Only when God pours out His Spirit upon us in the fulfillment of Tabernacles will we find the perfection and immortality we seek." (The Millennium Question, Dr. Stephen Jones)

O DEATH, WHERE IS YOUR STING? O GRAVE, WHERE IS YOUR VICTORY?

April 22

WHAT IS THE KINGDOM OF GOD?

According to J. Preston Eby: "The dictionary defines "kingdom" as "a government or country headed by a king or queen; a monarchical state; a realm or domain." The word "kingdom" is made up of the noun "king", and the suffix "dom". "Dom" is a noun-forming suffix to express rank, position, or domain. For example, a "dukedom" is the domain over which a duke has authority or exercises rule, and in the abstract the rank of a duke. In like manner a "kingdom" is the domain and the people within that domain over which a king exercises authority and rule. It is the "king's domain". "Kingdom" is thus a contraction of "king's domain". The term, "Kingdom of God", can mean no other than the domain over which God exercises rule as King. As well, the word "kingdom" is from the Greek word "BASILEIA" meaning "rule" or "reign"." (To Be The Lord's Prayer, J. Preston Eby)

Can you see it yet? The Kingdom of God is the domain over which, and in which God rules and reigns in SUPREME POWER AND AUTHORITY (SOVEREIGNTY)! The Kingdom of God is the sovereign rule of God within the hearts and lives of His people.

The Kingdom of God is NOT "in the sweet by-and-by"! It is not a place you go to after you die! IT IS IN THE HERE-AND-NOW! IT IS CHRIST IN YOU, THE HOPE OF GLORY!

It is the inward working of the Spirit of God to bring you to the place where you will begin to say:

1. THY KINGDOM COME!
2. THY WILL BE DONE!

The Kingdom of God is WITHIN YOU (INSIDE OF YOU, Luke 17:21)! It is the Spirit of God performing MAJOR SURGERY on your soul, which is your:

1. MIND
2. WILL
3. EMOTIONS

We must let go of our kingdom, and our will, which is the throne of our inner will and heart.

According to J. Preston Eby: "So, if I sincerely, earnestly, and genuinely beseech the Spirit of God to rule in my life and experience, there to establish His Kingdom, I can only expect that there will be a most tremendous confrontation. It is a foregone conclusion that there will follow a formidable conflict between His divine sovereignty and my self-willed ego. And this, precious friend of mine, is the true BATTLE OF ARMAGEDDON!" (What is the Kingdom of God, J. Preston Eby)

In conclusion, we can see that the Kingdom of God is:

1. THE DOMAIN (RULE) OF GOD
2. THE PEOPLE OF GOD
3. THAT IN WHICH GOD EXERCISES SOVEREIGN RULE
4. IN THE HERE-AND-NOW
5. WITHIN (INSIDE OF) YOU
6. AN INWARD WORKING OF THE SPIRIT OF GOD WITHIN HIS PEOPLE
7. THE BATTLE OF ARMAGEDDON WITHIN THE HEART AND LIFE OF MAN
   (This battle takes place between our kingdom and will, and the Kingdom and will of God).

What is the final result of the working of the Kingdom of God in our lives? Romans 14:17 states…For the kingdom of God is not meat and drink (anything external): but righteousness, peace, and joy in the Holy Spirit…

THAT IS THE KINGDOM OF GOD!

April 23

SALVATION IS OF THE LORD

Jonah 2:9 states…But I will sacrifice unto You with the voice of thanksgiving; I will pay that that I have vowed. Salvation is of the Lord…Psalm 3:8 states…Salvation belongs unto the Lord: Your blessing is upon Your people…

What a blessed day it is when we come to the understanding that SALVATION IS OF THE LORD! We must understand that salvation is authored and finished by God. In no way can man take any credit for his salvation, for it is by the grace of God. Remember…He (Jesus) is the AUTHOR and FINISHER of our faith! Salvation is authored and finished by God alone, not us, and not even our faith. Our faith is also a gift from God. Remember…HE IS THE AUTHOR OF OUR FAITH!!! God is the One Who is responsible to begin in us a good work, and to complete it until the day of Jesus Christ. SALVATION DEPENDS FOR ITS COMPLETION ON GOD, AND NOT ON MAN.

Man is only able to bring forth death (carnality). IN CHRIST ALONE IS LIFE AND SALVATION. Salvation was completed in the mind of God before the foundation of the world, and was manifested through Jesus Christ and His cross. We are now being awakened (spirit, soul, and body) to the salvation of our loving Father!

CAN WE BE HONEST IN ADMITTING THAT WE CAN NOT SAVE OURSELVES? Thank God for HIS salvation! What a Savior He is!

SALVATION IS OF THE LORD!

April 24

THE HIGH CALLING

Philippians 3:10-21 speaks of the high calling of God. What is the apostle Paul talking about? What is the high calling? What is he pressing toward? What is he wanting to apprehend? What is it he wants to attain? Is he talking about heaven and hell? NO!

Philippians 3:11 states…If by any means I might attain unto the RESURRECTION OF THE DEAD…This could also be classified as:

1. A BETTER RESURRECTION (Hebrews 11:35)
2. THE FIRST RESURRECTION (Revelation 20:4-6)

This is the high calling! Those with the spirit of wisdom and revelation in the knowledge of Him (God) have had the eyes of their understanding enlightened. These same people KNOW THE

HOPE OF THEIR CALLING. It is a call out of darkness into His marvelous light to be made into the image of the Son of God. This corporate remnant will be raised up in the first resurrection to rule and reign with Christ on the earth. The purpose of this is to set THE ENTIRE CREATION FREE (Romans 8:18-23)!

Let us forget those things which are behind, and reach forth unto those things which are before. We have been called to PRESS toward the mark for the prize of the high calling of God in Christ Jesus (Philippians 3:13,14). What a hope!

WHAT A CALLING!

April 25

SEEK FIRST THE KINGDOM OF GOD

Matthew 6:31 states…take no thought for the things you have need of…Matthew 6:33 states…But seek first the kingdom of God, and His righteousness; and all these things shall be added unto you…

WHAT A PROMISE!

We have here before us a <u>command</u> and a <u>promise</u>. We are told to SEEK FIRST the Kingdom of God, and then we are given the promise from God that He will supply all of our needs.

Our Heavenly Father is giving us the key to a successful and overcoming life. We must seek first the invisible realm, and then we shall have all the things that we need in the visible realm. This thought (way of life) does not make sense to our carnal mind, for we are always seeking first: food, drink, clothing, employment, and shelter. O Heavenly Father, SET US FREE from all anxiety, fear, and worry, for after all these things do the Gentiles (Nations) seek.

Don't you want to be a believer? Ask God to make you a believer today! Ask Him to increase your faith, and to help your unbelief concerning the things of this life. He actually wants you to not even think about: food, drink, clothing, and shelter. TAKE NO THOUGHT FOR YOUR LIFE! BUT SEEK FIRST THE LIFE OF CHRIST, FOR IN DOING THIS YOU SHALL ENTER IN TO GOD'S ABUNDANT LIFE! THIS WILL SET YOU FREE FROM WORRYING ABOUT YOUR LIFE, FOR YOU ARE DEAD, AND YOUR LIFE IS HID WITH GOD IN CHRIST!

Start believing God today! Seek first His glorious Kingdom, which is: righteousness, peace, and joy in the Holy Spirit. Our Heavenly Father knows what we have need of before we can even ask. He is not going to provide everything you need, but rather, HE HAS <u>ALREADY PROVIDED</u> EVERYTHING YOU NEED! We must learn to step forth in faith into the invisible realm of God. The material things of this life will be there when we need them.

HAVE FAITH IN GOD!

April 26

THE VICTORY THAT OVERCOMES THE WORLD

1ST John 5:4,5 states...For whatsoever is born of God overcomes the world: and this is the victory that overcomes the world, even our faith. Who is he that overcomes the world, but he that believes that Jesus is the Son of God?...

The journey of the overcomer is one of believing on the Lord Jesus Christ. In turn, we are born of the Spirit (spiritually awakened) to see (perceive) the Kingdom of God. This results in an overcoming lifestyle that is fueled by BEING a believer. Our faith is to be continually placed in the person and work of the Lord Jesus Christ.

It is IMPERATIVE that we see this as a PROCESS! We are overcomers in Christ, but we are also **becoming** overcomers in Christ. We have been justified, and we are now being sanctified. We have been declared an overcomer in Christ, and now we are becoming what we have been declared to be (an overcomer). As we stated earlier, this is all made possible by our faith in the person and work of the Lord Jesus Christ. Remember...Without faith it is impossible to please God: for he that comes to God must believe that He is, and that He is a rewarder of them that diligently seek Him (Hebrews 11:6)...It would do you well to read all of Hebrews chapter 11.

An overcomer is one who diligently and continually puts his or her faith in Jesus Christ. As well, an overcomer is one who HAS believed in Jesus Christ, IS believing, and SHALL continue to believe. THIS IS THE VICTORY THAT OVERCOMES THE WORLD! WE ARE LEARNING TO BE BELIEVERS! WE ARE HAVING FAITH IN THE SON OF GOD! The lifestyle of an overcomer is also to be seen and explained from Galatians 2:20, which states...I am crucified with Christ: nevertheless I live; yet not I, but Christ lives in me: and the life which I now live in the flesh I live by the faith of the Son of God, Who loved me, and gave Himself for me...May we understand and grasp what it is to...

LIVE BY THE FAITH OF THE SON OF GOD!

April 27

CALL ON THE NAME OF THE LORD

Acts 2:21 states...And it shall come to pass, that whosoever shall call on the name of the Lord shall be saved...What a wonderful day it is when a person calls on the name of the Lord! From that moment on their life will never be the same. After calling on the name of the Lord you are introduced to a way of life that you have not previously known. You are awakened out of death and introduced to the way, the truth, and the life. We are of course speaking of a personal relationship with the Lord Jesus Christ! O HAPPY DAY...WHEN JESUS WASHED ALL MY SINS AWAY!

After initially calling on the name of the Lord you are then introduced to justification. This is to be seen as a PASSOVER experience in God with PENTECOST and TABERNACLES to follow. Remember…These three feasts that took place in the Old Testament represent our full salvation process (spirit, soul, and body).

The key to this verse is in understanding that our salvation is a process. DO NOT LIMIT CALLING ON THE NAME OF THE LORD TO A ONE TIME EXPERIENCE THAT TOOK PLACE AT SOME POINT IN THE PAST! That type of thinking leads to a form of godliness and to spiritual death. CALL ON HIM NOW! CALL ON HIM TODAY! He is your Savior today, not just a Savior that did something for you at some point in your past. The Lord Jesus Christ will save you out of every temptation, and deliver you from all evil. He is your daily bread. TODAY IS THE DAY OF SALVATION!

You must recognize that you are still in the process of BEING SAVED. This is called sanctification. Call on the name of the Lord and you shall be saved. He is not just the Savior of your spirit, but also your soul and your body. We must STOP limiting God to the past and the future. Calling on the name of the Lord is a <u>NOW THING</u>!

CALL ON HIS NAME TODAY!

April 28

<u>GOD'S SACRED SECRET!</u>

Ephesians 1:9,10 states…Having made known unto us <u>the mystery of His will</u>, according to His good pleasure which He has purposed in Himself; that in the dispensation of the fullness of times He might gather together in one <u>all things in Christ, both which are in heaven, and which are on earth;</u> even in Him…

Ephesians 1:9,10 (Rotherham's Emphasized Bible) states…making known to us <u>THE SACRED SECRET OF HIS WILL</u>, According to His good pleasure which He purposed in Him, - For an administration of the fullness of the seasons to reunite for Himself   (under one head) <u>the all things in the Christ, The things upon the heavens, And the things upon the earth, In Him…</u>

Did you know that God has a SACRED SECRET? You just read about it! It is the mystery (sacred secret) of His will. So…What is this sacred secret?

According to Joseph Rotherham: "The "sacred secret" of this dispensation has been divulged (Ephesians 3:3-9) and should be blazed abroad (Romans 16:25,26; Ephesians 6:19); but yet is of a nature unlikely to interest any who are careless of God's dispensational ways…" (Joseph Rotherham)

The sacred secret speaks of the dispensation of the fullness of times. This is also referred to (in the original Greek) as the Age of the Ages! It is the gathering together in one of <u>ALL THINGS IN CHRIST</u>! It is the promise that even beyond the Kingdom Age (The Millennium), there is an

Age of the Ages. This is the Age (The Age of the Ages) in which EVERY KNEE SHALL BOW, AND EVERY TONGUE SHALL CONFESS THAT JESUS CHRIST IS LORD, TO THE GLORY OF GOD THE FATHER! This final age (the dispensation of the fullness of times) will prove to be the GOOD PLEASURE of our Father, in which HIS MAGNIFICENT PURPOSE OF THE AGES WILL COME TO AN END, GUARANTEEING THE SALVATION OF ALL MEN!

This must come to you through DIVINE REVELATION! Many do not understand that God's judgments and man's torment (period of severe trial and testing) are age-lasting (of the ages / "aionios"), and that they are for the purpose of correction. This can be easily discovered as one embarks on a journey to study the purpose of the ages. The key words that will UNLOCK the mystery of God's Sacred Secret are: the Hebrew word "olam", and the Greek words "aion", and "aionios". A careful and unbiased study of these words will prove beyond a shadow of a doubt that Jesus Christ is indeed THE SAVIOR OF THE WORLD, AND THAT HIS SALVATION INCLUDES ALL MEN, AND THAT IT IS UNIVERSAL IN ITS SCOPE!!!

Ask the Father to reveal this GREAT TRUTH to you! Ask Him for the spirit of wisdom and revelation in the knowledge of Him (Ephesians 1:17-23). Your Heavenly Father will gladly reveal HIS SACRED SECRET TO YOU as you humble yourself in studying to show yourself approved. O THANK YOU FATHER FOR THE DISPENSATION OF THE FULLNESS OF TIMES (THE AGE OF THE AGES), FOR YOU SHALL GATHER TOGETHER IN ONE…

ALL THINGS IN CHRIST!

April 29

LOGOS AND RHEMA

According to Ray Knight: "These two Greek words ("Logos" and "Rhema") are both translated "word" in English, but they have a different meaning which is important to recognize for this is a foundation for growth, wisdom, and understanding. "LOGOS" = The "word" which contains the full intent of the speaker. "RHEMA" = The "word" from the Logos that is presently being spoken to the hearer." (Literal Word Or Spiritual, Ray Knight)

There is a difference between a Logos and Rhema word from the Lord. The Logos is the written or spoken Word of God, which is personified in the person of the Lord Jesus Christ. A Rhema word from God is the revealed (unveiled) Word of God to the heart and life of a person. In essence, a Rhema word from God is the unveiling of the Logos. It is the Logos being uncovered, manifested, quickened (made alive), and revealed to the heart and life of man.

How many times have you read a passage of scripture from the Bible and it has meant absolutely nothing to you? Then, ALL OF A SUDDEN, it jumps off the page and tackles you. It becomes so plain to you what is being said. It becomes a revelation to you. This is to be seen as more than intellect at work. THIS IS A RHEMA EXPERIENCE IN GOD!

We must learn to pray for, seek for, and cherish our Rhema experiences with the Father. Many people do not believe there is any such thing as God revealing to us what His Word (Logos) means. Sadly to say, for them THERE IS NO SUCH THING! They remain in intellect, theology, the carnal mind (death), man's traditions, Bible colleges, and never see the true meaning of the scriptures. THEY ARE EVER LEARNING, BUT NEVER COMING TO THE KNOWLEDGE OF THE TRUTH!

May the Father deliver us from our futile, fleshly, and failing attempts to approach Him in raw intellect. It is absolutely necessary for us to have Rhema experiences in God!

O FATHER, RAIN ON US WITH RHEMA FROM ON HIGH!

April 30

THE AFFLICTIONS OF THE RIGHTEOUS
(PSALM 34)

Psalm 34:19 states…Many are the afflictions of the righteous: But the Lord delivers him out of them all…Not only do the righteous have afflictions, but they are many. The English word "afflictions" comes from the Hebrew word "Ra", which means: misfortune, adversity, calamity, and sadness. Why afflictions? Why many? Why the righteous? The key is to be found in Psalm 119:71, which states…It is good for me that I have been <u>AFFLICTED</u>; that I might <u>LEARN YOUR STATUTES</u>…

We can now see that we are going through afflictions, fiery trials, tribulations, judgments, and chastisements, that we might LEARN the ways of our Father! How else could we learn to:

BLESS THE LORD AT ALL TIMES…
MAKE OUR BOAST IN THE LORD…
EXALT HIS NAME…
SEEK THE LORD…
CRY UNTO THE LORD…
SEE THAT THE LORD IS GOOD…
FEAR (REVERENCE) THE LORD…
HAVE NO WANT OF ANY GOOD THING…
KEEP OUR TONGUE FROM EVIL…
DEPART FROM EVIL, DO GOOD, AND SEEK PEACE…

Our Father is bringing us through many afflictions to break us of our ways (self and sin), and to crush the spirit of antichrist that is within us. Remember…The Lord is near to them that are of a broken heart, and saves such as be of a contrite spirit (the crushed in spirit)…God is crushing the carnality in us through many afflictions. This is all done for our benefit, and that we might LEARN!

Remember…The apostle Paul told us to glory in our tribulations…As well, the apostle Peter told us to THINK IT NOT STRANGE CONCERNING OUR FIERY TRIALS…We must grow in maturity to be able to recognize the PROCESS OF GOD'S DEALINGS with us and within us. He is bringing us through HIS CONSUMING FIRE! This is the very reason that…Many are the afflictions of the righteous…

THAT WE MIGHT LEARN!

May 1

I AND MY FATHER ARE ONE

John 10:31,32 states…I (Jesus is speaking) and My Father are one. Then the Jews took up stones again to stone Him…Let us remember that the scriptures refer to Jesus as the:

1. SON OF GOD
2. SON OF MAN

In essence, Jesus was the perfect revelation of God and man. He was God manifested in the flesh. Jesus, the Son of God, showed man what God was really like. Jesus, the Son of man, showed man the perfect relationship with the Father. Hence, Jesus would say…I AND MY FATHER ARE ONE…

Jesus laid down the pattern for all who would follow in His footsteps. Whether we understand it or not, we are being drawn into a love relationship with our Heavenly Father. We are being brought to the place where we can say…I AND MY FATHER ARE ONE!

Do you remember what Psalm 82:6 says about man? It states…I HAVE SAID, YOU ARE GODS; ALL OF YOU ARE CHILDREN OF THE MOST HIGH…

WOW!

(LET THAT SINK IN FOR A MINUTE!)

Jesus quoted this same verse in John 10:34,35 (As well, read John 10:30-36). We are to see ourselves as IN CHRIST, for **_IN HIM_** we are part of the very Son of God. We are His body (the body of Christ). WE ARE GODS! THIS IS OUR TRUE IDENTITY!

You are a spirit, you have a soul, and you live in a body. With this being said though, your true essence is spirit. This leads us to the understanding that God is our Father, FOR GOD IS A SPIRIT. HE IS THE FATHER OF SPIRITS! ACCEPT IT! BELIEVE IT! RECEIVE IT! WALK IN IT! IT IS YOUR TRUE IDENTITY! YOU ARE GODS! YOU AND THE FATHER ARE BECOMING ONE! THIS IS YOUR DESTINY!

Just as Jesus was persecuted for revealing His relationship with the Father for what it truly was, so will you be persecuted. Do not be upset or surprised when you are stoned   (spiritually speaking) and persecuted by others for the sake of righteousness, BUT RATHER REJOICE, AND BE EXCEEDING GLAD: FOR GREAT IS YOUR REWARD IN HEAVEN: FOR SO PERSECUTED THEY THE PROPHETS WHICH WERE BEFORE YOU (Matthew 5:12)…

YOU AND THE FATHER ARE (BECOMING) ONE!

May 2

ENDURING TEMPTATION

James 1:2 states…Blessed is the man that endures temptation: for when he is tried, he shall receive the crown of life, which the Lord has promised to them that love Him…Let us try to dissect this verse, in which we will discuss the meaning of the words: blessed, endures, temptation, tried, and the crown of life.

Blessed: happy, fully satisfied.

Endures: to remain under; to endure a load of miseries, adversities, and persecutions in faith and patience.

Temptation: testing, trial for the purpose of proving someone.

Tried: to be proved, to be tried as metals are tried by fire and thus are purified. It refers to being approved as acceptable men in the furnace of adversity.

The Crown of Life: the crown of life (the victor's crown) is symbolic of royalty-- kingship-- and is a symbol of honor. It represents the prize of the high calling of God in Christ Jesus, which is the first resurrection. This involves ruling and reigning with Jesus Christ on the earth to gather in the nations. It finally involves the Age of the Ages, in which all things (through the sons of God) will be gathered in Christ.

We must understand that THE SPIRIT OF GOD DRIVES US INTO THE WILDERNESS (Luke 4:1,2) TO BE TEMPTED OF THE DEVIL. The purpose for this is to remain under adversities (enduring) and testing (temptation). This enables us to be approved (tried), purified, and purged by the consuming fire of God. These fiery trials are what God uses to make us into a vessel of honor. We then become profitable for the Master's use, whether now, or in the ages to come.

Remember…The sufferings of this present time are not worthy to be compared with the glory which shall be revealed in us (Romans 8:18)…

PRESS TOWARD THE MARK FOR THE PRIZE OF THE HIGH CALLING!

May 3

THE SERMON ON THE MOUNT PART 1
- BLESSED -

Jesus sees the multitudes. He goes up into a mountain (The Mountain, The Mount of Olives). He is set, and His disciples come unto Him to hear Him teach. Jesus opens His mouth and begins to teach, saying…<u>BLESSED</u>…WHAT AN INTRODUCTION!

This most famous sermon (The Sermon On The Mount) by the Lord Jesus Christ is also referred to as the BEATITUDES. The word "Beatitudes" means: supreme blessedness, exalted happiness, blissful, peace, the declarations of blessedness pronounced by Jesus Christ. Considering that the very last word in the Old Testament (Malachi 4:6) is the word CURSE, this is quite an introduction. Jesus starts out His first sermon with the word BLESSED!

The Old Covenant left a curse over man's head due to the fact that he could not keep the law (The Law of Moses). Jesus came to fulfill the law and to pronounce a blessing to all those who would believe on Him. So…Let us talk about the word blessed.

The word "blessed", which is many times translated happy, actually means: TO BE FULLY SATISFIED, as opposed to happy in the world sense of the definition. As well, it means: the state of the believer in Christ, the joy that comes from salvation, and inner peace which is not based on external circumstances.

Jesus began His Sermon On The Mount by telling man of a condition that is available to him, whereby he might be fully satisfied. Jesus was giving us the key to a life of true fulfillment, which can only be found inside the confines of a relationship with our Heavenly Father. His sermon points to the fact that the things of this world can never FULLY SATISFY us. Man is created to worship God, and the only thing that will fully satisfy this longing and craving is a relationship with His Creator.

Let us leave the realm of being partially satisfied, which leads to emptiness and frustration. Jesus came to invite men into a STATE OF TRUE BLESSEDNESS AND FULFILLMENT. We are of course speaking of the magnificent Kingdom of God that is available to all men in the here-and-now. It is your Father's good pleasure to give you the Kingdom. In Adam we are cursed. In Christ we are…

BLESSED!

May 4

THE SERMON ON THE MOUNT PART 2
- THE POOR IN SPIRIT -

Matthew 5:3 states…Blessed are the poor in spirit…This is where our relationship with the Father begins. The word "poor" that is used in this scripture means: one who is helpless, or one who has fallen from a better state. The blessing that awaits us is not just being poor in spirit, but in RECOGNIZING that we are poor in spirit.

We must recognize that we are helpless, and that we have fallen from a better state. Without God we are helpless, hopeless, wretched, poor, blind, naked, and most miserable. THIS IS NOT A PITY PARTY, FALSE HUMILITY, OR A LOAD OF CONDEMNATION THAT WE MUST CARRY AROUND. IT IS THE TRUTH! Remember when the apostle Paul said…For I know that in me (that is, in my flesh,) dwells no good thing…O WRETCHED MAN THAT I AM! WHO SHALL DELIVER ME FROM THE BODY OF THIS DEATH?…Was Paul having a pity party and feeling sorry for himself? NO! He was coming to the knowledge of the truth concerning his fallen state (condition). The man of sin was being revealed to him, and the Lord was destroying him (the man of sin, the carnal mind) by the brightness of His coming (presence)!

When we begin to recognize that the very nature that we were born with is our problem, then we have diagnosed the ROOT OF OUR PROBLEM. Ephesians 2:3 states…and we were BY NATURE the children of wrath…So…We must then come to the conclusion that we have a nature problem. This is referred to as the ADAMIC NATURE (the nature we INHERITED from Adam), or the SIN NATURE. The good news is that there is a solution. The solution is GOD'S DIVINE NATURE! 2ND Peter 1:4 tells us that we have been made partakers of the DIVINE NATURE. This is the answer and solution that <u>brings us out</u> of the grip of the ADAMIC NATURE.

After coming to this revelation (the revelation that we were born with a fallen nature, there is no good thing in our flesh, and that we are SPIRITUALLY BANKRUPT) we are on our way to higher ground in God. To be poor in spirit is to realize that except we abide in Christ, WE CAN DO NOTHING! Being poor in spirit could also be referred to as THE BADGE OF BROKENNESS. Those who truly are poor in spirit are broken and crushed in their spirit over their current condition, and do always look to God for their help in every situation of this life. The poor in spirit are fully aware of their inability to do what only God can do. Their realization of this is what makes them so strong in God, for God's strength is made perfect in our weakness!

As was stated earlier, this is not a load of condemnation. It is just the opposite. IT IS LIBERTY AND FREEDOM FROM DEATH! Romans 8:1,2 states…There is therefore now NO CONDEMNATION to them which are in Christ Jesus, who walk not after the flesh, but after the Spirit. For the LAW OF THE SPIRIT OF LIFE IN CHRIST JESUS has made me FREE from the law of sin and death…

The sooner we recognize that we are poor in spirit (helpless), the sooner we will realize that we are…

RICH IN CHRIST!

May 5

THE SERMON ON THE MOUNT PART 3
- THE KINGDOM OF HEAVEN -

Matthew 5:3 states…for theirs is the kingdom of heaven…SOUNDS GREAT! So…What is this Kingdom of heaven?

Matthew refers to it as the Kingdom of heaven, while the other Gospel writers (Mark, Luke, and John) refer to it as the Kingdom of God. The term "Kingdom of heaven" tells us where this Kingdom is from, and the term "Kingdom of God" tells us Who is in charge of the Kingdom. In other words, the Kingdom is from heaven (the heavens, or heavenly realm), and it is ruled by God. It is the heavenly Kingdom of (belonging to) God!

Let us try to define this Kingdom that is from heaven, is ruled by God, and belongs to the poor in spirit. The apostle Paul CLEARLY DEFINES IT for us in Romans 14:17. It states…FOR THE KINGDOM OF GOD IS…RIGHTEOUSNESS, PEACE, AND JOY IN THE HOLY SPIRIT…The Kingdom, in essence, is God's sovereign rule and reign within the hearts and lives of His children. The first work of the Spirit of God is to convince us that we are spiritually bankrupt in and of ourselves. His next work is to assure us that He loves and forgives us, even in our present fallen state. Finally, He wants us to possess the present reality of His Kingdom.

The Kingdom work of the Father is a deep and internal work. It is like major surgery, in which the Father removes our cancerous nature, and then writes His laws on our hearts and lives. The Kingdom of God is not a location that you go to after you die, but rather, it is the realm in which God rules and reigns. THAT REALM IS <u>YOU</u>!!! Remember…THE KINGDOM OF GOD IS WITHIN YOU (Luke 17:21)!!!

The key to apprehending the Kingdom of God in the here-and-now is in recognizing our spiritual poverty. Those who see themselves as WRETCHED outside of God are the very ones that God calls RIGHTEOUS. Let us press into the Kingdom of God. It is the Father's GOOD PLEASURE…

TO GIVE YOU THE KINGDOM! (Luke 12:32)

May 6

THE SERMON ON THE MOUNT PART 4
- THEY THAT MOURN -

Matthew 5:4 states…Blessed are they that mourn: for they shall be comforted…This verse carries with it a similar meaning as that of the beginning of verse three. The idea is: to grieve because of one's moral poverty, and to recognize one's moral imperfection.

We are to recognize and sorrow over our sin nature (our inherent inability to achieve godliness in and of ourselves). This leads us to the realization that we are by nature a sinner (one who misses the mark of God's nature). As it stands, WE ARE IN NEED OF A SAVIOR! We are to sorrow over our sinful condition, knowing that the wages of sin is death (the carnal mind).

While all this is true, God does not want us to remain in this condition. He does not want us to remain in our perished state of death, and neither should we want to stay in that state of mind. This mourning that takes place inside of us is a godly mourning and sorrow that leads to a CHANGE IN OUR LIVES. This is called REPENTANCE! 2ND Corinthians 7:9,10 states…Now I rejoice, not that you were made sorry, BUT THAT YOU SORROWED TO REPENTANCE: FOR YOU WERE MADE SORRY AFTER A GODLY MANNER, that you might receive damage by us in nothing. FOR GODLY SORROW WORKS REPENTANCE TO SALVATION NOT TO BE REPENTED OF: but the sorrow of the world works death…

This passage of scripture describes the mourning process that leads to repentance and salvation in our lives. THIS IS NOT TO BE SEEN AS A ONE TIME THING! It is a PROCESS of seeing who we are outside of our Heavenly Father, which then leads us to see Who our Father is , and shall be, inside of us. This mourning then leads us to be comforted by the Spirit of God. Remember…The Holy Spirit of God is spoken of as THE COMFORTER. After showing us our condition of moral poverty, the Spirit of God then does a work within us to replace our lack of godliness with HIS DIVINE NATURE. This gives us ALL THINGS that pertain to life and godliness!
This is a work of the Spirit. The Father:

1. DRAWS US
2. CONVICTS US (shows us that we are a sinner, and in need of salvation)
3. COMFORTS US (by giving us His life)

Mourning (godly sorrow) leads to repentance (change), repentance leads to salvation (salvation from our condition of missing the mark of God's nature), and salvation leads to life (the life of God's nature within us). This then leads to comfort, which is the very Spirit of God. HE IS OUR COMFORTER! WHAT A PROCESS! WHAT A SALVATION!

THANK GOD FOR THE COMFORTER!

May 7

THE SERMON ON THE MOUNT PART 5
- BLESSED ARE THE MEEK -

Matthew 5:5 states…Blessed are the meek…Psalm 37:11 states…But the meek shall inherit the earth; And shall delight themselves in abundance of peace…

The word "meek" means: the patient oppressed ones, lowly, the attitude or spirit in which we accept God's dealings with us as good and do not dispute or resist. Meekness is not weakness, BUT

IT IS GENTLENESS IN POWER. IT COULD ALSO BE REFERRED TO AS CONTROLLED STRENGTH! Meekness is not a lack of strength in God, BUT IT IS CONTROLLED STRENGTH IN GOD!

Remember…Moses was referred to as VERY MEEK, ABOVE ALL THE MEN WHICH WERE UPON THE FACE OF THE EARTH (Numbers 12:3)…In other words, he was the meekest man on the face of the earth. We also know that Moses was a VERY POWERFUL man of God. He was used mightily by God to do many miracles. The reason that God was able to put such power in the hands of Moses was because of his meekness. Moses experienced the power of God flowing through him to a greater degree than maybe any other man who ever lived (except for Jesus of course). As was previously stated, this power from God was entrusted to Moses as a result of his meekness. His meekness was the fruit of his forty years in the wilderness, in which God, by His Spirit, did CRUSH the self-will of Moses.

Remember what took place when Jesus was arrested in the garden of Gethsemane? Speaking to Peter, He said…Put up again your sword into its place: for all they that take the sword shall perish with the sword. Do you not know that I can pray to My Father, and He shall presently give Me more than twelve legions of angels? But how then shall the scriptures be fulfilled, (Matthew 26:52-54)?…What a demonstration of meekness by our Lord and Savior Jesus Christ! He could have asked the Father to send over twelve legions (about 72,000) of angels (messengers), BUT DID NOT DO SO! Jesus was the perfect example of meekness in His submission to the will of the Father. As well, His meekness was seen in His controlled strength toward sinful man.

Meekness is followed by those who are poor in spirit, and by those who mourn over their sin. The spirit of meekness will always result in a proper response toward God and our fellow man.

BLESSED ARE THE MEEK!

May 8

THE SERMON ON THE MOUNT PART 6
- THEY SHALL INHERIT THE EARTH -

Matthew 5:5 states…for they shall inherit the earth…What a promise! The meek shall inherit the earth. So…Why is everyone so anxious to fly off to heaven?

Modern day Christianity teaches us that the purpose and plan of God for our individual lives is nothing more than staying out of an eternal hell. O HOW WE HAVE MISSED THE TRUE GOSPEL OF THE LORD JESUS CHRIST!!! Not only is the "so-called" gospel of salvation from everlasting torture a LIE, but it would prove to be a very SHALLOW message if indeed it were true. Surely God has some greater purpose in store for the human race than just trying to keep them out of an eternal torture pit!

Revelation 5:9,10 states…You (Jesus) have redeemed us unto God by Your blood out of every kindred, and tongue, and people, and nation; And have made us unto our God kings and priests:

AND WE SHALL REIGN ON THE EARTH…Revelation 11:15 states…The kingdoms of this world are become the kingdoms of our Lord and of His Christ…Psalm 2:8 states…Ask of me, and I shall give You the heathen for Your inheritance. And the uttermost parts of the earth for Your possession…

The inheriting of the earth also spiritually refers to the inheritance of our bodies. Remember… We have a treasure hidden in an EARTHEN VESSEL! The meek shall ultimately inherit their glorified bodies at the first resurrection. They shall also inherit the physical earth. This will result in a great harvest of ALL NATIONS BEING BROUGHT UNTO THE SAVING KNOWLEDGE OF THE LORD JESUS CHRIST. This is the beginning of the ministry of the Ages of the Ages.

Can we begin to see that the earth is the Lord's and the fullness thereof; the world, and they that dwell therein? (Psalm 24:1)…God is the owner of the earth and all that are in it. He has left His possession for the meek to inherit. What an unbelievable purpose the Father has for those that love Him! He has put all that He owns into the hands of the meek. The meek are truly blessed in that they…

SHALL INHERIT THE EARTH!

May 9

THE SERMON ON THE MOUNT PART 7
- BLESSED ARE THEY WHICH DO HUNGER AND THIRST FOR RIGHTEOUSNESS -

Matthew 5:6 states…Blessed are they which do hunger and thirst for righteousness: for they shall be filled…ARE YOU HUNGRY? ARE YOU THIRSTY? Well…Sure you are!

We are all hungry and thirsty from the moment we are born. We are hungry to know our true identity. We are hungry to know where we came from and where we are headed. WE ARE HUNGRY AND THIRSTY FOR RIGHTEOUSNESS! Blessed are those who recognize what they are hungry for. Many who are hungry for life's answers do not see their need for God's righteousness. They know they are hungry and thirsty to discover the true meaning of this life, but many do not know what it is that will bring true inner peace and happiness (the state of being fully satisfied). The blessing that Jesus spoke of is not just being hungry and thirsty, for we all seek to be happy (fully satisfied) from the moment we are born. The blessing is in HUNGERING AND THIRSTING FOR GOD'S RIGHTEOUSNESS!

What does it mean or imply to be hungry and thirsty? The phrase, "who hunger and thirst", means: intense desire, even as a man starving for natural food. He must receive sustenance or he will die. This verse shows the poverty, emptiness, and complete lack of God's righteousness within our lives. WE MUST BE AWAKENED TO HIS RIGHTEOUSNESS!

The word "righteous" or "righteousness" simply means: that which is right according to God's standards, conformity to all that God commands or appoints. In and of ourselves, we are void of

God's righteousness. That is why we must hunger and thirst for it. God's righteousness comes to us through faith. It is imputed to us by grace through faith. Remember…Abraham believed in the Lord; and He counted it to him for righteousness (Genesis 15:6)…

Faith in Christ and Him crucified gives us the righteousness which is through the faith of Christ, the righteousness which is of God by faith: (Philippians 3:9)…As we previously stated, this righteousness (God's righteousness) is imputed (attributed or ascribed) to us upon placing our faith in the person and work of the Lord Jesus Christ. This is referred to as justification by faith (being declared righteous or right in the eyes of God). The next step in our Christian walk is that of sanctification by faith (being made righteous or right in the eyes of God), and is to be seen as a process. As we go through the sanctification process, in essence, we are BECOMING WHAT WE HAVE BEEN DECLARED TO BE. In order for us to experience justification or sanctification we must place our faith in Christ and Him crucified. THAT IS THE ONLY WAY! To see the difference between God's righteousness and man's self-righteousness read Luke 18:9-14.

As we hunger and thirst for God's righteousness, we are then filled. IT IS A PROMISE!!! As a matter of fact, we are filled, and filled, and filled, and filled. Remember…Our salvation is a process (justification: the salvation of our spirit; sanctification: the salvation of our soul; and glorification: the salvation of our body).

God's imputed righteousness is THE ONLY THING that can completely satisfy our hunger and thirst. O WHAT A GLORIOUS PROCESS OF BEING FILLED WITH THE RIGHTEOUSNESS OF OUR FATHER!

WE SHALL BE FILLED!

May 10

THE SERMON ON THE MOUNT PART 8
- BLESSED ARE THE MERCIFUL -

Matthew 5:7 states…Blessed are the merciful: for they shall obtain mercy…The word "merciful" means: compassionate, one who is tenderly compassionate, and one who grieves within for the condition and need of another.

This attribute is the result of the indwelling of God within. Those who understand and have experienced the mercy of God will be merciful to others. Mercy is not just a feeling of pity, but it is expressed in ACTION that goes far beyond just mere words! It causes a person to act on behalf of another to restore them, help them, save them, deliver them, forgive them, heal them, and bless them.

We must first recognize that our Father is merciful. Many people do not see God as merciful. They see Him as vindictive, spiteful, and hungry for revenge. THAT IS VERY SAD, ISN'T IT? The majority of what is preached in the realm of Evangelical Christianity is a gospel of NO MERCY. They preach a God Who will torture and torment most of humanity forever, and even say that He will be glorified in doing it. That, my friend, is SICK! THAT IS NOT MERCY! YES…There will be judgment for the purpose of correction, BUT MERCY WILL TRIUMPH OVER JUDGMENT!

Ephesians 2:4 states…BUT GOD, WHO IS <u>RICH IN MERCY</u>, FOR HIS GREAT LOVE WHEREWITH HE LOVED US…What a merciful and loving Father! Don't you want to be like your Father? Our merciful and loving Father LOOKED BEYOND OUR FAULTS AND SAW OUR NEED FOR A SAVIOR!!! THAT IS MERCY! Come and dine at the Father's table today! PARTAKE OF HIS GREAT LOVE AND MERCY!

GOD IS RICH IN MERCY!

May 11

THE SERMON ON THE MOUNT PART 9
- BLESSED ARE THE PURE IN HEART -

Matthew 5:8 states…Blessed are the pure in heart…The phrase "pure in heart" refers to a clean heart and clean hands. It speaks of innocence before God. Psalm 73:1 states…Truly God is good to Israel, even to such as are of a clean heart…Psalm 24:3,4 states…Who shall ascend into the hill of the Lord? Or who shall stand in His holy place? HE THAT HAS CLEAN HANDS, AND A PURE HEART; WHO HAS NOT LIFTED UP HIS SOUL UNTO VANITY, NOR SWORN DECEITFULLY…

A pure heart speaks of a person after God's own heart. This means that our goal is to know the heart of God, and then to apply it to our lives. A pure heart is one that has NO AGENDA of its own, but to do the will of the Father. The pure in heart are seeking ONLY FOR SPIRIT AND TRUTH. Their motives are pure (clean) in the eyes of God.

This is why denominations and man-made religions are so limited in their experience, teaching, and manifestation of God in the earth. <u>THEY HAVE AN AGENDA</u>! THEIR AGENDA IS TO PROMOTE THEIR PARTICULAR DENOMINATIONAL DOCTRINES AND BELIEFS! Your heart will either pledge allegiance to God (His Spirit and truth), or your heart will pledge allegiance to your denominational doctrines and beliefs. Why do most people avoid the "pure in heart experience" with God? They avoid this experience because <u>THEY LOVE THE PRAISES OF MEN</u>!!! Most would rather remain impure in heart due to their love for their personal agenda. As well, they do not want to go through the purifying fire of God. In order to be <u>pure</u> in heart you must be <u>PURIFIED</u>! Surely that makes sense, doesn't it?

Let us not be afraid to search our heart, asking the Father to show us what condition it is in. As we bask in His presence, He will expose to us all that is not pure within us. Someone who is pure in heart can not go wrong. If we veer off the road (and we will) our Father will lovingly put us back on the strait and narrow path that leads to life. YOU CAN NOT GO WRONG WITH A PURE HEART!

BLESSED ARE THE PURE IN HEART!

May 12

THE SERMON ON THE MOUNT PART 10
- THEY SHALL SEE GOD -

Matthew 5:8 states…for they shall see God…What does it mean to see God? The word "see" comes from a Greek word "optomai", which comes from a Greek word "horao", which means: to experience, behold, perceive, take heed, and mentally perceive.

This word ("see") is not talking about mere physical sight. IT IS TALKING ABOUT SPIRITUAL SIGHT! TO SEE GOD is to perceive and grasp Him with your mind, which then transforms your mind from the carnal mind to the mind of Christ! SEEING GOD is a spiritual thing. It is to understand Him.

Remember…Jesus told Nicodemus…Except a man be born again (born from above, or spiritually awakened) he cannot <u>see</u> (perceive with the mind, understand, or know experientially) the kingdom (royal dominion, the spiritual Kingdom of God within the human heart, or God's rule within) of God (John 3:3)…

The word "see" in this passage comes from a different Greek word "eido", but carries with it the similar meaning of PERCEPTION OF GOD. In essence, to SEE God's Kingdom is to UNDERSTAND or PERCEIVE His Kingdom.

So…Can you "SEE" what the word "SEE" means? Don't you want to see God? Many people know about God, but very few people can see God. Their minds are blinded by the god of this world (2nd Corinthians 4:4). If we are not seeing (perceiving) God, then what is it we are seeing? There is only one other thing that we can see, and that is the traditions and doctrines (teachings) of men. We become able to see only a FORM OF GOD, which is really nothing more than our own preconceived ideas about God. This is idolatry!

Let us come out of the idolatrous ideas of man about God and enter into His Kingdom. As we stated earlier, we must be born again in order to see our God for Who He really is! The pure in heart are beginning to see their Father, not according to the way the organized church presents Him, but according to Who He truly is. We are seeing God, and…

GOD IS LOVE!

May 13

THE SERMON ON THE MOUNT PART 11
- BLESSED ARE THE PEACEMAKERS -

Matthew 5:9 states…Blessed are the peacemakers…The word "peacemakers" is a very beautiful and unique word that is used in Matthew 5:9. It comes from the Greek word "eirenopoios", and is used only once in the entire canon of scripture. It means: one who makes peace in others, having first received the peace of God in his own heart.

The Bible speaks of two kinds of peace. They are:

1. PEACE WITH GOD
2. THE PEACE OF GOD

We must first receive and experience peace **with** God, and the peace **of** God, before we are able to be a peacemaker in the lives of others. We must partake of our Father's divine nature in order to receive of His peace. This enables us to then be a distributor of His heavenly peace.

Romans 5:1 states…being justified by faith, we have PEACE WITH GOD through our Lord Jesus Christ…This is a justifying peace that comes from our Father and results in us being declared righteous. After having placed our faith in the person and work of the Lord Jesus Christ we will then receive peace **with** God. Philippians 4:7 states…And the PEACE OF GOD, which passes all understanding, shall keep your hearts and minds through Christ Jesus…This is a sanctifying peace that comes from our Father and results in us being made righteous. It is accessed in the same manner as that of peace with God (justifying peace). Upon placing faith in the Lord Jesus Christ we shall receive the peace **of** God. This peace is that which brings us through the fiery trials and tribulations of this life. IT IS PEACE IN THE MIDST OF THE STORM!

The word "peace" means: rest, denoting the absence or end of strife, to be untroubled, undisturbed, and in a state of well-being. After partaking (on a daily basis) of God's peace we are then ready to become a peacemaker. The very peace that has come to us is that which is to be given to others.

God's peace brings an end to the strife that exists within the heart of man. It brings an end to our anxiety, fear, torment, and internal striving, in which we are always trying to work out the situations of life in our own strength. THANK GOD FOR THE PEACE OF GOD! THANK GOD FOR HIS PEACEMAKERS! Romans 10:15 states…How beautiful are the feet of them that preach the gospel of PEACE, and bring glad tidings of good things…Ephesians 6:15 states…And (having) your feet shod with the preparation of the gospel of PEACE…

May we go forth preaching the GOSPEL OF PEACE to all men. We have enough troublemakers in the world. We need more…

PEACEMAKERS!

May 14

THE SERMON ON THE MOUNT PART 12
- THE CHILDREN (SONS) OF GOD -

Matthew 5:9 states…for they shall be called the children of God…WHAT AN HONOR! WE SHALL BE CALLED THE CHILDREN OF GOD! This word "children"   (sometimes translated as "sons") comes from the Greek word "huios", which means: a fully mature son. This is to be distinguished from the Greek word "teknon", which means: a child.

There is a difference between a child and the placing of a full grown son. Both could be classified as a son, but a child is to be looked at as a son in training. A fully mature son is one that is ready to speak and to act on his Father's behalf. The word "huios" (a fully mature son) gives evidence of the dignity of one's relationship and likeness to God's character. The word "teknon" (a child) refers to a new believer (babe) in Christ who is but a child. A new believer is one that is in need of much maturing. The new believer is a son of God, but must grow up into the character and nature of his Father. This PROCESS of maturing is referred to as SONSHIP, and does show us that salvation IS INDEED A PROCESS!

According to Bill Britton: "Sonship begins with a new birth! In order for there to be a new birth, there must be a death of the old life. In order for there to be a resurrection out of that watery grave of baptism, you must first go down. The flesh doesn't want death and God says sonship can not come by the will of the flesh, nor the will of man, nor of blood. It cannot come by being born to a certain family. It doesn't come by being one of the sons of Aaron or one of the sons of David or because your blood happens to be the right nationality. SONSHIP COMES BY THE WILL OF GOD. The birthing of a son comes by the will of God. And the making of a son has something beautiful in it - it is relationship with the Father." (The Making Of A Son, Bill Britton)

Romans 8:19 states…For the earnest expectation of the creature (creation) waits for the manifestation of the sons ("huios") of God…What a journey! We are going from a "teknon" to a "huios"!

WE SHALL BE CALLED THE SONS ("HUIOS") OF GOD!

May 15

THE SERMON ON THE MOUNT PART 13
- PERSECUTED -

Matthew 5:10,11 states…Blessed are they which are persecuted for righteousness' sake: for theirs is the kingdom of heaven. Blessed are you, when men shall revile you, and persecute you, and shall say all manner of evil against you falsely, for My sake…Being persecuted for righteousness' sake is a sure sign that you have tapped into the very life of the Father.

A manifestation of the Spirit of God does one of two things:

1. It softens the hearts of men.
2. It hardens the hearts of men.

Those who are softened by the Spirit of God will surrender their lives and come to the Lord in brokenness. Those who are hardened by the Spirit of God will preserve their lives and reject God (for the time being). Remember the many times that Jesus was persecuted for simply telling people the truth? He was even accused of performing miracles by the power of Satan, even though that was not the case.

The word "persecute" means: to subject to harassing or cruel treatment because of religion, race, or beliefs, to annoy or trouble persistently, and to pursue closely.

What is it about the true righteousness of God that brings on persecution? When the true righteousness of God is brought forth in word or deed it convicts man of his self-righteousness. When he is convicted he either repents and surrenders, or he remains hardened and persecutes the messenger of righteousness.

What is it about being persecuted for righteousness' sake that is a blessing? The blessing is this: When you are persecuted for righteousness' sake you are following in the footsteps of the prophets and of your Lord and Savior Jesus Christ. The scriptures testify that they were persecuted for righteousness' sake, and surely we will be persecuted as well. When a person is persecuted and does not fight back it is a sign of TRUE MATURITY IN GOD! THIS IS THE HIGHEST LEVEL OF MATURITY IN GOD! This is how we learn to become a creditor like our Lord and Savior. We learn to say…FATHER FORGIVE THEM, FOR THEY KNOW NOT WHAT THEY DO (OR SAY)…

The next time you are persecuted for righteousness' sake you should count yourself as GREATLY BLESSED. The prophets and Jesus were persecuted, and so shall we be persecuted. <u>FORGIVE</u> YOUR PERSECUTORS!!! A person who is persecuted for righteousness' sake is truly…

BLESSED!

May 16

THE SERMON ON THE MOUNT PART 14
- REJOICE -

Matthew 5:12 states…Rejoice, and be exceeding glad: for great is your reward in heaven: for so persecuted they the prophets which were before you…Not only are we called blessed when we are persecuted for righteousness' sake, but we are told by the Lord to REJOICE! DO WHAT? REJOICE? YES…REJOICE!

The word "rejoice" means: to be cheerful, calmly happy, well-off, glad, or full of joy. The next time you are persecuted for righteousness' sake it should make you CHEER UP! Be cheerful, happy, glad, and REJOICE!

The next part of this scripture verse tells us that our reward is to be great. What kind of reward do you think it would be? Our reward could be nothing less than THE LORD HIMSELF! Genesis 15:1 states…the Lord came unto Abram in a vision, saying, fear not, Abram: <u>I AM YOUR SHIELD, AND YOUR EXCEEDING GREAT REWARD…</u>Well…There you have it. Our reward is the Lord Himself.

This reward is the very life of the Lord Jesus Christ. It is His life that is to be revealed inside of us. This life is available to us now, and is the same life that shall sustain us in the ages to come. It is referred to as ETERNAL LIFE (THE LIFE OF THE AGES). This is the very abundant life that Jesus spoke about. It is available to us now in the form of a down payment (the earnest of our inheritance…Ephesians 1:14), and in its fullness in the ages to come. We have begun to tap into His resurrection life. His resurrection life is raising us out of death in three phases, which are: spirit, soul, and body. We are raised with Christ, we are being raised, and we shall be raised. The final stage of His resurrection life will be the resurrection of our bodies.

Listen to the persecution of the Hebrew people, and what they were pressing toward. Hebrews 11:33-35 states…Who through faith subdued kingdoms, wrought righteousness, obtained promises, stopped the mouths of lions, Quenched the violence of fire, escaped the edge of the sword, out of weakness were made strong, waxed valiant in fight, turned to flight the armies of the aliens. Women received their dead raised to life again: and others were tortured, not accepting deliverance; THAT THEY MIGHT OBTAIN A <u>BETTER RESURRECTION</u>…

Let us rejoice when we are persecuted for righteousness' sake. Our reward is the very resurrection life of the Lord Jesus Christ. Don't you want to obtain a better resurrection? PRESS IN CHILD OF GOD! And again, I say…

REJOICE!

May 17

THE SERMON ON THE MOUNT PART 15
- CONCLUSION -

THE SERMON ON THE MOUNT...O WHAT A SERMON! What more could be said other than what Jesus has said? This sermon covers every aspect of our Christian walk. It takes us from the new birth to a fully mature son of God. It speaks of the sons of God as being able to even FORGIVE AND LOVE THEIR ENEMIES. We are told to rejoice when we go through times of persecution for the sake of righteousness. This sermon is to be seen as a process which the sons of God must pass through.

IT IS A PROGRESSIVE AWAKENING AND MATURING INTO THE VERY IMAGE OF OUR FATHER! It takes us on a journey from:

1. POOR IN SPIRIT...to
2. MOURNING...to
3. MEEK...to
4. HUNGERING AND THIRSTING FOR RIGHTEOUSNESS...to
5. MERCY...to
6. PURENESS IN HEART...to
7. PEACEMAKING...to
8. PERSECUTED...to
9. REJOICING...!

Let us note that we are <u>BLESSED</u> throughout this entire process! This means that the Spirit of God is bringing us to a place where we are FULLY SATISFIED IN HIM! This satisfaction comes from our personal relationship with our Father.

The journey of growing in grace and in the knowledge of the Lord results in us:

1. RECEIVING THE KINGDOM OF HEAVEN...
2. BEING COMFORTED...
3. INHERITING THE EARTH...
4. BEING FILLED...
5. OBTAINING MERCY...
6. SEEING GOD...
7. BECOMING THE CHILDREN OF GOD...
8. BEING PERSECUTED...
9. RECEIVING A GREAT REWARD...

WHAT A SERMON! WHAT A JOURNEY! WHAT A PROCESS! WHAT A REWARD! Our reward is nothing less than the LORD HIMSELF! This will result in the infilling and final manifestation of His resurrection life. We are BLESSED, BLESSED, BLESSED...!

REJOICE! GREAT IS YOUR REWARD!

May 18

I PLEDGE ALLEGIANCE
(By Dr. Harold Lovelace)

I Pledge Allegiance
To The Lord Of All
Creation
And To The Purpose
Which He Has Planned;
With Righteousness, Peace
And Joy For All,
In One Kingdom
Under His Command!

What marvelous theology is contained within this passage! Take some time today to meditate on these words and what they mean. Within this pledge is found the entire purpose and plan of God for all of His creation, and for all of time. Surely you would want to voluntarily pledge your allegiance to SUCH A GREAT GOD!!!

AMEN!

May 19

THE CALL OF ABRAM

Genesis 12:1-3 states…Now the Lord said unto Abram, Get out of your country, and from your kindred, and from your father's house, unto a land that I will show you: And I will make of you a great nation, and I will bless you, and make your name great; and you shall be a blessing: And I will bless them that bless you, and curse him that curses you: AND IN YOU SHALL ALL THE FAMILIES OF THE EARTH BE BLESSED…WHAT A WONDERFUL SCRIPTURE PASSAGE OF GOOD NEWS! IN ABRAM SHALL <u>ALL THE FAMILIES OF THE EARTH</u> BE BLESSED!

Let us take a close look at the call of Abram. The name "Abram" means high father. His name was later changed to "Abraham", which means father of many. This passage of scripture is referred to as the Abrahamic Covenant. Notice the Word of the Lord to Abram.

There is to be a separation from:

1. HIS COUNTRY
2. HIS KINDRED (FAMILY)
3. HIS FATHER'S HOUSE

Let us pay special attention to the fact that God did not approach Abram to curse him, but to bless him. He did not "hang him over the (so-called) eternal flames of hell". He did not threaten Abram to serve Him or else…But rather, He told Abram…I AM GOING TO BLESS YOU, AND NOT ONLY YOU, BUT ALL THE FAMILIES OF THE EARTH! WHAT GOOD NEWS! WHAT A PROMISE! WHAT A COVENANT! WHAT A BLESSING!

We must understand that our Father is not out to "get us", but to BLESS US! God approaches man in order to reconcile man unto Himself. He does not need to be reconciled unto us, BUT WE NEED TO BE RECONCILED UNTO HIM! Remember…God has reconciled us unto Himself by Jesus Christ, and has given to us the ministry of reconciliation; To wit, that God was in Christ, RECONCILING THE WORLD UNTO HIMSELF, not imputing their trespasses unto them, (2nd Corinthians 5:18,19)…

This is all a result of the original promise that God made to Abram. Do you believe it? Can you receive it? The Lord Jesus Christ, Who came through the loins of Abraham, TOOK AWAY THE SIN OF THE WORLD. He was made to be sin for us, Who knew no sin; that we might be made the righteousness of God in Him (2nd Corinthians 5:21)…Jesus (through the blood of His cross) has purchased all the families of the earth. He has reconciled all things unto Himself (Colossians 1:20)!

Thank God for the call of Abram! His call does signify and point to a blessing upon all the families of the earth. Abraham truly is the FATHER OF US ALL (Romans 4:16)! The blessing of Abraham will extend into the ages to come, until God shall be ALL IN ALL! ALL THE FAMILIES OF THE EARTH SHALL BE BLESSED!

ABRAHAM IS THE HEIR OF THE WORLD (Romans 4:13)!

May 20

LOVE
(By Emmet Fox)

Love Will Conquer

There is no difficulty that enough love will not conquer;
no disease that enough love will not heal;
no door that enough love will not open;
no gulf that enough love will not bridge;
no wall that enough love will not throw down;
no sin that enough love will not redeem . . .

It makes no difference how deeply seated may be the trouble;
how hopeless the outlook;

how muddled the tangle;
how great the mistake.
A sufficient realization of love will dissolve it all.
If only you could love enough
you would be the happiest and most powerful being in the world . . .

Emmet Fox

What a beautiful poem about the love of God! WE MUST EVER SEEK TO BASK IN THE LOVE OF GOD! Remember…LOVE is the fulfilling of the law (Romans 13:8).

Jeremiah 31:3 states…The Lord has loved you with an everlasting love: therefore with lovingkindness will He draw you…Bask in the love of your Father today. Partake of His lovingkindness. He will grow you up into a tree of righteousness, that you might bear the fruit of the Spirit, which is…

LOVE!

May 21

ORGE

According to Elwin Roach: "The English word "wrath" comes from the Greek word *"orge"* (pronounced…or-gay). Strong's Exhaustive Concordance tells us that *"ORGE"* means: *desire, (as a reaching forth or excitement of the mind), i.e. (by analogy) violent passion....* If we follow the word to its derivatives we find that *it is akin to 'airo,' which implies a deliverance from sin, and is comparable to 'ornis,' which means 'a bird' (as rising in the air). "Orge" is active. "Orge" reaches out and accomplishes its burning desire.* The passion *("orge"/"wrath")* we see in the scriptures is usually in the context of heated determination. Wrath in the Biblical sense is not a condition of rage, as the word implies in the English, but is generally associated with adamant punishment toward those in rebellion; yet it does not end with punishment alone. We see that it ends in deliverance, especially at the judgment of the Last Death, the Lake of Fire. The passion of Christ, the wrath of the Lamb, is no doubt grievous to the carnal man, for it means the end of his lustful, self-indulging life. It is similar to a father's wrath when he punishes his rebellious son. It is not enjoyable to either of the two; yet it is done with understanding and in love, knowing the pain is but for a season and very necessary for the spirit of rebellion to be broken. This is in all of God's judgments toward His fallen creation." (Hell & The Lake Of Fire, Elwin R. Roach)

It is now plain to see what is meant by the "WRATH" OF GOD. IT IS THE VERY PASSIONATE LOVE OF OUR FATHER! In essence, this love says…I LOVE YOU TOO MUCH TO LEAVE YOU IN YOUR CONDITION! I WILL CORRECT YOU BECAUSE I LOVE YOU!

As was stated earlier, "wrath" is the passionate love of God. It is His stored up desire and passion to see all of His creation set free. This is to be understood in the same sense of a man's passionate love for his bride. How would he react if his bride were to be wooed into the arms of another lover? He would go after his unfaithful bride in order to win her back again. In essence, he would unleash his "wrath" upon his bride. This "wrath" would not be to destroy her, but rather to bring her back in union with her true love. The man would pour out his passionate love in an effort to gain back his lover. He would exhaust all necessary means to draw her into his loving arms. HE WOULD STOP AT NOTHING, UNTIL SHE COULD FINALLY SEE HIS UNCONDITIONAL AND UNFAILING LOVE! After being a witness to this, the bride would voluntarily return to her one and only love. HOW COULD SHE RESIST SUCH FORGIVENESS, PASSION, DETERMINATION, AND LOVE?

There is no doubt that the Bible speaks of the "wrath" of God. The GOOD NEWS is that there is a purpose for the *WINEPRESS OF THE FIERCENESS AND "WRATH" OF ALMIGHTY GOD!* It is for the purpose of <u>correction</u>! It is His…

DETERMINED, PASSIONATE LOVE!

May 22

THE TALE OF TWO CITIES

Revelation 18:2 states…And he cried mightily with a strong voice, saying, Babylon the great is fallen, is fallen, and is become the habitation of devils, and the hold of every foul spirit, and a cage of every unclean and hateful bird…Revelation 18:4 states…And I heard another voice from heaven, saying, Come out of her (Babylon), MY PEOPLE, that you be not partakers of her sins, and that you receive not of her plagues…Revelation 21:2 states…And I John saw the holy city, new Jerusalem, coming down from God out of heaven, prepared as a bride adorned for her husband…

So…The Bible is really the TALE OF TWO CITIES:

1. BABYLON
2. JERUSALEM

The two cities represent:

1. THE FLESH (CORRUPT NATURE OF MAN)
2. THE SPIRIT (DIVINE NATURE OF GOD)

Let us take a closer look at the flesh and the Spirit. Romans 8:4-8 states…That the righteousness of the law might be fulfilled in us, who walk not after the flesh (Babylon), but after the Spirit

(Jerusalem). For they that are after the flesh do mind the things of the flesh; but they that are after the Spirit the things of the Spirit. FOR TO BE CARNALLY MINDED IS DEATH; but to be spiritually minded is life and peace. Because the carnal mind is enmity against God: for it is not subject to the law of God, neither indeed can be. So then they that are in the flesh cannot please God...

The words "flesh", "carnally minded", and "carnal mind" all come from the same Greek word "sarx", which means: the corrupt nature of man, the earthly nature of man apart from divine influence, and therefore prone to sin and opposed to God. The flesh always represents the efforts and achievements of man outside of the Spirit of God. The result is always failure and death, which is separation from God in your mind. The Spirit that is spoken of in Romans chapter eight is the very Spirit of God. HIS SPIRIT IS LIFE! THERE IS NO LIFE OUTSIDE OF THE SPIRIT OF GOD! There is no life in Babylon! There is only life in Jerusalem!

Can you see that you are on a journey? Our journey is one of coming out of Babylon and into Jerusalem. We are being brought from the ADAM NATURE to the DIVINE NATURE! Can you hear the call? God is saying...COME OUT OF BABYLON, MY PEOPLE!

JERUSALEM AWAITS US!

May 23

WHAT IS SIN?

Do you know what sin is? Are you still trying to figure out what is a sin and what is not? Do you approach your every word, thought, and action by checking to see whether or not it is on the "sin list"? Do you have a sin list? What is on it?
Here is a typical "sin list" from the realm of Evangelical Christianity:

DANCING	SPEEDING
ALCOHOL	TARDINESS
CERTAIN CLOTHES	SUING
GAMBLING	OVER-EATING
BEING STINGY	ADULTERY
SMOKING	DRUG ABUSE
TAX CHEATING	OVER-SPENDING
REMARRIAGE	NOT VOTING
HOMOSEXUALITY	CURSING
IMMORALITY	GOSSIPING
R RATED MOVIES	STEALING
PREMARITAL SEX	LAZINESS

So…Is this the "sin list" that we should go by? Is this what sin is? NO! As a matter of fact, NONE OF THESE THINGS ARE SIN! This particular list (or any other list) happens to be the RESULT OF SIN, BUT NOT SIN ITSELF! Most of what people call sin is not sin, but the symptoms (or results) of sin. These symptoms point to THE ROOT OF THE PROBLEM. They are actually not the problem itself. In fact, a list of dos and don'ts has never been the solution to man's problem. Man's problem is SIN! In actuality, it is a SIN NATURE that he is born with.

So…What is sin? The word "sin" comes from the Greek word "hamartia", which means: to miss the mark, and to miss the true goal and scope of life (and so not to share in the prize). SIN IS NOT A LIST OF DOS AND DON'TS! It is a missing of the mark of the very nature and character of God. Sin is not what we do or don't do. IT IS WHAT WE ARE!!!

Due to Adam's transgression we are all born with a nature that can do nothing but come short of the glory of God. Romans 3:23 states…that we have all sinned and come short of the glory of God…This idea of sinning and coming short of the glory of God is not one or many specific acts of sin, but rather it is a nature that we operate out of. IT IS THE SIN NATURE. IT IS WHO WE ARE OUTSIDE OF CHRIST. The good news is to be found in 2nd Corinthians 5:17, which states… Therefore if any man be IN CHRIST, he is a new creature: old things are passed away; behold, all things are become new…

Outside of Christ we miss the mark of God's nature. We are a sinner. In Christ we press toward the mark for the prize of the high calling of God in Christ Jesus. We become a new creature. We no longer depend on our nature, but we now place our faith in Christ, becoming partakers of God's divine nature. We leave the defeated realm of sin, and step into the unlimited realm of salvation.

THANK YOU JESUS for coming to save us from missing the mark of God!

YOU HAVE SAVED US FROM SIN!

May 24

A DEEPER LOOK INTO THE AGES (EONS)

According to Joseph Kirk and A. E. Knoch: "The teaching of the scriptures concerning the eons has been concealed from many by the inconsistencies of the translators. An understanding of the eons and God's eonian purpose, results in a revelation of God that is most enlightening and edifying. His every attribute becomes more wonderful and glorious. The truth on this subject reveals undreamed of value and success in the saving work of our Lord Jesus Christ. It leads to the solution of many difficult problems which exercise the hearts and minds of spiritual believers. The meaning of the word "eon" is clearly indicated by the way God has used it in the scriptures.

I. What is meant by an Eon?

An eon is a long period of time; an age.

II. The Eons have a beginning.

LITERAL TRANSLATION	KING JAMES VERSION
(Heb. 1:2) God made the eons…	God made the worlds…
(1 Cor. 2:7) Before the eons…	Before the world…
(2 Ti. 1:9) Before eonian times…	Before the world began…

III. The Eons end, individually and collectively.

(Heb. 9:26) The end of the eons…	The end of the world…
(1 Cor. 10:11) The ends of the eons…	The ends of the world…
(Mat. 24:3) The end of the eon…	The end of the world…

IV. How many eons are there?

(Col. 1:26) Hid from eons…	Hid from ages…
(Lu. 20:34) This eon…	This world…
(Eph. 2:7) Eons to come…	Ages to come…

*So…Seven distinct divisions are indicated, pre-eonian time (2 Tim. 1:9), five eons, two of which are future (referred to as the eons of the eons), and time after the conclusion of the eons (Heb 9:26; 1 Cor. 15:28). There are past eons, this present eon, eons to come, and that which is before and after the eons.

V. The purpose of the eons.

(Eph. 3:8-11) Purpose of the eons…	Eternal purpose…
(Eph. 1:9-10; Phil. 2:9-11; Col. 1:15-21; I Cor. 15:22-28)	

Apart from a knowledge of these eons or ages, God's plans and purpose are shrouded in darkness and doubt. In their light He is transformed from a heartless fiend into a most affectionate Creator and Reconciler, Who does all in love, Who will bring His creatures to Himself, through sin and suffering, and severe judgment for the unbeliever, on the basis of the blood of Christ's cross." (Quotes and excerpts on, The Eons or Ages, from Joseph E. Kirk and A. E. Knoch)

The eons are the longest periods of time referred to in the scriptures. They should be distinguished from the eras and dispensations. The dispensations within the eons are:

1. INNOCENCE
2. CONSCIENCE
3. HUMAN GOVERNMENT
4. PROMISE
5. LAW
6. GRACE
7. THE MILLENNIUM (THE EON)
8. THE AGE OF THE AGES (THE EON OF THE EONS)

Enjoy your search concerning the eons of our GREAT GOD! Throughout this search you will discover the purpose of your Father, WHICH IS TO BE ALL IN ALL!

READ ROMANS 11:36!

May 25

TRUE SUCCESS

What is true success? Is it…

MONEY?
FAME?
EDUCATION?
MATERIAL POSSESSIONS?
A LONG LIFE?
TO BE HANDSOME OR BEAUTIFUL?
HAPPINESS?
A GREAT CAREER?

The above mentioned list is the way in which the world defines true success. We are taught from the time we are born that if we do not achieve these things that we are a failure. Are these things really true success? Do they really make you the complete and total person that you long to be?

True success is found in none of the things listed above. The things of this world are but dung compared to the excellency of the KNOWLEDGE OF CHRIST (Philippians 3:7-21). So…What is true success? Let us look to the words of Jesus, for He clearly and simply defines it for us.

Matthew 25:21 states…His lord said unto him, Well done, you good and faithful servant: you have been faithful over a few things, I will make you ruler over many things: enter into the joy of the Lord…Did you catch the key word in that passage? Jesus said…you have been *FAITHFUL* over a few things…There it is! That is the definition of true success. IT IS FAITHFULNESS!

The word "faithful" means: trustworthy, trustful: believing, a believer, sure, and true. The word "faithful" carries with it the idea of someone who believes, and continues to believe. It speaks of someone who trusts, and continues to trust. As well, it speaks of diligence, and of a continued faith in the Lord Jesus Christ. True success is not just faith in God, but faithfulness to God in all that He requires of us. It is a submission to God along with a total abandonment of the self-life. It is to do the will of the Father in all things. We are to be faithful to where God places us, and to what God asks us to do.

Hebrews 11:6 states…he that comes to God must believe that He is, and that He is a rewarder of them that diligently seek Him…THIS IS FAITHFULNESS TO GOD! This is…

TRUE SUCCESS!

May 26

MERE HUMAN NATURE

Matthew 16:16,17 states…You, replied Simon Peter, are the Christ, the Son of the ever-living God. Blessed are you, Simon Bar-Jonah, said Jesus; for mere human nature has not revealed this to you, but My Father in Heaven (The New Testament In Modern Speech)…

The words spoken here by Jesus are VERY IMPORTANT! They inform us how that we receive understanding from the Father concerning His Kingdom. They also tell us what will not inform us and give us understanding concerning His Kingdom.

These two opposing forces are:

    1. MERE HUMAN NATURE (FLESH AND BLOOD)
    2. REVELATION FROM OUR FATHER

The words "mere human nature" refer to flesh and blood. This refers to all that is within our corrupt nature that we inherited from Adam. Our mere human nature cannot inherit the Kingdom of God. It is IMPOSSIBLE to grasp (perceive) the Kingdom of God from the standpoint of our human nature. Remember…The natural (carnal) man cannot discern the things of the Spirit, FOR THEY ARE SPIRITUALLY DISCERNED! That means that: intellect, education, Bible college, theology, and anything else for that matter CAN NOT cause you to see that Jesus is the Christ! The only thing that can bring about the understanding that Jesus is the Christ is to have it *REVEALED* to you by the Father! Did you hear what was just said? Without revelation from our Father we are doomed to stay in the realm of intellect and the traditions and doctrines of men!!! As well, we will continue to operate out of the carnal mind. Revelation knowledge from our Father causes us to be LIBERATED. We are then introduced to spirituality, revelation truth, and the mind of Christ.

The word "revealed" in this passage means: to uncover, lay open what has been veiled or covered up, disclose, make bare, to make known, make manifest, and to disclose what was before unknown. We must be honest and admit that the understanding of Christ and His Kingdom is unknown and covered up to our natural mind. Christ remains a mystery to us UNTIL the Father reveals Him to us. It is with this attitude that we must approach our Heavenly Father. We are to recognize our mere human nature, and that we are helpless to understand spiritual things unless the Spirit of God reveals them to us. Colossians 1:26 states…Even the mystery which has been hid from ages and from generations, but now is made manifest to His saints…which is CHRIST IN YOU the hope of glory…

MAY THE FATHER GIVE YOU A REVELATION OF THE CHRIST!

May 27

THE LORD'S PRAYER - PART 1
WHEN YOU PRAY

According to J. Preston Eby: "Someone has said that prayer is helplessness casting itself upon power; it is misery seeking peace; it is unholiness embracing purity; it is hatred desiring love. Prayer is corruption panting for immortality; it is the eagle soaring heavenward; it is the dove returning home; it is the prisoner pleading for release; it is the mariner steering for the haven amid the dangerous storm; it is the soul, oppressed by the world, escaping to the empyrean, and bathing its ruffled plumes in the ethereal and the divine." (To Be The Lord's Prayer, J. Preston Eby)

So…Let us learn how to pray. Let us learn the purpose of prayer. In order to do this we must look to the PRAYER OF PRAYERS. We are of course speaking of the Lord's Prayer. This prayer was delivered to us by the Lord Jesus Christ Himself.

Matthew 6:7,8 states…But when you pray, use not vain repetitions, as the heathen do: for they think that they shall be heard for their much speaking. Be not therefore like unto them: for your Father knows what things you have need of, before you ask Him…

We are told by the Lord to not use vain repetitions, for our Father knows what things we have need of before we ask Him. This means that our prayers should not consist solely of just asking God to give us things. HE ALREADY KNOWS WHAT WE HAVE NEED OF BEFORE WE EVEN ASK! Remember…Jesus told us to take no thought for what we would eat, drink, or be clothed with. BUT SEEK FIRST the Kingdom of God, and His righteousness; and ALL THESE THINGS SHALL BE ADDED UNTO YOU…

Our prayers should have substance to them, rather than just presenting a grocery list to our Heavenly Father. We must seek His face, and not just His hand. To seek the face of God is to know Him in a personal and intimate way. To seek the hand of God is to petition Him for specific needs. While it is necessary and correct to ask God to meet our needs, most of our praying should be for the purpose of seeking His face.

The Lord's Prayer teaches us to focus on God's will and Kingdom. In essence, we are instructed to TAKE NO THOUGHT for tomorrow or our personal needs. So…When you pray, seek first the Kingdom of God, and His righteousness. This is the very heart of the…

LORD'S PRAYER!

May 28

THE LORD'S PRAYER - PART 2
(Matthew 6:9-13)
OUR FATHER

The word "Father" means: an author, creator, or initiator of anything. How fitting it is that the Father, Who is the Creator and beginning of all things, is also to be the beginning of our prayer. The very first words of the Lord's Prayer are…OUR FATHER! How beautiful is the word Father! How beautiful it is to call Him "THE FATHER"! It is especially beautiful to call Him OUR FATHER!

This gives evidence to the fact that He is our Creator. We are of Him, through Him, and to Him (Romans 11:36). In Him we live, and move, and have our being (Acts 17:28).

So…If God is our Father, then that means that we are His sons and daughters. In essence, WE ARE HIS CHILDREN…ALL OF US! Acts 17:28,29 states…For in Him we live, and move, and have our being; as certain also of your own poets have said, FOR WE ARE HIS OFFSPRING. Forasmuch then as we are the offspring of God, we ought not to think that the Godhead is like unto gold, or silver, or stone, graven by art and man's device…As well, we are told in Ecclesiastes 12:1 to remember our Creator in the days of our youth.

Referring to God as your Father implies that there is to be an intimacy in your relationship with Him. Romans 8:14,15 states…For as many as are led by the Spirit of God, they are the sons of God. For you have not received the spirit of bondage again to fear; but you have received the Spirit of adoption, whereby we cry, ABBA, FATHER…

Don't you want to personally know God as YOUR Father? There is so much awaiting us due to the fact that we have received the Spirit of adoption (sonship)! Let us recognize God as our Father and Creator in all things. We are able to call Him our Father through the blood and cross of the Lord Jesus Christ. What a privilege! He is OUR FATHER!

The Lord's Prayer teaches us to first and foremost direct our heart and attention to the Author and Creator of all things. If God is our Father, then He truly loves us, cares for us, wants the best for us, and desires to be intimate with us. He longs to have a relationship with us. We know that a good earthly father desires to be all these things to his children. HOW MUCH MORE does God want to be everything to us? Let us confidently refer to God as…

OUR FATHER!

May 29

THE LORD'S PRAYER - PART 3
(Matthew 6:9-13)
WHICH ART IN HEAVEN

According to J. Preston Eby: "The English word "heaven" is derived from the old Anglo-Saxon term "heave-on," meaning to be lifted up, up-lifted. It means to be "heaved-up" or "heaven." Not only is God our Father, but He is our Father *in heaven*. By saying God is in heaven, Jesus does not mean to localize or locate God. He is not telling us of a place where God is and where God lives apart from any other place in the universe. Those who think of heaven as a place, usually think of Him as being very distant. Somehow we have gotten the idea that heaven is a long way off. This error has crept into many songs sung by the church world. In the Pentecostal Church where I was raised as a boy two of the favorite songs were "When We All Get To Heaven" and "Won't It Be Wonderful There." Another with which many who read these lines will be familiar says, "There is a happy land, far, far way." And even in that popular hymn, "The Old Rugged Cross," we sing, "He will call me some day to that home far away..." How did we get that conception? Certainly not from Jesus or the apostles!" (To Be The Lord's Prayer, J. Preston Eby)

John 3:13 states…And no man has ascended up to heaven, but He that came down from heaven, even the Son of man *Which is in heaven*…

WOW!

Did you hear what Jesus said? He said that He came down from heaven, but was STILL IN HEAVEN (THE SON OF MAN WHICH IS IN HEAVEN)!

According to J. Preston Eby: "Our Lord was in heaven; He came down from heaven, and still was in heaven; and this heaven is, in the Greek, OURANOS. It is something a person can be in, can descend from, and still possess. And the meaning of the word is "elevation, height, exaltation." Our Lord was the King of the universe. But He descended from that state. He humbled Himself, and took upon Himself the form of sinful flesh. He became despised and rejected. But nevertheless, in His humiliation He was still the Lord of the universe. All things were subject to Him. He still could command the winds and waves and they obeyed Him to the astonishment of those men who saw it. He still could control the atoms, multiply the loaves and fishes, raise the dead, and was Master of all laws of nature. He still saw into the unseen realm of spirit, was consciously aware in both the earthly and spiritual dimensions, unlimited by the physical world. He was still elevated, exalted; He was still *in heaven*!" (To Be The Lord's Prayer, J. Preston Eby)

Many are waiting until the day that they physically die to "go to heaven". May our Father deliver us from this type of CARNAL THINKING! So…If our Father is in heaven (elevated and exalted), how do we access this heaven in which He is? Do you remember the vision that Jacob had in the Old Testament? He laid his head upon a stone and saw a ladder that went from the earth to heaven, and from heaven to earth. He saw the angels of God ascending and descending upon the ladder. What (or Who) is this ladder? Jesus told us that HE WAS THE LADDER! John 1:51 states…Verily, verily, I say unto you, Hereafter YOU SHALL SEE HEAVEN OPEN, AND THE ANGELS OF GOD ASCENDING AND DESCENDING UPON THE SON OF MAN…

Jesus is the ladder to heaven! It is in and through Him that we have access to the heavenly realm. The heavenly realm is the place in which our Father dwells. This heavenly realm is opened to us in and through Christ. YOU DO NOT HAVE TO WAIT UNTIL YOU DIE TO GO TO HEAVEN! *HEAVEN IS IN CHRIST*!

Let us turn from the fairytale idea that heaven is some geographical location off in the "sweet by-and-by". IT IS HERE-AND-NOW! It is where our Father is! It is in Christ! Ephesians 2:6 tells us that God has raised us up together, and made us sit together *IN "HEAVENLY PLACES" IN CHRIST JESUS*!!!

THIS IS HEAVEN!

May 30

THE LORD'S PRAYER - PART 4
(Matthew 6:9-13)
HALLOWED BE THY NAME

According to J. Preston Eby: "What a depth of thought, what a wealth of meaning, what a world of reality, the model prayer contains that the firstborn Son of God has given for His many brethren with the opening words, "Our Father which art in heaven, *hallowed be Thy name*!" This is the first petition of the Lord's prayer." (To Be The Lord's Prayer, J. Preston Eby)

The word "hallowed" means: sanctified, set apart. We are to enter into prayer recognizing and sanctifying the name of our Heavenly Father. "YHWH" is a name that is usually translated as "LORD". It is used approximately 7,000 times in the Bible, more than any other name for God. It is also referred to as the "Tetragrammaton" which means "The Four Letters" because it comes from four Hebrew letters: (Yod, He, Waw, and He). The four characters are the four Hebrew letters that correspond to "YHWH" and are transliterated "IAUE" or "YAHWEH". Some pronounce "YHWH" as "Jehovah", which is a form of "Yahweh" produced by blending the letters of the "Tetragrammaton" with the vowels from "ADONAI", which means "my lord" in Hebrew. We must also keep in mind that the God of the Old Testament ("Yahweh" or "Jehovah") finally revealed Himself to man in the form of the SAVIOR. He did this with the name of "JESUS" ("Iesous"), which is of Hebrew origin "Joshua" ("Yehowshua"), which means "Yahweh" (or "Jehovah") is salvation!

Jesus was obviously the God of the Old Testament MANIFESTED IN THE FLESH! The name "Yahweh" (or "Jehovah") means: to be, to exist, to become, the self-existent One, and independent.

So...Let us hallow (sanctify and set apart) the name of our Heavenly Father. The name of "Yahweh" (or "Jehovah") was manifested in the person of the Lord Jesus Christ as the SAVIOR OF THE WORLD! Our Father is the self-existent One, Who after being manifested in the flesh, did TAKE AWAY the sin of the world! Our Father is THE SAVIOR OF THE WORLD!!!

This is the reason that we should HALLOW HIS GREAT NAME! His name is worthy to be sanctified, hallowed, praised, worshipped, and adored. Jesus told us in John 17:6 that He had manifested His Father's name to the men which were given to Him. What name did He manifest? The name of "Jesus", of course!

Thank you Father for loving us! Thank you Father for saving us!

HALLOWED BE THY NAME!

May 31

THE LORD'S PRAYER - PART 5
(Matthew 6:9-13)
THY KINGDOM COME

Matthew 6:10 states…Thy kingdom come. Thy will be done in earth, as it is in heaven…The Lord's Prayer begins with the introduction of our Father, where He is (in the heavenly realm), and that His name is to be hallowed (sanctified). Then Jesus immediately turns our attention to God's KINGDOM AND WILL. The Kingdom of God was at the very heart of everything that Jesus said and did. He began His ministry by announcing …Repent: for the kingdom of heaven is at hand (Matthew 4:17)…As well, all of His parables were in one way or another related to the Kingdom of God. Read Matthew chapter 13 to see what Jesus likened the Kingdom of God unto. He likened it unto: a sower, a man who sows, a mustard seed, yeast, buried treasure, a pearl, and a net. The message of Jesus Christ was THE KINGDOM OF GOD! THERE IS NO DOUBT ABOUT IT!

The words "THY KINGDOM COME" and " THY WILL BE DONE" are the very heart, center, and focal point of the entire prayer. Imagine the Lord's Prayer as a picture. The words "THY KINGDOM COME" would be the portrait. All the other words before and after these would serve as the frame and mat for the portrait itself. With this in mind, let us attempt to define the Kingdom of God.

Many people see the Kingdom of God as nothing more than a geographical location that they will fly away to after they die. They think of it as something that is futuristic and totally out of reach. This is very sad. If that were the case, that would mean that there is very little purpose for the Christian's existence here on this earth. The majority of the church is not praying for the Kingdom of God to come to the earth, but rather that they will be "raptured" off to a Kingdom that is supposed to be somewhere in the sweet by-and-by. This is the <u>exact opposite</u> of what Jesus told us to pray. He said…THY KINGDOM <u>COME</u>!

According to Kelley Varner: "Most Christians in this nation do not understand the basic truths about God's Kingdom. The term "Kingdom Now" was invented to conveniently and negatively dismiss what men do not comprehend. In fact, that is one of the hot "issues". Jesus is not our "soon-coming King;" He is King right now! All things are under His feet. Men ask, "So is His Kingdom now or in the future?" To that I answer, "Yes! It's both." The Kingdom of God is the extension of God's rule and dominion in the earth and universe, and is in the Holy Spirit

(Romans 14:17). Simply stated, it is the Lordship of Jesus Christ. God's Kingdom is a theocracy, not a democracy, and is ruled by God through His delegated representatives, not by the people. The term "Kingdom of Heaven" shows us where it is from, and the term "Kingdom of God" shows us Who runs it!" (The Issues Of Life, Kelley Varner)

According to J. Preston Eby: "The dictionary defines "kingdom" as "a government or country headed by a king or queen; a monarchical state; a realm or domain." The word "kingdom" is made up of the noun "king," and the suffix "dom". "Dom" is a noun-forming suffix to express rank, position, or domain. For example, a "dukedom" is the domain over which a duke has authority or exercises rule, and in the abstract the rank of a duke. In like manner a "kingdom" is the domain and the people within that domain over which a king exercises authority and rule. It is the "king's domain". "Kingdom" is thus a contraction of "king's domain". The term, "Kingdom of God", can mean no other than the domain over which God exercises rule as King. It is God's declared purpose therefore that His *people*, His *holy nation*, His *peculiar treasure*, should be the domain over which He would rule as King, and ultimately all the earth and all things and every creature. The Lord's greatest dominion at this time is in the lives of His elect and chosen ones. Millions sanctimoniously and religiously pray, "Thy Kingdom come," thinking it is something outside of themselves, is some distant age, under other conditions — and have no intention whatever of abdicating the throne of their own inner wills and hearts to the King of Glory. It is a foregone conclusion that there will follow a formidable conflict between His divine sovereignty and my self-willed ego. And this, precious friend of mine, is the true BATTLE OF ARMAGEDDON!" (To Be The Lord's Prayer, J. Preston Eby)

As was just stated, the conflict is between our kingdom and His Kingdom. It is between our will and His will. So...Let us submit to the Kingdom and will of our Heavenly Father, for in doing so we become partakers of His divine nature. For so an entrance shall be ministered unto us abundantly into the EVERLASTING KINGDOM (THE KINGDOM OF THE AGES) of our Lord and Savior Jesus Christ.

THY KINGDOM COME!

June 1

THE LORD'S PRAYER - PART 6
(Matthew 6:9-13)
GIVE US THIS DAY OUR DAILY BREAD

According to J. Preston Eby: "What meaning do you attach to the word "daily"? For what is it that you ask, exactly, when you pray, "Give us this day our *daily bread*?" What is "daily bread"? Around the Greek word translated "daily" ("EPIOUSION") much controversy has circled. The word is a coined word. It is not found elsewhere in the New Testament. It is not found in the Greek translation of the Old Testament. It is not found in Greek literature. The early Church Father, Origen, less than two hundred years after our Lord spoke, reported that he could not find the word either in the works of classical writers or in the common speech of the uneducated. It is not likely that in this prayer, intended by our Lord to be a model for His disciples, He would introduce an unknown word manufactured by Him for the occasion. Jesus never did that. It looks as though our Lord had indeed spoken in Aramaic, the common language of Galilee, and that when the apostles began to write their Gospels in Greek they coined this word to represent what Jesus said sort of a transliteration, and yet not that. The phrase "daily bread" comes to us from the Latin; it was adopted by Tyndale and Luther, and so passed into the King James Version. Scholars suggest various shades of meaning for the word, and each has his reasons. The four primary ones are: (1) daily bread (2) necessary bread (3) dependable bread (4) bread for the morrow." (To Be The Lord's Prayer, J. Preston Eby)

Whatever meaning is most correct, we can be sure that this bread comes from our Father, and it is essential that we have it on a daily basis to be spiritually nourished. What is this bread? Who is this bread? Let us first look to the Old Testament and then to the New Testament.

Exodus 16:15,21 states…And when the children of Israel saw it, they said one to another, It is manna (a whatness, what is it?): for they did not know what it was. And Moses said unto them, This is the bread which the Lord has given you to eat…And they gathered it every morning, every man according to his eating: and when the sun became hot, it melted…John 6:31-35 states…Our fathers did eat manna in the desert; as it is written, He gave them bread from heaven to eat. Then Jesus said unto them, Verily, verily, I say unto you, Moses gave you not that bread from heaven; but My Father gives you the true bread from heaven. For the bread of God is He Which comes down from heaven, and gives life unto the world. Then said they unto Him, Lord, evermore give us this bread. And Jesus said unto them, I AM THE BREAD OF LIFE: he that comes to Me shall never hunger; and he that believes on Me shall never thirst…

The daily bread that we seek IS A PERSON! It is He Which comes down from heaven. The daily bread that we seek is the Lord Jesus Christ. Jesus is our bread, our spiritual sustenance, our life, our everything, and our all in all. O Heavenly Father…Give us this day of Who YOU ARE. You are bread and water unto our souls. Give us this day…

OUR DAILY BREAD!

June 2

THE LORD'S PRAYER - PART 7
(Matthew 6:9-13)
FORGIVE US, AS WE FORGIVE

According to Dr. Stephen Jones: "The Jubilee is all about forgiveness. The law itself speaks of the cancellation and forgiveness of DEBTS on this day, but in the Bible, all sin is reckoned as a debt. If a man stole a thousand dollars, the thief normally *owed* his victim two thousand dollars (Exodus 22:4). His sin was reckoned as a debt, according to Biblical justice. And so the New Testament writers speak of debts as the equivalent of sin. For example, in the Lord's Prayer, we read in Matthew 6:12, "*And forgive us our <u>debts</u>, as we also have forgiven our <u>debtors</u>.*" In Luke 11:4, it reads, "*And forgive us our <u>sins</u>, for we ourselves also forgive everyone who is <u>indebted</u> to us.*" (<u>The Laws Of The Second Coming</u>, Dr. Stephen Jones)

As was just stated, the word "forgive" carries with it the idea of releasing someone from a debt that they are not able to pay. It means: to send forth, omit, send away, remit, dismiss, to liberate, and to release from a debt.

Every Christian must first understand that he (or she) has been forgiven by their Heavenly Father. He has released us from our sin debt by the cross of the Lord Jesus Christ. We are then to show forth this same forgiveness to all others. Ephesians 4:32 states…And be kind to one another, tenderhearted, FORGIVING ONE ANOTHER, even as God for Christ's sake has forgiven you…1st Corinthians 6:20 states…For you are bought with a price: therefore glorify God in your body, and in your spirit, which are God's…Romans 5:10 states…For if, when we were enemies, WE WERE RECONCILED TO GOD BY THE DEATH OF HIS SON, <u>much more</u>, being reconciled, we shall be saved by His life…

Let us rejoice and embrace God's forgiveness. We have been forgiven, bought, and reconciled. THIS IS GOOD NEWS!!! Our sin debt has been <u>paid in full</u>. We have been forgiven by God for Christ's sake!

Now…It is our turn. Our turn for what? It is our turn to extend this same forgiveness that has been FREELY GIVEN to us! Many people have a hard time forgiving others. Why is this? When it comes right down to it, they do not understand the forgiveness that has been given to them. (Read Matthew 18:23-35.) Someone who will not forgive others is clueless as to the forgiveness that their Heavenly Father has given to them. Don't you want to be a forgiver, a lover, and a reconciler? You have been forgiven, loved, and reconciled. Let us be kind one to another, tenderhearted, FORGIVING ONE ANOTHER!

According to Dr. Stephen Jones: "The overcomers are people who have experienced the Jubilee. That is, they have learned to release men from bondage and the prison house of sin (debt). They have learned not to hold grudges against their persecutors, but to rejoice that God has found them worthy to undergo these trials of faith. These are overcomers." (<u>The Laws Of The Second Coming</u>, Dr. Stephen Jones)

FORGIVE!

June 3

THE LORD'S PRAYER - PART 8
(Matthew 6:9-13)
LEAD US NOT INTO TEMPTATION

Lead us not into temptation! What does this statement mean? This statement must be rightly divided and understood in the context and light of other scriptures concerning temptation. At first glance it appears to be difficult to understand this statement. This is due to the fact that there are many scriptures that declare that God does lead man into seasons of trial, testing, and temptation. Let us take a look at some of these scriptures, attempting to reconcile all the thoughts that pertain to temptation. This will cause us to properly understand God, man, and the purpose for our temptation.

Matthew 4:1 states…Then was Jesus LED UP OF THE SPIRIT into the wilderness to be tempted of the devil…1st Corinthians 10:13 states…There has no temptation taken you but such as is common to man: But God is faithful, Who will not allow you to be tempted above that you are able; but will with the temptation also make a way to escape, that you may be able to bear it…1st Peter 1:6 states…Wherein you greatly rejoice, though now for a season, if need be, you are in heaviness through manifold temptations: That the trial of your faith, being much more precious than of gold that perishes, though it be tried with fire, might be found unto praise and honor and glory at the appearing of Jesus Christ…1st Peter 4:12 states…Beloved, think it not strange concerning your fiery trial which is to try (same Greek word that was translated tempt, or temptation in other areas) you, as though some strange thing happened unto you…2nd Peter 2:9 states…The Lord knows how to deliver the godly out of temptations, and to reserve the unjust unto the day of judgment to be punished…Revelation 3:10 states…Because you have kept the word of My patience, I also will keep you from the hour of temptation, which shall come upon all the world, to TRY THEM that dwell upon the earth…James 1:12 states…Blessed is the man that endures temptation: for when he is tried, he shall receive the crown of life, which the Lord has promised to them that love Him…

According to J. Preston Eby: "The apostle James tells us that God does not tempt anyone, yet the scriptures speak more than once of men who were tempted of God. The apparent contradiction vanishes when we remember that the word is commonly used with two meanings and covers two distinct spheres of thought. When *we* speak of temptation we most often think of an enticement to commit sin. We are tempted when we are attracted to that which is wrong, or is beneath our privileges, contrary to God's will, or inconsistent with His character, and sometimes the scriptures use the term in that sense. This is precisely the case when James tells us that God does not tempt any man. "For God cannot be tempted **with evil**, neither tempts He any man: but every man is tempted (with evil) when he is drawn away of his *own lust*, and enticed" (James 1:13-14). The subject here is being tempted *with evil*, or seduced to commit evil, and GOD DOES NOT SO TEMPT ANY MAN. God does not solicit people to do wrong. But the underlying meaning of the word is more specific than that and the Greek word in the New Testament indicates the idea of **trial, testing,** or **proof** — that which tests or examines or proves the moral or spiritual quality, character, condition or standing of a person. In this sense it is perfectly true that OUR HEAVENLY FATHER DOES LEAD US INTO TEMPTATION! There are times when the ways of God refuse to be confined within the bounds of man's logic. They make statements that appear to be mutually contradictory but are nonetheless true. The Lord says, "You need to be led into temptation," and He also says, "You need to pray, Lead us not into temptation." Both of these statements are true! "Lead us not into temptation" is not a cry to escape temptation and testing. It is the longing within every son to PASS THE TEST, to pass EVERY TEST, to pass the LAST GREAT TEST, to obtain the victory at last over every vestige of the world, the flesh and the Devil. We are walking out and fulfilling our period of trials and chastisement, and are being prepared by those trials. The hope and promise of full salvation is our goal, for Father has chosen us to receive that promise. This prayer articulates the desire in the breast of every son to come at last to the full stature of Jesus Christ, to be a full overcomer, to have completely and only the mind of Christ, to stand in the power of the resurrection as the image and likeness of God. It asks to be led BEYOND TEMPTATION. It anticipates the formation of the eternal, unchangeable, *untemptable* nature of God as our very own reality. Almighty Father! Lead us not into temptation, lead us beyond the temptable realm, deliver us from all evil, let every lesson be fully learned, that we may stand on mount Zion with the Father's name written in our foreheads. This is the goal and the consummation of the life of sonship. This is the power and the glory of the Kingdom of God." (To Be The Lord's Prayer, J. Preston Eby)

LEAD US NOT INTO TEMPTATION!

June 4

THE LORD'S PRAYER - PART 9
(Matthew 6:9-13)
DELIVER US FROM EVIL

   According to J. Preston Eby: "As Jesus was in the world, so are we in the world, and it is an evil world facing us on every side. Therefore we need a power beyond our natural selves to help us through the temptation that it may not overpower us. DELIVER US FROM EVIL! We know what was in the mind of the Son of God. To Him evil meant one thing. Not the evil of sorrows, calamities, sickness, accidents, crime, drugs, hatred, persecution, war and tragic events which the world calls evil. The problem is not Russia, Fidel Castro, Saddam Hussein, the humanists, gangs, abortionists and politicians. **The evil which we are to fear is the corruption of our own hearts.**" (To Be The Lord's Prayer, J. Preston Eby)

   Jeremiah 17:9 states…The heart is deceitful above all things, and desperately wicked: who can know it?…Matthew 15:19,20 states…For out of the heart proceed evil thoughts, murders, adulteries, fornications, thefts, false witnesses, blasphemies: These are the things which defile a man…

   Well…There you have it! Evil is in the heart of man. We must be awakened to this sobering fact. People are always looking outside of themselves, pointing the finger at certain groups of people such as: homosexuals, certain religions and denominations, certain political groups, the masons, terrorists, atheists, scientists, and even those who strive to advance technology. When will we WAKE UP and realize that none of these people, groups, or things are the evil that we are longing to be delivered from? These things are but symptoms of the root of our problem! The evil that we are to be delivered from is the nature that is within us. Ephesians 2:2,3 states…Wherein in time past you walked according to the course of this world, according to the prince of the power of the air, the spirit that now works in the children of disobedience: Among whom we all had our conversation in times past in the lusts of our flesh, fulfilling the desires of the flesh and of the mind; AND WERE <u>BY NATURE</u> the children of wrath, even as others…

The reason that we see evil in this world is because it is in the heart of man. Once we are delivered from the evil that is within, we will cease to see it without. The apostle Paul came to this grand revelation when he said…For I know that in me (that is, in my flesh,) dwells no good thing…O wretched man that I am! Who shall deliver me from the body of this death? (Romans 7:18,24)…

We must also realize that we have within us the spirit of antichrist, which is the man of sin who sits in the temple of God, whose temple WE ARE. This must be revealed to you! (2nd Thessalonians 2:3,4)

According to J. Preston Eby: "The devil will never come as a hideous spirit creature in a funny red suit to seduce or rape your wife, but *the devil in some man* may surely attempt it. I must tell you frankly that I have not had any problem with that devil out there someplace, but I have had a great deal of difficulty with that devil whose countenance I behold when I look in the mirror!" (<u>To Be The Lord's Prayer</u>, J. Preston Eby)

Evil, and deliverance from evil, both take place in the heart of man. For we all, with open face beholding as in a glass the glory of the Lord, ARE CHANGED into the same image from glory to glory, even as by the Spirit of the Lord (2nd Corinthians 3:18)…

THAT IS DELIVERANCE! God has promised to change us into His image from glory to glory! As well, He has promised to give us all things that pertain to life and godliness…that by these things we might be partakers of His divine nature (2nd Peter 1:3,4)…Not only will He give us deliverance, but it shall be DIVINE DELIVERANCE. OUR DELIVERANCE IS THE VERY DIVINE NATURE OF GOD HIMSELF!!! O Father…

DELIVER US FROM EVIL!

June 5

THE LORD'S PRAYER - PART 10
(Matthew 6:9-13)
YOURS IS THE KINGDOM, AND THE POWER, AND THE GLORY

This doxology is rooted in David's doxology in 1st Chronicles chapter 29. 1st Chronicles 29:11,12 states…Yours, O Lord, is the greatness, and the power, and the glory, and the victory, and the majesty: for all that is in the heaven and in the earth is Yours; Yours is the kingdom, O Lord, and You are exalted above all. Both riches and honor come of You, and You reign over all; and in Your hand is power and might; and in Your hand it is to make great, and to give strength unto all…Daniel 4:34,35 states…The Most High lives for ever, Whose dominion is an everlasting dominion, and His kingdom is from generation to generation. All the inhabitants of the earth are reputed as nothing: AND HE DOES ACCORDING TO HIS WILL in the army of heaven, and among the inhabitants of the earth: and no one can stay His hand, or say unto Him, What do You do?…

According to J. Preston Eby: "God is saying to us that HE IS SOVEREIGN. Another way to express that truth is: God owns the earth and everything in it — He does what He wants to do and nobody can stop Him from doing it. In particular He is sovereign with what He does with the earth. God does not have to ask anybody's permission to do anything He wants with any part of the earth — and none can hinder or resist Him!" (<u>To Be The Lord's Prayer</u>, J. Preston Eby)

This shows and tells us of the AWESOME, ALMIGHTY, AND INDISPUTABLE POWER OF GOD! He owns and controls everything! The Kingdom is His! The glory is His! The power is His! EVERYTHING IS HIS!!! This is good news! If everything is God's, then we know that everything is in good hands. We know that everything will eventually be subdued unto Him. The final outcome is not left up to man, but to our GREAT GOD! Aren't you glad that the Kingdom, power, and glory are His?

The words "for ever" at the end of this prayer come from the Greek word "aion", which means an age. In this case it should read…to the ages…We can now see that the Kingdom, power, and glory belong to God for all the ages of time, and that this is to take place until God shall be ALL IN ALL! To this our response should be a resounding AMEN! The word "amen" means: it is so!…so let it be!

LET IT BE THAT THE KINGDOM, AND THE POWER, AND THE GLORY BELONG UNTO OUR FATHER THROUGHOUT ALL AGES OF TIME, UNTO THE AGE, EVEN UNTO THE AGE OF THE AGES!

AMEN!

June 6

READ ROMANS CHAPTER 5...I DARE YOU!

The beautiful words of Romans chapter 5 attest to the truth of Adam and Christ. They teach us of the fall and redemption of man. This chapter portrays the offence and the free gift, judgment and grace, death and life, and disobedience and obedience. Romans chapter 5 speaks of only two men.

These two men are:

1. THE FIRST ADAM
2. THE LAST ADAM

There are only two men as far as God is concerned. The key to understanding this chapter (and the entire Bible for that matter) is to see all of the human race as having been placed in each of these two men. You must see yourself as having been placed in Adam. You must also see yourself as having been placed in Christ. This means that the fall of Adam (the human race) was: universal, total, complete, and corporate. This also means that the redemption of man was: universal, total, complete, and corporate.

Many people will scream from the hilltops that this is not so. They will chime in immediately when they are told that the fall of man was universal, but will bitterly deny that the redemption of man was just as universal. If the fall of man in Adam included all men, which it did, but the redemption of man in Christ did not include all men, then what would that tell us?

This would mean that the fall of man was more powerful than the cross and blood of the Lord Jesus Christ. This would also mean that Satan (the spirit that now works in the children of disobedience), the most subtle beast of the field which the Lord God had made, would have to be declared as more powerful than the God that created him. IT WOULD MEAN THAT GOD LOST, AND THAT SATAN WOULD HAVE TO BE DECLARED AS HAVING BROUGHT DOWN MORE SOULS THAN JESUS CHRIST COULD SAVE!!!

Thank God that this is not the case! It does not matter what the Babylonian church system says. THIS IS NOT THE CASE! ***THE TEACHING OF ETERNAL TORTURE IS NOT TRUE!!!*** There will not be more people lost than there will be saved. The same amount of people that were lost in Adam shall be saved in Christ! Romans chapter 5 states that judgment and condemnation came to all, but it also states that THE FREE GIFT AND JUSTIFICATION came to <u>all</u>!

1st Corinthians 15:22 states...For as in Adam ALL DIE, even so IN CHRIST SHALL ALL BE MADE ALIVE. ***BUT EVERY MAN IN HIS OWN ORDER***...Take some time today to meditate on these things. Read Romans chapter 5.

I DARE YOU!

June 7

PHILIPPIANS CHAPTER 3
(The Process Of Salvation)

What a wonderful journey that Philippians chapter 3 takes us on. It is the journey of salvation. It is the journey of our full salvation! Full salvation?…Yes! FULL SALVATION!

In Philippians chapter 3:1-6 the apostle Paul gives us a list of credentials that he had accumulated in his years previous to his encounter with the Lord Jesus Christ. He then goes on to say that these things were but dung compared to the EXCELLENCY of the knowledge of Christ Jesus. He further states, that we are to have NO CONFIDENCE in the flesh, but we are to worship God in the Spirit, and to rejoice in Christ Jesus. Paul then begins to speak of a process in which he finds himself in. This process which he speaks of is the process of his salvation.

Paul characterizes his salvation as being found in Him (Christ), not having his own righteousness, but having the righteousness which is through the faith of Christ. He goes on to state his earnest desire to know Him in the power of His resurrection, and the fellowship of His sufferings. Paul acknowledges that he has not fully attained his goal, nor is he perfect yet, but rather he determines to forget the things that are behind him, pressing toward the mark for the prize of the high calling of God in Christ Jesus.

Paul makes it clear to us that he has not yet attained his final blessed state in Christ, neither is he already perfect. SURELY WE CAN SEE THAT HE CONSIDERS HIMSELF TO BE IN THE PROCESS OF GOD'S SALVATION! It is a process that brings us from recognizing our flesh, having no confidence in the flesh, and to worshipping God in the Spirit. Can we be honest with ourselves in admitting that we have not fully attained to this, nor have we fully apprehended the One Who has apprehended us? We are not fully saved yet! WE ARE BEING SAVED!!!

The key to growing in the Lord is in realizing that you have much growing in the Lord to do. If Paul had already arrived at the fullness of his salvation, then what was he pressing toward? Why was he saying that he counted himself as not having apprehended the fullness of his salvation yet? Paul understood and taught that man was made up of spirit, soul, and body. He knew that his spirit was saved, his soul was being saved, and that his body was yet to be saved. These three aspects of salvation are referred to as justification, sanctification, and glorification. No wonder that Paul said that he counted himself not to have apprehended. He knew that his salvation process would continue until the Lord Jesus Christ did change his vile body, that it would be fashioned like unto His glorious body (Philippians 3:21).

Let us rejoice in our salvation. We have been saved, we are being saved, and we shall be saved.

WHAT A HOPE!

WHAT A SALVATION!

June 8

ALL IN ALL POEM
(By Derek Calder)

All in All

Every nation, every tongue,
Every person, old and young.
All the dead, and all the living,
Astonished at the Father's giving.
Hearts laid bare before the Throne,
Cleansed and salted to the bone.
Raised to life and clothed with white,
Gaze at Jesus with delight.
Every pain and every tear,
All the worries and every fear,
Melt beneath unending Love,
Banished by the heaven'ly Dove.
Every family born to sin,
Crowned by liberty within.
God now All in All Creation,
Joyful Reconciliation!

Derek Calder

God was, is, and always will be ALL. But He did not stop there. He created another all. He created all things (Colossians 1:16). His end goal is to be ALL IN ALL. He will be ALL (everything) in the ALL (everything) that He created!

READ 1ST CORINTHIANS 15:22-28!

GOD SHALL BE ALL IN ALL!

June 9

PURE RELIGION

James 1:26,27 states…If any man among you seem to be religious, and bridles not his tongue, but deceives his own heart, this man's religion is vain. Pure religion and undefiled before God and the Father is this, to visit the fatherless and widows in their affliction, and to keep himself unspotted from the world…Religion is not bad, but impure religion is. We can seem to be religious, but it can all be in vain. Let us attempt to look at what characterizes impure and pure religion.

The word "religion" means: a careful follower of the observances connected with one's belief. This tells us that pure religion is more than just mere words. It is a way of life. It is a lifestyle. This lifestyle should match up with the words that a person speaks about his or her religion. Pure religion is a demonstration and a manifestation of the words and faith that we speak of. We can see this in the writings of James, for he went on to say that faith without works is dead. In essence, faith that is properly placed in the person and work of Jesus Christ will produce true works. Pure religion is characterized as: quick to hear, slow to speak, slow to anger, righteous action, rejecting vile and evil influences, a humble spirit in accepting God's message, obedient, looking into the perfect law, a hearer who remembers, an obedient doer, blessed, one who curbs his tongue, something that gives a person revelation truth, and of great worth.

On the other hand, impure religion is to be seen as the exact opposite of the list mentioned above. The world has seen enough impure religion. May our Father remove the *scars* that it has left on us and the world! Let us strive to be a part of the religious service that is pure and stainless in the sight of our God, which is to: visit the fatherless and widows in their time of trouble, and to keep one's own self unspotted from the world. In short, it is a DEMONSTRATION OF THE LOVE OF GOD that reaches out to those in need. Pure religion is the love of God in action.

THIS IS PURE RELIGION!

June 10

DAMN "?"

According to Gary Amirault: "The words "damn" and "hell" are among favorite words spoken by theologians of the "hell-fire" type, that is, as long as they are used in church. These same words used in the local bar or on the athletic field would constitute "cussing" which would not be considered proper. If you are a little uncomfortable even reading about the word "damn" just remember the "Authorized" King James Bible uses it quite frequently. Let us look into the etymology of this word "damn." We may find some interesting surprises.

The Dictionary of Word Origins written by John Ayto and published in 1990 states the following about the word "damn":

Damn: "Damn" comes via Old French "damner" from Latin "damnare," a derivative of the noun "damnum." This originally meant 'loss, harm' (it is the source of the English 'damage'), but the verb damnare soon spread its application to 'pronounce judgment upon,' in both the legal and the theological sense. These meanings (reflected also in the derived 'condemn') followed the verb through Old French into English, which dropped the strict legal sense around the 16th century but has persisted with the theological one and its more profane offshoots. Condemn, damage, indemnity." (<u>Etymology Of The Word "Damn"</u>, Gary Amirault)

According to Gary Amirault: "The words "damn" and its derivative do not once occur in the Old Testament. In the New Testament they are the exceptional and arbitrary translation of two Greek verbs or their derivatives; which occur 308 times. These words are "apollumi" and "krino." "Apolleia" (destruction or waste) is once rendered "damnation" and once "damnable." (2 Peter 2:3, and 2 Peter 2:1); "krino," (judge) occurs 114 times, and is only once rendered "damned." (1 Thess. 2:12) "Krima, (judgment or sentence) occurs 24 times, and is 7 times rendered "damnation." "KataKrino," (I condemn) occurs 24 times, and is twice only rendered "be damned." (<u>Etymology Of The Word "Damn"</u>, Gary Amirault)

The word "damn" does not mean what it has come to mean today in the realm of Christianity. It means: loss, harm, or judgment, but is definitely does not mean eternal torture in a literal hell (torture pit) away from the presence of God. THAT IS ABSURD, AND THAT IS WHAT RELIGION DOES! Man has a religious agenda, and it is this: to make the Bible conform to his ideas about God, rather than forming his ideas about God based on what the Bible actually teaches.

According to Gary Amirault: "As we can see, originally the word was neither a "cuss" word nor did it have theological significance. It was a perfectly good word with which to translate the Biblical Greek words "apollumi," "krino," and "apolleia." But when theologians twisted this word out of its original meaning, it became a word which would smear the character of our Father. The world followed the church and used it as a "cuss" word, but it should be noted, that it was the church that turned it into its present meaning, not unbelievers…In conclusion, it is time for many preachers to stop blaspheming our Father. When they say that hordes of humanity are "damned to hell," they themselves are actually guilty of misrepresenting the Creator's role as Judge. The scriptures declare that the earth will learn righteousness when His judgments are in the earth. It is we, who call ourselves Christians, who need to clean up our mouths and hearts far more than the unbeliever drowning his miseries at the local bar." (<u>Etymology Of The Word "Damn"</u>, Gary Amirault)

WE MUST STOP DAMNING PEOPLE, AND START ***LOVING*** PEOPLE!

June 11

UNDERSTANDING SCRIPTURE

2ND Timothy 3:15-17 states…And that you from a child have known the Holy Scriptures, which are able to make you wise unto salvation through faith which is in Christ Jesus. All Scripture is given by inspiration of God, and is profitable for doctrine, for reproof, for correction, for instruction in righteousness: That the man of God may be perfect, thoroughly furnished unto all good works...

THANK GOD FOR THE HOLY SCRIPTURES! Without the Holy Scriptures we would be totally in the dark concerning the things of God. We should read the scriptures daily, pouring over them in an attempt to know the true heart of our Heavenly Father. The question is though, if so many people claim to read and study the scriptures, then why are there so many different denominations and such confusion over the scriptures? It must be due to the fact that there is a lack of understanding in those who are reading the scriptures. Most people know the scriptures (as the Pharisees did). They are able to recite many passages from memory, but they are lacking one very important thing. THEY DO NOT UNDERSTAND THE SCRIPTURES! Why is this?

According to Miles Coverdale: "It shall greatly help you to understand scripture if you mark, not only what is spoken and written, but of whom, and to whom, with what words, at what time, where, to what intent, with what circumstances, considering what goes before and what follows." (Miles Coverdale in his introduction to his Bible translation)

It would do us well to meditate on the words of Miles Coverdale, for they do explain to us the reason why so few people truly understand the Bible. We are so accustomed to reading our Bibles with our denominational minds already made up. We have put God in our nice, pretty, and religious box with a beautiful pharisaical bow on top. When we read the Bible we learn very little of its true meaning, for in our minds we already have God all figured out. WE MUST STOP DOING THIS! WE MUST STOP PULLING SCRIPTURES OUT OF CONTEXT TO SUIT OUR DENOMINATIONAL AGENDAS! DO WHAT THE MAN SAID! Take the advice of Miles Coverdale.

Matthew 13:23 states...But he that received seed into the good ground is he that hears the word, AND UNDERSTANDS IT; which also bears fruit, and brings forth, some a hundredfold, some sixty, some thirty...We must seek to understand the scriptures that we might bear the fruit of the Spirit.

According to Millar Burrows: "What we really need, after all, is not to defend the Bible but to understand it." (Millar Burrows)

SEEK TO UNDERSTAND THE SCRIPTURES!

June 12

WHAT GOD HATES

Proverbs 6:16-19 states...These six things does the Lord hate: seven are an abomination unto Him: A proud look, a lying tongue, and hands that shed innocent blood, A heart that devises wicked imaginations, feet that are swift in running to mischief, A false witness that speaks lies, and he that sows discord among the brethren...Yes...There are things that God does hate, and these are among the top of the list. Let us draw our attention to one in particular...A PROUD LOOK.

Psalm 18:27 states…For you will save the afflicted people; but will bring down high looks… Psalm 101:5 states…Whoever slanders his neighbor, him will I cut off: he that has a high look and a proud heart will I not allow…

A proud look obviously speaks of PRIDE in one's heart and life. Is that what God hates? YES! Among the things that God hates, PRIDE TOPS THE LIST! You would think that there are many other things that would top the list other than pride, but that is not the case. Remember…Jesus had no harsh things to say to notorious sinners, harlots, thieves, murderers, and such like. His harsh words were to the RELIGIOUS LEADERS of the day. The religious leaders (the Pharisees, Sadducees, and scribes) were those whose hearts were full of pride and self-righteousness. The word "proud" in Proverbs 6:17 means: to rise, rise up, be high, lofty, exalted, and to be lifted up. This is what God hates. HE HATES PRIDE! Pride screams of…ME, MYSELF, I, GIVE TO ME, AREN'T I SOMETHING, ME, ME, _ME_! Are you sick yet? GOD IS! Read Luke 18:9-14 to see what Jesus had to say about a proud look. In verse 14 it states…for everyone that exalts himself shall be abased; and he that humbles himself shall be exalted…

Let us strive for the opposite of a proud look. Our trust in self-righteousness (self) is what STINKS to the world and God.

According to George MacDonald: "I am so tired about the things said about God. I understand God's patience with the wicked, but I do wonder how He can be so patient with the pious." (George MacDonald)

HUMBLE YOURSELF!

June 13

EATING WITH SINNERS

Do you hang around sinners? Do you hang around notorious sinners? I SURE HOPE SO! Matthew 9: 10-13 states…And while He was reclining at table, a large number of tax-gatherers and notorious sinners were of the party with Jesus and His disciples. The Pharisees noticed this, and they inquired of His disciples, Why does your teacher eat with the tax-gatherers and notorious sinners? He heard the question and replied, It is not men in good health who require a doctor, but the sick. But go and learn what this means, it is mercy that I desire, not sacrifice; for I did not come to appeal to the righteous, but to sinners (The New Testament In Modern Speech)…

Why did Jesus eat with sinners? Why did He not come to appeal to the righteous? WHO ELSE COULD HE POSSIBLY EAT WITH? WHO ELSE COULD HE SPEND HIS TIME WITH? _WE ARE ALL SINNERS! THERE IS NONE RIGHTEOUS, NO, NOT ONE!!!_ For all have sinned, and come short of the glory of God; (Romans 3:23)…

We are all sinners and unrighteous before our Father. There is not one person (other than the man Christ Jesus) who can say that they are holy and righteous in and of themselves. Many think that after they become a Christian that they are righteous in and of themselves, but this is still not the case. It is the LORD'S RIGHTEOUSNESS that has been imputed to us based upon faith in the person and work of the Lord Jesus Christ.

With this in mind, we can now understand why that Jesus ate with notorious sinners, and why He did not come to call the righteous, but sinners unto repentance. HE HAD NO ONE ELSE TO EAT WITH OR SPEND HIS TIME WITH, FOR WE ARE ALL SINNERS AND UNRIGHTEOUS OUTSIDE OF GOD! If Jesus did not fellowship with sinners there would have been no one for Him to fellowship with.

Now you know it is alright to hang out with sinners. This is who Jesus came for. He came for us all. The Pharisees were *so blind* that they could not fathom that they too were sinners. Let us strive to be like our Savior in spending time with notorious sinners. We have nothing to be ashamed of in doing this. The purpose for this type of fellowship is to demonstrate the love of God to the very people that He came to save. Jesus did not come to call the righteous...

BUT SINNERS (ALL PEOPLE) TO REPENTANCE!

June 14

UNBELIEF

Matthew 13:57,58 states...And they were offended in Him. But Jesus said unto them, A prophet is not without honor, except in his own country (His native country: i.e. Galilee), and in his own house. And He did not many mighty works there because of their unbelief...Mark 6:5,6 states... And He could do there no mighty work, except that He laid His hands upon a few sick people, and healed them. And He marveled because of their unbelief...Mark 16:14 states, Afterward He appeared unto the eleven as they sat at meat, and upbraided them with their unbelief and hardness of heart, because they believed not them which had seen Him after He was risen...Romans 11:20 states...Well; because of unbelief they (Israel) were broken off...Hebrews 4:3,6 states...For we which have believed do enter into rest...seeing therefore it remains that some must enter therein, and they to whom it was first preached entered not in because of unbelief...

As you can see, unbelief is not real high on God's list. As a matter of fact, it is not on His list of likes at all. Remember...Without faith it is impossible to please God (Hebrews 11:6)...As was stated earlier, Jesus did not perform many mighty works in His own country. This would tell us that unbelief hinders, blocks, and stops the power of God from coming forth in our midst. It does not hinder God, as much as it hinders us from experiencing God in our own personal lives. We must understand that unbelief is a very serious matter to our Father. It puts us in a position of not being able to enter into God's rest. As well, it causes us not to apprehend that which is ours (our inheritance) in Christ.

God does not deal with man on the basis of intellect, but rather gives each man a measure of faith to approach Him. This faith is what unlocks the door to justification, sanctification, and glorification. Remember…It is by grace THROUGH FAITH that we are to experience the life of our Heavenly Father. FAITH is the key that unlocks the door of grace, whereby, giving us access to heavenly places in Christ Jesus. Unbelief quenches the flow of God's Spirit and keeps us in bondage to the hell of the carnal mind. In simple terms…UNBELIEF DISPLEASES GOD, AND FAITH (BELIEVING) PLEASES GOD!

Let us be honest in admitting that we all struggle with unbelief at times. Thankfully, our loving Father is patient, forgiving, and ever ready to…

HELP OUR UNBELIEF!

June 15

PECULIAR PEOPLE

1ST Peter 2:9 states…But you are a chosen generation, a royal priesthood, a holy nation, a peculiar people; that you should show forth the praises of Him Who has called you out of darkness into His marvelous light…1st Peter 2:9 (Amplified Bible) states…But you are a chosen race, a royal priesthood, a dedicated nation, (God's) own purchased, special people, that you may set forth the wonderful deeds and display the virtues and perfections of Him Who called you out of darkness into His marvelous light…

Well…There you have it. YOU ARE NOT NORMAL! YOU ARE PECULIAR AND SPECIAL TO GOD! You are called out of darkness into His marvelous light to *show forth* His praises. You are: a chosen generation, a royal priesthood, a holy nation, and a peculiar people. The word "peculiar" means: acquisition, purchased, a possession.

We must see ourselves as a peculiar people of God for a treasure. He has purchased us and we are His possession. We are not our own, but we have been bought with a price. We are therefore to glorify God in our bodies and in our spirits, which belong to God (1st Corinthians 6:20)…This means that not only are we peculiar, but we have a peculiar purpose. That purpose, as we have already stated, is to SHOW FORTH HIS PRAISES IN THE EARTH! In essence, we are being brought from a revelation of Jesus Christ to a manifestation of Jesus Christ. This is the very reason why we have been purchased by God. It is to distribute the very DIVINE NATURE of God for all to see. We are peculiar for a purpose, and that purpose is to be a <u>partaker</u>, <u>sharer</u>, and <u>operator</u> in the very nature of God. You are not called to be natural or normal, but supernatural and abnormal, bringing the world what it so desperately needs. It is this peculiar aspect of God's people that draws others out of darkness, bringing them into His marvelous light.

So…Settle it in your spirit. You are called to be a distributor of God's nature. This is not a normal calling.

IT IS PECULIAR!

June 16

ARE YOU PREJUDICED?

According to Charles Pridgeon: "The spirit of prejudice stands in the way of all new views of truth. "Prejudice" has been defined as "a judgment or opinion formed without due examination of the facts or reasons that are essential to a just and impartial determination."…There are those who will not accept any truth unless it is ministered in a certain conventional manner or supported by certain great names…One of the words that Prejudice uses is, "That is unorthodox." "Orthodoxy" means "right thinking;" to nearly every one it has come to mean "to think as I do."…Unless there are deepenings and enlargement, vital and new openings of truth, orthodoxy becomes dead… Prejudice stands in the way of even a conservative and constructive advance. May God's Holy Spirit alone be our Teacher." (Is Hell Eternal, Or Will God's Plan Fail?, Charles Pridgeon)

If there was one word to characterize modern day Christianity as a whole, it is this: PREJUDICE! Most Christians base their beliefs on what others say. They care more about what their pastor, family, and friends say than what the Bible says. They do not want to go through the process of checking into facts and reasons that are essential to a just and impartial determination.

It is not enough to just believe something. WE MUST KNOW WHY WE BELIEVE WHAT WE BELIEVE! When people are presented with something they have never heard they immediately discard it as false. If it is something they do not understand they are sure to label it as deception. All of this is done WITHOUT DUE EXAMINATION AND PRAYER. ***THIS IS PREJUDICE!*** WE DESPERATELY NEED TO STOP DOING THIS! Most people do not read, meditate on, or study the Bible, but they are quick to assure you that they have God all figured out. Why is this? They are held captive by the spirit of prejudice! This is what Jesus referred to when He said…the traditions and doctrines of men make the Word of God of none effect (Mark 7:13)…

May our Heavenly Father deliver us from prejudice, for the body of Christ is drowning in a sea of religious confusion, refusing to properly examine the facts or reasons that are essential to a just and impartial determination. It is time to examine whether or not we are in "the faith" (2nd Corinthians 13:5). It is time to prove all things (1st Thessalonians 5:21). It is time to be a ***"BEREAN"***, being more noble than others, in that we receive the Word with all readiness of mind, searching the scriptures daily, looking to see whether the things we hear are correct or not (Acts 17:11)…

According to Charles Pridgeon: "It ought not to be counted strange that new discoveries might be found in God's Word and that modification of some things which we regarded as truth had to be made. In this way alone will truth remain living and have power." (Is Hell Eternal, Or Will God's Plan Fail?, Charles Pridgeon)

Let us lay down our prejudice and worship God…

IN SPIRIT AND TRUTH!

June 17

DUNG

Have you ever wondered about Ezekiel chapter four? The Lord asks Ezekiel to do several things, one of which was very strange. The Lord tells Ezekiel in verse nine to take wheat, barley, beans, lentils, millet, and fitches, and put them in one vessel, and make bread. The Lord then tells Ezekiel to eat it as barley cakes, and to bake it with DUNG that comes out of man (verse twelve). The Lord further clarifies Himself in verse fifteen by saying...I have given you cow's dung for man's dung, and you shall prepare your bread with it. This is a very strange request, don't you think? What could be the purpose for this request? Did it symbolize something concerning the spiritual state of Israel? What did it represent or speak of?

According to Dr. Stephen Jones: "In the fourth chapter of Ezekiel, at the beginning of his ministry, the prophet is told to eat food cooked with dung. The word "dung" is from the Hebrew word "*gelel*" (#1561 in Strong's Conc.). It is a variation of the basic root word "*galal*", which also means "dung."

This Bible passage teaches us the contrast between good food and dung. God's Word is the good food; man's traditions, that which proceeds from his rebellious heart, are only dung. Those who eat food cooked with dung are those who believe in God, who do eat God's Word, but they mix it with the dung of men's traditions, men's understanding of God and His Word. This is one of the most basic moral problems of all time. The Hebrew word for "idols" is "*gillul*", which is just a slight variation of "*galal*" ("dung"). Ezekiel is really telling us that **idols are dung**. "Dung" was the popular euphemism for idols. This dung was only a physical manifestation of that which he and the entire nation had already eaten spiritually." (Heart Idolatry And Dung, Dr. Stephen Jones)

Ezekiel chapter fourteen addresses the problem of idolatry that had plagued the nation of Israel. The Lord tells Ezekiel that the people have set up *idols in their heart*, and that He will answer them according to the multitude of their idols. Idolatry was something that was primarily seen outwardly during Old Testament times. Man would try to liken the Godhead unto physical things such as gold, silver, or stone graven by art and man's device. The idolatry of this day and age happens to be more subtle, but in both cases it is a condition of the heart. In simple terms, "idolatry" is to be seen as a preconceived idea or assumption about God that is not true. It keeps a person estranged from knowing the TRUE GOD, His true nature, and His true character.

The true nature and character of God is LOVE! Anything that replaces this idea of God is idolatry. We must understand that God does not want to destroy us, but rather He wants to destroy the idols that are in our heart. Like the prophet Ezekiel, we have all eaten the dung of man's traditions. For those of you that are reading this, you are no doubt being shown revelation truth from the Father. It is the spirit of wisdom and revelation in the knowledge of Him that destroys the idolatry in our lives. We must have compassion toward those who are still saturated in idolatry, praying for their deliverance. Are you ready for the good food? It is...

GOD'S WORD!

June 18

MATTHEW, MARK, LUKE, AND JOHN

Have you ever considered why there are four accounts of the life of Jesus? These four gospel accounts are referred to as Matthew, Mark, Luke, and John. But why four? Why not one, three, five, six, or seven? What is the significance of having four gospel accounts? Does it represent something? Is it a fulfillment of prophecy? What does it symbolize?

According to Robert Beecham: "The book of the prophet Ezekiel begins with a dramatic vision. He saw the heavens opened and in the middle of dazzling brightness he saw four living beings. He describes them as follows: 'Their faces looked like this: Each of the four had the face of a man, and on the right side each had the face of a lion, and on the left the face of an ox; each also had the face of an eagle' (1: 10). John had a similar vision, recorded in Revelation 4: 6, 7: "In the centre, around the throne, were four living beings, and they were covered with eyes, in front and behind. The first living being was like a lion, the second was like an ox, the third had a face like a man, the fourth was like a flying eagle." (The Four Living Beings, Robert Beecham)

The occupations of Matthew, Mark, Luke, and John were:

1. MATTHEW…A TAX COLLECTOR
2. MARK…UNKNOWN OCCUPATION
3. LUKE…A DOCTOR
4. JOHN…A FISHERMAN

These four gospels correspond to the four living beings! Matthew's gospel speaks of Jesus as a lion. This represents Jesus as a **_KING_**. Mark's gospel speaks of Jesus as an ox. This represents Jesus as a **_SERVANT_**. Luke's gospel speaks of Jesus as a man. This represents Jesus as a **_MAN_** (the humanity of Jesus). John's gospel speaks of Jesus as an eagle. This represents Jesus as **_GOD_** (the deity of Jesus).

As you can see, the purpose of the four gospels is to portray Jesus in His fullness. He is to be seen as a: KING, SERVANT, MAN, AND GOD! With this in mind, the gospel accounts will mean much more to you from here on out. Pay close attention to how each gospel portrays Jesus in its own unique way.

According to Robert Beecham: "Only Matthew records the visit of the wise men, and their words: 'where is the One Who has been born **king** of the Jews? Mark's gospel is all about action. Jesus is serving His Father. Appropriately, for a servant, Mark's gospel is the shortest. Only Luke gives us all the human details of Jesus' birth. He tells the story of Gabriel's visit to Mary and her conception. Only Luke mentions the inn at Bethlehem and the manger where Jesus first slept. Only Luke recounts how Jesus sweated drops of blood in Gethsemane. John is the gospel of 'I am'. Only John records the great claims of Jesus. 'I am the bread of life.' 'I am the light of the world.' 'I am the door.' 'I am the good shepherd.' 'I am the resurrection and the life.' 'I am the way, the truth and the life.' 'I am the true vine.' 'Before Abraham was, I am.' Who but God can say such things? No other teacher or religious leader before or since has ever spoken words like these." (The Four Living Beings, Robert Beecham)   WHAT AN AWESOME JESUS!

June 19

WE THE FOLLOWING...PROCLAIM

We the following, stand before the peoples of the earth to bear witness to the Good News of Jesus Christ, and proclaim:

1. That God the Creator loves and cares for each individual with a Parent's love.
2. In the spiritual authority and leadership of Jesus Christ, the Son of God.
3. In the trustworthiness of the Bible as containing a revelation from God.
4. In the certainty of just retribution for sin.
5. In the final harmony of all souls with God.

The Universalist Christian's Association

Those who have dedicated their lives to an intense study of the Bible are sure to come to an understanding of the statements mentioned above. These five statements do summarize and characterize all that the Bible stands for and teaches. They represent the very heart of our Heavenly Father! As well, these statements spell out our Father's *purpose of the ages*, showing Him to be the Creator and Reconciler of ALL THINGS. Take some time today to meditate on, study, and pray about these declarations. They point to the absolute and complete victory of the cross of the Lord Jesus Christ, signifying Who He is, and what He has accomplished. We will humbly attempt over the next five days to give an explanation of each statement.

O FATHER...OPEN THE EYES OF OUR HEART!

June 20

#1 - GOD THE CREATOR LOVES
That God the Creator loves and cares for each individual with a Parent's love.

This statement is the theme of the entire Bible. There are many that read the Bible and do not understand that God the Creator loves and cares for each individual with a Parent's love. This is sad and also ironic. It is equivalent to looking into the sky on a cloudless day and saying that you are not able to see the sun. The book of Genesis is a book of beginnings. Genesis 1:1 states...In the beginning God created the heaven and the earth...This assures us that God is the Creator! As well, we are able to see that God the Creator loved and cared for the human race. Not only did God create Adam, but He gave him everything that he needed, including the promise to redeem the human race from their fallen state. This (fallen state) was due to the disobedient act and transgression of

Adam. When mankind was at it lowest point, GOD WAS AT HIS BEST, promising to bruise the head of the serpent, thereby delivering humanity from its bondage.

The love of God is greater far than tongue or pen can ever tell;
It goes beyond the highest star, and reaches to the lowest hell.
The guilty pair, bowed down with care, God gave His Son to win;
His erring child He reconciled, and pardoned from his sin.

(The Love Of God, Frederick M. Lehman)

Colossians 1:16 plainly tells us that God created "*all things*" by Jesus Christ. Colossians 1:20 tells us that God will reconcile the same "*all things*" to Himself through the cross of Jesus Christ. This passage of scripture (Colossians 1:16-20) portrays God as the Creator and Reconciler of all things. WHAT A LOVING CREATOR!

As was stated earlier, God's love is that of a Parent's love. A Parent's love is to be characterized as: a love that births, nurtures, develops, teaches, corrects, and causes one to fully mature. In addition to all of this, ***GOD'S LOVE NEVER FAILS!!!***

Is this how you see God? Unfortunately, many people do not. Many people see God as an angry monster Who is eager to torture the majority of His created beings forever. This is due to the incorrect teaching of eternal torture that has all but permeated Evangelical Christianity. Does this teaching (eternal torture) glorify God??? ***SURELY IT DOES NOT!!!***

Let us focus our attention back on the love of a Parent. Does a Parent punish his child? YES! Why does he punish his child? He punishes his child TO CORRECT HIM! THAT IS A PARENT'S LOVE! THAT IS THE LOVE OF GOD THE CREATOR! Will there be punishment in the ages to come? YES! With that being said though, we must understand that this punishment is a means to an end. IT IS FOR THE PURPOSE OF CORRECTION AND FOR THE BETTERING OF THE OFFENDER!

There are those who would ask the question…How do you know that there is a Creator? The answer is simple. IT IS IMPOSSIBLE TO HAVE CREATION WITHOUT A CREATOR! As well, there are those that would ask the question…How do you know that God loves you? The answer is simple. God DEMONSTRATED His love toward us in coming to this earth, being manifested in the flesh to take away the sin of the world.

GOD THE CREATOR LOVES!

June 21

#2 - JESUS CHRIST, THE SON OF GOD
In the spiritual authority and leadership of Jesus Christ, the Son of God.

The Bible clearly teaches the spiritual authority and leadership of Jesus Christ, the Son of God. This truth is to be seen from Genesis through Revelation. Hebrews 10:7 tells us that Jesus came (in the volume of the book it was written of Him,) to do the will of His Father…

John 1:1 states…In the beginning was the Word, and the Word was with God, and the Word was God…John 1:14 states…And the Word was made flesh, and dwelled among us, (and we beheld His glory, the glory as of the only begotten of the Father,) full of grace and truth…1st Timothy 3:16 states…And without controversy great is the mystery of godliness: God was manifest in the flesh, justified in the Spirit, seen of angels, preached unto the Gentiles, believed on in the world, received up into glory…1st John 1:1-3 states…That which was from the beginning, which we have heard, which we have seen with our eyes, which we have looked upon, and our hands have handled, of the Word of life; (For the life was manifested, and we have seen it, and bear witness, and show unto you that eternal life, which was with the Father, and was manifested unto us;) That which we have seen and heard declare we unto you, that you also may have fellowship with us: and truly our fellowship is with the Father, and with His Son Jesus Christ…

It is now clear to see that Jesus Christ was none other than GOD MANIFESTED IN THE FLESH. He is the Yahweh of the Old Testament that came to this earth, taking on human form. Remember…"Jesus" means: Yahweh saves, or Yahweh is salvation! HOW PLAIN CAN IT BE? As we delve into the writings of the apostle John it becomes even more plain.

According to Robert Beecham:

"As we stated in an earlier teaching (Matthew, Mark, Luke, and John), John is the gospel of 'I am'. Only John records the great claims of Jesus. 'I am the bread of life.' 'I am the light of the world.' 'I am the door.' 'I am the good shepherd.' 'I am the resurrection and the life.' 'I am the way, the truth and the life.' 'I am the true vine.' 'Before Abraham was, I am.' Who but God can say such things? No other teacher or religious leader before or since has ever spoken words like these." (The Four Living Beings, Robert Beecham) As well, Thomas referred to Jesus as his Lord and his God in John 20:28. Jesus accepted these words without protesting.

The Bible obviously testifies to the Deity of Jesus Christ, the Son of God. It is imperative that we understand the spiritual authority of Jesus Christ, recognizing Who He is and what He has accomplished. ALL POWER (AUTHORITY) IS GIVEN UNTO HIM IN HEAVEN AND EARTH (Matthew 28:18)…

ALL HAIL THE POWER OF THE NAME OF JESUS!

June 22

#3 - THE TRUSTWORTHINESS OF THE BIBLE
In the trustworthiness of the Bible as containing a revelation from God.

According to Keith Newman: "The authenticity of the Holy Bible has been attacked at regular intervals by atheists and theologians alike but none have explained away the mathematical seal beneath its surface. It would seem the Divine Hand has moved to prevent counterfeiting in the pages of the Bible in a similar manner to the line that runs through paper money. Bible numerics appears to be God's watermark of authenticity." (Is God A Mathematician?, Keith Newman)

According to Ray Knight: "Dr. E.W.Bullinger was a direct descendant of the Bullinger of the Swiss Reformation. He lived from 1837 - 1913 and was a mighty spiritual man as well deep into the Word of God. He discovered numerical patterns in scripture and creation which led him to believe that His God had purposely placed it there for a reason. His insight to creation and the numerical patterns in God's Word are especially precious. Dr. Ivan Panin, a converted Russian Nihilist, later a Harvard scholar, professor and mathematician . . . he once tutored Albert Einstein . . . learned Greek and Hebrew in four years. He then added Aramaic to his skills. He, quite separately from Bullinger, discovered the mathematical construction of scripture as seen in the two languages used . . . Hebrew and Greek. These two men of God spent many years recording their works and we have access to their findings today and are sincerely blessed by the insight that they have shown us. The 'seal of sevens' on all scripture of our Bible was mind-boggling . . . Panin and his assistant were converted through their discovery. Panin died in 1942 after spending the remainder of his life in the Word unveiling its mighty treasures." (Bible Numbers Are Mighty, Ray Knight)

According to Keith Newman: "Let's take the number seven as an illustration of the way the patterns work. Seven is the most prolific of the mathematical series which binds scripture together. The very first verse of the Bible "In the beginning God created the heaven and the earth" (Gen 1:1), contains over 30 different combinations of seven. This verse has seven Hebrew words having a total of 28 letters 4 x 7. The numeric value of the three nouns "God", "heaven" and "earth" totals 777. Any number in triplicate expresses complete, ultimate or total meaning. Also tightly sealed up with sevens are the genealogy of Jesus, the account of the virgin birth and the resurrection. Seven occurs as a number 187 times in the Bible (41 x 7), the phrase "seven-fold" occurs seven times and "seventy" occurs 56 times (7 x 8). In the Book of Revelation seven positively shines out: there are seven golden candlesticks, seven letters to seven churches, a book sealed with seven seals, seven angels standing before the Lord with seven trumpets, seven thunders and seven last plagues. In fact there are over 50 occurrences of the number seven in Revelation alone." (Is God A Mathematician?, Keith Newman)

According to Ray Knight: "The *'Wonderful Numberer'* showed forth His great care by making the total for **every** paragraph in the Bible have its total value that was **exactly divisible by 7**. A true 'seal' on His word. A modern computer was used to try and copy God's supernatural pattern in just writing a single paragraph: it failed miserably! It was estimated that the chance of succeeding was one in many billions!" (Bible Numbers Are Mighty, Ray Knight)

If all this undeniable information was not enough, the Bible itself clearly states that it is the literal "God-breathed" living Word of the Creator. (Read 2nd Timothy 3:16 and 2nd Peter 1:20,21.)

THE GLORY OF GOD & THE HONOR OF KINGS

The Holy Scriptures are a miracle of God. They are trustworthy, inspired, and contain a revelation from God to man. They are to be read, studied, and cherished above all other writings on planet earth. The Bible is a lamp unto our feet, and a light unto our path (Psalm 119:105).

THANK GOD FOR THE BIBLE!

June 23

#4 - CERTAIN, JUST RETRIBUTION
In the certainty of just retribution for sin.

The Bible clearly teaches us of the certainty of just retribution for sin. The word "retribution" speaks of the distribution of rewards and punishments that are to be administered by our Lord. In this case we are of course referring to the punishment aspect of retribution that is to be distributed accordingly in the ages to come.

A careful study of Luke 12:42-48 will shed much light on this topic. This passage of scripture is very enlightening and informative, giving us an understanding of just retribution.

It tells us of three classes of people:

1. OVERCOMERS (A FAITHFUL AND WISE STEWARD OR SERVANT)
2. NON-OVERCOMERS (AN UNFAITHFUL SERVANT)
3. UNBELIEVERS (ONE WHO DOES NOT KNOW THE LORD)

Luke 12:47,48 states…And that servant, which knew his lord's will, and prepared not himself, neither did according to his will, shall be beaten with many stripes. But he that knew not, and did commit things worthy of stripes, shall be beaten with few stripes. For unto whomsoever much is given, of him shall be much required: and to whom men have committed much, of him they will ask the more…The faithful and wise steward is destined to rule and reign with Jesus Christ in the ages to come, having power over the nations. He shall rule them with a rod of iron; as the vessels of a potter shall they be broken to shivers: even as Jesus received of His Father (Revelation 2:26,27)…The non-overcomer and unbeliever are destined for certain, just retribution for sin. This is referred to as the resurrection of judgment or second resurrection. It is a resurrection that includes fiery judgment for the purpose of correction and restoration. It is the Lake of Fire! This is not a literal fire, but a cleansing, purifying, and spiritual fire that will consume their wood, hay, and stubble (the carnal mind). Remember…***GOD IS A CONSUMING FIRE!!!*** His very presence is a LAKE OF FIRE to the non-overcomer and the unbeliever.

This is to be seen as God's passionate, corrective LOVE! The certainty of just retribution for sin is for THE PURPOSE OF CORRECTION, not to eternally torture someone. The teaching of eternal torture (as we know it today) is rooted in Greek Mythology, Bible mistranslations, a literal interpretation of some of the metaphors of scripture, the complete neglect of a proper study of the scriptures, and is fueled by the carnal mind.

We must see that there is going to be retribution for sin, but we must also see that it is going to be JUST! In other words, THE PUNISHMENT MUST FIT THE CRIME! Those who know to do the will of the Father and do not do it will be corrected *more severely*! Those who go against the will of the Father in ignorance will be corrected, but with less severity! The levels of correction are to vary due to the amount of light that a person was given concerning the things of the Lord. But rest assured, there is going to be retribution for sin! GOD WILL NOT BE MOCKED (Galatians 6:7,8)!

That which is at stake is the opportunity for a <u>better resurrection</u> (Hebrews 11:35)! In essence, those who voluntarily serve the Lord now are already experiencing His consuming Lake of Fire. They are being brought through the process of purification and correction that they might be profitable for the Master's use. It is called sanctification!

According to Dr. Harold Lovelace: "Since God has revealed His plan and purpose, we should ask, "How do we live now and what do we do with this knowledge? Are we more responsible now to do something with this knowledge? Do we listen to the carnal mind and think that since God is going to restore all we might as well live like we want to live?" The answer is "NO!" His correction is severe. The carnal views are against the character, qualities, and nature of God. The knowledge of His plan is given to those who will be trusted to take it to others. It is His knowledge and glory that is to cover the earth." (<u>Read And Search God's Plan</u>, Dr. Harold Lovelace)

Remember…To whom much is given…

MUCH IS REQUIRED!

June 24

#5 - THE FINAL HARMONY OF ALL SOULS WITH GOD
In the final harmony of all souls with God.

The majority of those in Evangelical Christianity teach that God is going to eternally torture most of the human race. According to their teaching, not only is God going to torture over 95% of all the people who have ever been born, but He is going to separate, punish, and torture them FOREVER! They claim that God is going to burn them (unbelievers) in a literal fire causing them to SCREAM OUT IN AGONY FOREVER AND EVER. These torturous flames are said to fall on all who do not believe in the Son of God.

Why is it that God's people can not see that He is victorious? Why do so few people believe in the salvation of all men? Why is it that Christians can not see that Jesus Christ is the SAVIOR OF THE WORLD?

According to George Hawtin: "The inability of God's people to understand and accept the restitution of all things, which was spoken of by all the prophets since the world began, may be traced to three great faults in our traditional teaching. Firstly, very, very few people are familiar with the truth that there is a coming age which the Bible names the dispensation of the fullness of times (Eph. 1: 10), and that that age above all others has been specially set aside for the work of reconciling all things in heaven and in earth and bringing all things into Christ. The age, as I will point out presently, is the Age of the Ages. It is the greatest age of all ages and is the time in which the Almighty God brings to completion the unfailing Word spoken before time began, "Let Us make man in Our image and after Our likeness." Secondly, God's people fail to see the final restitution of all things because they also fail to see the greatness of the work of Christ and the all-inclusive faith which God the Father has in that marvelous work of redemption. Thirdly, and perhaps most important of all, is the failure of God's people to see that all things are of God, that He is working all things according to the Counsel of His own will. Nothing has ever gone wrong with the merciful purpose of God. Once these three truths become clear to the spiritual mind of a devout child of God, then the mysteries of the ages disperse like mists before the rising sun and all the parts of the puzzle begin to fall into their appointed place to form a perfect blueprint of the progression of God's purpose through the ages. It is also important for us to understand the difference between time and eternity. Time is not eternity. There are many times and many dispensations, but there is only one eternity. Eternity does not begin; neither does it end, but times, dispensations, and ages all have beginnings and all have ends. It is wrong to assert that, when time ends, eternity will begin, because eternity has no beginning. Neither did it end when time began, as so many charts indicate. Ages have their place in eternity in the same way that minutes have their place in years, except that years end and eternity does not. Therefore it is very important that we make a clear distinction between ages, which belong to time, and eternity, which is timeless. It is more important still that we, in our study of the Bible, search out diligently those passages which refer to time and those which refer to eternity. In making this search, I strongly recommend that wherever possible the searcher avail himself of a good, exhaustive concordance such as Young's Analytical or Strong's, available at almost any good book store. Both of these give the correct meaning of every Greek and Hebrew word in the Bible." (<u>The Restitution Of All Things</u>, George Hawtin)

In addition to all of this, one must do a proper, unbiased study of the origin of the English word "hell", following up with an in-depth study of the words "Sheol" (Hebrew), "Hades", "Gehenna", and "Tartaroo" (Greek). You will be pleasantly surprised to find out that the true meanings of these words in no way denote a place of eternal torture! Finally, the words "olam" (Hebrew), "aion", and "aionios" (Greek) must be studied in order to uncover God's purpose of the ages.

You have been challenged with the thought that there will be a final harmony of all souls with God! Do you believe it? Do you care enough to study the things that have been presented to you to see whether or not they are so? What would glorify God the most? Some souls, many souls, or…

ALL SOULS?

June 25

THE MYSTERIES OF GOD

1ST Corinthians 4:1,2 states…Let a man so account of us, as of the ministers of Christ, and stewards of the mysteries of God. Moreover it is required in stewards, that a man be found faithful…

According to Ray Prinzing: "The word "mystery" also bears examination, for it comes from the Greek word "musterion", meaning: what is known only to the initiated, from a derivative of "muo," to shut the mouth. Through the idea of silence imposed by initiation, it comes to refer to a secret, or mystery. From the noun "mystery" comes the adjective "mystic" in reference to one who has been initiated into those secrets. We also have the adjective "mystical" as in reference to the **MYSTICAL BODY OF CHRIST**. This is defined as: Having a spiritual meaning, reality, neither apparent to the senses nor obvious to the intelligence (of the carnal mind). But it refers to an individual's direct communion with God through contemplation, vision, an inner light, giving spiritual insight." (Whispers Of The Mysteries, Ray Prinzing)

We are to see ourselves as stewards of the mysteries of God. The word "steward" means: a person who manages the domestic affairs of a family. We must first come to the understanding that God is a mystery to the carnal mind. The word "mystery" is also referred to as a "sacred secret". Wow! How awesome is that! God is a sacred secret, not known, understood, or perceived by human intellect. The mysteries of God must be "REVEALED" to a person by the Spirit of God. The revelation of the Spirit then enables us to become a steward (manager) of His mysteries, raising us up to be a faithful manager of these mysteries. WHAT A CALLING! WHAT AN AWESOME RESPONSIBILITY! WHAT AN EXCITING JOURNEY!

God's mysteries remain LOCKED to the spirit of pride, carnality, and human intellect. We must humble ourselves, asking the Father to reveal His mysteries to us. The goal is to avoid a lifetime of ever learning and never coming to the knowledge of the truth. We have not because we ask not. SO ASK, SEEK, AND KNOCK! It is our Father's good pleasure to give us of the mysteries of His Kingdom.

Over the next several days we will take a look into some of the wonderful mysteries of our Father's Kingdom. We should be filled with awe that God would entrust HIS MAGNIFICENT MYSTERIES to us, asking us to be faithful stewards over them!

SHOW US YOUR MYSTERIES O GOD!

June 26

THE MYSTERY OF BABYLON

Revelation 17:5,6 states…And upon her forehead was a name written, MYSTERY, BABYLON THE GREAT, THE MOTHER OF HARLOTS AND ABOMINATIONS OF THE EARTH. And I saw the woman drunk with the blood of the saints, and with the blood of the martyrs of Jesus: and when I saw her, I wondered with great admiration…

According to Ray Prinzing: "It takes the illumination of the Holy Spirit, imparting divine revelation, to discern between the true and the false. **So CONFUSED** has it all become, so interwoven is truth with error, that the nominal church-goer is not even aware of how much of his religion is actually anti-christ, against the truth. Only those who are "initiated" into God's Kingdom will be able to see clearly how vast Nimrod's kingdom has become. Furthermore, today Babylon is a union of religious, political, and economical mire-- expressed through three different avenues, yet all under the same Anti-Christ spirit. Catholicism, with all of her Protestant daughters, bespeak of the religious part of Babylon. Socialism, expressed through its various forms, has gripped all governments. While Zionism has certainly grabbed hold of the economical realm. All three are very intertwined: money, politics, religion all go hand in hand. This is evident in the little community church at the crossroads, to the vast denominations of our times. One man enterprises, to the vast dictatorial regimes. BABYLON!" (<u>Whispers Of The Mysteries</u>, Ray Prinzing)

The spirit of antichrist (Babylon) has infiltrated all areas of our society. It is present in our religion, economics, and politics. It is a spirit that says…I WANT TO MAKE A NAME FOR MYSELF, MY DENOMINATION, MY FORTUNE, AND MY POLITICAL AGENDA. This spirit can be traced all the way back to the book of Genesis. Genesis 11:4-9 tells us of the story of Nimrod, *his kingdom*, and of the Tower of Babel. The word "Babel" that is used in this passage of scripture means: confusion (by mixing). The word "Babylon" comes from the word "Babel" and means the same thing. The people spoken of in Genesis 11:4-9 wanted to build a city and a tower, whose top would reach unto heaven. They did all this that they might MAKE A NAME FOR THEMSELVES. The Lord stopped their plans of building a physical tower, but mankind has continued to go forward with the spirit of Babylon in his heart.

The city of Babylon was once a literal city. It is now a spiritual city that is made up of one man. That man is ADAM. "Babylon" represents the flesh, the efforts and thoughts of human intellect, and the carnal mind. It speaks of the spirit of antichrist that now operates in the children of disobedience (Ephesians 2:1,2). We must stop looking to the Middle East for a literal city called Babylon. As well, we must stop looking for the rise of one literal man who is supposed to be "The Antichrist". LOOK TO YOURSELVES (2ⁿᵈ John 1:8)!!!

It is time for the body of Christ to awaken to a proper understanding of Babylon (confusion) and the spirit of antichrist. It is time to hear the Father's call…***COME OUT OF HER, MY PEOPLE*** (Revelation 18:4)!!! Let us come out of the confusion of the Babylonian church system and into the revelation truth of our Heavenly Father!

COME OUT OF HER!

June 27

THE MYSTERY OF INIQUITY

According to Ray Prinzing: "For the mystery of iniquity does already work, only there is one who restrains now, until he may become from the midst. And then shall be revealed the lawless one, whom the Lord Jesus shall slay with the breath of His mouth and bring to nought by the manifestation of His presence." [2 Thessalonians 2:7-8, Clementson]. The King James Version gives "until he be **TAKEN OUT** of the way." But the Greek word here is **"BECOME"**. There is that which is **BECOMING FROM THE MIDST**, it is now in the process of being formed and brought to maturity, and until it has fully **BECOME**, all else is in restraint. **Creation is waiting-- for what?** The unveiling of the man of lawlessness? No ! Such does have an appointed time, but he cannot be revealed until those who are the **"WITHHOLDING" force have first BECOME. Creation is waiting for the manifestation of the sons of God."** (Whispers Of The Mysteries, Ray Prinzing)

So…What is this mystery of iniquity? What is iniquity? The word "iniquity" means LAWLESSNESS. This speaks of the condition that exists in the hearts of carnal men and women. As well, it speaks of the spirit of antichrist that now works in the children of disobedience. This is referred to as the prince of the power of the air. It is the fallen nature in man that opposes and exalts itself above all that is called God, or that is worshipped; so that he as God sits in the *temple of God*, showing himself that he is God (2ⁿᵈ Thessalonians 2:4)…Remember…WE ARE THE *TEMPLE* OF GOD!

This mystery of lawlessness remains a mystery to most people because they continue to look outside of themselves for this mysterious man of sin. They are waiting for him (the man of sin) to pop up in the Middle East at any moment, not realizing that this man of sin is ***WITHIN THEM!!!*** It is the sin in our members that remains in rebellion to the law of God. THIS IS INIQUITY! THIS IS LAWLESSNESS! THIS IS THE KEY THAT UNLOCKS THE MYSTERY! THE MAN OF SIN IS NOW BEING REVEALED TO YOU! LOOK IN THE MIRROR! IT IS ***YOU!*** IT IS YOUR CARNAL MIND!

REJOICE! The Lord is at work within you, destroying the carnality in you by the manifestation of His presence. He is filling "THE TEMPLE" with His glory!

According to Ray Prinzing:

"For after all is said and done,
The mystery fulfilled,
The universe shall know the depth
Of handiwork so skilled.
Iniquity shall have an end,
The Word on this is pure,
Its work complete, God shall be praised,
His grace shall e'er endure."
(Whispers Of The Mysteries, Ray Prinzing)

MAY GOD BE PRAISED!

June 28

THE MYSTERY OF GODLINESS

1ST Timothy 3:16 states…And without controversy great is the mystery of godliness: God was manifest in the flesh, justified in the Spirit, seen of angels, preached unto the Gentiles, believed on in the world, received up into glory…

According to Ray Prinzing: "The first key in understanding this mystery, as it relates to us, is in the fact that the word translated as "God" in the King James version, is not **"THEOS"** in the Greek text, but it is "hos" which means "who, or which," even as Wuest translates it, "**WHO** was made visible in the sphere of flesh." For while it gives the process as wrought out in our Lord Jesus Christ, it is also to be shared by those who are apprehended to become **ONE IN HIM.** Yes, "in all things He shall have preeminence." [Colossians 1:18]. Yet He is "the firstborn among many brethren," [Romans 8:29], for He is "bringing many sons unto glory." [Hebrews 2:10]. (Whispers Of The Mysteries, Ray Prinzing)

This transformation that takes us from sinfulness to godliness is definitely a mystery. IT IS A GLORIOUS MYSTERY! It is a mystery that is hidden from the natural man and from the natural mind. Remember…The natural man receives not the things of the Spirit of God: for they are foolishness unto him: neither can he know them, because they are spiritually discerned (1st Corinthians 2:14)…

John 1:1 states…In the beginning was the Word, and the Word was with God, and the Word was God…John 1:14 states…And the Word was made flesh, and dwelled among us…As you can see, the Word (God) was manifested in the flesh. God was personified in our Lord and Savior Jesus Christ. This was the beginning of the mystery of God being manifested unto the world. It was necessary for God to be manifested in the flesh for His mystery to come to the light. Jesus, as the "PATTERN SON OF GOD", has paved the way for the sons of God. We must follow in His footsteps. GOD MUST BE MANIFESTED IN OUR FLESH AS WELL!

Colossians 1:26 states…Even the mystery which has been hid from ages and from generations, BUT NOW IS MADE MANIFEST TO HIS SAINTS…the glory of this mystery among the Gentiles, WHICH IS CHRIST IN YOU, the hope of glory…This mystery of godliness is the process in which our Heavenly Father is to be manifested in and through His people. This results in a people who display the very nature of God, being justified in the Spirit, seen of angels (messengers), preached unto the Gentiles, believed on in the world, and received up into glory.

GREAT IS THE MYSTERY OF GODLINESS!

June 29

THE MYSTERY OF OUR CHANGE

1ST Corinthians 15:51-53 states…Behold, I show you a mystery; We shall not all sleep, but we shall all be changed, In a moment, in the twinkling of an eye, at the last trump: for the trumpet shall sound, and the dead shall be raised incorruptible, and we shall be changed. For this corruptible must put on incorruption, and this mortal must put on immortality…

According to Ray Prinzing: "Now, Paul spoke of our change also as threefold, **"in a moment, in the twinkling of an eye, IN (Greek is in not at) the last trump."** In a moment has dealt with substance, our being changed in the atoms to be of His own substance. Next we find that "in the twinkling of an eye" is concerned with condition, while "in the last trump" refers to time. Reading this verse superficially, we might be inclined to believe that the bodily change of God's people will take place in a split second, or in the time it takes to wink the eye. This may have its application, too, but as we have already stated, there is a being changed by degrees, from glory to glory, so that being changed is not just some drastic one-moment event, it is a process with a climax, the speed of the climax still to be revealed with the happening." (Whispers Of The Mysteries, Ray Prinzing)

This is the mystery of our change. IT IS A PROCESS WITH A CLIMAX! It is a total and complete change that involves our spirit, soul, and body. It is FULL AND COMPLETE REDEMPTION! It is a gradual change from glory to glory that will have a sudden and climactic conclusion. This process takes place in three stages. They are: justification, sanctification, and glorification. Our spirit is reborn as a result of believing on the Lord Jesus Christ, our soul is being transformed, and our bodies shall be changed.

This process remains a mystery to many due to the fact that they do not understand that salvation is a *process!* Most Christians have been taught that they are completely saved the moment that they walk an aisle to ask Jesus to forgive them. They are then taught to "hang on" and wait for a rapture that will cause them to go sailing through the clouds into eternal bliss while God pounds the earth with His wrath. This is very carnal teaching and causes many to remain as spiritual infants in Christ.

Ask the Father to reveal to you the mystery of your change. 2nd Corinthians 3:18 states…But we all, with open face beholding as in a glass the glory of the Lord, ARE CHANGED into the same image from glory to glory, even as by the Spirit of the Lord…WHAT A CHANGE! WHAT A PROCESS! WHAT A CLIMAX! We are being brought through God's three great love feasts.

They are:

    1. PASSOVER…THE SALVATION OF OUR SPIRIT
    2. PENTECOST…THE SALVATION OF OUR SOUL
    3. TABERNACLES…THE SALVATION OF OUR BODY

THANK GOD FOR OUR CHANGE!

June 30

THE MYSTERY OF HIS WILL

Ephesians 1:9,10 states…Having made known unto us the mystery of His will, according to His good pleasure which He has purposed in Himself: That in the dispensation of the fullness of times He might gather together in one all things in Christ, both which are in heaven, and which are on earth; even in Him…

Ephesians 1:9,10 (The New Testament In Modern Speech) states…He made known to us the secret of His will. And this is in harmony with God's merciful purpose for the government of the world when the times are ripe for it - the purpose which He has cherished in His own mind of restoring the whole creation to find its one Head in Christ; yes, the things in Heaven and things on earth, to find their one Head in Him…

This is one of the most powerful scriptures in the Bible. It gives us insight into THE MYSTERY OF GOD'S WILL. So…What is this mystery (sacred secret) of God's will? It is this: In the dispensation of the fullness of times God will gather together in one <u>ALL THINGS IN CHRIST</u>! YES…YOU HEARD IT RIGHT! ***ALL THINGS IN CHRIST!***

This remains a mystery to many due to the power of the traditions and doctrines of men. Christianity continues to conveniently find ways to *explain away* simple declarations in scripture that boldly proclaim the salvation of the entire human race in the ages to come. This is a result of the falling away that started with Constantine about 1,700 years ago. Constantine was instrumental in the legalization of Christianity. Christianity became a matter of fashion. The number of hypocrites and formal professors rapidly increased; strict discipline, zeal, self sacrifice, and brotherly love proportionally ebbed away; and many heathen customs and usages, under altered names, crept into the worship of God and the life of the Christian people. (<u>The Story Of Church History</u>, Community Bible Chapel)…This downward spiral of heathen and pagan influence in the church continued on into the Dark Ages. During this time the teaching of eternal torture became the primary message of the Catholic Church. This same message (eternal torture) was later adopted by the Protestant Church. It is ironic that this took place, for the Protestant Church prides itself in the fact that it broke away from the Catholic Church, not realizing that the very message of eternal torture that it preaches has its roots in the Catholic Church.

According to George Hawtin: "The dispensation of the fullness of times is the eighth dispensation. The dispensations of Innocence, Conscience, Human Government, Promise, Law, Grace and the Kingdom - these seven will have run their course and all will end in judgment, but the dispensation of the fullness of times is the eighth dispensation, and it will conclude all former things. It will end death, judgment, pain and tears, and its final act will be the delivering up of a perfect Kingdom to the Father of all. Then time will have reached its fullness and will be no more. The number eight in scripture is the number of new beginnings." (<u>The Restitution Of All Things</u>, George Hawtin)

GOD WILL MAKE ALL THINGS NEW!

July 1

THE MYSTERY OF FAITH

1ST Timothy 3:9 states…Holding the mystery of faith in a pure conscience…

According to Ray Prinzing: "Faith" is more than a tenet, a creed, a doctrine of theology. "Faith" is a living, vital confidence founded in the revelation of divine truth. When we possess and hold the mystic secret of "the faith", it does not refer to just "any faith," **but of "THE FAITH".** The identifying article **"the"** is used in the Greek text, and specifically identifies it as a certain faith, that **TRUTH** which was kept hidden from the world until revealed at the appointed time, and which is secret to ordinary eyes, but is made known by divine revelation. It bespeaks of truth which is only understood by the illumination of the Holy Spirit." (Whispers Of The Mysteries, Ray Prinzing)

The key to understanding "THE FAITH" is to be found in a person. The person that we are speaking of is the Lord Jesus Christ. The mystery of "the faith" is found in Who He is and what He has accomplished..

Many people have faith, but not "the faith". Some have faith in themselves, the stock market, their intelligence, their good looks, their riches, their job, their abilities, their denomination, their Pastor, and so on. As was just stated, this is faith, but not "the faith". True faith is exhibited when it is placed in the person and work (the cross) of the Lord Jesus Christ. All else is faith, but not "the faith".

Faith remains a mystery to many people due to the fact that they do not associate their faith with Christ and Him crucified. It is imperative that our faith be placed in the crucified and risen Christ. Colossians 2:14,15 states…Blotting out the handwriting of ordinances that was against us, which was contrary to us, and took it out of the way, nailing it to His cross; And having spoiled principalities and powers, He made a show of them openly, triumphing over them in it…2nd Corinthians 13:5 states…Examine yourselves, whether you are in "the faith"; prove your own selves…

ARE YOU IN "THE FAITH"?

July 2

THE MYSTERY OF THE GOSPEL

Ephesians 6:19,20 states…And for me, that utterance may be given unto me, that I may open my mouth boldly, to make known the mystery of the gospel, For which I am an ambassador in bonds: that therein I may speak boldly, as I ought to speak…

According to Ray Prinzing: "Galatians 5:11, "If I yet preach circumcision, why do I yet suffer persecution?" One might preach creed, politics, clothes-line holiness, etc. fighting this and that "ism", but there is no **GOOD NEWS** in any such preaching. Let those who do not have any **GOSPEL** proclaim such things, and let those who are being initiated into the good news, faithfully declare it." (Whispers Of The Mysteries, Ray Prinzing)

Within the meaning of the word "gospel" lies the understanding of the mystery of the gospel. The word "gospel" literally means good news or glad tidings.

According to Dr. E. W. Bullinger: "The "good news" was first heralded by angels sent specially from heaven; and the exact terms of the proclamation are recorded. The angel of Jehovah spoke from the glory of Jehovah, and said: "Behold I bring you good tidings of great joy, which shall be to all people. For unto you is born this day, in the city of David, a SAVIOR, which is CHRIST, THE LORD." Thus the good news concerned a Person, Who would "save His people from their sins" (Matthew 1:21): the Savior Whom God had anointed (Messiah), appointed, given, and sent." (Dr. E. W. Bullinger)

We are now able to see and admit that the gospel is the person and work of the Lord Jesus Christ, and that it results in GOOD TIDINGS OF GREAT JOY, WHICH SHALL BE TO <u>ALL PEOPLE</u>! Our failure to see that the effects of the gospel shall be extended to ALL PEOPLE is what causes many not to understand the mystery of the gospel. 2nd Corinthians 5:18,19 states…And all things are of God, Who has reconciled us to Himself by Jesus Christ, and has given to us the ministry of reconciliation; To wit, that God was in Christ, reconciling the world unto Himself, not imputing their trespasses unto them, and has committed unto us the word of reconciliation…WOW!

THAT IS GOOD NEWS! THAT IS GOOD TIDINGS OF GREAT JOY, WHICH SHALL BE TO <u>ALL PEOPLE</u>! THAT IS THE GOSPEL! Let us stop preaching our lists of dos and don'ts to people. THAT IS BAD NEWS! Let us tell the world that they are forgiven, saved, and reconciled, having been bought with a price. When people hear the TRUE GOSPEL they will *want* to repent and surrender their lives to the Lord of glory!

PREACH THE GOSPEL!

July 3

THE MYSTERY OF THE CHURCH

Ephesians 5:32 states…This is a great mystery: but I speak concerning Christ and the church…

According to Ray Prinzing: "You might "join" or "un-join" some man-made group, but **THE CHURCH is not something that can be joined. "The Lord added to the church daily such as should be saved." [Acts 2:47]. THE CALLED OUT ONES ARE GOD'S. He gives the calling, and He works it out experientially in each one.** The first time the word "church" is used in the New Testament, is found in Matthew 16:18, when Jesus said, "-- and upon this rock I will build My church; and the gates of hell shall not prevail against it." **The context reveals that it is upon the solid, divine revelation that HE is "the Christ, the Son of the living God,"** [Matthew 16:16], that the church is founded." (<u>Whispers Of The Mysteries</u>, Ray Prinzing)

The Greek word "ekklesia" means: assembly, or a gathering of called out ones. This would mean that the church is to be seen as a living and breathing organism. It is not a denomination, a building, or any certain religion. It is made up of people. WE ARE HIS CHURCH! Many people think that when they get up on Sunday morning that they are preparing to "go to church". It is hard to go to something that we already are. We must see ourselves as the very CHURCH OF THE LORD JESUS CHRIST. We have been called out of darkness into His marvelous light to show forth His praises in the earth. When we assemble ourselves together with other believers we are bringing "the church" to where we go. We are not going to a place to "have church", but we **are** the church, coming together to corporately share in the presence of God. In essence, we are coming together to form the Lord's body. ***IT IS TIME TO STOP HAVING CHURCH AND TO START BEING THE CHURCH!!!*** There is a difference.

The called out ones are those that have received a revelation from God. They have received the revelation that JESUS IS THE CHRIST (THE ANOINTED ONE), and that they are part of the many membered body of Christ. This understanding of the Lord's church remains a mystery to many due to the fact that they continue to look in the physical realm for a definition and explanation of the church. When you realize that you are the church of the Lord Jesus Christ you will stop waiting to press into His Kingdom. We must STOP limiting our relationship with the Lord to a building that we go to on Sunday morning or Wednesday night. WE ARE THE BUILDING OF THE LORD! WE ARE A SPIRITUAL HOME FOR THE PRESENCE OF THE LORD!

YOU ARE HIS CHURCH!

July 4

THE MYSTERY OF CHRIST

Colossians 4:3,4 states…praying also for us, that God would open unto us a door of utterance, to speak the mystery of Christ, for which I am also in bonds: That I may make it manifest, as I ought to speak…

According to Ray Prinzing: "For as the body is one, and has many members, and all members of that one body, being many, are one body; **SO ALSO IS THE CHRIST**. For by one Spirit (His) are we all baptized into one body . . . and have been all made to drink into one Spirit." [1 Corinthians 12:12-13]. There is a corporate Christ body of which **HE** is the Head. And to become a part of this body in its full expression of reality means more than just to have the beginnings of an anointing. It included the whole process of our identification in His death and resurrection, till even our body is changed like unto His glorious body. He went into the grave as Jesus, but He certainly came forth as **THE CHRIST**. There is dimension beyond dimension, in one glorious expression after another, until **HE** becomes the fullness that fills **ALL IN ALL**." (Whispers Of The Mysteries, Ray Prinzing)

The understanding of Christ remains a mystery to many due to the fact that they do not see the CORPORATE ASPECT and expression of the Christ. They recognize that Jesus is the Christ, which is right and proper, but they do not see that they too are a part of the Christ! Remember…

Christ is one, but has many members. Jesus is the head and we are His body. We are His fullness that fills all in all. Think about that. Jesus, the Christ, is not complete without His body. Once again, His body is the fullness of Him that fills all in all.

We must see that Jesus is THE CHRIST and we are HIS CHRIST. The word "Christ" means: the anointed One. Jesus is the anointed One, and in Him, we are His anointed ones. He is the anointed One with many anointed ones. THIS IS THE CHRIST!

Colossians 1:26,27 states…Even the mystery which has been hid from ages and from generations, but now is made manifest to His saints…which is CHRIST IN YOU, the hope of glory…We must see that the Christ has enlarged Himself. He is now a many membered man. The anointed One is in us.

THIS IS THE MYSTERY OF CHRIST!

July 5

THE MYSTERY OF THE KINGDOM

Matthew 13:10,11 states…And the disciples came, and said unto Him, Why do You speak unto them in parables? He answered and said unto them, Because it is given unto you to know the mysteries of the kingdom of heaven, but to them it is not given…

According to Dr. E. W. Bullinger: "The term "the Kingdom of heaven", occurs only in Matthew, where we find it thirty-two times. Matthew was divinely guided to retain the figure of speech literally ("heaven"), so as to be keeping with the special character, design, and scope of his gospel. But in the parallel passages in the other gospels we find, instead, the expression "the Kingdom of God". In other words, the term " the Kingdom of heaven" tells us where it is from, and the term "the Kingdom of God" tells us Who this Kingdom has for its Ruler." (Dr. E. W. Bullinger)

According to Ray Prinzing: "Paul taught very clearly that "the Kingdom of God is not meat and drink; but righteousness, and peace, and joy in the Holy Spirit." [Romans 14:17]. Meat and drink pertain to natural, earthly things. Righteousness, peace, and joy are spiritual, heavenly qualities. Righteousness does not spring out of carnal flesh, for such is corruptible. But righteousness can be made manifest in the sphere of our mortal flesh as an expression of **HIS INNER DWELLING**, for He is our righteousness." (Whispers Of The Mysteries, Ray Prinzing)

Luke 17:20,21 states…And when Jesus was demanded of the Pharisees, when the kingdom of God should come, He answered them and said, The kingdom of God comes not with observation: Neither shall they say, Lo here! Or, lo there! For, behold, the kingdom of God is within you…This is probably one of the most beautiful statements that Jesus ever made. Unfortunately, many people do not understand what Jesus was actually saying. Most people think that the Kingdom of God is a planet that they are going to "fly away to" one day. They always speak of it as though it is something off in the future, not realizing that it is WITHIN THEM. It is even more shocking that Jesus spoke these words to the PHARISEES. Have you ever stopped and thought about that? Jesus told the PHARISEES that the Kingdom of God was WITHIN THEM. WOW! How could that be true?

According to J. Preston Eby: "The Pharisees were treating as future what was already present. The Kingdom of God was right there *within them* if they could have understood it. "But," someone objects, "surely the Kingdom of God was not within those carnal, hateful, legalistic, Christ-rejecting Pharisees!" Some say that the correct translation should be: For the kingdom of God is *"in your midst,"* or *"among you,"* meaning that the Kingdom was present in their midst in the person of Jesus, "among" them but not "within" them. It cannot be denied—the Kingdom was indeed present among them in the very life of the Son of God, the King of glory! **But that is not the meaning of this passage.** The clearest meaning of the Greek can always be ascertained by *usage*. The way a word is *used* reveals its true meaning—the meaning that the Holy Spirit of inspiration puts upon it, not the meaning our English translators give it. It is a thing of wonder—the Holy Spirit has faithfully, powerfully, wisely and indisputably recorded for us the precise meaning of the word here translated "within". The Greek word is "ENTOS" meaning simply, according to Strong's Concordance, "inside; within". The word is used in only one other place in the New Testament, in Matthew 23:26. It is the Lord Jesus Himself that uses the word on both occasions, and notice what He says. "Woe unto you, scribes and Pharisees, hypocrites! for you make clean the *outside* of the cup and platter, but *within* they are full of extortion and excess. You blind Pharisee, cleanse first that which is *within* ("entos") the cup and platter, that the *outside* of them may be clean also." No one can argue that "ENTOS" means "in the midst" or "among" in this place—it clearly means "within". "Within" is contrasted with the "outside" of the cup and platter and plainly speaks of the pollution *within* the hearts of men, not *in their midst* or *among* them. The evil in men is not something apart from them or outside of them but something rooted deeply in the inward nature. The question follows—how could Jesus say to the same Pharisees that both corruption was within them and the Kingdom of God was within them! It sounds like an obvious contradiction. But it isn't. Paul spoke of a dual reality within man when he said, "For I delight in the law of God after the *inward man:* but I see another **law *in my members,*** warring against the law of my (spiritual) mind, and bringing me into captivity to the law of sin which is in my members" (Rom. 7:22-23). Little wonder that in desperation he cried out, "O wretched man that I am!" It is really very simple. The carnal, soulish heart of man is the seat of all uncleanness, just as the deeper spirit of man is the root of all godliness. So it is not surprising that the Pharisees failed to discover the presence of the Kingdom within them, for they were not walking after the spirit, but after the flesh." (The Kingdom Of God, J. Preston Eby)

THE KINGDOM IS WITHIN *YOU*!

THE GLORY OF GOD & THE HONOR OF KINGS

July 6

THE MYSTERY OF GOD

Revelation 10:7 states…But in the days of the voice of the seventh angel, when he shall begin to sound, the mystery of God should be finished, as He has declared to His servants the prophets…

According to Ray Prinzing: "The mystery began in Genesis, chapter one, and through all the processings, as mentioned in the various fragments of these mysteries that we have touched upon, we now come to its glorious fulfillment-- **THE MYSTERY OF God is to be accomplished, brought to the full, and ready for revelation. All of that which has been done in secret, the inner hidden work, is to be climaxed and made ready for all the universe to behold. We stand in awe before Him Who has worked so marvelous a purpose-- bringing forth "man in our image, after our likeness." [Genesis 1:26]. HE is bringing forth after His own kind, that He might be God of gods, King of kings, Lord of lords."** (Whispers Of The Mysteries, Ray Prinzing)

The mystery of God begins with Genesis 1:26 (Let Us make man in Our image) and ends with 1st Corinthians 15:28 (God shall be all in all). In order to make man into the image of God it takes God and man. It is a collective effort that involves man being radically changed into the image of His Creator. This is brought about by the SOVEREIGNTY OF GOD. With that being said though, man is not to be seen as a robot. Man does indeed play a part. His part is one of SUBMISSION to the sovereign will of God. His choices, if you will, are being brought in line with the sovereign will of God. Man is not being forced to serve God, but rather, he is being DRAWN by the Spirit of God to submit and relinquish his kingdom and his will to that of his Creator. God is bringing man to the place where he says…YOUR KINGDOM COME! YOUR WILL BE DONE IN ME! The making of man (the human race) into the image of God is to be seen as a process. It began with Adam in the Garden of Eden and will continue until God is all in all. The fall of Adam was NECESSARY! It was a schoolmaster to lead man through God's purpose of the ages.

Through the fall of Adam we learned that:

1. GOD IS SOVEREIGN
2. GOD CREATED ALL THINGS (GOOD AND EVIL)
3. GOD SUBJECTED THE CREATION TO VANITY
4. GOD WILL DELIVER THE CREATION FROM BONDAGE AND CORRUPTION

The mystery of God is being carried out according to His purpose one dispensation at a time. The recognized dispensations are: Innocence, Conscience, Human Government, Promise, Law, Grace, Kingdom, and the Dispensation of the Fullness of Times. Within these dispensations, God is drawing the creation to Himself in three great harvests. They are: Remnant, Nations, and World (all things).

The mystery of God can be seen and understood by reading the book of Job, especially the last chapter. The latter end of the creation will be greater than its former. This is the mystery and purpose of the ages, in which our God shall be everything to everyone.

HOW AWESOME IS OUR GOD!

July 7

THE MYSTERY OF ISRAEL'S BLINDNESS

Romans 11:25-27 states...For I would not, brethren, that you should be ignorant of this mystery, lest you should be wise in your own conceits; that blindness in part is happened to Israel, until the fullness of the Gentiles be come in. And so all Israel shall be saved: as it is written, There shall come out of Sion the Deliverer, and shall turn away ungodliness from Jacob: For this is My covenant unto them, when I shall take away their sins...

The apostle Paul tells us that we are to consider the mystery of Israel's blindness, not remaining in ignorance to the fact that they are not forgotten, but that they are still a special people to God, for they shall all be saved after God's dealings with them in the ages to come. If we do not understand this mystery we will be wise in our own conceits. This speaks of being wise in our own eyes, but not having the wisdom of the Lord.

According to Ray Prinzing: "Consider the uniqueness of God's operation, **"For God has concluded them all in unbelief, that He might have mercy upon all."** [Romans 11: 32]. The Greek word here for "concluded" literally means "shut up together." Israel was called and chosen to be God's special people, and through whom He would bless all nations. And then comes this rarity of His operation, He took Israel, scattered her among all nations, hardened their hearts and shut them up in unbelief with all nations, and then purposes to have **MERCY UPON ALL**-- upon all Israel, and upon all nations among whom they have been scattered." (Whispers Of The Mysteries, Ray Prinzing)

Why would God operate in this manner concerning His chosen people? Let us consider a few scriptures that do shed some light on this mystery.

Romans 11:11,12 states...I say then, Have they stumbled that they should fall? God forbid: but rather through their fall salvation is come unto the Gentiles, for to provoke them to jealousy. Now if the fall of them be the riches of the world, and the diminishing of them the riches of the Gentiles; how much more their fullness?...Romans 11:15 states...For if the casting away of them be the reconciling of the world, what shall the receiving of them be, but life from the dead?...Romans 11:26 states...And so all Israel shall be saved...Romans 11:30-32 states...For as you in times past have not believed God, yet have now obtained mercy through their unbelief: Even so have these also now not believed, that through your mercy they also may obtain mercy. For God has concluded them all in unbelief, that He might have mercy upon all...Romans 11:32 (Today's English Version) states...FOR GOD HAS MADE ALL PEOPLE PRISONERS OF DISOBEDIENCE, SO THAT HE MIGHT SHOW MERCY TO THEM ALL...

CAN YOU SEE IT? DO YOU GRASP IT? The blindness of Israel in part will result in the RECONCILING OF THE WORLD! Romans 11:33 states...O the depth of the riches both of the wisdom and knowledge of God! how unsearchable are His judgments, and His ways past finding out!...

FOR OF HIM, AND THROUGH HIM, AND TO HIM, ARE ALL THINGS: TO WHOM BE GLORY FOREVER. AMEN!

July 8

THE MYSTERY OF THE FATHER

Colossians 2:2,3 states…That their hearts might be comforted, being knit together in love, and unto all riches of the full assurance of understanding, to the acknowledgement of the mystery of God, and of the Father, and of Christ; In whom are hid all the treasures of wisdom and knowledge…

According to Ray Prinzing: "I came forth from the Father, and am come into the world: again, I leave the world, and go to the Father." [John 16:28]. Furthermore, "It is expedient for you that I go away." [John 16:7]. What was He saying? God, omnipotent, omnipresent Spirit, invisible, **THE FATHER SOURCE,** dwelled in the man Christ Jesus, manifested as **SON.** In this realm there was limitation, "The Son can do nothing of Himself, but what He sees the Father do." [John 5:19]. As the Spirit (Father) directed, so He did. Faithful, obedient, He sought not His own will, but only to fulfill the will of the Father. Men knew Him as Jesus, they could not see the Father in Him. But furthermore, it was necessary to leave the realm of limitation (sonship) behind, and to return into **His FATHERHOOD POSITION,** so that He might fulfill those purposes which were beyond the realms of sonship. The very fact of "being in the form of a servant, made in the likeness of men," [Philippians 2:7] meant limitation. Jesus knew His position as a **SON,** but He also knew of His position as **FATHER,** and that it was expedient for Him to return to that realm from which He would be able to impart, pour out of Himself, as the Source for every need." (Whispers Of The Mysteries, Ray Prinzing)

YES…Jesus was the Father manifested in the flesh. The understanding of the Father remains a mystery to many people due to the common, traditional error of trying to make the Father and the Son as two separate beings. When we use the term "THE SON OF GOD", we are to understand this as God in the form of the Son. God, the eternal Word, was made flesh, and dwelled among us. Here is a list of some other scriptures to help you understand the mystery of the Father: Isaiah 9:6, John 10:30-33, and John 14:8-9.

The mystery of the Father was manifested in the Son. Jesus, the everlasting Father (Isaiah 9:6), was the Word made flesh, Who dwelled among us, (and we beheld His glory, the glory as of the only begotten of the Father,) full of grace and truth (John 1:14).

WHEREBY WE CRY, ABBA, FATHER!

July 9

THE MYSTERY OF THE SEVEN STARS

Revelation 1:20 states…The mystery of the seven stars which you saw in My right hand, and the seven golden candlesticks. The seven stars are the angels of the seven churches: and the seven candlesticks which you saw are the seven churches…

According to Ray Prinzing: "Revelation 2:1 carries right on with this, adding one more word to the phrase, "These things says He that **HOLDS** the seven stars in His right hand . . . " We note the word "holds"-- from the Greek "krateo" **TO LAY HOLD ON.** God has, and **IS** laying hold of, apprehending a people for Himself. **They are becoming a part of His RIGHT HAND COMPANY.** They are so held by Him, that His hand cannot move without them being moved with it. Furthermore, they don't move until the hand moves. But becoming totally one in the **WILL** of the right hand, when moved it is with all the ability, power, authority of that hand." (Whispers Of the Mysteries, Ray Prinzing)

Let us now try to point out a few things concerning this mystery. We are told that the seven stars are the seven angels of the seven churches. We are then told that they are in the Lord's right hand. The Greek word for "angel" is "aggelos", literally a messenger. The word "angel" is not the translation of the Greek word, only its English spelling. The term "right hand" speaks of power and strength. "Hereafter shall we see the Son of Man sitting on the RIGHT HAND OF POWER" (Matthew 26:64)…The term "seven churches" speaks of the seven (spiritual perfection) church ages:

1. EPHESUS - APOSTOLIC CHURCH
2. SMYRNA - MARTYR CHURCH
3. PERGAMOS - STATE CHURCH
4. THYATIRA - PAPAL CHURCH
5. SARDIS - REFORMATION CHURCH
6. PHILADELPHIA - MISSIONARY CHURCH
7. LAODICEA - APOSTATE CHURCH

We can now see and understand that the mystery of the seven stars speaks of God, throughout the church ages, laying hold of a remnant (His messengers), and elevating them to a position of power, strength, and authority.

According to Ray Prinzing: "**These stars shall give forth His light, HIS MESSAGE,** to stand and feed in the strength of the Lord, in the power of His right hand. They shall abide-- not like unto those who rise up in a brilliant display to dash across the heavens, and burn out-- these are **FIXED in God**, positioned in the place He has prepared for them, and prepared them for. They are His sign of **PEACE** when the enemy would tread in the palace-- seeking to usurp the dominion. They shall destroy the adversaries with the brightness of their shining, and they shall restore righteousness in all the earth. "Peace on earth, good will toward men." (Whispers Of The Mysteries, Ray Prinzing)

READ DANIEL 12:3!

July 10

THE FELLOWSHIP OF THE MYSTERY

Ephesians 3:9 states…And to make all men see what is the fellowship of the mystery, which from the beginning of the world has been hid in God, Who created all things by Jesus Christ…

According to Ray Prinzing: "Fellowship-- the act of sharing in common. **"For as in Adam all die, even so in Christ shall all be made alive. But every man in his own order."** [1 Corinthians 15:22-23]. As every man is regenerated, to receive the **LIFE** of Jesus Christ, and oneness with the Father, they shall also be enriched with the knowledge of **HIS mysteries--they shall KNOW.** Because, Moffatt goes on, in his translation, He is **"intending to let the full sweep of the divine wisdom be disclosed now by the church (His called out)."** The Amplified-- "The purpose is that through the church the complicated, many-sided wisdom of God in all its infinite variety and innumerable aspects might now be made known…" (<u>Whispers Of The Mysteries</u>, Ray Prinzing)

Many at this present time do not comprehend the mysteries of God. They are too enchanted by their denominational ideas about God. When they are exposed to the deeper truths of God they suddenly say…"That's too deep for me. I think I will just go back to the basics." This is a normal reaction that we are to expect from people when they are exposed to the deeper things of God. We must not be offended or upset at this person. THEY ARE HELD CAPTIVE, BEING IN BONDAGE TO THE CARNAL MIND. THEY ARE IN BABYLONIAN CAPTIVITY! We must love and forgive them as they go through the process of coming out of Babylon.

According to Ray Prinzing: "On the other hand, there are some truths which can only be **SHARED IN COMMON** by those who have been duly processed by the way of the cross, death to self, set apart unto the Lord, and led by His Spirit into more truth. When someone suddenly says, "that's too deep for me," if you want to share fellowship with them, you have to leave the mystery truths and find a common basis on what they do know, as far as they have gone in their walk with Christ. An adult can enjoy a short conversation with a child, but they also need that in-depth sharing with their own peers. Therefore we are admonished to grow up into Him, and be no more children." (<u>Whispers Of The Mysteries</u>, Ray Prinzing)

This is the fellowship of the mystery. It is lonely at times, but God will be faithful to bring truth-seeking people into our path who are of the same mind. God will also bring us into the path of others who need to be encouraged. SO BE READY! The fellowship of the mystery will eventually include all men. Of this we are sure, for the scripture tells us so. In the meantime, be encouraged in knowing that it is given unto you to know the mysteries of the Kingdom of heaven (Matthew 13:11). Blessed are your eyes, for they see: and your ears, for they hear (Matthew 13:16)…

TO GOD BE THE GLORY!

July 11

THE LAKE OF FIRE

Most people who read about, talk about, or preach about the lake of fire do not have the foggiest idea what these words mean. They assume that it is a literal lake of fire designed for the purpose of perpetually tormenting people. Let us take a fresh look at this lake. We will be pleasantly surprised to find out the true meaning of these words.

We must ask ourselves these questions:

  1. WHAT IS THE NATURE OF THIS FIRE?
  2. IS IT LITERAL OR SYMBOLIC?
  3. WHAT IS THE DURATION OF THIS FIERY JUDGMENT?

Daniel 7:9,10 states…I beheld till the thrones were cast down, and the Ancient of Days did sit, Whose garment was white as snow, and the hair of His head like the pure wool: His throne was like the fiery flame, and His wheels as burning fire. A fiery stream issued and came forth from before Him: thousand thousands ministered unto Him, and ten thousand times ten thousand stood before Him: the judgment was set, and the books were opened…Revelation 20:11-15 states…And I saw a great white throne, and Him that sat on it, from Whose face the earth and the heaven fled away; and there was found no place for them. And I saw the dead, small and great, stand before God; and the books were opened: and another book was opened, which is the book of life: and the dead were judged out of those things which were written in the books, according to their works. And the sea gave up the dead which were in it; and death and hell (Hades - the grave) delivered up the dead which were in them: and they were judged every man according to their works. And death and hell (Hades - the grave) were cast into the lake of fire. This is the second death. And whosoever was not found written in the book of life was cast into the lake of fire…

According to Dr. Harold Lovelace: "The lake of fire has been used to scare people, and it was not meant to do so. The lake of fire is only recorded a number of five times in Revelation 19, 20, and 21 by the Greek word #4442 pur. Check again in your Concordance, and you will find that the verses that read "Holy Ghost and fire, hell fire, unquenchable fire, ministers a flame of fire, fiery indignation, God is a consuming fire, lake of fire and brimstone, and the overcomers stand on a sea of glass mingled with fire." These terms are from this same word pur. Therefore it is the same fire in all these places. Now notice that in Mark 14:54 when Peter warmed himself by a fire, it is a different Greek word. Another word used to bring fear is brimstone. Yet when its meaning is looked up in a dictionary, you will discover that its meaning today is sulphur. It is called the king of chemicals. Even in recent years it has been used for medical purposes. What is interesting is that in your Concordance it is listed as #2303, theion, and its root word is #2304, theios, meaning Godlike, divine power. Its root word is #2316 which is theos, meaning God or divinity. Now we can see the importance of being baptized with the Holy Ghost and FIRE and understanding Hebrews 12:29, "For our God is a consuming FIRE." For sure, He knows how to cleanse / purify us to make us in His image." (Read And Search God's Plan, Dr. Harold Lovelace)

As we can see, the words "lake of fire and brimstone" mean: DIVINE PURIFICATION! Daniel saw it as a stream and John saw it as a lake. Can we now see that the words "lake of fire and brimstone" are to be understood symbolically, portraying a spiritual fire that is by nature corrective, and for the purpose of purification? This lake of fire speaks of God Himself and His ministers, for our God IS a consuming fire, making His ministers a flaming fire (Hebrews 12:29 and Psalm 104:4).

This experience of purification is to be for a period of time. IT IS NOT FOREVER! This can be discovered by studying the words "olam", "aion", and "aionios", which words do show that God's judgments are "of the ages", but not to continue past the ages, for the ages shall come to an end, and God shall be ALL IN ALL! -OUR GOD IS A CONSUMING FIRE!-

July 12

THE FIRST AND SECOND RESURRECTION - PART 1

Revelation 20:4-6 states…And I saw thrones, and they sat upon them, and judgment was given unto them: and I saw the souls of them that were beheaded for the witness of Jesus, and for the Word of God, and which had not worshipped the beast, neither his image, neither had received his mark upon their foreheads, or in their hands; and they lived and reigned with Christ a thousand years. But the rest of the dead lived not again until the thousand years were finished. This is the first resurrection. Blessed and holy is he that has part in the first resurrection: on such the second death has no power, but they shall be priests of God and of Christ, and shall reign with Him a thousand years…

Revelation 20:14,15 states…And death and hell (Hades - the grave) were cast into the lake of fire. This is the second death. And whosoever was not found written in the book of life was cast into the lake of fire…(This is the second {general} resurrection)

John 5:28,29 states…Marvel not at this: for the hour is coming, in the which all that are in the graves shall hear his voice, And shall come forth; they that have done good, unto the resurrection of life; and they that have done evil, unto the resurrection of damnation (judgment)…(This speaks of the righteous and wicked in the second resurrection)

Daniel 12:2 states…And many of them that sleep in the dust of the earth shall awake, some to everlasting (age-lasting) life, and some to shame and everlasting (age-lasting) contempt…(This speaks of the righteous and wicked in the second resurrection)

The apostle John tells us in the book of Revelation that there is a "first" resurrection. This would then tell us that there is a "second" resurrection to come at a later time. The first resurrection happens 1,000 years before the second (general) resurrection. Hebrews 11:35 tells us that the Hebrew people served God in order to obtain a *BETTER RESURRECTION*. If there is a better resurrection, then there is also another resurrection that is less desirable. It is important to understand and distinguish between these two resurrections.

Over the next few days we will attempt to look at, understand, and dissect the all-important subject of resurrection, including the nature of resurrection, seeking to understand the spiritual and physical aspects of the term resurrection. But rest assured. There shall be a first and second resurrection, in which lies the hope of all humanity, whether just or unjust.

THANK GOD FOR THE FIRST AND SECOND RESURRECTION!

July 13

THE FIRST AND SECOND RESURRECTION - PART 2

According to Dr. Stephen Jones: "The apostle Paul clearly speaks of a single resurrection in which both "the righteous and the wicked" are raised. This cannot be the first resurrection, wherein only those "blessed and holy" shall be raised. Paul must be referring to the general resurrection of ALL the dead, small and great, including both righteous and wicked people—all who did not inherit the first resurrection. Paul makes it very clear (as does Jesus) that in this general resurrection there will be found both Christians and non-Christians. The Christians will be found written in "the book of life;" the rest will be judged and "cast into the lake of fire." And so it is clear that there will be Christians raised in BOTH the first and the second resurrections. Those raised in the first will reign with Christ for a thousand years; the others will miss this, yet will receive life (immortality) at that later time. Hence, the scriptures make a distinction between the overcomers and the church in general." (The Purpose Of Resurrection, Dr. Stephen Jones)

Luke 12:35-50 sheds much light on the subject of resurrection, ruling and reigning, and judgment for the purpose of correction. This passage speaks to us of three classes of people:

1. FAITHFUL SERVANT - made ruler over all that God has…those in the first resurrection (Revelation 2:26).
2. UNFAITHFUL SERVANT - appointed his portion with the unbelievers to be corrected… those in the second resurrection (1st Corinthians 3:12-15).
3. UNBELIEVER - appointed for correction and purification…those in the second resurrection (Revelation 20:11-15).

We must take note of these three classes of people. There are "overcomers", "unfaithful servants", and "unbelievers". We must also take note of their just retribution. The overcomers are rewarded with the first resurrection, being given the privilege of ruling and reigning with Jesus Christ. The unfaithful servants and unbelievers await fiery judgment for the purpose of correction. The unfaithful servant is saved like as by fire (1st Corinthians 3:12-15), and the unbeliever is cast into the lake of fire. Remember…Our God is a consuming fire! This fire is a purifying, cleansing, and spiritual fire that consumes wood, hay, and stubble (the carnality within man). As well, take note of the different levels or degrees of correction. Some are beaten with few stripes, and some are beaten with many stripes. This is not talking about a literal beating, but is referring to heavy or light correction (judgment). This is the second (general) resurrection that includes just and unjust people.

According to Dr. Stephen Jones: "1st Corinthians 3:12-15 does not deal with the judgment of unbelievers. It deals strictly with believers who have laid Jesus Christ as the Foundation of their "temples." Once that foundation is laid, the man is a Christian. Paul then discusses the works of the Christian in terms of what he builds upon that Foundation. He makes it clear that Christians, at least some of them, will find their works judged by the fire of God. If his works are unacceptable, he will still be saved, yet will suffer loss, for the fiery law of God will burn up all the dross. This passage is interesting, because it shows there will be Christians in the second resurrection. Further, these Christians will be judged by the same law, the "lake of fire" that will judge the unbelievers. The only difference is that they will be given Life after their works have been tested and revealed in the fire, while the unbelievers themselves will be brought into a longer and more severe judgment as prescribed in the law." (The Purpose Of Resurrection, Dr. Stephen Jones)

PRESS IN…FAITHFUL AND WISE STEWARD!

July 14

QUALIFYING FOR THE FIRST RESURRECTION - PART 1

In light of the fact that there is a <u>first</u> and <u>second</u> resurrection, and that the first resurrection is a *better resurrection*, the next logical line of thought would be:

1. How do I obtain a better resurrection?
2. How does one qualify for the first resurrection?

Luke 14:12-14 states…Then said He also to him that bade Him, When you make a dinner or a supper, call not your friends, nor your brethren, neither your kinsmen, nor your rich neighbors; lest they also bid you again, and a recompense be made to you. But when you make a feast, call the poor, the maimed, the lame, the blind: And you shall be blessed; for they cannot recompense you: for you shall be recompensed at the resurrection of the just…As well, Matthew 18:21-35 sheds much light on what qualifies a person to be raised in the first resurrection. This passage (parable) is about FORGIVENESS! In light of Luke 14:12-14 and Matthew 18:21-35, we can see that an OVERCOMER is a LOVER and a FORGIVER. An overcomer is one who does things for others, being motivated by the love (agape) of God, not expecting anything in return. As well, he is one who FORGIVES (releases others from their debt) ALL PEOPLE!

According to Dr. Stephen Jones: "To attain the first resurrection, "the resurrection of the just," one must know and practice the principle of grace and *agape* love. This is the highest form of love, for it is the love of God. More importantly, he who would qualify for the first resurrection must have the grace to hold no grudges. He must forgive from his heart the sins (debts) of those who have transgressed against him. This is made plain in many of Jesus' parables, most notably the one in Matt. 18:21-35. There we find that God will cancel the debts (sins) of those who appeal to Him for grace. He must learn the principle of the Jubilee, the cancellation of all "debt," for this is the key to receiving one's inheritance, the promise of God." (The Purpose Of Resurrection, Dr. Stephen Jones)

WE ARE CALLED TO LOVE AND FORGIVE!

July 15

QUALIFYING FOR THE FIRST RESURRECTION - PART 2

As we have already established, an OVERCOMER (one who qualifies for the first resurrection) is a LOVER and a FORGIVER. Let us continue with this thought, delving deeper into the specifics of a lover and a forgiver.

The key to understanding love and forgiveness is to be found in the law of God, more specifically, the law of Jubilee. The Jubilee is about forgiveness, including the cancellation and forgiveness of debts. This can be found in Leviticus 25:8-10. This law was a type and shadow of Jesus Christ. He, as God manifested in the flesh, came to this earth to forgive and cancel the sin debt of the whole world. JESUS IS THE JUBILEE! WE ARE FORGIVEN! WE ARE LOVED! We have been reconciled (2nd Corinthians 5:18-21) and made to be reconcilers.

According to Dr. Stephen Jones: "God has made all men victims of injustice in some manner. All have experienced the injustice of sin. Most men become angry and often quite bitter over these injustices. But those who know the heart of God and the character of Jesus Christ may learn how to deal with these injustices in a somewhat unusual manner. They understand that God is sovereign, and that nothing happens to them, except that God has the knowledge and the power to work it out for their good (Romans 8:28). Those who truly believe this are the ones who do not become angry when they are personally subjected to injustice. They have learned to forgive those who wrong them and to rejoice when men persecute them. More than that, the overcomers are people who have experienced the Jubilee. That is, they have learned to release men from bondage and the prison house of sin (debt). They have learned not to hold grudges against their persecutors, but to rejoice that God has found them worthy to undergo these trials of faith. These are overcomers. The primary qualification of an overcomer--one who aspires to attain to the Feast of Tabernacles--is to be a forgiver." (The Laws Of The Second Coming, Dr. Stephen Jones)

God is going to place the overcomers in a position of rulership (Revelation 2:26) in His Kingdom. THIS IS THE FIRST RESURRECTION! They will administer the law of God in righteousness to all the earth.

WE SHALL RULE THE NATIONS!

July 16

WHAT WILL THE RESURRECTION BE LIKE? - PART 1

What type of body will we have in the resurrection? Will our resurrected body be physical or spiritual? What will be the nature of our resurrected body? Does the Bible answer these questions? Is there a pattern or type for us to look at to determine what our resurrected bodies will be like?

According to Dr. Stephen Jones: "The first and most important pattern is that Jesus was raised bodily from the tomb. The disciples came to the tomb to look for Him, but He had risen. His resurrection was NOT the same thing as His ascension, or going to heaven. It was a physical, literal event, "as He said" (Matt. 28:6). In other words, when Jesus talked of the resurrection prior to that time, He meant to convey the literal meaning of the term, not a "spiritual" event in the sense that some take it. The only real question is "with what body do they come?" (1 Cor. 15:35?) Is the resurrected body physical or spiritual? The answer is: **BOTH**. He had a heavenly Father and an earthly mother, and the resurrected body was the culmination of that relationship. He could enter the spiritual dimension ("heaven") or the physical, earthly dimension at will. His Father had given Him all authority in BOTH realms, even as He said in Matt. 28:18 (NASB), [18] **. . . All authority has been given to Me in heaven and on earth.** As a result, He could take a physical form where the disciples could touch Him and see the wounds of His crucifixion (John 20:27). He could also eat food with the disciples (John 21:13; Luke 24:43). Then He could vanish (Luke 24:31) just as suddenly by taking spirit form. The question of whether Jesus was merely a spirit or if He had physical characteristics is faced and answered squarely in Luke 24:36-43." (The Purpose Of Resurrection, Dr. Stephen Jones)

Luke 24:36-43 states…And as they spoke, Jesus Himself stood in the midst of them, and said unto them, Peace be unto you. But they were terrified and affrighted, and supposed that they had seen a spirit. And He said unto them, Why are you troubled? and why do thoughts arise in your hearts? Behold My hands and My feet, that it is I Myself: handle Me, and see; for a spirit has not flesh and bones, as you see me have. And when He had spoken, He showed them His hands and His feet. And while they yet believed not for joy, and wondered, He said unto them, Have you here any meat? And they gave Him a piece of a broiled fish, and of an honeycomb. And He took it, and did eat before them…

Notice that Jesus said nothing about having blood. He only mentions flesh and bone. We must see the reality that Jesus was raised with a physical body. This physical body, though, was not limited to the physical world. He had access to the physical and spiritual realms. As well, we must see His resurrection as the *PATTERN* for our resurrection, for Jesus is the PATTERN SON OF GOD. His body has become the pattern for our own resurrected body!

WE SHALL BE LIKE HIM!

July 17

WHAT WILL THE RESURRECTION BE LIKE? - PART 2

Ezekiel 44:15-19 states…But the priests the Levites, the sons of Zadok, that kept the charge of My sanctuary when the children of Israel went astray from Me, they shall come near to Me to minister unto Me, and they shall stand before Me to offer unto Me the fat and the blood, says the Lord GOD: They shall enter into My sanctuary, and they shall come near to My table, to minister unto Me, and they shall keep My charge. And it shall come to pass, that when they enter in at the gates of the inner court, they shall be clothed with linen garments; and no wool shall come upon them, while they minister in the gates of the inner court, and within. They shall have linen bonnets upon their heads, and shall have linen breeches upon their loins; they shall not gird themselves with any thing that causes sweat. And when they go forth into the utter court, even into the utter court to the people, they shall put off their garments wherein they ministered, and lay them in the holy chambers, and they shall put on other garments; and they shall not sanctify the people with their garments…

According to Dr. Stephen Jones: "Ezekiel is telling us that these "sons of Zadok" have authority to move in the inner sanctuary of God (which represents the spiritual realm) as well as the outer court (the earthly realm). In other words, they will move with the same calling and anointing that Jesus had after His resurrection. They will have authority in both the spiritual and the physical worlds. Thus, when they minister to God in the spiritual realm, they put on their linen "garments;" but when they come into the physical world, they put on their "woolens" (fleshly bodies). In essence, when Jesus suddenly appeared to His disciples in that closed room, He had simply "put on His woolen garments." Wool comes from animals; linen comes from plants. In His woolen garments, He showed the disciples His hands and feet, and He ate fish and honey in their presence. When He finished ministering to His disciples in the "outer court," dressed in His "woolens," He simply changed into His linen garments (spiritual body), stepped into the sanctuary of heaven, and disappeared before their eyes." (The Purpose Of Resurrection, Dr. Stephen Jones)

As you can see, our resurrected bodies will be fashioned like unto the glorious resurrected body of our Lord and Savior Jesus Christ, for He is the *pattern* for all things that pertain to the sons of God. There will be no more limitations. We will be able to be seen and able to vanish. These bodies will not be limited by time and space. This is what Paul referred to as the *MANIFESTATION OF THE SONS OF GOD.* Jesus Christ will be manifested in and through the overcomers in all His fullness. Philippians 3:21 states…Who shall change our vile body, that it may be fashioned like unto His glorious body, according to the working whereby He is able even to subdue…

ALL THINGS UNTO HIMSELF!

July 18

THOSE WHO DO NOT BELIEVE IN THE RESURRECTION, OR SAY IT IS ALREADY PAST - PART 1

Some say there is to be no resurrection. Others spiritualize the resurrection, saying it has already taken place in their lives. They claim that there is no bodily resurrection that is yet futuristic. Let us look to the scriptures to see if these statements are valid or not.

Matthew 22:23,29 states…The same day came to Him the Sadducees, which say that there is no resurrection, and asked Him…Jesus answered and said unto them, You do err, not knowing the scriptures, nor the power of God…1st Corinthians 15:12-19 states…Now if Christ be preached that He rose from the dead, how say some among you that there is no resurrection of the dead? But if there be no resurrection of the dead, then is Christ not risen: And if Christ be not risen, then is our preaching vain, and your faith is also vain. Yes, and we are found false witnesses of God; because we have testified of God that He raised up Christ: whom He raised not up, if so be that the dead rise not. For if the dead rise not, then is not Christ raised: And if Christ be not raised, your faith is vain; you are yet in your sins. Then they also which are fallen asleep in Christ are perished. If in this life only we have hope in Christ, we are of all men most miserable…(As well, read verses 20-28.) Daniel 12:2 states…And many of them that sleep in the dust of the earth shall awake, some to everlasting life (age-abiding life), and some to shame and everlasting contempt (age-abiding abhorrence)…John 5:28,29 states…Marvel not at this: for the hour is coming, in the which all that are in the graves shall hear His voice, And shall come forth; they that have done good, unto the resurrection of life; and they that have done evil, unto the resurrection of damnation (judgment)…

According to Dr. Stephen Jones: "Paul makes it clear that the resurrection of Jesus Christ is the pattern for our own resurrection as well. The only reason we shall be raised from the dead is because Christ was raised as the Pattern Son. Paul's argument shows the inherent contradiction of this Sadducee doctrine. If there is no such thing as resurrection, but that man simply goes to heaven when he dies, then Jesus was not raised. But if Jesus was not raised, then we are yet in our sins, because he "*was raised again for our justification*" (Rom. 4:25). So the only way we attain the promise of God is if Jesus was raised from the dead. But if He was, it is the pattern of our own resurrection as well. That is the path of Paul's logic." (The Purpose Of Resurrection, Dr. Stephen Jones)

HOW CAN WE SAY THERE IS NO RESURRECTION OF THE DEAD?

July 19

THOSE WHO DO NOT BELIEVE IN THE RESURRECTION,
OR SAY IT IS ALREADY PAST - PART 2

There are those who say that the first resurrection is already past. Some believe that it has already taken place, and use Matthew 27:50-54 to justify their teaching. Others spiritualize the idea of resurrection, using passages of scripture such as Ephesians 2:6, claiming that resurrection is a spiritual thing only. There are even some who believe the first resurrection took place in 70 A.D. at the destruction of Jerusalem. As well, some believe it took place before World War I . The apostle Paul had to deal with this issue even in his day. He is recorded as having denounced certain teachers who said that the resurrection was already past.

2nd Timothy 2:17,18 states…And their word will eat as does a canker: of whom is Hymenaeus and Philetus; Who concerning the truth have erred, saying that the resurrection is past already; and overthrow the faith of some…It is not possible that they were referring to the resurrection of Christ, for Paul would have agreed with that. They were obviously referring to the first resurrection, the resurrection of the righteous (just), to which Paul did not agree. Paul clearly stated that he had not attained to the resurrection yet in Philippians 3:11,12.

According to Dr. Stephen Jones: "Some Christians spiritualize the first resurrection. This is accomplished by <u>redefining</u> resurrection in terms of justification by faith. Once spiritualized, it is an easy transition into a total denial of the bodily resurrection of the dead. The scriptures do tell us that through faith we move from death into life. However, the actual word "resurrection" (Gr. *anastasis*) is never used to describe the process by which one becomes a Christian. Every passage clearly speaks of resurrection in a literal sense, where those who have died rise to stand upon the earth." (<u>The Purpose Of Resurrection</u>, Dr. Stephen Jones)

DON'T LET YOUR FAITH BE OVERTHROWN!

July 20

THE 1,700-YEAR NIGHTMARE

According to Jim Rutz: "The 1,700-year nightmare is over: the Constantinian Shift is shifting back. Under Emperor Constantine, the church became an imperial audience, but is now finally freeing itself from the corset of state control. An unprecedented transfer of divine power is underway, from clerics into the hands of ordinary people. This is giving rise to an entirely new form of Christianity - with far greater repercussions than the Protestant Reformation. **The church is transforming itself from an organization to an organism.** After 1,700 years of institutional structure, the body of Christ is emerging in the form described in the New Testament. People are rediscovering the original forms and functions in an open, participatory system mostly consisting of house churches." (Megashift, Jim Rutz)

The words "1,700-year nightmare" refer to the rise of Constantine and the legalization of Christianity. This took place from about 313 A.D. to 325 A.D. This resulted in the union of church and state and the secularization of the church. Christianity became a matter of fashion. Many heathen customs and usages, under altered names, crept into the worship of God and the life of the Christian people. This downward spiral away from the original message of the early apostles was the falling away that the apostle Paul spoke of in 2nd Thessalonians 2:3.

According to Dr. Harold Lovelace: "This Great Truth of the salvation of All Creation by God was denounced by the Fifth General Council of the Catholic Church held in Constantinople from May 4, A.D. 553 until June 2, A.D. 553. The Dark Ages, as they are known, came upon the world for about 1,000 years, and this Great Truth was hidden." (Read And Search God's Plan, Dr. Harold Lovelace)

The teaching of eternal torture, that was developed by the Catholic Church, has been the primary message of Christianity ever since. It attached itself to the Protestant Reformation and continued to be the primary message that was taught. The teaching of eternal torture is the CORE DECEPTION OF MODERN DAY CHRISTIANITY! It is the strong delusion that Paul spoke of in 2nd Thessalonians 2:11. It is also the seducing spirits and doctrines of demons that Paul taught about in 1st Timothy 4:1,2. The teaching of eternal torture has SEARED OUR CONSCIENCES WITH A HOT IRON TO THE LOVE OF GOD! It is a damnable heresy that denies the Lord who **bought us** (2nd Peter 2:1)!

The church has been under this delusion for 1,700 years. As we look back on church history we can surely see that it was a disastrous nightmare of killing, bondage, and fear. BUT THANK GOD THAT HE IS REVEALING THE TRUTH TO THOSE WHO HAVE EARS TO HEAR. The Spirit of God is calling HIS PEOPLE OUT OF BABYLON (CONFUSION), and out of the 1,700-year nightmare. The only way out of a nightmare is to **wake up!** SO…AWAKE!

According to Jim Rutz: "God has called us to stop going with the flow, and decide to actively turn away from the outdated control structures (clerics & laypeople). He wants us to pay the price of being a pioneer, learn to LOVE OTHERS, help carry the burdens of others, not become stagnate, and take small steps forward every day." (Megashift, Jim Rutz)

THE NIGHTMARE IS OVER! AWAKE!

July 21

THE SPIRITUAL MIGRATION OF THE CHURCH

According to Robert Burgess: "For many years now there has been a slow transition coming upon the minds of believers in Christ, this has been a "Spiritual Migration" as it were; from an earthly perception of a Heaven that is "Up There, and we are Down Here," to the realization that

"Heaven is where WE ARE IN CHRIST." As new creatures in Christ, we have been "Raised up together with Him, and He has made us sit together in Heavenly Places (Ephesians 2:6)..." (The Kingdom Of God, Robert Burgess)

This transition and migration (a moving from one thing to another) can be summed up and characterized by a moving from the carnal (fleshly) to the spiritual. This spiritual migration is a journey from the carnal mind to the mind of Christ. The migration brings us from a mindset of "having church" to "BEING THE CHURCH"! THERE IS A BIG DIFFERENCE!

This transition takes place as we begin to look in the mirror at ourselves. We begin to see that the root of our problem is SELF. It is our ADAMIC NATURE (the nature that we inherited from Adam). It then becomes apparent that the man of sin is within us. Our problem is then revealed to us as an internal sin nature that sits in the temple of God, opposing and exalting itself above all that is called God. This is the spirit of antichrist, the mark of the beast, the prince of the power of the air, and the spirit that now works in the children of disobedience. This is our adversary. It is not something "out there", but rather, it is WITHIN US!

Once this has been revealed to us by the Father, we are then led (by the Spirit) to an..."O WRETCHED MAN THAT I AM EXPERIENCE" (Romans 7:24)! This experience then launches us toward the power source that pertains to life and godliness. This power source is God's DIVINE NATURE. This is the very nature of God at work within us.

We are now leaving the earth (spiritually speaking) and being "caught up" into the heavens, being seated in heavenly places in Christ Jesus. "Heaven" must be understood as a state of being rather than a physical location that is somewhere off in the "sweet by-and-by".

Then, and only then, can we begin to understand the Bible, God, and His purpose for the whole creation. As our minds are transformed by the Spirit of God, we are then able to grasp and see (perceive) the Kingdom of God. Until these things take place in our lives, the Kingdom of God remains a mystery to our carnal (hellish) mind, FOR THE CARNAL MIND IS HELL! We can then see that the mind of Christ is HEAVEN! What a joy to be liberated from the bondage that is **within!**

WHAT A MIGRATION!

July 22

1ST CORINTHIANS 13 - PART 1

According to J. Preston Eby: "It is my deep conviction that this opening of Divine Love will melt more hearts for God than any other exercise. A mother may forget her child, but the Word says, "For God SO LOVED THE WORLD that He gave His Son" (Jn. 3:16). How can God ever forget the world, or give up on the world with a love so fierce as that! The scripture declares, "But God commends His love toward us, in that, while we were yet sinners, Christ died for us" (Rom. 5:8). And again, "In this the love of God was made manifest, where we are concerned, in that

God sent His Son, the only begotten or unique Son, into the world so that we might live through Him. In this is love, *not that we loved God*, but that HE LOVED US and sent His Son to be the propitiation for our sins; and not for ours alone, but also for the sins of THE WHOLE WORLD" (I Jn. 4:9-10; 2:2, Amplified)." (<u>God Is Love</u>, J. Preston Eby)

Over the next several days we are going to try to dissect 1st Corinthians chapter 13. This passage of scripture, like no other, goes into great detail in describing the love of God. It portrays the true heart of our loving Father, FOR GOD IS LOVE! It also portrays the hearts and lives of His true disciples, for Jesus said…A new commandment I give unto you, That you love one another; as I have loved you, that you also love one another. By this shall all men know that you are My disciples, if you have love one to another (John 13:34,35)…

With this in mind, we are now able to see that 1st Corinthians chapter 13 is one of the most important passages in the Bible. It speaks of the very **essence** and **nature** of God. It represents all that God is, including all that He desires for us to be in Him. LOVE IS THE FULFILLING OF THE LAW (Galatians 5:14)!

This is what an overcomer is! HE IS A LOVER AND A FORGIVER! Remember…The fruit of the Spirit is **love!** For all the law is fulfilled in one word, even this; YOU SHALL LOVE YOUR NEIGHBOR AS YOURSELF (Galatians 5:14)…

O FATHER…TEACH US TO LOVE!

July 23

1ST CORINTHIANS 13 - PART 2

1st Corinthians 13:1-3 states…Though I speak with the tongues of men and of angels, and have not charity (love), I am become as sounding brass, or a tinkling cymbal. And though I have the gift of prophecy, and understand all mysteries, and all knowledge; and though I have all faith, so that I could remove mountains, and have not charity (love), I am nothing. And though I bestow all my goods to feed the poor, and though I give my body to be burned, and have not charity (love), it profits me nothing…

The word "charity" ("love") comes from the Greek word "agape", which means: spontaneous, unconditional love that always seeks what is best for the recipient, not expecting anything in return, and having not been given on the basis of merit. "**Agape**", being the highest and most mature form of love, speaks of the love that comes from God. In essence, it tells us of the very nature and character of God, FOR GOD <u>IS</u> LOVE ("AGAPE")! This love is possessed only by God and those whom He has revealed it to. It is to be distinguished from the other forms of love, which are: "storge", "philia", and "eros". "**Agape**" is all giving, not getting.

The other forms of love are as follows:

1. storge - affection between members of a family.
2. philia - friendship.
3. eros - sexual and romantic love between people "in love".

It is important and necessary to bring out that "**agape**" (God's love) is not something that we can *work up*, for "**agape**" is in total contrast with our Adamic Nature. "**Agape**" must first be revealed to us from our Heavenly Father, then being realized, received, experienced, and distributed to others. Our nature is void of this type of love. This love is only to be found in partaking of God's divine nature (2nd Peter 1:4).

With this in mind, we can now see what is being said in verses 1-3 of 1st Corinthians. If we do any or all of the things mentioned in these verses, not being motivated by "**agape**", then we are:

1. A noisy gong or a clanging cymbal…
2. A useless nobody…
3. Gaining nothing…

This tells us that the most important thing that we are to derive from the Bible is…**GOD IS LOVE!** If we do not see this as the heart and message of the Bible, then we have missed the very essence and meaning of the Holy Scriptures! Without "**agape**", there is nothing in our treasure chest but wood, hay, and stubble. Let us lay down our lives that we might become partakers of this life-changing power, for GOD <u>IS</u>…

"AGAPE"!

July 24

1ST CORINTHIANS 13 - PART 3

1ST Corinthians 13:4-7 states…Charity (love) suffers long, and is kind; charity (love) envies not; charity (love) vaunts not itself, is not puffed up, Does not behave itself unseemly, seeks not her own, is not easily provoked, thinks no evil; Rejoices not in iniquity, but rejoices in the truth; Bears all things, believes all things, hopes all things, endures all things…

This detailed description of "love" ("agape") shows and tells us of the fruit of the Spirit in action. Remember…This love is **all giving**, not getting! This love is not just in word, but it is also in deed as well. 1st John 4:9 tells us that God's love was manifested toward us, because that God sent His only begotten Son into the world, that we might live through Him. In essence, we could say that Jesus, the Word made flesh, was a manifestation of 1st Corinthians chapter 13. He was the perfect revelation and manifestation of the love of God that we have to look at. Jesus told us that

His commandment was for us to love one another, AS HE HAD LOVED US! He then told us that there is NO GREATER LOVE THAN THAT A MAN LAY DOWN HIS LIFE FOR HIS FRIENDS (John 15:12,13). Jesus showed us true love in the laying down of His life for the sin of the world, then asking us to learn of, partake of, and to distribute this same love to all.

1st Corinthians 13:4-7 speaks of a person who is DEAD TO SELF. It then goes on to list the fruit of the Spirit that is to flow from such a person. This can be seen in verses 4-7. Love bears up under anything and everything that comes, is ever ready to believe the best of every person, its hopes are fadeless under all circumstances, and it endures everything [without weakening]. (The Amplified Bible)

God's love is the only thing that will melt the hearts and lives of people, causing them to turn from their carnal (fleshly) ways, including the carnal ideas that they have about their Heavenly Father. As His love melts our hearts, we will discover that He is a loving Father to a degree that we never imagined possible. HIS LOVE INCLUDES ALL, CORRECTS ALL, RESTORES ALL, AND SAVES ALL, UNTIL HE IS **ALL IN ALL!**

O LOVE OF GOD, HOW RICH AND PURE!

July 25

1ST CORINTHIANS 13 - PART 4

1ST Corinthians 13:8 states…Charity (love) never fails: but whether there be prophecies, they shall fail; whether there be tongues, they shall cease; whether there be knowledge, it shall vanish away…

LOVE NEVER FAILS! What a statement! These words should give us reason to greatly rejoice! Unfortunately, most do not believe or understand this statement. Most that say they believe that love never fails, in essence, really do not believe this is the case, for they preach and teach that God's love will fail most of humanity. They (Christians) claim that the vast majority of God's creation will be tortured for ever and ever in a burning hell. This comes from the simple fact that most have never done a word study on the words "hell", "fire", and "for ever" ("eternal", "everlasting"). If a proper study is done of these three words, then the truth will rise to the top, causing the traditions and doctrines of men to crumble before your very eyes. You must do a word study on the Hebrew word "Sheol" and the Greek words "Hades", "Gehenna", and "Tartaroo". These are the words that have been translated into the English word "hell". As well, you must do a word study on the Greek word "pur". This is the Greek word for "fire". Finally, you must do a word study on the Hebrew word "olam" and the Greek words "aion" and "aionios". These words pertain to the "ages", **but many have misunderstood and mistranslated these words, causing much confusion.**

After an unbiased study is done concerning these words, the truth of the salvation of all men will become quite clear. You will then see (perceive) your Heavenly Father for Who He truly is…THE SAVIOR OF THE WORLD!!! Then, and only then, will you understand the statement…LOVE

NEVER FAILS! This means that God's love never fades out, or becomes obsolete, or comes to an end! Remember…Nothing can separate us from the love of God, NOT EVEN DEATH (Romans 8:35-39)!

Romans 8:38,39 states…For I am persuaded, that neither death, nor life, nor angels, nor principalities, nor powers, nor things present, nor things to come, Nor height, nor depth, nor any other creature, shall be able to separate us from the love of God, which is in Christ Jesus our Lord…(DO YOU BELIEVE THIS?)

The love of God could be summed up best by the old song that states:

> The love of God is greater far
> Than tongue or pen can ever tell;
> It goes beyond the highest star,
> And reaches to **the lowest hell.**

LOVE <u>NEVER</u> FAILS!

July 26

1ST CORINTHIANS 13 - PART 5

1ST Corinthians 13:9-13 states…For we know in part, and we prophesy in part. But when that which is perfect is come, then that which is in part shall be done away. When I was a child, I spoke as a child, I understood as a child, I thought as a child: but when I became a man, I put away childish things. For now we see through a glass, darkly; but then face to face: now I know in part; but then shall I know even as also I am known. And now abides faith, hope, charity (love), these three; but the greatest of these is charity (love)…

As we run the race of life, marching toward a deeper relationship with our Lord, we are accompanied by **three great friends**. Their names are FAITH, HOPE, AND LOVE. These three friends help us as we walk through the wilderness of this Christian journey. They guide us through the seasons of this life, helping us to be able to see through a glass, darkly. Sometimes it appears that these three friends have abandoned us, but they are always watching us. Many times they are closer to us then we realize. They work behind the scenes, helping, strengthening, and encouraging us in ways that we do not realize until later down the road. These three friends are bringing us from being able to see in part, to being able to see our Father in all His fullness. They are bringing us to a grand, glorious, and climactic conclusion, in which we will see our Heavenly Father as ALL IN ALL!

There is coming a day when two of these friends will leave us. These two are FAITH and HOPE. They are not leaving us to desert us, but rather, they are leaving simply because we will not need them any more. They will have finally brought us to the desired end of the journey. This "end of the journey", as we will call it, is to know our Father even as we are known of our Father.

Our third and greatest friend of all, Who is LOVE, **WILL ALWAYS BE WITH US**! He will never fail us! NEVER, NEVER, NEVER! He goes by the name of love, but He is also known as the Lord Jesus Christ, for He is God, AND GOD IS LOVE!

If at the end of time there remains just one person who is estranged from the love of God, then that person has defeated the love of God, and God's love will have failed. ***BUT GOD WILL NOT FAIL! HE CAN NOT FAIL! HIS LOVE GOES BEYOND THE HIGHEST STAR, AND REACHES TO THE LOWEST HELL!!!*** He has promised that He will draw (drag) all men unto Himself. What a promise! What a God!

HIS LOVE IS <u>INESCAPABLE</u>!

July 27

GO IN TO POSSESS THE LAND

Joshua 1:10,11 states…Then Joshua commanded the officers of the people, saying, Pass through the host, and command the people, saying, Prepare you victuals (provisions); for within three days you shall pass over this Jordan, to go in to possess the land, which the LORD your God gives you to possess it…

"Joshua", which means **Jehovah The Savior,** was about to lead the children of Israel into the promised land of Canaan. The Lord spoke unto Joshua in reference to Moses, saying…Moses My servant is dead…The Lord also encouraged Joshua by telling him to be strong and of a good courage; be not afraid, neither be dismayed: for the Lord your God is with you, wherever you go…Joshua sent officers to command and to prepare the people to be ready to pass over the Jordan river. God would miraculously part the waters of the Jordan, causing the priests that bare the ark of the covenant of the Lord to stand firm on dry ground in the midst of the Jordan, and all the Israelites passed over on dry ground, until all the people were passed clean over Jordan. What an awesome miracle this was! Let us now look at what this story represents for the followers of Christ today.

The key words or phrases that we will take note of are: "Joshua", "Moses", "Be strong and of a good courage", "Within three days", and "Pass over this Jordan". We must understand that the Old Covenant (Moses, the letter of the law) is dead (fulfilled in Christ). The One Who has accomplished this is Jesus (Joshua). We are now called to be overcomers (strong and of a good courage) through faith in the finished work of Jesus Christ (Joshua). In addition to this, we are coming out of death (Jordan), which is the carnal mind. This is all made possible by the death (cross) and resurrection (represented by the statement…within three days) of the Lord Jesus Christ (Joshua). As well, we shall also be resurrected according to the same pattern in which the Lord Jesus was resurrected. THIS IS OUR FULL SALVATION, WHICH IS THE PROMISED LAND OF CANAAN THAT FLOWS WITH MILK AND HONEY! This spiritual promised land is to be found IN CHRIST, FOR HE IS THE TRUE PROMISED LAND! **In Him** we live and move and have our being (Acts 17:28)…

Let us go in to possess THIS LAND at once! After continually putting our faith in Christ, we will see the giants (our flesh and carnal mind) fall, causing us to totally and completely inherit the land (our glorified bodies). The taking of this land is a process. It is called SALVATION! It involves the salvation of our spirit, soul, and body. This is the promised land!

Thank God for our Heavenly Joshua (Jesus), Who is the PATTERN SON, and Who has already paved the way for us, becoming the firstborn of every creature (Colossians 1:15).

GO IN TO POSSESS THE LAND!

July 28

REFORMATION

According to Bob Evely: "We need Reformation within the church today as badly as in Luther's day. We need to understand that "orthodoxy" is not truth as compared with falsehood ... it is simply the majority opinion, and it can be wrong. We cannot cling to a set a beliefs or interpretations simply because the majority that preceded us has worked through these issues and developed what they have passed down to us as orthodoxy ... the "majority opinion." "Orthodoxy" is widely viewed as a safeguard against heresy. But what if the "majority opinion" is wrong, and what if orthodoxy now prevents us from rooting error out of the teachings of the church? Consider this ... *When in scripture was the majority opinion correct?* Were the Jewish leaders (the majority) correct, when God's prophets (the minority ... like Jeremiah) were proclaiming things that were "unorthodox" in their day? Were the Pharisees (the majority) correct when Jesus and later His apostles were proclaiming things that were "unorthodox" in their day? Were the majority of believers correct as they clung to legalism, as Paul spoke of things that were "unorthodox?" (See Acts 21:20-21 when the majority of believers in Jerusalem opposed Paul when he returned to Jerusalem .)" (How Can You Be Right, And The Whole Church Wrong?, Bob Evely)

The word "reform" means: the improvement or amendment of what is wrong, corrupt, or unsatisfactory. This is what is now taking place in the body of Christ. Those who have EARS TO HEAR are coming out of Babylon (confusion)! They are hearing the call of the Spirit to come out of deception and STRONG DELUSION, for most of the established visible church is to be found in this state. Remember…If it were possible, the **very elect** (God's own people) would be deceived (Matthew 24:24)…

There is only one road that leads to REFORMATION. This road is revelation truth! The words "revelation truth" mean: unveiled reality. This combination of Spirit and truth is essential to be a true worshipper of God. It takes the Spirit to reveal truth to a person. In essence, they (Spirit and truth) go hand in hand. The teachings of Evangelical Christianity are **pitiful**, for most of what they teach is nothing more than the traditions and doctrines of men. We must admit that…

IT IS TIME FOR A REFORMATION!

July 29

THE PROBLEM OF PAIN

Why is this life full of emotional and physical pain? Why is there so much evil? What is the purpose of pain, evil, and suffering? The Bible gives us concrete answers to these questions.

The problem of pain is obviously a tough thing for the human race to come to terms with. It is difficult to understand and comprehend all the reasons why certain things happen to certain people. It would seem that there is no logical reason for much of the pain, evil, and suffering that we are subjected to. But the Bible does not leave us in the dark on this subject. As a matter of fact, it is very clear in its explanation concerning the reasons for the creation having been subjected to pain, evil, and suffering.

Psalm 119:71 is a KEY VERSE that unlocks the problem of pain, evil, and suffering. It states… **IT IS GOOD FOR ME THAT I HAVE BEEN AFFLICTED; THAT I MIGHT <u>LEARN</u> YOUR STATUTES**…It is not that we welcome or enjoy pain, evil, and suffering, for we certainly do not! But the Bible gives us hope in stating that there is a *purpose* for everything that we go through. The purpose for our affliction is that we might LEARN! This concept is also to be seen in the story of Job.

All of Job's friends bemoaned him and comforted him over all the EVIL THAT <u>THE LORD HAD BROUGHT UPON HIM</u>: (Job 42:11)…Why did God afflict Job and bring pain into his life? It is important that we see why, for Job represents the entire creation and its afflictions. Job was afflicted that he might LEARN. What did he learn? He said…I have heard of You (God) by the hearing of the ear: But now my eye sees (understands) You (God). Wherefore I abhor myself, and repent in dust and ashes (Job 42:5,6)…What was the result of what Job learned? The Lord BLESSED THE LATTER END OF JOB MORE THAN HIS BEGINNING (Job 42:12)…

This is where we are headed. Unfortunately, there will be some pain, evil, and suffering along the way. We must see as Job eventually did, that all of God's methods are <u>corrective</u> in nature. He afflicts us not to be vindictive, but corrective.

The key that causes us to grow in grace and in the knowledge of the Lord is this: We must see (as Job did) that everything that happens to us, whether good or evil, is under the control of the SOVEREIGN HAND OF ALMIGHTY GOD! God either causes or allows EVERYTHING! We are afflicted that we might …

LEARN!

July 30

THE THREE GREAT TRAPS

After much reading and studying of the Bible, I think you will agree that there are things that we are to guard against. There are "traps", if you will, that we are to avoid falling into. These are things that the Bible warns us to stay away from. I am convinced that the three most dangerous things that the Bible speaks of are:

1. PRIDE
2. BITTERNESS
3. ISOLATION

These three traps will ruin a life, a relationship, and our witness for God. They are to be viewed as a spiritual cancer that eats away at the very essence of God's life within us. "Pride", "isolation", and "bitterness" will surely cause us to be a clogged vessel, leaving us in a condition that will always frustrate the grace of God.

The Bible continually urges us to humble ourselves, not being lifted up in "pride". Proverbs 6:16,17 tells us that GOD HATES "PRIDE"! The words "proud look" in verse 17 speak of "pride", referring to one who is lifted up and exalted in and of themselves. The Bible is very clear on this issue. Everyone who exalts himself shall be abased; and he that humbles himself shall be exalted (Read Luke 18:9-14).

Ephesians 4:31 and Hebrews 12:15 tell us to guard against a "root of bitterness". The word "bitterness" speaks of being harsh and disagreeable, showing intense hostility, being resentful or cynical. Psalm 1:1 calls it the "SEAT OF THE SCORNFUL". "Bitterness" is a result of "pride", being a more harsh form of "pride". "Bitterness" then leads to "isolation".

Matthew 5:13-17 tells us that a believer is salt and light to the world, and that we are to let our light shine before men. "Isolation" is the final and **most deadly** form of "pride", for it says…I NEED NO ONE BUT MYSELF! It is a celebration of self, which leads to spiritual death! It is a recipe for disaster!

"Pride", "bitterness", and "isolation" are, without a doubt, the three greatest stumbling blocks that stop people from entering into the Kingdom of God. Not only do they hinder the one whom they have attached themselves to, but they hinder others as well. Let us be on guard for these three deadly traps. We must…

HUMBLE OURSELVES!

July 31

GROW

2ND Peter 3:18 states…But grow in grace, and in the knowledge of our Lord and Savior Jesus Christ. To Him be glory both now and for ever (to the day of the age). Amen…

The Bible is full of passages that tell us to mature, progress, and to grow up into a mature son of God. The growth that is being spoken of is a spiritual growth. It is a growing up into the fullness of God that must take place in our lives. We must see ourselves as individually and corporately coming into the unity of the faith, and of the knowledge of the Son of God, unto a perfect man, unto the measure of the stature of the fullness of Christ: That we henceforth be no more children, tossed to and fro, and carried about with every wind of doctrine, by the sleight of men, and cunning craftiness, whereby they lie in wait to deceive; but speaking the truth in love, may GROW UP INTO HIM in all things, which is the Head, even Christ: (Ephesians 4:13-15)…

This is what is taking place within the true members of the body of Christ. WE ARE GROWING UP INTO HIM! We are not to remain as children (spiritual infants) in our understanding and knowledge of God, but we are to learn how to access the VERY GRACE OF GOD in our Christian walk. Our knowledge of God and His purpose for the creation should also increase. This should take place to where we are beginning to understand the mysteries of the Kingdom of God.

Why is it that **so many** of God's people are afraid, even scared to death, to learn, progress, and grow in grace and in the knowledge of their Lord? We must understand this about man and his fallen condition: Carnal man is eager to remain stagnant in his comfort zone. Anything that seems to be unorthodox or challenging to man is immediately discarded and thrown to the side. It is regarded as "off the deep end".

We ought to guard against believing everything we hear, but we must also guard against discarding everything new that we hear. Many times we may be discarding revelation truth. WE MUST STRIVE TO HAVE A **TEACHABLE SPIRIT**, being led by the Spirit, testing everything we hear and experience by the Holy Scriptures. Let us not be afraid to learn, consider, study, and…

GROW!

August 1

LAY NOT THIS SIN TO THEIR CHARGE

Acts 7:57-60 states…Then they cried out with a loud voice, and stopped their ears, and ran upon him with one accord, And cast him out of the city, and stoned him: and the witnesses laid down their clothes at a young man's feet, whose name was Saul. And they stoned Stephen, calling upon God, and saying, Lord Jesus, receive my spirit. And he kneeled down, and cried with a loud voice, Lord, lay not this sin to their charge. And when he had said this, he fell asleep…

The beautiful secret to understanding this passage of scripture is to be found in the name STEPHEN. The name "Stephen" means crown. The word "crown" means: a headdress symbolizing royalty, achievement, or victory, a reigning monarch, pertaining to royal status and reward.

Revelation 2:26 tells us that the overcomers will be given power over the nations: And they shall rule them with a rod of iron…The next logical question would be, what causes one to qualify and be classified as an overcomer? The answer to this is found in the meaning of Stephen's name.

"Stephen", whose name means crown, symbolizing royalty, ruling, and reigning, dealt with his persecutors in LOVE AND FORGIVENESS. **THIS IS AN OVERCOMER!** He cried to the Lord with a loud voice, saying…Lord, LAY NOT THIS SIN TO THEIR CHARGE…THOSE ARE

THE WORDS OF AN OVERCOMER! Do they sound familiar? Remember…Jesus said…Father, **forgive** them; FOR THEY KNOW NOT WHAT THEY DO (Luke 23:34)…These are the words of the overcomer of all overcomers. As well, Jesus said…Be of good cheer; I HAVE OVERCOME THE WORLD (John 16:33)…How did He do it? He submitted His life to do the Father's will, being a lover and a forgiver.

In the same sense, we must lose our life for His name's sake, being a lover and a forgiver. Someone who operates in this manner has truly grasped that heart of the Father. This person is truly an OVERCOMER! God is raising up a STEPHEN COMPANY of people who truly understand what is involved in *qualifying* for the CROWN OF LIFE. It is…

SUBMISSION, LOVE, AND FORGIVENESS!

August 2

HELL - PART 1

According to J. W. Hanson: "Does the Bible teach the idea commonly held among Christians concerning "hell"? Does the "hell" of the Bible denote a place of torment, or a condition of suffering without end, to begin at death? What is the "hell" of the Bible? Manifestly the only way to arrive at the correct answer is to trace the words translated "hell" from the beginning to the end of the Bible, and by their connections ascertain exactly what the divine Word teaches on this important subject. It seems incredible that a wise and benevolent God should have created or permitted any kind of an endless "hell" in His universe. Has He done so? Do the scripture teachings concerning "hell" stain the character of God and clothe human destiny with an impenetrable pall of darkness, by revealing a state or place of endless torment? Or do they explain its existence, and relieve God's character, and dispel all the darkness of misbelief, by teaching that it exists as a means to a good end? It is our belief that the Bible "hell" is not the heathen, nor the "orthodox hell", but is one that is doomed to pass away when its purpose shall have been accomplished, in the reformation of those for whose welfare a good God ordained it." (The Bible Hell, J. W. Hanson)

Before getting into the Hebrew and Greek words that were translated into the English word "hell", we will first take a look at the origin of the English word "hell", and how it grew into its present meaning. Over the coming days we are going to search for what the Bible actually teaches about "hell". We are going to study to show ourselves approved unto God (2nd Timothy 2:15). We are going to put our beliefs to the test in order to see whether or not the orthodox teaching of Evangelical Christianity concerning "hell" is truth or tradition.

After carefully examining the facts that will be presented, we will seek to prove that the modern day teaching on "hell" is INCORRECT, and does in fact malign the character of our Heavenly Father, Who is not to be looked at as the eternal torturer, but is in fact…

THE SAVIOR OF THE WORLD!

HELL - PART 2

According to J. W. Hanson: "The English word "hell" grew into its present meaning. Horne Tooke says that "hell", "heel", "hill", "hole", "whole", "hall", "hull", "halt" and "hold" are all from the same root. "Hell", any place, or some place covered over. "Heel", that part of the foot which is covered by the leg. "Hill", any heap of earth, or stone, etc., by which the plain or level surface of the earth is covered. "Hale", i.e., healed or whole. "Whole", the same as "hale", i.e., covered. It was formerly written "whole", without the w, as a wound or sore is healed, or "whole", that is, covered over by the skin, which manner of expression will not seem extraordinary if we consider our use of the word "recover". "Hall", a covered building, where persons assemble, or where goods are protected from the weather. "Hull", of a nut, etc. That by which a nut is covered. "Hole", some place covered over. 'You shall seek for holes to hide your heads in.' "Holt", "holed", "hold", "holt". A rising ground or knoll covered with trees. "Hold", as the hold of a ship, in which things are covered, or the covered part of a ship. **The word was first applied to the "grave" by our German and English ancestors, and as superstition came to regard the "grave" as an entrance to a world of torment, "hell" at length became the word used to denote an imaginary realm of fiery woe.** Dr. Adam Clarke says: "The word "hell", used in the common translation, conveys now an improper meaning of the original word; because "hell" is only used to signify the place of the damned. But as the word "hell" comes from the Anglo-Saxon "helan", to cover, or hide, "henee" the tiling or slating of a house is called, in some parts of England (particularly Cornwall), "heling", to this day, and the corers of books (in Lancashire), by the same name, so the literal import of the original word "Hades" was formerly well expressed by it." (The Bible Hell, J. W. Hanson)

With just a little bit of research, we can already begin to see the confusion concerning the word and teaching of "hell" begin to clear up. After taking a look at the origin and meaning of the English word "hell", we will now attempt to look at and dissect the four words that are translated into the one English word "hell". They are: The Hebrew word "Sheol", and the Greek words "Hades", "Gehenna", and "Tartaroo".

Most people have NO IDEA that there are **FOUR DIFFERENT WORDS IN THE ORIGINAL LANGUAGES OF THE BIBLE THAT HAVE BEEN TRANSLATED INTO THE ONE ENGLISH WORD "HELL"**. After finding this out, the next most logical thing to do would be to seek to understand the meaning of each word from the original languages of the Bible. We are going to do just that. So...HANG ON! We are going to take...

A JOURNEY THROUGH "HELL"!

HELL - PART 3

JUST WHAT THE HELL IS HELL?
(By Gary Amirault)

There once was a time, 'twas plain to see
Just what the hell, Hell was meant to be.
But then theologians got into the act
And Hell no longer was a simple fact.

Hell formerly was a dark hidden space
Imperceivable, covered, a true hiding place.
It could be a place, as crude as a shed
Or could be a *hel*met, to cover your head.

Smoochers and kissers oft needed a hell
For hidden in darkness, no one could tell.
Hall, hole, and hull come from the same root
Along with a heel covered with a boot.

"Too simple!" So theologians once said
And now from their scheming, confusion has spread.
They hired the Dantes and Michaelangelos
To paint pretty pictures of many great woes.

Fire and torment, with much superstition
Was added to pagan mythology and fiction.
The Goddess of Hel from Norse mythology
Became Satan, hero of most eschatology.

Jesus the Savior, delivered mankind
He came not for few, but for ALL men to find.
His portion became a rather small lot
While most of mankind, in Hell-fire would rot.

The way to this Hell became broad and wide
The gift of God's grace was at its low tide.
Clothes, creeds and days, the right denomination
Became the sole means, the way to salvation.

Gehenna, Hades, Tartaroo, and Sheol
All became places that could swallow your soul.
Preachers now had us, right where they wanted
"Obey or to Hell with you" they often taunted.

Countless denominations of devilish preachers
Forsook the Gift and became Satan's teachers.
Thousands of ways of deliverance from "Hell"
In common they all have a self-righteous smell.

"Finished" He cried, "I will draw all mankind"
The Father's desire, "all saved" in His mind.
The task He was given, He accomplished it all
And as His witness, He commissioned St. Paul.

Paul's Gospel was different, it's easy to tell
Because never once did he use the word "hell."
So "hell" is no more, it's becoming a bore
It's taking its place along with common folklore.

Punish He will, for our Father is just
In age-long correction, you surely can trust.
On vindictive torment our Father's not bent
Mercy will, *yes!* triumph over judgment.

Well…You did it! You have been to "hell" and back. You have taken a journey through "hell". You have seen the origin of the English word "hell", its distortion by theologians, and how that it grew into its present meaning. You can also see that one English word was used to pitifully portray one Hebrew word and three Greek words. As we journey through "hell", our next stop will be to look at each one of the words that were translated into the English word "hell". They are: "Sheol", "Hades", "Gehenna", and "Tartaroo".

This study will shed even more light on the confusion that has spread concerning what the Bible teaches about "hell". So…HANG ON! The next stop on our journey through "hell" is…"SHEOL"!

ENJOY YOUR SEARCH!

August 5

HELL - PART 4

SHEOL

According to J. W. Hanson: "That the Hebrew "Sheol" never designates a place of punishment in a future state of existence, we have the testimony of the most learned of scholars, even among the so-called orthodox. We quote the testimony of a few:

Rev. Dr. Whitby: "**Sheol** throughout the Old Testament, signifies not a place of punishment for the souls of bad men only, but the grave, or place of death."

Dr Chapman: "**Sheol**, in itself considered has no connection with future punishment."

Dr. Allen: "The term "Sheol" itself, does not seem to mean anything more than the state of the dead in their dark abode."

Dr. Firbairn, of the College of Glasgow: "Beyond doubt, "Sheol", like "Hades", was regarded as the abode after death, alike of the good and the bad."

Edward Leigh, who says Horne's, "Introduction," was "one of the most learned understanding of the original languages of the scriptures," observes that "all learned Hebrew scholars know the Hebrews have no proper word for "hell", as we take **hell**."

Prof. Stuart: "There can be no reasonable doubt that "Sheol" does most generally mean the underworld, the grave or sepulchre, the world of the dead. It is very clear that there are many passages where no other meaning can reasonably be assigned to it. Accordingly, our English translators have rendered the word "Sheol" grave in thirty instances out of the whole sixty-four instances in which it occurs."

Dr. Thayer in his Theology of Universalism quotes as follows: Dr. Whitby says that "hell" "throughout the Old Testament signifies the grave only or the place of death." (The Bible Hell, J. W. Hanson)

Well…There you have it! The word "Sheol" means: **the grave, or the place of the dead**. In no way does it denote a place of punishment, torment, or torture. The idea that "Sheol" signified a place of punishment entered in through pagan mythology. We are now on our way to understanding the "hell" of the Bible. Our next stop on our journey through "hell" will be to look at and dissect the Greek word "Hades". We will see that "Hades" is the Greek equivalent to the Hebrew word "Sheol". It is the New Testament word that signifies the grave, or the place of the dead.

O WHAT A DIFFERENCE THE TRUTH MAKES!

August 6

HELL - PART 5

HADES

According to J. W. Hanson: "The Greek Septuagint, which our Lord used when He read or quoted from the Old Testament, gives "Hades" as the exact equivalent of the Hebrew "Sheol", and when the Savior, or His apostles, use the word, they must mean the same as it meant in the Old Testament. When "Hades" is used in the New Testament, we must understand it just as we do ("Sheol" or "Hades") in the Old Testament.

Dr. Campbell well says: "In my judgment, it ought never in scripture to be rendered "hell", at least, in the sense wherein that word is now universally understood by Christians. In the Old Testament, the corresponding word is "Sheol", which signifies the state of the dead in general without regard to the goodness or badness of the persons, their happiness or misery. In translating that word, the seventy have almost invariably used "Hades". It is very plain, that neither in the Septuagint version of the Old Testament, nor in the New, does the word "Hades" convey the meaning which the present English word "hell", in the Christian usage, always conveys to our minds."

Le Clere affirms that "neither "Hades" nor "Sheol" ever signifies in the Sacred Scripture the abode of evil spirits, but only the sepulchre, or the state of the dead." (The Bible Hell, J. W. Hanson)

According to J. W. Hanson: "That "Hades" is the kingdom of death, and not a place of torment, after death, is evident from the language of Acts 2:27, "You will not leave my soul in hell: neither will You suffer Your Holy One to see corruption." Verse 31: "His soul was not left in "hell", neither His flesh did see corruption," that is His spirit did not remain in the state of the dead, until His body decayed. No one supposes that Jesus went to a realm of torment when He died. Jacob wished to go down to "Hades" to his son mourning, so Jesus went to "Hades", the under-world, the grave. The Apostle's Creed conveys the same idea, when it speaks of Jesus as descending into "hell". He died, but His soul was not left in the realms of death, is the meaning." (The Bible Hell, J. W. Hanson)

1st Corinthians 15:55 tells us that "hell" ("Hades") will be destroyed. It states…O death, where is your sting? O grave ("Hades", "hell"), where is your victory? So we can see that "hell" ("Sheol", "Hades") is the grave, or the place of the dead. We can also now see that "hell" ("Sheol", "Hades") is not to endure forever, but is destined to be destroyed. This is also in harmony with Revelation 20:13,14, which tells us that death and "hell" ("Hades") shall be consumed by the fire of God. This is speaking of the purifying fire of God. AWESOME!

O "HELL" ("HADES", GRAVE), <u>WHERE IS YOUR VICTORY</u>?

August 7

HELL - PART 6

GEHENNA
(Hope For All Generations And Nations, Gary Amirault)

"Israel, during one part of its history, began to mix the worship of Yahweh with some of the customs of the pagan nations around them. They molded a statue which was half man and half bull. They called this god, MLK. (The original Hebrew had no vowels. One had to put in the vowels from memory.) Some scholars render these three consonants Molock or Molech, others believed it was the word Melech, which means "king" in Hebrew. The latter view would mean that Israel had made an image of Yahweh (their king) in the image of being half man and half animal. Either way, they felt they had *not* abandoned the worship of Yahweh. They felt this new practice was harmonious with the other religious traditions of the Hebrew faith. Regardless of whether he was called Moloch, Molech or Melech, the Israelites took their own babies and placed them in the hands of this statue. Beneath the hands was a pot under which was a very hot fire. The child would fall out of the hands of MLK into the burning pot. As the child screamed with pain, the adults would go into a sexual frenzy as the sounds of the burning children mixed with the beating of drums. MLK was a fertility god. In other Jewish rites, the Jews were commanded to offer up the first-fruits of a harvest unto Yahweh that He might bless the rest of the harvest. The Israelites extended this practice by offering up some of their children as a burnt-offering. Yahweh told Jeremiah the prophet He was going to destroy the city in which they were committing these horrible acts. The location where these rites were performed was in the Valley of the Son of Hinnom (also called Tophet in the Bible) right outside the Southwest wall of *Jerusalem!* When speaking of Israel burning their own children, Yahweh said that such a thing never entered His mind. *If God prepared a place in which He was going to torture billions of the human beings He created, how could He say it never entered His mind. Obviously, God never intended, nor ever will eternally burn and torture the men and women He created!* This cruel teaching came from the same place from which Israel got the idea of burning their own children, that is, from a mind which was not subject to the true God; from a depraved mind. When Jesus in the New Testament used the word which has been incorrectly translated "hell" in most Christian Bibles, the place He was referring to was this valley in which *Israel* burned their own children, not God. The place called "Gehenna" (translated "hell") was the Greek form of the Hebrew "Ge Hinnom". This valley became a disgraceful reminder to Israel of what their forefathers did. It became the city dump. Jesus warned the very generation in which He lived that if they did not repent, they would find themselves thrown into this valley of garbage which burned night and day. To tell a Jew something like this was the absolute worst of insult. It meant that their lives were worthless. A Jew's honor was very important to him, especially at his death. It was not uncommon to hire professional mourners at one's funeral. Imagine paying someone to cry tears at your funeral. This is an example of how vain God's own people were during Jesus' physical presence on earth. Jesus told some of the most religious people of His day, their lives were only fit to be thrown into the city dump! What an insult! *And* what a prophecy! The very people who heard these words would find their bodies thrown over the Southwest wall of Jerusalem during the siege against the city in 70AD. Because they did not follow Christ and participated in His crucifixion, their lives truly did become worthless." (Gary Amirault)

Now that we are educated as to the literal history and meaning of "Gehenna", understanding that it is a place on this earth, let us take a look at what this literal valley represents spiritually and metaphorically.

FIRST THE NATURAL, THEN THE SPIRITUAL!

HELL - PART 7

GEHENNA CONTINUED

According to J. Preston Eby: "In the New Testament there appears the word "GEHENNA" referring to the "Valley of Hinnom", or "Gehenna", which was the city dump outside the walls of Jerusalem, a place of constant burning of refuse. It is interesting to note that those who are pictured as going into "Gehenna" are, without exception, not the sinners of the world, but the SINNERS AMONG GOD'S PEOPLE. How precise the type! "Gehenna" was the city dump of Jerusalem, the Holy City, where every unclean and unnecessary thing was burned and consumed. The antitypical "Gehenna" to which our Lord alluded in His teaching is the process of PURIFICATION by which every unclean and unnecessary thing in the lives of His Holy People is purged and consumed by the fires of His judgment. "The Lord Whom you seek, shall suddenly come to HIS TEMPLE ... but who may abide the day of His coming? and who shall stand when He appears? for He is like a REFINER'S FIRE, and like fuller's soap: and He shall sit as a refiner and purifier of silver: and He shall PURIFY the sons of Levi (the Priesthood), and PURGE them as gold and silver, that they may offer unto the Lord an offering in righteousness" (Mal. 3:1-3). "Gehenna" stands as a type of the place or process of the PURIFICATION OF GOD'S PEOPLE. It is referred to in the Old Testament by the name of "Tophet," located in the "Valley of Hinnom", a place where many sacrifices were made and dead bodies consumed." (Hell, J. Preston Eby)

The idea of God's people being purified in and through fire is also to be found in the apostle Paul's writings. 1st Corinthians 3:12-15 states…Now if any man build upon this foundation gold, silver, precious stones, wood, hay, stubble; Every man's work shall be made manifest: for the day shall declare it, because it shall be revealed by fire; and the fire shall try every man's work of what sort it is. If any man's work abide which he has built thereupon, he shall receive a reward. If any man's work shall be burned, he shall suffer loss: but he himself shall be saved; yet so as by fire…

This is obviously speaking of a spiritual fire, of which GOD IS! Remember…GOD IS A CONSUMING FIRE (Hebrews 12:29)…Now we can begin to see that Jesus pointed to the literal fire of "Gehenna", which did consume literal refuse, to teach us about **the spiritual fire of God**. He used "Gehenna" to *typify, symbolize, and portray* what the fire of God was like. HE USED "GEHENNA" AS A METAPHOR!

The fire of God is His judgment in our lives that consumes the refuse in us, which is WOOD, HAY, AND STUBBLE! God's fire is for PURIFICATION, **NOT ETERNAL TORTURE!** Nothing was tortured in "Gehenna", only consumed and **changed into another form**. Can you now begin to see your <u>FIERY</u> TRIALS as the process in which God is consuming your carnality and CHANGING YOU INTO THE VERY IMAGE OF THE SON OF GOD? As you believe on the Lord Jesus Christ, you are being consumed by the Holy Ghost and FIRE, being changed from glory to glory. This is what "Gehenna" represents. It speaks of the ALL-CONSUMING FIRE OF GOD!

THANK GOD FOR THE FIRE OF "GEHENNA"!

August 9

HELL - PART 8

FACTS ABOUT GEHENNA
(<u>The Bible Hell</u>, J. W. Hanson)

"Gehenna" was a well-known locality near Jerusalem, and ought no more to be translated "hell", than should Sodom or Gomorrah. See Josh. 15:8; II Kings 17:10; II Chron. 28:3; Jer. 7:31, 32; 19:2.

"Gehenna" is never employed in the Old Testament to mean anything else than the place with which every Jew was familiar.

The word should have been left untranslated as it is in some versions, and it would not be misunderstood. It was not misunderstood by the Jews to whom Jesus addressed it. Walter Balfour well says: "What meaning would the Jews who were familiar with this word, and knew it to signify the "Valley of Hinnom", be likely to attach to it when they heard it used by our Lord? Would they, contrary to all former usage, transfer its meaning from a place with whose locality and history they had been familiar from their infancy, to a place of misery in another world? This conclusion is certainly inadmissible. By what rule of interpretation, then, can we arrive at the conclusion that this word means a place of misery and death?"

Neither Christ nor His apostles ever named it to Gentiles, but only to Jews which proves it a locality only known to Jews, whereas, if it were a place of punishment after death for sinners, it would have been preached to Gentiles as well as Jews.

It was only referred to twelve times on eight occasions in all the ministry of Christ and the apostles, and in the gospels and epistles. Were they faithful to their mission to say no more than this on so vital a theme as an endless "hell", if they intended to teach it?

Only Jesus and James ever named it. Neither Paul, John, Peter nor Jude ever employ it. Would they not have warned sinners concerning it, if there were a "Gehenna" of torment after death?

Paul says he "shunned not to declare the whole counsel of God," and yet though he was the great preacher of the gospel to the Gentiles he never told them that "Gehenna" is a place of after-death punishment. Would he not have repeatedly warned sinners against it were there such a place?

When Jesus warned against the judgment of "Gehenna" in Matthew 23:33, He immediately explained it as about to come in this life (vs. 36...All these things shall come upon **this generation**...)" (<u>The Bible Hell</u>, J. W. Hanson)

The damnation (judgment) of "hell" ("Gehenna") did come upon the Jews in 70-73 A.D. In July of 70 A.D. the Roman Army, led by Titus, attacked and overran the city of Jerusalem. According to Josephus, over 1,000,000 Jews perished in the siege. The prophecy of Jeremiah 7:30-34 came to pass in 70-73 A.D. The "Valley of the Son of Hinnom" became the valley of slaughter. The Roman Army destroyed Jerusalem, leveled the Temple, and burned the city to the ground. As Jesus prophesied in Matthew 23:33-36, the Jews did not escape the JUDGMENT OF "GEHENNA", FOR THEIR BODIES WERE PILED UP IN THE VERY VALLEY OF "GEHENNA". Let us stop teaching the traditions of men about "Gehenna". Let us...

TEACH THE TRUTH!

August 10

HELL - PART 9

TARTAROO

According to J. Preston Eby: "Next we consider the Greek word "TARTAROO" - the English form is "Tartarus." The passage where this word is found is II Pet. 2:4. "God spared not the angels (messengers) that sinned, but cast them down to "hell" ("Tartarus"), and delivered them into *chains of darkness* to be *reserved unto* judgment." Jude also presents the same truth without mentioning the name as he writes, "And those angels (messengers) who kept not their first position of power and authority, but left their habitation, He has kept *in chains under thick darkness*, for the judgment of the great day" (Jude 6). The whole thought is of a restraint, a confinement, a prison, a condition in which apostates are held for a specific period of time, in the same manner as prisoners are often held in jail awaiting the day of trial. "Tartarus" is not the judgment itself, but a state or condition in which persons are inescapably held over unto a day of judgment." (Hell, J. Preston Eby)

According to J. W. Hanson: "Peter alludes to the subject just as though it were well-known and understood by his correspondents. "If the angels that sinned."-what angels? "were cast down to "Tartarus," where is the story related? Not in the Bible, but in a book well-known at the time, called the Book of Enoch. It was written some time before the Christian Era, and is often quoted by the Christian fathers. But no one can fail to see that the apostle employs the legend from the Book of Enoch to illustrate and enforce his doctrine of retribution. As though he had said: "If, as is believed by some, God spared not the angels that sinned, do not let us who sin, mortal men, expect to escape." If this view is denied, there is no escape from the gross doctrine of "Tartarus" as taught by the pagans and that, too, on the testimony of a solitary sentence of scripture! But whatever may be the intent of the words, they do not teach endless torment, for the chains referred to only last unto the judgment." (The Bible Hell, J. W. Hanson)

It is believed by many that Peter and Jude were referring to sinning messengers in the days of Noah. These sinning messengers were referred to as "the sons of God" who took "the daughters of men" as wives and produced children by them (Genesis 6:2). As to the nature of these angels (messengers), there are many different thoughts and opinions. Some believe that the flood, in Noah's day, was brought on and designed by God for the very purpose of thwarting these fallen angels (messengers) in their design.

The important point to see though, is that "Tartarus" does in no way teach endless torment, for the chains referred to only last **unto the judgment**. It is to be seen as a state or condition in which persons are held over unto a day of judgment for the purpose of correction. The Lord knows how to reserve...

THE UNJUST UNTO THE DAY OF JUDGMENT!

August 11

HELL - PART 10

CONCLUSION

The English word "hell" is to be found 54 times in the original "Authorized Version" of the King James Bible. This one English word is used to represent **four different words** in the original languages of the Bible. The one Hebrew word is "Sheol", and the three Greek words are "Hades", "Gehenna", and "Tartaroo". After an in-depth study on each one of these words, we have discovered that none of these words support the idea of the modern day teaching of an endless "hell of torture". After studying the origin of the English word "hell", we found it to mean: a hidden place, or to hide. This meaning is in no way harmonious with the present day meaning that it has grown into. We must see that the "hell" preached by Evangelical Christianity **IS NOT THE "HELL" THAT THE BIBLE TEACHES.**

According to J. W. Hanson: "Canon Farrar truthfully says, in his "Eternal Hope": "And, finally, the word rendered "hell" is in one place the Greek word 'Tartarus,' borrowed as a word for the prison of evil spirits not after but before the resurrection. It is in ten places 'Hades,' which simply means the world beyond the grave, and it is twelve places 'Gehenna,' which means primarily, the "Valley of Hinnom" outside of Jerusalem in which after it had been polluted by Moloch worship, corpses were flung and fires were lit; and, secondly, it is a metaphor not of final and hopeless but of that purifying and corrective punishment which as we all believe does await impenitent sin both here and beyond the grave. But be it solemnly observed, the Jews to whom and in whose metaphorical sense the word was used by our blessed Lord, never did, either then or at any other period attach to that word 'Gehenna,' which He used, that meaning of endless torment which we have been taught to apply to "hell". To them and therefore on the lips of our blessed Savior Who addressed it to them, it means not a material and everlasting fire, but an intermediate, a metaphorical and a terminal retribution." (The Bible Hell, J. W. Hanson)

After evaluating the **FACTS**, we can now see that "Sheol", "Hades", and "Tartaroo" speak of literal death (the grave) or the consequences of sin, and "Gehenna" was the city dump used in a metaphoric way by our Lord to explain the consuming fire of God.

O DEATH, WHERE IS YOUR STING? O "HELL" ("HADES"), WHERE IS YOUR VICTORY?

August 12

THE RICH MAN AND LAZARUS - PART 1

<u>IT IS A PARABLE!</u>

The first and most important thing that we must see concerning the story of The Rich Man and Lazarus is: IT IS A PARABLE! A "parable" is: a short allegorical story designed to illustrate or teach a spiritual truth, religious principle, or moral lesson.

Matthew 13:34 tells us that **Jesus spoke to the multitudes in parables** (figurative language); **and without a parable did He not speak unto them: That it might be fulfilled which was spoken by the prophet, saying, I will open My mouth in PARABLES; I will utter things which have been kept secret from the foundation of the world…** With this in mind, we can now approach the teachings of Jesus in a proper way. Remember…Jesus always spoke in parables when He opened His mouth in public before the multitudes.

Starting with Luke chapter fifteen Jesus begins to speak a five-part parable. Notice who His audience is. He is speaking to the: publicans, sinners, Pharisees, and scribes.

The five parables are:

1. THE LOST SHEEP
2. THE LOST COIN
3. THE TWO LOST SONS (THE PRODIGAL SON)
4. THE UNJUST STEWARD
5. THE RICH MAN AND LAZARUS

The first three parables are spoken to encourage the publicans and sinners concerning God's love for them. The last two parables are spoken to warn the Pharisees and scribes (the religious leaders) of God's disapproval of their self-righteous behavior, which would ultimately lead to the Kingdom of God being stripped from the Jews and given to the Gentiles.

The reason it is so important that we understand that Jesus spoke to the multitudes in parables is because of this: **Many people literalize things in scripture that are to be understood spiritually, or in a metaphoric sense.** This is the MISTAKE that is often made by most concerning the parable of The Rich Man and Lazarus. We must also understand that the meaning of a parable is LOCKED to the mind of human intellect, which is the carnal (fleshly) mind.

1st Corinthians 2:14-16 states…But the natural man receives not the things of the Spirit of God: for they are foolishness unto him: neither can he know them, because they are spiritually discerned. But he that is spiritual judges all things, yet he himself is judged of no man. For who has known the mind of the Lord, that he may instruct Him? **But we have the mind of Christ…**

MAY WE APPROACH THIS PARABLE WITH THE MIND OF CHRIST!

August 13

THE RICH MAN AND LAZARUS - PART 2

THE MEANING OF THE PARABLE

Now that we have established that the story of The Rich Man and Lazarus is a PARABLE, let us seek to understand its true meaning.

The meaning of the parable is as follows:

A CERTAIN RICH MAN: This represents the Jewish Nation as a whole (Judah…More specifically: The Priesthood), for they were spiritually rich in the things of God (Romans 3:1,2… Romans 9:3-5).

CLOTHED IN PURPLE AND LINEN: This statement further clarifies who the Rich Man is, for purple represents royalty, and fine linen represents the priesthood. The Nation of Israel was to be a nation of kings (purple) and priests (linen) before God (Exodus 19:5,6).

FARED SUMPTUOUSLY EVERY DAY: This once again reaffirms that the Jews were a blessed people, having been given the adoption, glory, covenants, law, service, promises, and of whom as concerning the flesh Christ came (Romans 9:4,5).

A CERTAIN BEGGAR: This represents the Gentiles (Nations) as a whole, for they were spiritual Beggars concerning the things of God (Ephesians 2:11,12). The Gentiles (Nations) were referred to as the *Uncircumcision*. They were without Christ, being aliens from the commonwealth of Israel, and strangers from the covenants of promise, having no hope, and without God in the world.

LAZARUS: The name "Lazarus" comes from the Hebrew name "Eleazar", which means: "WHOM GOD HELPS". The reason Jesus used the name of "Lazarus" in this parable is for this very reason. The Gentiles (Nations) are those WHOM GOD HAS HELPED.

AT HIS GATE…FULL OF SORES…FED WITH CRUMBS…THE DOGS LICKED HIS SORES: These phrases all point to a description of the Gentiles (Nations), and how they were viewed by the Nation of Israel during the time that Jesus walked the earth. The Gentiles (Nations) were referred to as "dogs", and were considered to be uncircumcised filth by the Jews (Matthew 15:21-28…Mark 7:25-30).

THE BEGGAR DIED: This represents a **change** in the Beggar's condition. The Gentiles (Nations) died to their old condition of a Beggar, and would now be included and brought into the blessings of God (Ephesians 2:13-22).

ABRAHAM'S BOSOM: "Abraham's Bosom" is NOT a physical location. The term represents a place of **spiritual favor and honor**. The Gentiles (Nations) were now given the opportunity to become the children of Abraham. This represented the death of their Beggar status.

THE RICH MAN DIED, AND WAS BURIED: This represents a change in the Rich Man's condition. It signifies the death of Judaism (their religion). We must see that the Rich Man and Lazarus **changed places**. The Rich Man became a Beggar, and the Beggar became a Rich Man. Jesus took the Kingdom from the Jews (the Rich Man) and gave it to the Gentiles (Lazarus…the Beggar…the dogs). (Matthew 21:33-43…Matthew 8:12…Matthew 23:13-39…Mark 12:1-12… Acts 13:46,47…Luke 13:28,29).

IN HELL: The English word "hell" (used here) comes from the Greek word "Hades". The word "Hades" simply means: **"the grave, or the place of the dead"**. It carries with it the idea or meaning of **"un-perception"**. The Rich Man, along with his religion (Judaism), was now to be buried, finding himself in a place of un-perception, which refers to not being able to "see" (understand) or grasp the Kingdom of God (John 3:3).

LIFTED UP HIS EYES...IN TORMENTS...SEES ABRAHAM AFAR OFF...LAZARUS IN HIS BOSOM: This represents the Jews suffering the punishment of their sins, in the destruction of their city (70-73 A.D.) and temple, and the sore calamities which have befallen on them ever since. As we now know, the Jews have been through torment for the last 2,000 years due to the rejection of their Messiah. Their religion is dead, and they are currently in un-perception (outer darkness). The Rich Man now sees that Abraham (their spiritual roots) is afar off (cut off), and that Lazarus (the Gentiles / Nations) is in his bosom (a place of favor with God).

FATHER ABRAHAM...MERCY ON ME...SEND LAZARUS...DIP HIS FINGER IN WATER...COOL MY TONGUE...I AM TORMENTED IN THIS FLAME: This is all metaphoric language to show the change of positions and current conditions of the Rich Man and Lazarus. The Jews are now tormented in the flame of having rejected their Messiah. The Rich Man (the Jews) is now asking Lazarus to come and help (comfort) him, whereas before he wanted nothing to do with him, even referring to him as a dog.

THERE IS A GREAT GULF: The great gulf is explained by the apostle Paul in Romans 11:25-36. It is simply this: GOD BLINDED ISRAEL IN PART, UNTIL THE FULLNESS OF THE GENTILES (NATIONS) BE COME IN. Until then, the Rich Man can not pass from where he is (his condition) to where Lazarus is (his condition), and Lazarus can not pass from where he is to where the Rich Man is.

SEND HIM TO MY FATHER'S HOUSE...I HAVE FIVE BRETHREN...LEST THEY ALSO COME TO THIS PLACE OF TORMENT: This represents that the Jew learns mercy and compassion after his season of torment. The terminology "five brethren" gives us another undeniable clue as to the meaning of this parable. Modern day Israel, at the time of Jesus, was referred to as Judah (Note: After Solomon died, his Kingdom fell apart - Judah in the South and Israel in the North. What was a strong and united empire broke in two. God divorced Himself from Israel {the Northern Kingdom} in 745 B.C., causing them to be invaded by the Assyrian Empire and deported to the region of Nineveh.). God would later divorce Himself from Judah (the Southern Kingdom) in 70-73 A.D., causing them to be invaded by the Roman Army. This resulted in the destruction of Jerusalem. In this parable, Jesus was speaking to Judah (the Southern Kingdom). He was actually warning them of their destruction that was about to come if they did not repent. It is **extremely interesting** to note that Judah (in the Old Testament) had **FIVE FULL-BLOODED BROTHERS!** They were: Reuben, Simeon, Levi, Issachar, and Zebulun. The words "five brethren", used by Jesus, were a direct clue as to the identity of the Rich Man.

MOSES AND THE PROPHETS: This represents the law and the prophets, which could also be said to represent the Old Testament Scriptures. Jesus said...Let them hear them!

IF ONE WENT TO THEM FROM THE DEAD, THEY WILL REPENT: Jesus here alluded to HIS DEATH AND RESURRECTION from the dead, knowing that even though He would rise from the dead, yet would the Jews (as a whole) still not believe and repent.

---

*<u>**NOTE:**</u> Notice how that the Rich Man referred to Abraham as Father, and how that Abraham referred to him as son. This further clarifies the identity of the Rich Man.

Now that we have had our minds renewed (concerning this parable) to the mind of Christ, being brought to a proper understanding of this parable, we can discard the foolish ideas of the traditions and doctrines of men (concerning this parable), which state that this story is about eternal torture in hell. **THAT IS NOT CORRECT!** It is simply a <u>parable</u> which talks about...

THE JEWS AND GENTILES!

August 14

THE KINGDOM OF GOD IS WITHIN YOU - PART 1

Luke 17:20,21 states...And when He (Jesus) was demanded of the Pharisees, when the kingdom of God should come, He answered them and said, The kingdom of God comes not with observation: Neither shall they say, Lo here! or, lo there! for, behold, the kingdom of God is within you...

According to J. Preston Eby: "Some say that the correct translation should be: For the kingdom of God is *"in your midst,"* or *"among you,"* meaning that the Kingdom was present in their midst in the person of Jesus, "among" them but not "within" them. It cannot be denied—the Kingdom was indeed present among them in the very life of the Son of God, the King of glory! **But that is not the meaning of this passage.** The clearest meaning of the Greek can always be ascertained by *usage.* The way a word is *used* reveals its true meaning—the meaning that the Holy Spirit of inspiration puts upon it, not the meaning our English translators give it. It is a thing of wonder—the Holy Spirit has faithfully, powerfully, wisely and indisputably recorded for us the precise meaning of the word here translated "within". The Greek word is "ENTOS" meaning simply, according to Strong's Concordance, "inside; within". The word is used in only one other place in the New Testament, in Matthew 23:26. It is the Lord Jesus Himself that uses the word on both occasions, and notice what He says. "Woe unto you, scribes and Pharisees, hypocrites! for you make clean the *outside* of the cup and platter, but *within* they are full of extortion and excess. You blind Pharisee, cleanse first that which is *within* ("entos") the cup and platter, that the *outside* of them may be clean also." No one can argue that "ENTOS" means "in the midst" or "among" in this place—it clearly means "within". "Within" is contrasted with the "outside" of the cup and platter and plainly speaks of the pollution *within* the hearts of men, not *in their midst* or *among* them. The evil in men is not something apart from them or outside of them but something rooted deeply in the inward nature." (The Kingdom of God, J. Preston Eby)

If the Kingdom of God was in the Pharisees, how could they not see it or understand it? How could the Kingdom of God be in the Pharisees? Is the Kingdom of God in every man? What is the Kingdom of God? What does it mean to "see" the Kingdom of God? We will try to answer these questions in the coming days concerning the...

KINGDOM OF GOD!

August 15

THE KINGDOM OF GOD IS WITHIN YOU - PART 2

It is extremely important that we come to the understanding that the Kingdom of God is **within us**. Unfortunately, <u>most</u> Christians believe that the Kingdom of God is a planet that they are going to fly away to one day. They view it (the Kingdom of God) as something "out there", "up there", or "over there in the sweet by-and-by". They constantly sing songs that say…"Won't it be wonderful *there*". No wonder there is SO MUCH IMMATURITY in the body of Christ! It is time for God's people to see that the Kingdom of God is **within them**! It is not something external, but internal. All of the dealings of God (concerning man) begin within, and then are to be manifested without. Here are just a few scriptures that testify to this…

Colossians 1:26,27 states…Even the mystery which has been hid from ages and from generations, but now is made manifest to His saints: To whom God would make known what is the riches of the glory of this mystery among the Gentiles; which is <u>Christ</u> in <u>you</u>, the hope of glory…

2nd Corinthians 4:7 states…But we have this <u>treasure</u> in <u>earthen</u> <u>vessels</u>, that the excellency of the power may be of God, and not of us…

Galatians 1:15,16 states…But when it pleased God, Who separated me from my mother's womb, and called me by His grace, To <u>reveal</u> <u>His</u> <u>Son</u> <u>in</u> <u>me</u>, that I might preach Him among the heathen; immediately I conferred not with flesh and blood…

Ephesians 2:22 states…In Whom you also are built together for a <u>habitation</u> (dwelling place) of God through the Spirit…

1st Corinthians 6:19 states…What? know you not that <u>your</u> <u>body</u> <u>is</u> <u>the</u> <u>temple</u> <u>of</u> <u>the</u> <u>Holy</u> <u>Ghost</u> <u>which</u> <u>is</u> <u>in</u> <u>you</u>, which you have of God, and you are not your own?…

2nd Corinthians 6:16 states…And what agreement has the temple of God with idols? for <u>you</u> <u>are</u> <u>the</u> <u>temple</u> <u>of</u> <u>the</u> <u>living</u> <u>God</u>; as God has said, <u>I</u> <u>will</u> <u>dwell</u> <u>in</u> <u>them</u>, and <u>walk</u> <u>in</u> <u>them</u>; and I will be their God, and they shall be My people…

1st Peter 2:5 states…You also, as lively stones, are built up <u>a</u> <u>spiritual</u> <u>house</u>, a holy priesthood, to offer up spiritual sacrifices, acceptable to God by Jesus Christ…

These are just a few scriptures that show that God's dealings are within man, not outside of him. God's Kingdom is a Kingdom that operates within the hearts and lives of people, bringing about righteousness, peace, and joy in the Holy Spirit. The reason that many remain as spiritual infants is due to the fact that they do not see the Kingdom of God as something that is within. They are waiting to go to God's Kingdom "one day". WHY WOULD JESUS TELL US TO SEEK FIRST THE KINGDOM OF GOD IF IT WAS NOT AVAILABLE TO US IN THIS LIFE? (Think about it!)

THE KINGDOM OF GOD IS WITHIN <u>YOU</u>!

August 16

SEEING THE KINGDOM

John 3:3 states…Jesus answered and said unto him (Nicodemus), Verily, verily, I say unto you, Except a man be born again, he cannot see the kingdom of God…

This scripture verse is one of the most cherished verses in the Bible. It is often quoted and preached, but sadly, it is one of the most misunderstood verses in all of the Bible. It is quoted and read correctly, but it is explained and understood incorrectly. Listen to it again, for it states… Except a man be born again, HE CANNOT **"SEE THE KINGDOM OF GOD"**…Now…Let us talk about what all this means.

The words "born again" mean: to be begotten from above, or to be born from above. They speak of being <u>spiritually</u> <u>awakened</u> by the Spirit of God, or being quickened (made alive) to an awareness of the reality and presence of God in your own personal life. The word "see" means: to perceive, understand, or grasp with the mind. Now…Let us attempt to put all of this together.

Except a man be born again (have a spiritual awakening that is caused by the very Spirit of God Himself, resulting in being spiritually born from above), he cannot see (perceive, understand, or grasp with his mind) the Kingdom (the sovereign rule) of God. This is the very reason that the Pharisees could not see (perceive) that the Kingdom (the sovereign rule) of God was within them. They were thinking and looking in the physical realm for the Kingdom of God. This is why Jesus made the statement…The Kingdom of God does not come with observation…

The Kingdom of God is in every man, but he cannot see the Kingdom until he is born again to understand that God's seat of authority to rule and reign is within the heart of man. Jesus did not say that after being born again that we would die and go to the Kingdom, but rather, that we would "SEE" ("PERCEIVE") the Kingdom, and that the Kingdom would come to earth. The Kingdom is indeed coming to earth in the hearts of those that can…

SEE (PERCEIVE)!

August 17

PERCEPTION AND UN-PERCEPTION

After discussing the word "see", we have discovered that it means: to perceive, grasp, or understand with the mind. We are then led to the conclusion that: To "see" the Kingdom of God is to "perceive" the Kingdom of God. "SEEING" MEANS "PERCEIVING", OR "PERCEPTION". With this in mind, let us consider the opposite of "perception", which is "un-perception".

According to J. Preston Eby: "Concerning the literal meaning of the word "HADES" there can be no doubt. It comes from the Greek "A(I)DES". The "a" is a prefix which is equivalent to our "un-" and the stem "-id" means *"perceive"*. Thus we have "UN-PERCEIVE" or "imperceptible"; the *"unseen"*. That is "Hades" - the unseen world, the unknown realm. Our English word "hell" is derived from an Anglo-Saxon word "hillan" or "helan," meaning a cavern, anciently denoting a concealed or "UNSEEN" place. In parts of England men still say, "I plan to *"hell"* my potatoes," meaning to bury them in a hole or pit, that is, a covered place, out of sight. And in the old days a young couple seeking to be alone, sought a *"hell"*, a place where they could make love without being seen by prying eyes." (<u>Hell</u>, J. Preston Eby)

The reason the Pharisees (or any other person) could not "see" ("perceive") that the Kingdom of God was within them, was due to the fact that they were in "UN-PERCEPTION" ("Hades", "hell"). After having stated this, we should now be able to "see" that **"heaven" is "perception"** of God, and that **"hell" is "un-perception"** of God. It could also be said that "heaven" is the <u>mind of Christ</u>, and that "hell" is the <u>carnal</u> <u>mind</u>.

In conclusion, we are able to "see" that "heaven" and "hell" are not so much physical locations, as much as they are **a state or condition of the soul**. We can be found seated in "heavenly places" in Christ Jesus, having the <u>mind of Christ</u>, or we can be found having made our bed in "hell" ("Sheol", "Hades"), having <u>the carnal</u> (fleshly, hellish) <u>mind</u>. Remember…Except a man be born again, he cannot **"see" ("perceive")** the Kingdom of God. We must understand that only the Spirit of God can LIBERATE man from the **"HELL" ("UN-PERCEPTION")** of the carnal mind. Then, and only then, can we begin to "see"…

THE KINGDOM OF GOD!

August 18

DEFINING THE KINGDOM OF GOD

It is amazing that so many people have so little of an understanding of the Kingdom of God. If you were to ask people what the Kingdom of God was, you would get answers like:

We will know more about it in the "sweet by-and-by"…

Go ask a theologian, for I don't know…

It is a planet that we will "fly away" to "one day"…

It will come to earth "one day", but it is not for now…

It was among us when Jesus was here, but we must wait until His "second coming" to see it again…

It is a physical structure only, having no spiritual aspect to it…

It is isolated to a coming age only, and by the way, stay away from those "Kingdom Now" people who believe we can access it (the Kingdom) in this life…

With statements like these, it is quite clear that the majority of Christians (including the leadership of Christianity) HAVE ABSOLUTELY NO IDEA WHAT THE KINGDOM OF GOD IS! The Kingdom of God is probably **THE MOST IMPORTANT SUBJECT OF THE BIBLE**, for it was all that Jesus talked about! He was always pointing men to an understanding of the Kingdom of God.

According to J. Preston Eby: "The word "kingdom" is from the Greek word "BASILEIA" meaning "rule" or "reign". Remember when Jesus replied…My Kingdom is not of this world — that is, My Kingdom is not after the order and systems of earthly kingdoms. It is the rule of God by the Spirit…The dictionary defines "kingdom" as "a government or country headed by a king or queen; a monarchical state; a realm or domain." The word "kingdom" is made up of the noun "king," and the suffix "dom". "Dom" is a noun-forming suffix to express rank, position, or domain. For example, a "dukedom" is the domain over which a duke has authority or exercises rule, and in the abstract the rank of a duke. In like manner a "kingdom" is the domain and the people within that domain over which a king exercises authority and rule. It is the "king's domain". "Kingdom" is thus a contraction of "king's domain". The term, "Kingdom of God", can mean no other than the domain over which God exercises rule as King. It is God's declared purpose therefore that His *people*, His *holy nation*, His *peculiar treasure*, should be the domain over which He would rule as King, and ultimately all the earth and all things and every creature." (To Be The Lord's Prayer, J. Preston Eby)

As men are awakened to the Kingdom that is within them, they will arise to find that a battle is taking place within them. This battle is called…

THE BATTLE OF ARMAGEDDON!

August 19

THE BATTLE OF ARMAGEDDON

According to J. Preston Eby: "Millions sanctimoniously and religiously pray, "Thy Kingdom come," thinking it is something outside of themselves, is some distant age, under other conditions — and have no intention whatever of abdicating the throne of their own inner wills and hearts to the King of Glory. They are utterly unwilling to surrender the sovereignty of their lives to God. They are no more prepared to accept the sovereign rule of Christ than were those men who shouted at His crucifixion, "We have no king but Caesar!" So, if I sincerely, earnestly, and genuinely beseech the Spirit of God to *rule* in my life and experience, there to establish His Kingdom, I can only expect that there will be a most tremendous confrontation. It is a foregone conclusion that there will follow a formidable conflict between His divine sovereignty and my self-willed ego. And this, precious friend of mine, is the true BATTLE OF ARMAGEDDON!" (To Be The Lord's Prayer, J. Preston Eby)

To those who would seek first the Kingdom of God, let us seek His Kingdom with the understanding THAT THIS IS OUR MOST IMPORTANT TASK IN THIS LIFE! Jesus told us to put the Kingdom of God before food, clothing, drink, and anything else for that matter. IT IS TO BE OUR <u>CHIEF</u> <u>AIM</u>! As this takes place, let us not be surprised to find that a battle will begin to rage from within. This battle (The Battle of Armageddon) is a conflict between flesh and Spirit, for they do war against one another (Romans 8:1-10, Romans7:14-25).

We begin to find ourselves exposed to our Adamic Nature, and as well, to the divine nature, which is the **power source** to overcome the Adamic Nature. This process places us in the valley of decision (Joel 3:14), in which our soul is sanctified, and our decisions (choices) are purified. God exposes us to good and evil, while teaching us to overcome, choosing good. We will find that we are overcoming evil through the **tree of life** (Jesus Christ), and not through the **tree of the knowledge of good and evil** (our carnal mind).

The only way to overcome in this battle is to recognize that THE BATTLE IS THE LORD'S. We must fight the good fight of faith, which is to continually believe that THE BATTLE IS THE LORD'S. This is what it means to labor to enter into His rest (1st Samuel 17:47, 1st Timothy 6:12, Hebrews 4:1-11). When we rest we are changed from glory to glory, causing the flesh to become weak, which in turn open us up to the strength of the Spirit of God.

SEEK FIRST THE KINGDOM OF GOD!

August 20

THE ETERNAL PURPOSE - PART 1

THE PURPOSE OF THE AGES

It is our goal in this study to prove that **the teaching of eternal torture is a lie**, and that it is primarily based on the wrong and improper translation of three key words, which are: **"OLAM", "AION", AND "AIONIOS"**.

According to Nathaniel Scarlett: "This confused translation of "olam", and "aion", when it occurred as a substantive, and "aeonian", when it occurred as an adjective, and the want of discernment in readers, has been a means of propagating the doctrine of endless damnation, which states that God will kindle a fire, and so constantly supply it with combustible matter, brimstone, and by His all creating power, as to endure as long as He Himself shall exist; and that the subjects of future punishment, being raised incorruptible and indissoluble, shall for the same period endure burning in the lake of fire, God having no ultimate end in view but the endless misery of His creatures." (A Translation Of The New Testament, Nathaniel Scarlett)

Let us now turn our attention to Ephesians 3:11, which states...According to the *eternal purpose* which He purposed in Christ Jesus our Lord...The word "eternal" in this passage comes from the Greek word "aion", and should be literally rendered...**THE PURPOSE OF THE <u>AGES</u>**. With this being brought to our attention, we are now headed in the right direction. We are headed to a proper understanding of God's purpose of the ages.

To understand God's purpose for the creation, we must have an understanding of <u>DISPENSATIONS</u> and <u>AGES</u>, for God's purpose is the purpose of the ages. Without an understanding of AGES we are doomed and even forced to believe the teachings of men, who state that God cannot and will not save all mankind, but will in fact separate, punish, and eternally torture the MAJORITY of the human race, having no end goal or remedial (corrective) purpose in mind.

The goal of this study will be to prove, beyond a shadow of a doubt, that the teaching of eternal torture is FALSE! We will also prove that this teaching is based primarily on the mistranslation of the words "olam", "aion", and "aionios", which refer to the ages, and do not give validity to the BLASPHEMOUS IDEA that God would ever eternally torment any of His created beings. Let us study to show ourselves approved unto God! We are going to...

TAKE A JOURNEY THROUGH THE AGES!

August 21

THE ETERNAL PURPOSE - PART 2

DISPENSATIONS AND AGES

According to Joseph E. Kirk: "The teaching of the scriptures about the eons (ages) provides answers to frustrating questions concerning the meaning of human existence. God's purpose in creating man, and God's purpose of the eons (ages) are inseparably related. Many are unfamiliar with this important subject because the facts have been concealed by incorrect and misleading translations of the Bible from the original languages into English. The eons (ages) are the longest periods of time referred to in the scriptures. They should be distinguished from the eras and the dispensations. Time-wise they (the ages) are of indefinite duration, but event-wise they are distinctly marked off by great cataclysms which affect the whole earth. For example, an age may consist of several dispensations, in the same sense that a year does consist of several months.

We are to see that <u>the ages have a beginning</u>:

    Heb.1:2: God made the *eons*-vs-God made the *worlds*

    1 Cor.2:7: before the *eons* -vs- before the *world*

    Tim.1:9: before *times eonian* -vs- before the *world began*

<u>The ages end</u>, individually and collectively:

> Heb.9:26: the end of the *eons* -vs-the end of the *world*
>
> 1 Cor.10:11: the end of the *eons* -vs- the ends of the *world*
>
> Matt.24:3: the end of the *eon* -vs- the end of the *world*

<u>The Bible speaks of at least five ages</u>, which are: past ages, this present age, and the ages to come:

> Col.1:26: hid from the *eons* -vs- Past hid from *ages* (at least two ages have past)
>
> Luke 20:34: this *eon* -vs- this *world* (this present age)
>
> Eph.2:7: *eons* to come -vs- *ages* to come (At least two more to come, thus--a minimum of five eons indicated)" (The above information is from: <u>Eons Of The Bible</u>, Joseph E. Kirk)

As we have just stated, the Bible speaks of at least five ages. Within these ages are eight recognized dispensations. They are: Innocence, Conscience, Human Government, Promise, Law, Grace (Church), Kingdom (The Millennium), The Dispensation Of The Fullness Of Times (The Age Of The Ages).

According to Joseph E. Kirk: "The teaching of the scriptures concerning the eons (ages) has been concealed from many by the inconsistencies of the translators. An understanding of the eons (ages) and God's eonian purpose (the purpose of the ages), results in a revelation of God that is most enlightening and edifying. His every attribute becomes more wonderful and glorious. The truth on this subject reveals undreamed of value and success in the saving work of our Lord Jesus Christ. It leads to the solution of many difficult problems which exercise the hearts and minds of spiritual believers." (<u>Eonian: Everlasting Or Age-Lasting</u>?, Joseph E. Kirk)

Our next effort will be to show the many contradictions in some modern day translations. This is due to the mistranslation of the words...

"OLAM", "AION", AND "AIONIOS"!

August 22

THE ETERNAL PURPOSE - PART 3

CONTRADICTIONS IN SOME MODERN DAY TRANSLATIONS
(<u>Hell Is Leaving The Bible "Forever"</u>, Gary Amirault)

Now let's discover how long the "eternity" REALLY is in many leading "selling" English translations:

- Sodom's fiery judgment is "eternal" (Jude 7)--until--God "will restore the fortunes of Sodom" (Ezekiel 16:53-55).

- Israel's "affliction is incurable" (Jer. 30:12)-until--the Lord "will restore health" and heal her wounds (Jer. 30:17).

- The sin of Samaria "is incurable" (Mic. 1:9)-until-- the Lord "will restore ... the fortunes of Samaria." (Ez. 16:53).

- Ammon is to become a "wasteland forever" and "rise no more" (Zeph. 2:9, Jer. 25:27) --until-- the Lord will "restore the fortunes of the Ammonites" (Jer. 49:6).

- An Ammonite or Moabite is forbidden to enter the Lord's congregation "forever"-until--the tenth generation (Deut. 23:3):

- Habakkuk tells us of mountains that were "everlasting", that is -until-- they "were shattered" (Hab. 3 3:6).

- The Aaronic Priesthood was to be an "everlasting" priesthood (Ex. 40:15), that is-until-it was superceded by the Melchizedek Priesthood (Hebrews 7:14-18).

- Many translations of the Bible inform us that God would dwell in Solomon's Temple "forever" (1 Kings 8:13), that is,--until the Temple was destroyed.

- The children of Israel were to "observe the Sabbath throughout their generations, for a perpetual covenant" (Exodus 31:16)-until--Paul states there remains "another day" of Sabbath rest for the people of God (Heb. 4:8,9).

- The Law of Moses was to be an "everlasting covenant" (Leviticus 24:8) yet we read in the New Covenant the first was "done away" and "abolished" (2 Corinthians 3:11,13), and God "made the first old" (Hebrews 8:13).

- The fire for Israel's sin offering (of a ram without blemish) is never to be put out. It shall be a "perpetual"-- until-- Christ, the Lamb of God, dies for our sins. We now have a better covenant established on better promises (Lev. 6:12-13, Heb. 8:6-13).

- God's waves of wrath roll over Jonah "forever"-until--the Lord delivers him from the large fish's belly on the third day (Jonah 2:6,10; 1: 17); Egypt and Elam will "rise no more" (Jer. 25:27)-until--the Lord will "restore the fortunes of Egypt" (Ez. 29:14) and "restore the fortunes of Elam" (Jer. 49:39).

- "Moab is destroyed" (Jer. 48:4, 42)-until--the Lord "will restore the fortunes of Moab" (Jer. 48:47).

- Israel's judgment lasts "forever"-until--the Spirit is poured out and God restores it (Isa. 32:13-15).

- So, narrow is the way to life and few find it-until-- and His church confiscate the "strong man's" booty, setting the captives free so God becomes all in all (Isa. 61, Luke 11:21-22, Matt. 7:13; 16:18, 1 Cor. 15:24-28).

- The King James Bible, as well as many others, tells us that a bondslave was to serve his master "forever" (Exodus 21:6), that is,--until--his death.

- God is now calling out "a people for His name"--an "elect" or chosen priesthood people who will represent and reflect His loving nature. Many are called and few are chosen--until--the small chosen priesthood people, by the Spirit, restore "David's tabernacle" so ALL mankind may inquire of the Lord. Thus we see that the church is the first-born, the beginning--until--in ALL (later born new creatures in Christ) our Lord will have supremacy (Amos 9:11-12, Matt. 22:14, Acts 15:14-18, Eph. 3:15, Col. 1 18).

- All manner of sin will be forgiven in this AGE as well as in the AGE (not eternity) to come, except blasphemy against God's Spirit-until--such blasphemy finds pardon in the fullness of the times (or ages) when God unites all in Christ. For the Lord does not retain His anger forever because He delights in mercy (Matt. 12:32; 18:11,21-22, Eph. 1:9-11, Rev. 4:11; 5:13, Mic. 7:18-20).

- God's wrath has come upon Israel "to the uttermost" (1 Thess. 2:16). So there is a gulf between "the rich man in purple" (Royal Covenant "Son", Israel) and the saved gentiles (Lazarus) which no man can cross--until--Christ Himself crosses it to bring His promised restoration. For again, scripture promises that ALL Israel will be saved (Jer. 50:5, Luke 16:19-26, John 12:32, Romans 11:26-29). (Gary Amirault)

Hang on…

THERE ARE MORE TO COME!

August 23

THE ETERNAL PURPOSE - PART 4

CONTRADICTIONS IN SOME MODERN DAY TRANSLATIONS CONTINUED

Here are some more contradictions from leading "selling" English translations:

Matthew 24:3 (King James Version) states…And as He sat upon the mount of Olives, the disciples came unto Him privately, saying, Tell us, when shall these things be? and what shall be the sign of Your coming, and of **the end of the world**?…

Ephesians 3:21 (King James Version) states…Unto Him be glory in the church by Christ Jesus throughout all ages, **world without end**. Amen…

Now…Let us take a look at these two scripture verses from the King James Version. THIS IS AS CLEAR OF A CONTRADICTION AS YOU COULD POSSIBLY HAVE! Matthew 24:3 (King James Version) tells us that the **world will end**. Ephesians 3:21 (King James Version) tells us that **the world will be without end**. One verse (Matthew 24:3) tells us that the world will end, and the other (Ephesians 3:21) tells us that the world will not end. THAT, MY FRIEND, IS A CONTRADICTION, IF THERE EVER WAS ONE!

The reason there are many contradictions to be found in leading "selling" English translations, is due to the fact that certain words ("olam", "aion", "aionios") were not handled or translated correctly as they were brought from the original languages (Hebrew and Greek) into the English language. The meanings of these verses, in the original Greek, carry with them no hint of contradiction, and do indeed paint quite a beautiful picture of the purpose and plan of the ages.

Matthew 24:3 should be translated as follows…And as He sat upon the mount of Olives, the disciples came unto Him privately, saying, Tell us, when shall these things be? and what shall be the sign of Your coming, and of the end of the **age**? Ephesians 3:21 should be translated as follows… Unto Him be glory in the church by Christ Jesus throughout all **generations**, **unto** **the** **age** **of the** **ages**. Amen…

WOW! Now we can see that these passages are referring to the ages, and more specifically, GOD'S PURPOSE AND PLAN OF THE AGES.

According to Gary Amirault: "If one wants to get down right technical about it, many leading "selling" English Bible translations have just plain missed it when translating the Hebrew word "olam," the Greek word, "aion," and its adjective "aionios." These words simply should never have been translated by words which indicate an eternal state. Many leading scholars today readily admit that. I'll just quote one for this non-technical article just for the reader's sake. **Dr. R. F. Weymouth**, translator of the "New Testament in Modern Speech" states in that work, "Eternal, Greek aeonian, i.e., of the ages: Etymologically this adjective, like others similarly formed does not signify, "during" but "belonging to" the aeons or ages." (Hell Is Leaving The Bible "Forever", Gary Amirault)

NOW…LET US GO FROM CONTRADICTION TO CLARITY!

August 24

THE ETERNAL PURPOSE - PART 5

OLAM

According to C. Gary Reid and Ernest L. Martin: "The word "*olam*" is derived from the primitive root "*alam*", meaning to veil from sight, to conceal. An analysis of the passages where "*olam*" appears shows clearly that the word does not express "eternity" or "everlasting" as it has been frequently translated in the King James Version. Rather, it simply expresses a duration, a time during which a person, thing, or state of a thing exists — literally an age of time which has a definite beginning and conclusion. The duration of an age in scripture is sometimes defined and sometimes undefined. "*Olam*", including its usage in the singular and plural and with prepositions and negatives, is translated differently in the Old Testament of our English Version.

These various translations with their number of occurrences are tabulated below:

    "for ever and ever" - 24

    "from everlasting to everlasting" - 4

    "for ever" - 251

    "everlasting" - 60

    "of ancient times" "of old time" - 2

    "of old" or "ever of old" - 16

    "world without end" - 1

    "never" - 16

    "perpetual" - 22

    "evermore" - 15

    "old" or "ancient" - 13

    "of" or "in old time" - 3

    "always" or "alway" - 5

    "anymore" - 2

    "world" - 2

    "continuance" - 1

    "eternal" - 1

    "lasting" - 1

    "long time" - 1

    "at any time" - 1

    "the beginning of the world" - 1

    "ever" - 4

    "long" - 2

Total occurrences of olam - 448

The Time Periods for Salvation, Part 1
by C. Gary Reid and Ernest L. Martin, Ph.D., 1975
Typeset and footnoted by David Sielaff, November 2004"

    The following is an excerpt from: (The Power Of Life And Death In A Greek Four Letter Word - Aion, Gary Amirault)…"While studying this Hebrew word "olam," I came across some quotations from leading scholars which began to give me much understanding. The classical Wilson's Old Testament Word Studies by William Wilson gives as the meaning of "olam," "duration of time which is concealed or hidden," in other words, an unknown length of time. This unknown length of time could be 3 days and nights as in the case of Jonah, or the length of a man's life, or as long as the period of time the Aaronic Priesthood was in effect, which was around 1600 years. Well, that seemed to solve all the problems. This definition took care of all the clear contradictions between the Old and New Testament and got old Jonah out of "hell forever." From Jonah's point of view, while he was in the fish, he didn't know how long he was there since he couldn't see the sun and moon. (They didn't invent Timex watches until a few thousand years later.) But while the problem was solved in the Old Testament, it presented some different problems in the New Testament. The Greek equivalent for the Hebrew "*olam*" is the word "*aion*". We get the English word "eon" from this word. It seems that many Bible translators carried the error of mistranslating "*olam*" to the Greek word "*aion*". (Gary Amirault)

This brings us to our next stop on our journey through the ages. We will consider the Greek word "aion" next, giving its meaning, and showing how it too has been grossly mistranslated in many leading "selling" English translations. We are now beginning to see…

THE PURPOSE OF THE AGES COME TO LIGHT!

❖

August 25

THE ETERNAL PURPOSE - PART 6

AION

According to C. Gary Reid and Ernest L. Martin: "The noun "*aion*" means "age" or "eon" and is found 128 times in 105 passages of the New Testament. It doubly occurs in 23 of the 105 passages. In its simple form (noun only), it is found 37 times and with prepositions 68. "*Aion*" is translated as follows in the Authorized Version:

USAGE	NUMBER OF OCCURRENCES	REPRESENTATIVE SCRIPTURE
Age	2	Ephesians 2:7
Course	1	Ephesians 2:2
World	40	Hebrews 6:5
Ever	72	Jude 13
Never	7	John 11:26
Evermore	4	2 Corinthians 11:31
Eternal	2	1 Timothy 1:17

Here are seven different renderings of the word "*aion*" as it appears in the form of a noun. On the surface, it seems that the translators were confused as to the right meaning of this important word. The word "world" in the English language is used to describe the present arrangement of human life and activity, but it certainly indicates a terminable period. It had a beginning and will have an end. Indeed "world" conveys no duration of time whatever. Yet "*aion*" shows "time" — though the time is always indefinite as to length. It is just like "*olam*" in Hebrew. The usual words in English which best approximate the original meaning of "*aion*" are "age" and "eon" (the latter word is derived from the Greek original itself)."

The Time Periods for Salvation, Part 1
by C. Gary Reid and Ernest L. Martin, Ph.D., 1975
Typeset and footnoted by David Sielaff, November 2004

The following is an excerpt from: (The Power Of Life And Death In A Greek Four Letter Word - Aion, Gary Amirault)…"One of the major problems the King James translators have caused by their incorrect handling of this word, deals with the end of the world. It seems most Christians throughout the Christian era have been very interested in this time period. Martin Luther, in his time, was convinced he was living in "the end of the world." The King James translation contradicts itself using this phrase. Most present day Bible translations have corrected this error in many places, but not enough to clear up the confusion completely. In Hebrews 9:26 we read from the King James translation: "For then must He often have suffered since the foundation of the world; but now once in the end of the world has He appeared to put away sin by the sacrifice of Himself." According to this King James verse, the end of the world occurred 1900 years ago. If we are supposedly living in the end of the world, the "end of the world" has been going on for 1900 years of the 6000 year Biblical record! But this is not the end of the confusion, it gets worse. According to Ephesians 3:21(see also Isaiah 45:17), there is to be no end of the world: "Unto Him be glory in the church by Christ Jesus throughout all ages, world without end. Amen." The King James Bible tells us that the end of the world occurred 1900 years ago, yet at the same time tells us the world will never end! And we wonder why there are so many atheists out there! This problem is immediately cleared up when we discover "*aion*" should never have been translated world. The Greeks had a perfectly good word to describe "world", the word "cosmos". We use this word in the English today, but with a slightly different meaning than in the Greek of Biblical days. If the King's translators had done what most leading Bible translations today have done with the word "*aion*" in these cases where the KJV translated it "world," much of the confusion about the "end of the world" would disappear. The word "*aion*" should have been translated "age" (or something similar). Jesus would then have been living at the end of the Jewish "age." After that came a new "age," the one we are currently experiencing." (Gary Amirault)

When a word is translated correctly…

IT MAKES A "WORLD" OF DIFFERENCE!

August 26

THE ETERNAL PURPOSE - PART 7

AIONIOS

According to C. Gary Reid and Ernest L. Martin: "In the translation of the adjective in the King James Version there is not as much variation. "*Aionios*" is rendered into only four English words.

USAGE	# OF OCCURRENCES	SCRIPTURES
Eternal	42	Titus 3:7
Everlasting	25	2 Thessalonians 1:9
Ever	1	Philemon 15
World	3	Titus 1:2

The adjective form "*aionios*" cannot carry a force or express a duration greater than the "age" of which it speaks. It cannot mean "eternal" or "everlasting". It literally means "of the age" or "age-long." Once these meanings of the Hebrew "*olam*" and the Greek "*aion*" are understood, a flood of light will shine forth to show how God has been using various ages or strategic time periods to perfect His plan of salvation for man."

The Time Periods for Salvation, Part 1
by C. Gary Reid and Ernest L. Martin, Ph.D., 1975
Typeset and footnoted by David Sielaff, November 2004

The following is an excerpt from: (The Power Of Life And Death In A Greek Four Letter Word - Aion, Gary Amirault)…"There are some who after wrestling with the facts above will admit that the word "*aion*" means "an age," but they say its adjective "*aionios*" has to mean "eternal" because it is used so often to describe God. Professors in seminaries say these kind of **foolish things**. Anyone with a little bit of sense recognizes that an adjective cannot have a greater force or meaning than its noun. "Hourly" cannot mean "yearly," for example. The adjective gets its force from the noun. If the noun "*aion*" means "age", then the adjective "*aionios*" has to pertain to "age" and not to something greater than "age." It cannot therefore correctly represent "eternity". Just because "*aionios*" is used to describe God Who is "eternal" does not mean "*aionios*" means "eternal." God is the God of Abraham, Isaac, and Jacob. Does that mean He is not the God of the rest of us? Of course, not! God can be the God of **ages** as well as being **eternal**. The very nature of God commands the idea of "eternity". He doesn't have to be called "eternal" to make Him "eternal". That is part of His nature. The Bible has many other ways to express "endlessness" or not being exposed to the corruption of death. "Endlessness" is expressed in the scriptures by the simple phrase "no end" (Luke 1:33; Dan.

7:14; Isa. 9:7). The thought of permanence is also expressed in Hebrews 7:16, "the power of an endless or indissoluble life," and in 1 Peter 1:4, "an inheritance incorruptible, and undefiled, and that fades not away." (Gary Amirault)

HE IS THE GOD OF ETERNITY AND TIME (AGES)!

August 27

THE ETERNAL PURPOSE / PART 8

A PROPER TRANSLATION OF OLAM, AION, AND AIONIOS…
FINDING A GOOD BIBLE TRANSLATION
(L. Ray Smith)

"The first page of my Oxford University Press edition of the King James Bible says this:

Containing the Old and New Testaments Translated out of the Original Tongues and with the former Translations diligently compared and revised by His Majesty's special command

Notice that it "contains" the Old and New Testaments from the original tongues, but IT was not translated FROM the original tongues, but is rather, a revision of "former Translations!" Sadly to say, although we owe MUCH to the King James or Authorized Version of the scriptures, it is NOT a translation of the original Hebrew and Greek languages of the scriptures. To its credit, many (thousands) of inconsistencies have been corrected over the years. However, NOT ALL. There still remains some colossal errors that translators and scholars either are overlooking or are purposefully ignoring. The following Bible Translations are helpful in seeing the honest rendering of such King James words as, "everlasting", "evermore", "forever and ever", "eternal", "hell", etc. They either render these words properly or show in the margins what the literal Hebrew or Greek is, rather than attempting to prop up the fancied pagan doctrine of eternal torment in an ever-burning hell of literal fire. I am not recommending that you buy any of these Bible Versions. You can understand the truths of God by merely coming to understand the proper translation of two or three words in your King James Bibles. But, if you decide to actually buy one of these Versions, I would suggest Rotherham's over the others. Besides it may be the only one that you can find in a book store."

Ray

Rotherham's Emphasized Bible, 1959
Young's Literal Translation of the Holy Bible, 1898
The Holy Bible in Modern English (Fenton), 1903
The Emphatic Diaglott, 1912 edition (Greek/English Interlinear)

The New Covenant, 1884
The New Testament in Modern Speech, 1910
The Restoration of Original Sacred Name Bible, 1976
The New Testament of Our Lord and Savior Jesus Anointed, 1958
The New Testament a Translation, 1938
Concordant Literal New Testament, 1983
The Companion Bible, 1990 A King James Reference Bible

After a careful study of "olam", "aion", and "aionios" from the original Hebrew and Greek, along with these more accurate translations, the pagan idea and doctrine of eternal torment will disappear from the pages.

MAY THE LOVE OF GOD FILL YOUR HEART!

August 28

THE ETERNAL PURPOSE- PART 9

EXAMPLES OF OLAM, AION, AND AIONIOS TRANSLATED CORRECTLY

Let us now look to some of the more accurate translations of the Holy Scriptures for a proper rendering of "olam", "aion", and "aionios". In order to do this, we will consider Daniel 7:18 in the King James Version, The Emphasized Bible, and The Young's Literal Translation.

Daniel 7:18 (King James Version) states…But the saints of the MOST HIGH shall take the kingdom, and possess the kingdom for ever, even for ever and ever…(Note: Have you ever stopped and thought about the phrase "for ever and ever"? What is "for ever and ever"? Is it "eternity and eternity"? Does that really make any sense? Why would you need to place an "ever" on top of a "for ever"? Would not one "for ever" be enough? THINK ABOUT IT!)

Let us now look to Rotherham's Emphasized Bible. This Bible is a literal word by word translation from the original Hebrew and Greek. We will look at the same scripture to see if Rotherham is able to make more sense of our "for ever and ever" dilemma.

Daniel 7:18 (Rotherham's Emphasized Bible) states…But the holy ones of the Highest, shall receive the kingdom, - and shall possess the kingdom **for the age, yea for the age of ages…**

We are already beginning to go from confusion ("for ever, even for ever and ever"???) to clarity ("for the age, yea for the age of the ages"!!!)! We are now able to see that this scripture is referring to a coming "age", and then referring to an "age above all ages", which is referred to as the "AGE OF THE AGES". (Note: We will go into the meaning of the terminology…"for the age, yea for the age of the ages"…in greater detail in a future teaching.)

The Young's Literal Translation of the Holy Bible renders Daniel 7:18 as follows…And receive the kingdom do the saints of the Most High, and they strengthen the kingdom **unto the age, even unto the age of the ages…**

These two Bible **TRANSLATIONS** (The Emphasized Bible and The Young's Literal Translation) do properly and correctly represent the original Hebrew words used in Daniel 7:18. They (The Emphasized and The Young's) teach us of a coming "age", as well as an "age of the ages". This scripture (Daniel 7:18) does not refer to endlessness, as is incorrectly portrayed by the King James Version, but rather, it refers to the coming "Kingdom Age", as well as "The Age Of The Ages". The next stop on our journey through the ages will be in the book of Jonah. We must figure out…

HOW TO GET JONAH OUT OF THE BELLY OF HELL!

August 29

THE ETERNAL PURPOSE - PART 10

EXAMPLES OF OLAM, AION, AND AIONIOS TRANSLATED CORRECTLY

We now turn our attention to the book of Jonah. According to the King James Version of the Bible, the great prophet is to be found "in the belly of hell" crying out for God to hear his voice, and is said to be there "for ever". Wait…It gets even more confusing. According to Jonah 1:17, Jonah was in the belly of the fish three days and three nights. Jonah 2:6 tells us that Jonah went down to the bottoms of the mountains; the earth with her bars was about him **for ever…**The remainder of Jonah 2:6 states…**yet have You brought up my life from corruption, O Lord God…**

Well…The King James Version has ONCE AGAIN left us a *messy contradiction* that we must clean up! In essence, we find Jonah: in the belly of **hell**, going down to the bottoms of the mountains; the earth with her bars was about him **for ever: yet God brought up his life from corruption**. Let us begin our RESCUE MISSION! We must save Jonah from the "belly of hell", in which he is to be doomed "for ever", that is, unless we are able to find a way to get him out. It is important that Jonah is rescued from the belly of the great fish, for he must go to Nineveh, that great city, to preach God's message to them.

In order to save our good friend Jonah, we must do something <u>very</u> <u>courageous</u>! WE MUST READ FROM ANOTHER BIBLE TRANSLATION OTHER THAN THE KING JAMES VERSION! CAN YOU HANDLE IT? ARE YOU READY? We will look to two very accurate translations to help us solve our problem.

Jonah 2:2,6 (The Emphasized Bible) states…I cried - out of my distress - unto Yahweh, and He answered me, - Out of the belly of **Hades** (the grave, or the place of the dead…un-perception) called I, You did hear my voice…To the roots of the mountains, went I down, As for the earth, her bars, were about me, **age-abidingly**, - Then did You bring up - out of the pit - my life, O Yahweh my God…

Jonah 2:2,6 (Young's Literal Translation) states…I called, because of my distress, to Jehovah, And He did answer me, From the belly of **Sheol** ("Sheol" is the Hebrew equivalent of the Greek word "Hades"…they both mean the same thing) I have cried, You have heard my voice…To the cuttings of mountains I have come down, The earth, her bars [are] behind me **to the age**. And You bring up from the pit my life, O Jehovah my God…

After having consulted the Emphasized Bible and the Young's Literal Translation, our dilemma is solved, Jonah is released from "Sheol" (as well as the great fish), having been there **to the age** ("olam" - a hidden or concealed amount of time), and Nineveh will be preached to, so that they will repent.

WOW!…ALL THIS FROM READING SOME OTHER BIBLE TRANSLATIONS!

August 30

THE ETERNAL PURPOSE - PART 11

EXAMPLES OF OLAM, AION, AND AIONIOS TRANSLATED CORRECTLY

After having solved the "for ever and ever" dilemma, and rescuing Jonah from the belly of "eternal hell", we are now ready to continue our journey through the ages. We will cite one other contradiction in the King James Version concerning the word "olam". This contradiction refers to the Aaronic Priesthood as being an "everlasting" one, which we know is not true, for it has been replaced by the Priesthood after the order of Melchisedec.

Exodus 40:15 (King James Version) states…And you shall anoint them, as you did anoint their father, that they may minister unto Me in the priest's office: for their anointing shall surely be an **everlasting** priesthood throughout their generations…

Hebrews 7:14-19 (King James Version) states…For it is evident that our Lord sprang out of Juda; of which tribe Moses spoke nothing concerning priesthood. And it is yet far more evident: for that **after the similitude of Melchisedec there arises another priest**, Who is made, not after the law of a carnal commandment, but after the power of an endless life. For He testifies, **You are a priest for ever after the order of Melchisedec. For there is verily a disannulling** of the commandment going before for the weakness and unprofitableness thereof. For the law made nothing perfect, but the bringing in of a better hope did; by the which we draw near unto God…

Exodus 40:15 (Young's Literal Translation) states…And anointed them as you have anointed their father, and they have acted as priests to Me, and their anointing has been to be to them for a priesthood **age-during**, to their generations…

We can now see that after a proper translation of Exodus 40:15, that it is in total harmony with Hebrews 7:14-19. The Aaronic Priesthood was never to be an "everlasting" priesthood, but rather, it was to give way to the Priesthood after the order of Melchisedec. Hebrews 7: 14-19 makes this very clear. This is OBVIOUSLY another one of the many contradictions of the King James Version.

It is EASILY cleared up when we see that the Aaronic Priesthood was to be an **age-during (age-lasting)** priesthood. The mistranslation of the word "olam" in the Old Testament has caused many contradictions. But fear not, for with a little bit of research…

THEY ALL CLEAR UP!

August 31

THE ETERNAL PURPOSE - PART 12

EXAMPLES OF OLAM, AION, AND AIONIOS TRANSLATED CORRECTLY

We will now turn our attention to the New Testament, in which we will show and correct some of the mistranslations of the words "aion" and "aionios". We will begin by showing that there is NO SUCH THING as an "unpardonable sin". The words "unpardonable sin" are nowhere to be found in scripture, FOR THERE IS NO SUCH THING AS AN "UNPARDONABLE SIN" WITH OUR LOVING FATHER! Those words were later ADDED to study Bibles, causing many to believe this FALSE CONCEPT. Let us first quote from the King James **Version**, and then from a **translation** that deals with these passages (Matthew 12:31,32…Mark 3:28-30) in a proper way.

Matthew 12:31,32 & Mark 3:28-30 (King James Version) state…Wherefore I say unto you, All manner of sin and blasphemy shall be forgiven unto men: but the blasphemy against the Holy Ghost shall not be forgiven unto men. And whosoever speaks a word against the Son of man, it shall be forgiven him: but whosoever speaks against the Holy Ghost, it shall not be forgiven him, neither in this world, neither in the world to come…Verily I say unto you, All sins shall be forgiven unto the sons of men, and blasphemies wherewith soever they shall blaspheme: But he that shall blaspheme against the Holy Ghost has never forgiveness, but is in danger of eternal damnation. Because they said, He has an unclean spirit…

Let us now focus on the words: "world", "never", and "eternal damnation". According to the Young's Literal Translation, the word "world" in Matthew 12:32 should be translated…**age**, for it comes from the Greek word "aion". The words "never forgiveness" in Mark 3:29 should be translated…**no forgiveness to the age**. The words "eternal damnation" in Mark 3:29 should be translated…**age-during (age-lasting) judgment (the judgment of the ages)**.

So we can see that those who blaspheme the Holy Spirit will not be forgiven, neither in this "age", neither in the "age" to come. In essence, they have no forgiveness to the "age", and are in danger of "age-during" ("age-lasting") judgment. The GOOD NEWS is that the judgment is <u>not eternal</u>, but "age-during" ("of the ages", or "within the ages of time"). The other point that needs to be made concerning the words…"this age, or the age to come", is that this is also GOOD NEWS! The apostle Paul told us in Ephesians 2:7 that there are **AGES** to come, not just one more age to come. This would then show us that there WILL BE FORGIVENESS IN THE LAST AND FINAL

AGE FOR THIS SIN! The fact that there are ages to come, and that this sin is not to be forgiven only to the "age", leaves the door open for God's forgiveness in the following age, which is referred to in scripture as the AGE OF THE AGES, OR THE DISPENSATION OF THE FULLNESS OF TIMES. **O WHAT AN ALL-WISE, MERCIFUL, AND LOVING GOD! TO HIM BE GLORY...**

UNTO THE AGE OF THE AGES!

September 1

THE ETERNAL PURPOSE - PART 13

EXAMPLES OF OLAM, AION, AND AIONIOS TRANSLATED CORRECTLY

Matthew 18:8 (King James Version) states...Wherefore if your hand or your foot offend you, cut them off, and cast them from you: it is better for you to enter into life halt or maimed, rather than having two hands or two feet to be cast into everlasting fire...

The first and most important thing to take note of in this passage of scripture is: That Jesus is using metaphoric (figurative) language to describe what the punishment (correction) and the consuming fire of God is like. These words are not to be taken to heart in a literal sense, but in a metaphoric sense. For if they are meant to be taken literally, then we must at once begin to pluck out our eyes and cut off our hands and feet, so as to not end up in everlasting fire. Now that that point has been made, let us once again refer to a **more accurate translation** concerning these verses of scripture.

Matthew 18:8,9 (The New Testament In Modern Speech) states...If your hand or your foot is causing you to fall into sin, cut it off and away with it. It is better for you to enter into Life crippled in hand or foot than to remain in possession of two sound hands or feet but be thrown into the **fire of the Ages**. And if your eye is causing you to fall into sin, tear it out and away with it; it is better for you to enter into Life with only one eye, than to remain in possession of two eyes but be thrown into the **Gehenna** of fire...

Notice that the word "everlasting", when referring to fire, is correctly and properly translated as...**of the ages**...rather than "everlasting" or "eternal", which it should <u>not</u> be translated as, for it comes from the Greek word "aionios", which means: of the ages, or belonging to the ages of time. Jesus is here describing the consuming fire of God by pointing to the literal valley of "Gehenna", in which the fire did consume the refuse which was cast into it. But the point at hand is this: The fire that is spoken of is "aionios" (of the ages), not eternal, which shows us that this fire does indeed have a CORRECTIVE PURPOSE, and is not endless. This is the <u>same fire</u> spoken of in the words..."Holy Ghost and fire".

THANK GOD FOR THE FIRE OF THE AGES!

September 2

THE ETERNAL PURPOSE - PART 14

EXAMPLES OF OLAM, AION, AND AIONIOS TRANSLATED CORRECTLY

Let us now turn our attention to one of the most often quoted verses in the Bible in support of the teaching of eternal torture. This verse of scripture is none other than Matthew 25:46. We will first look at this verse from the King James Version, and then from the New Testament In Modern Speech (1910 Edition).

Matthew 25:46 (King James Version) states…And these shall go away into everlasting punishment: but the righteous into life eternal…

Matthew 25:46 (The New Testament In Modern Speech) states…And these shall go away into the punishment **of the ages**, but the righteous into the life **of the ages**…

Not only does the New Testament In Modern Speech translate this passage MORE ACCURATELY, but it also translates it MORE CONSISTENTLY. It renders both terms mentioned ("everlasting" and "eternal") as…**of the ages**…which is in total agreement with the meaning of the Greek word "aionios" used in this passage. "Aionios", beyond a shadow of a doubt, means: pertaining to, belonging to, or of the ages. **IT DOES NOT DENOTE ENDLESSNESS!** The strongest meaning it can possibly have is: **belonging to eternity, but not lasting through it.** "Aionios", in this passage, describes the kind of punishment (correction), and the kind of life. What is being contrasted in Matthew 25:46 is: **punishment (correction) within the ages of time, and life within the ages of time.** What is also worthy to note is that the word "punishment" used in this passage comes from the Greek word "kolasis", which means: **punishment for the bettering of the offender.** It also carries with it the idea of pruning a tree that has not previously brought forth fruit, that it would bring forth the desired fruit.

HOW RIDICULOUS are the words "eternal punishment"? They are actually a contradiction of one another, and not a proper collection of terms at all! That would be the same as saying… "eternal correction". If correction were to be "eternal" in nature, you would not be able to label it correction, but rather, you would have to refer to it as endless, senseless, and insane torture, having no purpose or end goal in mind but to torture someone for the sake of torture. **THAT IS INSANE!** The other interesting point about this passage of scripture (Matthew 25:31-46) is that it concerns the judgment of…

NATIONS, NOT INDIVIDUALS!

September 3

THE ETERNAL PURPOSE - PART 15

AUGUSTINE'S ARGUMENT

According to Louis Abbott: "Matthew 25:31-46 concerns the judgment of NATIONS, not individuals. It is to be distinguished from other judgments mentioned in scripture, such as the judgment of the saints (2 Cor. 5:10-11); the second resurrection, and the great white throne judgment (Rev. 20:11-15). The judgment of the nations is based upon their treatment of the Lord's brethren (verse 40). No resurrection of the dead is here, just nations living at the time. To apply verses 41 and 46 to mankind as a whole is an error. Perhaps it should be pointed out at this time that the Fundamentalist Evangelical community at large has made the error of gathering many scriptures which speak of various judgments which will occur in different ages and assigning them all to "Great White Throne" judgment. This is a serious mistake. Matthew 25:46 speaks nothing of "grace through faith." We will leave it up to the reader to decide who the "Lord's brethren" are, but final judgment based upon the receiving of the Life of Christ is not the subject matter of Matthew 25:46 and should not be interjected here. Even if it were, the penalty is "age-during correction" and not "everlasting punishment." (An Analytical Study Of Words, Louis Abbott)

According to Louis Abbott: "An argument was introduced by Augustine, and since his day incessantly repeated, that if "*aionios kolasis*" does not mean "endless punishment," then there is no security for the believer that "*aionios zoe*" means "endless life," and that he will enjoy the promise of endless happiness. But Matt. 25:46 shows the "eonian chastisement" and "eonian life" are of the same duration-lasting during the eons, and when the eons end, as scripture states they will (1 Cor. 10:11; Heb. 9:26), the time called "eonian" is past and the life called "eonian" is finished, but life continues beyond the eons, as Paul teaches at 1 Cor. 15:26: "The last enemy that shall be destroyed is death." That is, the last, the final one in order. How will it be destroyed? First Corinthians 15:22 gives the answer: "For as IN ADAM ALL are dying, even so IN CHRIST ALL shall be made alive." Death is destroyed when ALL have been vivified, or made alive, IN CHRIST. There will then be no more death. Just as life is destroyed by death, so death is destroyed by life. Our present bodies are mortal and corruptible (1 Cor. 15:44-55), but when mankind is made alive IN CHRIST they will be raised immortal and incorruptible." (An Analytical Study Of Words, Louis Abbott)

After a careful and unbiased study of the terms "olam", "aion", and "aionios", it is overwhelmingly clear that these terms in no way denote endlessness, but rather are time words, which do explain and portray…

THE PURPOSE OF THE AGES!

September 4

THE ETERNAL PURPOSE - PART 16

UNTO THE AGES OF THE AGES / UNTO THE AGE OF THE AGES

As we study God's purpose of the ages, we must recognize and consider what the apostle Paul talked about in Ephesians 2:7. This verse (Ephesians 2:7) speaks of the **ages to come**.

These **ages that are yet to come** are referred to and recognized as:

THE MILLENNIAL REIGN OF CHRIST (also referred to as…THE AGE or KINGDOM AGE)

THE AGE OF THE AGES (also referred to as…THE DISPENSATION OF THE FULLNESS OF TIMES)

Let us now focus our attention on the phrase…"UNTO THE AGES OF THE AGES"…that we might discover its meaning, understanding what it refers to.

According to Randy Bonacorso: "References to the five ages are hopelessly clouded in most translations of the Bible. (I prefer the Emphasized Bible because of its accuracy.) In the original Greek, the ages are set forth in a **variety of phrases, or configurations**. The phrase "age of the age" appears in Hebrews 1:8, "age of the ages" in Ephesians 3:21, and most often "ages of the ages", as in Revelation 11:15. Despite the fact that these configurations are highly technical, all three are translated "for ever and ever". To be consistent, why not translate them "for ever and evers" or "for evers and evers"? When one considers it, the translation "for ever and ever" is absurd. If "for ever" means *forever*, how can there be a "for ever and ever"? We should bear in mind that all scripture was penned in this present age with a view to the two future ages. THEREFORE "AGES OF THE AGES" MUST DESIGNATE THE REMAINDER OF TIME, **AN EXPRESSION THAT ENCOMPASSES BOTH COMING AGES.** The "age of the ages" is the final and ultimate age. (The "age of the age" also designates that final age. It is the "age" which evolves from the fruit of Christ's reign during the Millennium.)" (The Gospel Of Maturity, Randy Bonacorso)

Our goal in this ongoing study will be to take a brief look at (and to define) the ages to come. As we see God's purpose in the ages to come, we will see HIS GREAT PURPOSE OF THE AGES UNFOLD IN GREAT GLORY AND POWER, SEEING THE AGES CLIMAX WITH A TRIUMPHANT VICTORY, INCLUDING THE ENTIRE CREATION HAVING BEEN VIVIFIED AND MADE ALIVE IN CHRIST!

We will now, with great anticipation, dare to look beyond this present age…

LOOKING UNTO THE AGES OF THE AGES!

September 5

THE ETERNAL PURPOSE - PART 17

THE COMING AGE OF MIRACLES

According to Bill Britton: "There is a beautiful clue given us in Hebrews 6:5 about what will take place in the next age. "For in the case of those who have once been enlightened and have tasted of the heavenly gift and have been made partakers of the Holy Spirit, and have tasted the good Word of God and the powers of the age to come. (Hebrews 6:4-5 New American Standard Bible)." The Amplified Bible says: "the mighty powers of the Age and world to come." Wuest translation states: "tasted the good Word of God, also the powers (miracles) of the age that is about to come." King James says simply: "tasted the good Word of God, and the powers of the world to come." They all agree on this - there are Mighty powers reserved for the next age, and we are not there yet. Satan will be bound for 1,000 years, during which the sons of God -- that glorious company of saints without a spot or wrinkle -- will clean up the terrible mess his government has left. Glorious miracles and healings will abound; in fact, they will be the order of the day, the norm for the hour. There will be absolute dominion by the sons of God over all the natural and created forces, as well as over all the powers of darkness." (<u>Writings Of His Unlimited Glory</u>, Bill Britton)

This present age **(the barley harvest)** is for the purpose of gathering in a remnant. This remnant is to be used by God in the ages to come. The remnant will play a part in what the apostle Paul referred to as the MANIFESTATION OF THE SONS OF GOD, in which ALL the creation will be set free (Romans 8:18-23). The coming age will be for the purpose of gathering the nations unto God **(the wheat harvest)**. This can be seen through many Old Testament scriptures.

Isaiah 2:2-4 states…And it shall come to pass in the last days, that the mountain of the LORD'S house shall be established in the top of the mountains, and shall be exalted above the hills; and all nations shall flow unto it. And many people shall go and say, Come, and let us go up to the mountain of the LORD, to the house of the God of Jacob; and He will teach us of His ways, and we will walk in His paths: for out of Zion shall go forth the law, and the word of the LORD from Jerusalem. And He shall judge among the nations, and shall rebuke many people: and they shall beat their swords into plowshares, and their spears into pruninghooks: nation shall not lift up sword against nation, neither shall they learn war any more…

Zephaniah 3:8,9 states…Therefore wait upon me, says the LORD, until the day that I rise up to the prey: for My determination is to gather the nations, that I may assemble the kingdoms, to pour upon them My indignation, even all My fierce anger: for all the earth shall be devoured with the fire of My jealousy. For then will I turn to the people a pure language, that they may all call upon the name of the LORD, to serve Him with one consent…

What glorious promises concerning the coming age of miracles, in which ALL NATIONS shall call upon the name of the Lord, to serve Him with one consent.

According to Bill Britton: "Press on, saints of God! The purpose of God for His church is at hand. This present age of darkness is rapidly coming to a close. The next age, governed by Christ and His sons, is at the door. Praise the Lord!" (<u>Writings Of His Unlimited Glory</u>, Bill Britton)

GOD'S DETERMINATION IS TO GATHER THE NATIONS!

September 6

THE ETERNAL PURPOSE - PART 18

THE AGE OF THE AGES

According to George Hawtin: "Very, very few people are familiar with the truth that there is a coming age which the Bible names the "dispensation of the fullness of times" (Eph. 1: 10), and that that age above all others has been specially set aside for the work of reconciling all things in heaven and in earth and bringing all things into Christ. The age, as I will point out presently, is the "Age of the Ages". It is the greatest age of all ages and is the time in which the Almighty God brings to completion the unfailing Word spoken before time began, "Let Us make man in Our image and after Our likeness." There are yet at least two great ages to come, first, the "Kingdom Age", which in scripture is often referred to as "The Age", and following this there comes the "Age of the Ages", which in Eph. 1: 10 is named the "dispensation of the fullness of times". Our failure to recognize God's workings in that wonderful age of the fullness of times is the reason so many thousands of God's good people fail to see the restitution of all things. The "Age of Grace" or the "Church Age", of which we are now a part, runs from the resurrection to the setting up of the king- The "Kingdom Age", next in order, will last at least one thousand years. Rev. 20:4. Then follows the "Age of the Ages", or the "dispensation of the fullness of times". The term "Age of the Ages" identifies this age as the greatest of all the ages. No age, not even the "Kingdom Age", can be compared to it. Just as the Song of Solomon is the song of songs, that is, the greatest of all songs, and as the holy of holies is the holiest of all, so the "Age of the Ages" is the greatest age of all the ages, far surpassing even the "Millennial Kingdom" in its power and glory, its revelation of God, and its wonderful reconciliation and restitution. Men today use such terms as "the greatest day of my life," "our finest hour," or the "day of days." It is in this same sense that our Almighty Father speaks of the "dispensation of the fullness of times" as the "Age of the Ages". Now all ages have to do with time and times, but there comes an hour eventually when time has reached its fullness. When all other ages have run their course, then we have come at last to the fullness of times. Time is full, time is complete, and time shall be no more. At the consummation of the fullness of all time the purpose of God, laid down in the edict, "Let Us make man in Our image and after Our likeness," is complete, and time shall be no more. The "dispensation of the fullness of times" is the eighth dispensation. The dispensations of Innocence, Conscience, Human Government, Promise, Law, Grace and the Kingdom - these seven will have run their course and all will end in judgment, but the "dispensation of the fullness of times" is the eighth dispensation, and it will conclude all former things. It will end death, judgment, pain and tears, and its final act will be the delivering up of a perfect kingdom to the Father of all. Then time will have reached its fullness and will be no more." (The Restitution Of All Things, George Hawtin)

Incidentally, the number eight in scripture means **new beginning**.

BEHOLD, HE MAKES ALL THINGS NEW!

September 7

THE ETERNAL PURPOSE - PART 19

TIME AND ETERNITY

According to George Hawtin: "Lastly, let us consider briefly that great age which the Word of God describes as the dispensation of the fullness of times. Ephesians 1:10. Time is not eternity. There are many times and many dispensations, but there is only one eternity. Eternity does not begin; neither does it end, but times, dispensations, and ages all have beginnings and all have ends. It is wrong to assert that, when time ends, eternity will begin, because eternity has no beginning. Neither did it end when time began, as so many charts indicate. Ages have their place in eternity in the same way that minutes have their place in years, except that years end and eternity does not. Therefore it is very important that we make a clear distinction between ages, which belong to time, and eternity, which is timeless. It is more important still that we, in our study of the Bible, search out diligently those passages which refer to time and those which refer to eternity. In making this search, I strongly recommend that wherever possible the searcher avail himself of a good, exhaustive concordance such as Young's Analytical or Strong's, available at almost any good book store. Both of these give the correct meaning of every Greek and Hebrew word in the Bible." (The Restitution Of All Things, George Hawtin)

According to J. Preston Eby: "A concept we must immediately grasp in order to understand God's plan of the ages is that *time is a created phenomena* consisting of past, present, and future just as man is created phenomena having youth, middle age, and old age. No, you cannot smell, touch, or feel time, but it is there, ever-present, always marching into the future. Time was created; it had a beginning, it shall have an end. It is only one thing among countless other things that are part of the entire created universe. It is as much a "species" of creation as, for example, rocks, elephants, trees, and water are species of creation. Before the creation of the universe, there was no time; at the end of the ages when the present material universe is dissolved and replaced by a new, spiritual universe, time shall cease to be. It will be swallowed up into eternity just as all death will be swallowed up into victory, and there shall be no more death. Time - composed of milliseconds, seconds, minutes, hours, days, weeks, months, years, decades, centuries, millenniums, ages was created in the beginning, and will be dissolved at the end of the ages. ETERNITY IS A STATE OF ABSOLUTE TIMELESSNESS, not of unending time. Eternity is a STATE OF BEING, resident in the very nature and person of God in which such concepts as past, present, future, before, after, change, transition, growth, decay, etc. do not exist. It is wrong to assert that, when time ends, eternity will begin, because eternity has no beginning. Neither did it end when time began, as so many charts indicate. Therefore it is very important that we make a clear distinction between ages, which belong to time, and eternity, which is timeless." (Eternity, J. Preston Eby)

Eternity is that which IS! It is part of the very nature of God. It is for this reason that God refers to Himself as the GREAT I AM, not the I WAS, OR I WILL BE, but the **I AM**. He is that WHICH IS.

HE IS ETERNAL!

September 8

THE ETERNAL PURPOSE - PART 20

CONCLUSION

After a careful and unbiased study concerning God's purpose of the ages ("olam", "aion", and "aionios"), we have proved, beyond a shadow of a doubt, that all of God's dealings with man, whether it be reward or punishment, are within the confines of time. The Bible then, is God's purpose and plan for man throughout the ages of time. The concept of eternity is hardly to be found anywhere in the entirety of scripture. The **life** that is spoken of in the Bible is "the life of the ages", and the **punishment** (correction) that is spoken of is "the punishment of the ages". Both are said to be "aionios", that is, "of the ages", or "belonging to the ages". The **life** and **punishment** ("of the ages") are also to be seen as a **quality of life**, and a **quality of punishment** within the ages of time. This will indeed produce eternal results, that is, results that belong to the eternal realm, the realm in which God dwells. The reason that the **life** will continue and the **punishment** (correction) will not is due to what the apostle Paul taught us in 1st Corinthians 15:22-28. 1st Corinthians 15:25-28 states...For He must reign, till He has put all enemies under His feet. The last enemy that shall be destroyed is death. For He has put all things under His feet. But when He says all things are put under Him, it is manifest that He is excepted, which did put all things under Him. And when all things shall be subdued unto Him, then shall the Son also Himself be subject unto Him that put all things under Him, that God may be all in all...

If death, which is the carnal mind, is destroyed, including the second death, which is death and hell (Hades - the grave) cast into the lake of fire, then there is nothing left but life, and this is how God will be ALL IN ALL (EVERYTHING TO EVERYONE)!

The only remaining question that is left is...WHAT WILL **YOU** DO WITH THE KNOWLEDGE OF THIS GLORIOUS TRUTH??? Will you believe it, seek to understand it, proclaim it, and teach it? Or will you run from the knowledge of this glorious truth that is now being exposed to you? Many run from it (the truth of the salvation of all men), avoid it, ignore it, or say it isn't so. DO NOT BE BULLIED BY THE TRADITIONS AND DOCTRINES OF MEN!!! **STAND UP AND BE COUNTED!!! ARISE AND SHINE; FOR YOUR LIGHT IS COME, AND THE GLORY OF THE LORD IS RISEN UPON <u>YOU</u>! IT IS TRUE! BELIEVE IT! RECEIVE IT! WALK IN IT! GOD TRULY IS...**

THE <u>SAVIOR</u> <u>OF</u> <u>THE</u> <u>WORLD</u>!!!

❖

September 9

THE PURPOSE OF EVIL - PART 1

THE ORIGIN OF EVIL

According to A. P. Adams: "There is probably no subject in all the range of religious thought so hard to deal with as that of the purpose of evil. Writers on Biblical lore have tried to account of the **origin** of evil; but it seems to me that the real difficulty is the bare fact of its **existence,** whatever may have been its origin. The great question for theologians to wrestle with is this: **How can you account for the existence of evil alongside a supreme, all-wise, holy and benevolent God?** First let me say that there is no help out of this trouble in orthodoxy. In regard to this subject orthodoxy is hopelessly contradictory and utterly absurd. Thus it speaks: **"It was not in God's original plan that evil should exist, but evil has come into existence and done incalculable harm; yet God's plans cannot be thwarted nor disarranged in the least, because He is all-wise and almighty. Evil being in existence before man was created, God allows it to come into contact with the man He created when He might have prevented it, knowing full well what the result would be; yet He is in no wise responsible for the consequences of evil. In fact, it is blasphemy to entertain any such idea. Evil having come into existence contrary to God's will, He cannot put it out of existence, but it will continue as long as He exists, an eternal blot on His otherwise perfect universe and a perpetual offense unto all the purified; yet His will is absolute and sovereign and the redeemed will be perfectly happy. Thus, God is in no wise responsible for either the *origin, existence, consequences or continuance* of evil; yet He can have everything as He pleases, and is the Creator of all things."** And so Orthodoxy goes on, **stultifying** common sense, **throttling** human reason, and **stupidly expecting** that intelligent, thoughtful men and women will accept its idiotic patter as the infallible utterances of divine inspiration. Cannot everyone see that the entire orthodox view is contradictory and absurd in the extreme, and hence self-destructive and untenable?" (The Purpose Of Evil, A. P. Adams)

Now that we have heard the ABSURD thoughts of organized religion, let us next consider what the Bible has to say about this all-important subject. We will be pleased to discover that there is a grand and…

GLORIOUS PURPOSE FOR EVIL!

September 10

THE PURPOSE OF EVIL - PART 2

GOD CREATED EVIL

According to A. P. Adams: "Now I hold that the following proposition is self-evident. **Given a God of infinite power, wisdom and goodness, He is responsible for ALL things that exist. And this also follows from the wisdom and goodness of God: All things that exist are for an intelligent and benevolent end.** These conclusions are inevitable from the premises; they cannot be modified except by modifying the premises. For instance, if you say that some things exist contrary to God's will, then it follows that God is **not** all-powerful; and you cannot escape this conclusion by bringing in the orthodox doctrine of man's free moral agency, for whatever a free moral agent may do, He is responsible for it Who made him a free moral agent. If God made man a free moral agent, He knew beforehand what the result would be, and hence is just as responsible for the consequences of the acts of that free moral agent as He would be for the act of an irresponsible machine that He had made. Man's free moral agency, even if it were true, would by no means clear God from the responsibility of His acts since God is His Creator and has made him in the first place just what he is, well knowing what the result would be. **If God's will is EVER thwarted, then He is not almighty.** If His will is thwarted, then His plans must be changed, and hence He is not all-wise and immutable. **If His will is NEVER thwarted, then all things are in ACCORDANCE with His will and He is responsible for all things as they exist.** If He is all-wise and all-good, then all things, existing according to His will, **must** be tending to some **wise and benevolent end.** Thus we come back to my proposition again: If God is infinite in power, wisdom and goodness, then **He is responsible for ALL things that exist,** and all existing things are tending toward some wise and good end." (The Purpose Of Evil, A. P. Adams)

Having stated these things, let us now look to the Holy Scriptures to confirm what has been stated. Colossians 1:16,17 states…For **by Him were all things created**, that are in heaven, and that are in earth, visible and invisible, whether they be thrones, or dominions, or principalities, or powers: all things were created by Him, and for Him: And He is before all things, and by Him all things consist…

Isaiah 45:7 states…I form the light, and create darkness: I make peace, and **create evil**: I the LORD do all these things…

Isaiah 54:16 states…Behold, I have created the smith that blows the coals in the fire, and that brings forth an instrument for his work; and **I have created the waster to destroy**…

Amos 3:6 states…Shall a trumpet be blown in the city, and the people not be afraid? **shall there be evil in a city, and the LORD has not done it?**…

Job 42:11 states…Then came there unto him all his brethren, and all his sisters, and all they that had been of his acquaintance before, and did eat bread with him in his house: and they bemoaned him, and comforted him over **all the evil that the LORD had brought upon him**…

Job 12:16 states…With Him is strength and wisdom: the **deceived** and the **deceiver** are His…

Genesis 3:1 states…Now **the serpent was more subtle than any beast of the field** *which the* **LORD God had made**. And he said unto the woman, Yea, has God said, You shall not eat of every tree of the garden?…(Also read Revelation 20:2.)

2nd Thessalonians 2:11 states…And for this cause **God shall send them strong delusion**, that they should believe a lie…

2nd Corinthians 5:18 states…And **all things are of God**, Who has reconciled us to Himself by Jesus Christ, and has given to us the ministry of reconciliation…

We must be honest and come to the conclusion that GOD CREATED ALL THINGS (GOOD AND EVIL), and is responsible for all things.

ALL THINGS ARE OF GOD!

September 11

THE PURPOSE OF EVIL - PART 3

JOB

After having established that **God created all things, including evil**, let us now seek to understand the purpose of evil. This can be understood by looking at the book and story of Job. Job's experiences represent the creation and its experiences with evil as a whole. To understand the story of Job is to understand God's purpose and plan for the creation as a whole. This story involves a man being subjected to evil **by God** for a specific purpose. That God was responsible for bringing evil upon Job is UNDENIABLE, and can be seen throughout the entire story. The story ends with a dramatic climax of Job seeing himself for who he was, and seeing God for Who He was. His latter end was to be found MORE BLESSED than his beginning, and all due to the fact THAT THE LORD HAD BROUGHT EVIL UPON HIM!

With this being said, there is obviously a PURPOSE FOR EVIL. The purpose of evil is simply this: to cause us to see ourselves for who we are without God, to repent, turn to God, **learn**, to see God for Who He is, and in turn our latter end will be MORE BLESSED than our beginning. The entire book of Job gives us tremendous insight into God's purpose and dealings with man, especially of the PURPOSE OF EVIL. We will now call to attention some key scriptures from this book.

Job 1:8,12 states…**And the LORD said unto Satan, Have you considered My servant Job**, that there is none like him in the earth, a perfect and an upright man, one that fears God, and eschews (declines) evil?…**And the LORD said unto Satan, Behold, all that he has is in your power**; only upon himself put not forth your hand. So Satan went forth from the presence of the LORD…

Job 2:10 states…But he (Job) said unto her (his wife), You speak as one of the foolish women speak. What? shall we receive **good** at the hand of God, and shall we not receive **evil**? In all this did not Job sin with his lips…

Job 13:15 states…Though **He slay me**, yet will I trust in Him…

Job 42:5,6 states…**I have heard of You** by the hearing of the ear: but **now my eye sees You**. Wherefore I abhor myself, and repent in dust and ashes…

Job 42:11,12 states…Then came there unto him all his brethren, and all his sisters, and all they that had been of his acquaintance before, and did eat bread with him in his house: and they bemoaned him, and comforted him over **all the evil that the LORD had brought upon him**: every man also gave him a piece of money, and every one an earring of gold. So the LORD blessed the latter end of Job more than his beginning…

Can we now see that **God is in all things**, and works all things together for our good, including evil?

MAY GOD BE PRAISED IN ALL THINGS!

September 12

THE PURPOSE OF EVIL - PART 4

SUBJECTED TO VANITY

Romans 8:20-22 (The New Testament In Modern Speech) states…For the Creation fell into subjection to failure and unreality (not of its own choice, but by the will of Him Who so subjected it). Yet there was always the hope that at last the Creation itself would also be set free from the thraldom of decay so as to enjoy the liberty that will attend the glory of the children of God. For we know that the whole of Creation is groaning together in the pains of childbirth until this hour…

This is one of the most interesting, informative, and glorious scripture passages in all of the Bible. It does indeed declare God's purpose for the entire creation from beginning to end. It shows that GOD IS RESPONSIBLE FOR HAVING SUBJECTED THE CREATION TO FAILURE AND UNREALITY. We can also see that the creation was also CONDEMNED TO HAVE ITS ENERGIES MARRED AND FRUSTRATED. This was not the creation's choice, but it is to be seen as God's will and purpose, FOR HE IS THE ONE WHO SUBJECTED THE CREATION TO THIS STATE OF BEING. For it was God Who created all things, including: good, evil, principalities, powers, the tree of life, the tree of the knowledge of good and evil, and the serpent (Satan) who did deceive Eve. HE IS RESPONSIBLE FOR IT ALL. HE IS RESPONSIBLE FOR THE FALL OF MAN AND THE REDEMPTION OF MAN. It was God Who first created Adam (mankind) in the Spirit (Genesis 1:27), and then lowered him into the soulish realm, in which he became a living soul (Genesis 2:7). After having been lowered into this realm, it was then possible for Adam to fall. This would then enable God to carry out His purpose that is stated in 1ˢᵗ Corinthians 15:22,23, which states…For as in Adam all die, even so in Christ shall all be made alive. But every man in his own order…

After taking these things into account, it is easy to see the STUPIDITY of the traditions and doctrines of men, which state…God is responsible for nothing, but rather, He just reacts to man's choices and decisions. It is much better for us to **stop trying to protect God, for He does not need**

to be protected! He simply wants to be understood and known in the earth, for that is why He gave us the Holy Scriptures. It is time to start believing and proclaiming the scriptures, rather than man's **pitiful attempts**…

TO EXPLAIN AWAY THE PURPOSE OF EVIL!

September 13

THE PURPOSE OF EVIL - PART 5

THE PURPOSE OF EVIL

According to Randy Bonacorso: The following is a passage from: <u>The Gospel Of Maturity</u>, Randy Bonacorso…"When we begin to understand the purpose of evil in God's plan, we begin to see past the pain. The writer of Deuteronomy tells us that it was God Who "led Israel through the great and terrible wilderness, wherein were fiery serpents, and scorpions, and drought, where there was no water." Then we are told why: "That He might prove them, to do good to them at their latter end" (Deuteronomy 8:15,16). The deepest truths are often the simplest truths. And this one is simple: If it weren't for the darkness of sin we wouldn't know the light of God's grace. Good and evil are both gifts of love. The Samaritan was a "good" Samaritan because he performed an act of kindness to someone in need. Need provided the occasion. For God to have created a perfect world without sin and suffering would have been pointless. If God hadn't found us in the gutter, He would have had no opportunity to reveal His love. There would be no hymns of gratitude, no "Amazing Grace." Seeing that God created His own opposition, it's easy to see why He will reconcile the enemy in the end. What a miscarriage of justice it would be if God created Pharaoh to be the enemy and then sentenced him to endless torment for what he did. As we have seen, God did not merely allow Pharaoh to do what he did; Pharaoh was "raised up" to do it. Pharaoh provided an occasion for God to make a name for Himself throughout the earth. As well, Joseph's brothers cast him into a pit and left him for dead. A group of Midianites rescued Joseph and took him into Egypt where they sold him as a slave. Every child who has attended Sunday school knows the story of how Joseph rose from Pharaoh's dungeon to become the governor of Egypt. Years later, when Joseph was reunited with his brothers, he explained to them, "But as for you, you thought evil against me; but God meant it unto good" (Genesis 50:20). Joseph's brothers had merely performed God's will. God used them to demonstrate His power to take Joseph from the dungeon to the throne. And so, in the end, love will more than compensate for evil. It will "superabound!" Pain is the breaking of the shell that imprisons understanding. And one day we will see that pain and suffering were indispensable in bringing man to a full revelation of God's love." (Randy Bonacorso)

The purpose of evil…

IS TO BRING ABOUT GOOD!

September 14

THE PURPOSE OF EVIL - PART 6

LUCIFER

According to Ray Knight: "Tradition has taught over many years that "Lucifer" is Satan. This tradition, we are told, comes out of two chapters . . . Ezekiel 28 and Isaiah 14 which we will look into with great care. First of all let us acknowledge that the Devil or Satan (as laid out in 're-think' No.11) never did start out with any wisdom, holiness or glory. "Lucifer" was in the garden of Eden ... says Ezekiel's account; so "Lucifer" has to be either God (that's not possible) or the Serpent or Adam . . . there was just no-one else! It is between the Serpent (Devil) or Adam! Let us investigate this challenging problem. The word "Lucifer", from the Hebrew, is "HEYEL" and is translated *"Shining One"*, *"Morning-Star"* or *"Lucifer"*. "Morning-Star" equates with "Day-Star". Here is the only mention of "Lucifer". (12) *How are you fallen from heaven, O "Lucifer", son of the morning! How are you cut down to the ground, which did weaken the nations!* Adam was the 'son' of God, his Father. It was Adam who 'fell' from God's presence . . . the Devil is controlled! (13) *For you have said in your heart, I will ascend into heaven, I will exalt my throne above the stars of God: I will sit also upon the mount of the congregation, in the sides of the north:* 'Man' wants to 'run' the congregation! (14) *I will ascend above the heights of the clouds; I will be like the most High.* The Serpent offered this position to Adam and he fell for it! Page 777 (Amplified Bible), footnote 'n' informs us that "Lucifer" being Satan is erroneous. "Lucifer" comes from the Latin equivalent of "PHOSPHOROS" which is used of a title for Jesus in 2 Pet.1:19 and corresponds to the name "bright and morning star". Luke 10:18 has been incorrectly used to lead us astray. Adam had the ability to think heavenly thoughts and then he fell to the earthly realm of thinking producing demonic thoughts which can be overcome in us by the power that God has provided in Jesus Christ." (Lucifer?, Ray Knight)

As we do a proper study of the name "Lucifer", Isaiah 14, and Ezekiel 28, we will see that these all agree and point to ADAM'S FALL IN THE GARDEN OF EDEN. They do not speak of a fall of Satan, for Satan had no fall, but was a murderer from the **beginning** (John 8:44). It was **ADAM** who was in Eden, the Garden of God (Ezekiel 28:13), and was perfect **until** iniquity was found in him.

As we stated, the Devil was a murderer from the beginning: he sinned from the beginning; he was the father of lies, there was no truth in him. However, Adam was perfect, being in the image of God...**until iniquity was found in him**.

According to Ray Knight: "Adam was "Lucifer" who fell and lost all, dragging all mankind down with him . . . no longer being "The Shining One". "Lucifer" today is the fallen Adamic natural-reasoning carnal nature in us. The Second Adam (Christ) has restored all that the first "Lucifer-Adam" lost that we may be clothed upon with Light and Beauty (Psalm 52:1). So Adam fits the 'bill' of who "Lucifer" was! And so now, today, we see why 'carnal man' is so very responsive to the Devil's (Serpent's) authority and suggestions!" (Lucifer?, Ray Knight)

After a proper explanation of the name "Lucifer", we are now free to explore the true origin of Satan. We will look to the Holy Scriptures to understand and comprehend...

SATAN AND HIS PURPOSE!

September 15

THE PURPOSE OF EVIL - PART 7

THE DRAGON, THAT OLD SERPENT, WHICH IS THE DEVIL, AND SATAN

According to J. Preston Eby: "Orthodoxy had long taught that Satan was, in the beginning, a high and beautiful archangel in heaven. The theologians and preachers recite over and over how Satan was originally "the anointed cherub that covers ... the most beautiful and wise of all God's creation!" This being was, so they say, the ruler and leader of the angelic beings and apparently led them in their praise of God and shouts of joy ...the greatest being God ever created, one who had unequaled strength, wisdom, beauty, privilege, and authority, and was next to God Himself. This blameless, perfect one, named Lucifer, was created without any form of evil and with the greatest intelligence of any created being. Then, we are told, this Lucifer, suddenly realizing how beautiful and intelligent he was, became inflated with power and pride and his heart was lifted up in rebellion against God. According to the story, Lucifer gathered one-third of the heavenly angels to his cause, mustering an army with which he planned to knock God off His throne and supplant himself as king and god of the universe and there was war in heaven! Luckily, God won, cast Lucifer out of heaven and he became, instead of a holy angel, the Devil that he is today." (The Serpent, J. Preston Eby)

Is this the most ridiculous thing that you have ever heard in your life, or what? Can you imagine an all-powerful, all-knowing, all-present, and all-wise God, Who created all things, knowing the end from the beginning, being snuck up on by one of His created beings. As well, orthodoxy then leads us to believe that God found Himself in a war that He could barely overcome, hoping He would not be defeated. THAT IS INSANE, ABSURD, AND <u>DEFINITELY</u> <u>NOT</u> <u>THE</u> <u>TRUTH</u>! IT IS THE TRADITIONS AND DOCTRINES OF MEN, ALONG WITH TRYING TO INTERPRET SCRIPTURE BY MEANS OF THE CARNAL MIND!

Let us GROW UP! It is time to stop being swept away by the FOOLISH TEACHINGS OF MEN! The Bible clearly tells us about the origin of Satan. Our problem is that we have been **so indoctrinated** by the teachings of MYSTERY BABYLON THE GREAT (THE MAN-MADE, ORGANIZED CHURCH), that when we hear plain truth we think it is heresy and blasphemy.

Our next goal will be to show the origin of Satan, his purpose, and essence. It is much easier to believe the truth...

THAN TO BELIEVE THE LUDICROUS TEACHINGS OF MEN!

THE PURPOSE OF EVIL - PART 8

WHERE DID THE DEVIL COME FROM? - #1

According to J. Preston Eby: "Man says that Satan IN THE BEGINNING was holy, but later fell from that estate. JESUS said of Satan, "You are of your father the devil, and the lusts of your father you will do. He was a MURDERER (not an angel) **from the** BEGINNING, and abode not in the truth, because there is no truth in him. When he speaks a lie, he, speaks of his own: for he is a liar and the father of it. (Jn. 8:44). In these studies on the Garden of Eden we are searching out the BEGINNING, probing into the very midst of the past, the times before this age and past ages, that we might understand the grand and glorious purposes of our omnipotent and omniscient Heavenly Father which He has purposed from the beginning of the world. How authoritatively the Lord Jesus reveals that way back there, in THE BEGINNING, in even HIS beginning, Satan WAS A MURDERER! MAN says that Satan IN THE BEGINNING was perfect and sinless. But the apostle John, writing under the inspiration of the Holy Spirit, penned these words in regard to Satan's origin: "He that commits sin is of the devil; for the devil SINNED FROM THE BEGINNING" (I Jn. 3:8). This could not be rightly said of Adam. According to Genesis 2 and 3, it was not until **after** Adam was created in spirit essence, **after** he was lowered into the realm of flesh, **after** he was placed in the Garden, **after** he named all the animals, **after** the woman was taken from his side, **after** she listened to the serpent and ate the forbidden fruit - it was **AFTER** ALL THESE THINGS that Adam sinned. Adam was not a sinner from the beginning. But the Devil, according to I Jn. 3:8 **WAS A SINNER FROM THE BEGINNING!** Now, if we are to believe the Bible means what it says - and I believe it does - we must believe that from his very beginning SATAN WAS EVIL." (The Serpent, J. Preston Eby)

In our next teaching we will look at more scriptures that confirm that Satan was created by God, and that Satan's origin was that of evil from his very beginning. God did not (as we have stated) create Satan as a "good guy" at first and then he became a "bad guy". He was created evil ON PURPOSE, FOR A PURPOSE, THAT HE MIGHT BE A TOOL IN God's hands, being used to bring about the grand and glorious purpose that God had in store for the entire creation. GOD KNOWS EXACTLY WHAT HE IS DOING! HE IS IN CONTROL OF ALL THINGS, INCLUDING...

THE DEVIL!

September 17

THE PURPOSE OF EVIL - PART 9

WHERE DID THE DEVIL COME FROM? - #2

The following scriptures testify that God is responsible for ALL THINGS, has created ALL THINGS, AND THAT HE CREATED THE DEVIL, and that the Devil was evil from his beginning:

Genesis 3:1 states…Now **the serpent** was more subtle than any beast of the field which **the LORD God had made**…

Revelation 20:2 states…And He laid hold on the dragon, **that old serpent, which is the Devil, and Satan**…(Note: THE SERPENT, WHICH THE LORD GOD HAD MADE, WAS THE DEVIL.)

Job 12:16 states…With Him is strength and wisdom: **the deceived and the deceiver are His**…

Isaiah 54:16 states…Behold, I have created the smith that blows the coals in the fire, and that brings forth an instrument for his work; and **I have created the waster to destroy**…(Note: Remember…Satan comes to kill, steal, and to **destroy**.)

Colossians 1:16 states…For by Him were all things created, that are in heaven, and that are in earth, visible and invisible, whether they be thrones, or dominions, or principalities, or powers: all things were created by Him, and for Him…(Note: This would of course include Satan, for the words "all things" are all-inclusive.)

According to J. Preston Eby: "Did GOD create the Devil? Well, we know he did not create himself! And he did not "just happen"! The reason some have held the view that Satan was originally an angel is because it seems to relieve God of the responsibility of evil and sin in the world. When they are asked if a good God created a bad Devil, they can reply: "No, He did not create the Devil; He created a beautiful and powerful angel who later **became** the Devil!" This sounds good **on the surface,** but when the Spirit of wisdom and revelation comes from God, this line of reasoning is seen to be but shallow inductions of the natural mind." (The Serpent, J. Preston Eby)

In our next teaching we will define the terms: "Satan", "Devil", and "Serpent". After defining these terms, we will begin to see that Satan has a definite purpose, and was CREATED BY GOD to perform specific tasks. We will see that **OPPOSITION WAS NECESSARY** for God to produce overcomers. How could we, as believers in Christ, learn to overcome Satan IF THERE WAS NO SATAN TO OVERCOME??? (THINK ABOUT IT!)

WHAT AN ALL-WISE GOD!

September 18

THE PURPOSE OF EVIL - PART 10

THE PURPOSE OF SATAN - #1

According to Ray Knight: "SATAN — this title means ADVERSARY ... one who always GOES AGAINST or is opposed to YOU EXPRESSING CHRIST. SATAN DESPISES THE CROSS. WHEN PETER OPPOSED THE DEATH OF JESUS, he was addressed by Jesus as Satan .. *Get behind Me, Satan* (Mark 8:33). Subtle Satan operates in the RELIGIOUS realm for he is very religious! Well ... there is *the synagogue of Satan* (Rev.2:9) mentioned. "Synagogue" means ASSEMBLY or GATHERING ... thus the above title can be placed upon any gathering/fellowship that opposes or ignores the work of the cross in every life even to the point of opposing the Holy Spirit in His liberating work! **DEVIL** — this title means ACCUSER or SLANDERER. **SERPENT** — this title means TO HISS which is derived from a word meaning TO WHISPER ... just like a person speaking behind their hand to get your attention — saying *'Pssst'* (meaning *listen to this!*). The serpent started out preaching in the Garden of Eden ... but preaching the opposite to God's Word! ... And he is still doing it today! The serpent's word encompasses all the opposition consisting of lying, slandering, twisting utilizing scriptures against those who have been awakened to the plan and purposes of God. His greatest work is to replace the things of Christ ... hence expressing the **anti-Christ** (remember, "anti-Christ" simply means 'INSTEAD OF CHRIST'). The Devil is like a 'mallet' on God's carpenter bench. When the project is complete, the mallet is no longer needed. Because God is in control you will never be tested more than you can handle to overcome in order to walk victoriously. God's chastening rod is the Devil just like He used the Philistines mostly to spank His people Israel in the Old Testament. The enemy is used by God to test God's sons: however, you will not be tested above that which you can overcome and be the stronger for it." (The Devil - Satan - Serpent, Ray Knight)

If you can believe it, GOD CREATED SATAN FOR A PURPOSE. He is actually able to teach us, and is used by God for specific purposes in our lives. The apostle Paul understood this, not hesitating to tell us how that Satan was used of God in bringing about God's purpose in the lives of Hymenaeus and Alexander.

1st Timothy 1:19,20 states…Holding faith, and a good conscience; which some having put away concerning faith have made shipwreck: Of whom is Hymenaeus and Alexander; whom **I have delivered unto Satan, that they may <u>learn</u> not to blaspheme**…

1st Corinthians 5:5 states…**To deliver such a one unto Satan for the destruction of the flesh, that the spirit may be saved** in the day of the Lord Jesus…

So as we can see, Satan's purpose is to teach us not to blaspheme, destroy our flesh (carnality), and cause our spirit to be saved in the day of the Lord. WHAT AN INSTRUMENT OF GOD! WHAT A TOOL!

WHAT A PURPOSE!

September 19

THE PURPOSE OF EVIL - PART 11

THE PURPOSE OF SATAN - #2

According to J. Preston Eby: "Jesus declared of Satan, "The THIEF comes not, but for to steal, and to kill, and to destroy: I am come that they might have life, and that they might have it more abundantly" (Jn. 10:10). Out of God's own mouth proceeds the assertion, "I have created the WASTER to destroy" (Isa. 54:16). We gather from this passage that Satan is a created being with a definite purpose. That purpose is stated in the opening words of the above quoted verse: "I have created the smith (the Devil) that blows the coals in the fire, and that BRINGS FORTH AN INSTRUMENT for his work." The "Smith" that "blows upon the fire" is also the one who heats the furnace seven times hotter! "Beloved, think it not strange concerning the **fiery trial** which is to **try you,** as though some strange thing had happened unto you." (I Pet. 4:12). Our trials and testings are associated in the Word of God with the ministry of Satan. You never thought of Satan having a MINISTRY? "Then was Jesus led up of the Spirit into the wilderness to be TEMPTED (tested) OF THE DEVIL. And when the Tempter came to Him, he said, If You be the Son of God, command that these stones be made bread" (Mat.4:1-3). "Fear none of those things which you shall suffer: behold, the Devil shall cast some of you into prison, THAT YOU MAY BE TRIED ... be faithful... and I will give you a crown of life" (Rev. 2:10). "And the Lord said, Simon, Simon, behold, Satan has desired to have you, THAT HE MAY SIFT YOU AS WHEAT: but I have prayed for you, that your faith fail not: and when you are converted, strengthen your brethren" (Lk. 22:31-32). "Be sober, be vigilant; because your adversary the Devil, as a roaring lion, walks about, SEEKING WHOM HE MAY DEVOUR: whom resist steadfast in the faith, knowing that the same AFFLICTIONS are accomplished in your brethren that are in the world" (I Pet. 5:8-9)." (The Serpent, J. Preston Eby)

As you can clearly see, Satan has a definite purpose. His purpose is to be a force of OPPOSITION, giving the sons of God obstacles to overcome. These obstacles cause us to learn how to access the overcoming power that is available to us IN CHRIST. He is an instrument created by God, even being brought forth by God, in which he is to be used for a specific work in the hearts and lives of God's people. Let us recognize this truth by submitting to God…

FOR HE IS IN CONTROL OF SATAN!

September 20

THE PURPOSE OF EVIL - PART 12

THE ESSENCE OF SATAN

According to Ray Knight: "**SATAN IS A SPIRIT.** It is a known fact that **Satan is a spirit**, for in John 13:27 we read that Satan entered into Judas . . . 'man' cannot enter into man!" (Lucifer?, Ray Knight)

Let us remember that Jesus also referred to Peter as Satan in Matthew 16:23. Jesus said… Get behind Me **Satan**…Ephesians 2:2 refers to Satan as **the prince of the power of the air, THE SPIRIT** that now works in the children of disobedience…

Now we are able to see and understand the essence of Satan. We see who and what he is. HE IS THAT SPIRIT THAT NOW WORKS IN THE CHILDREN OF DISOBEDIENCE. He is not a winged creature with fangs, a pitchfork, a tail, horns, and a red cape. That idea of Satan was borrowed from Greek Mythology. HE IS A SPIRIT! HE IS THAT SPIRIT THAT NOW WORKS IN THE CHILDREN OF DISOBEDIENCE, CAUSING THEM TO ACT IN A WAY THAT IS ANTI-CHRIST (AGAINST, OR INSTEAD OF CHRIST).

As a spirit, Satan creates thoughts in people. These thoughts are anti-Christ. That is why the apostle Paul told us to **cast down imaginations, and every high thing that exalts itself against the knowledge of God, and bringing into captivity every thought to the obedience of Christ: (2ⁿᵈ Corinthians 10:5)…** This is what it means to see SATAN AS LIGHTNING FALL FROM HEAVEN (Luke 10:18). When Jesus made this statement (I saw Satan as lightning fall from heaven), He was not referring to a creature that He saw falling through the clouds. He was referring to His time of temptation in the wilderness for forty days and forty nights. During this time Jesus was tempted by the Devil. As the spirit of Satan came against His mind, bringing thoughts that were contrary to the will and Word of God, what did He do? HE CAST DOWN THOSE IMAGINATIONS, AND EVERY HIGH THING THAT DID EXALT ITSELF AGAINST THE KNOWLEDGE OF GOD, BRINGING INTO CAPTIVITY EVERY THOUGHT TO THE OBEDIENCE OF GOD. Jesus overcame the prince of the power of the air. In essence, HE SAW SATAN (THAT SPIRIT) FALL LIKE LIGHTNING FROM THE HEAVENLY REALM (HIS MIND). He then left out of the wilderness in the power of the Spirit of God, declaring the gospel of the Kingdom!

JESUS OVERCAME SATAN!

September 21

THE PURPOSE OF EVIL - PART 13

SATAN...A DOG ON A LEASH

According to J. Preston Eby: "Dear saints of God, don't believe for one moment that anything in all God's great universe is out of control! God is GOD, He IS in full control of every sphere of activity, and Satan himself is under the province of God. May God enlighten our minds to perceive the truth that Satan has no power at all except that which God delegates to him. Do you REALLY believe that Satan could cause all the trouble in the world UNLESS GOD HAD ORDAINED IT? My friend, if you believe Satan is a problem to Almighty God, then your God is entirely too small! Satan is no thorn in God's side Who made him in the first place, Who binds his hands daily, Who sets his boundaries and limits his power and marks his path. Oh, yes, those who would be sons of God MUST OVERCOME HIM. Beloved, when that purpose is accomplished, Satan will have completed his course as an INSTRUMENT in the hand of God Who has everything under control! Hallelujah!" (The Serpent, J. Preston Eby)

Yes...Satan is a dog on God's leash. He is only able to do what God either allows or commissions him to do. **STOP** thinking of Satan in terms of him being able to do anything he wants. He can only operate inside the boundaries of God's SOVEREIGNTY. IT IS GOD WHO WRITES HIS "PAYCHECK" AT THE END OF THE WEEK, FOR HE IS ON GOD'S PAYROLL! Satan does what he is told. (Read the story of Job.) If this is the case (and it is), then man will find his real battle to be with God and **not the Devil**.

The battle that man finds himself in is one of SUBMISSION TO GOD! James 4:7,8 states... Submit yourselves therefore to God. Resist the devil, and he will flee from you. Draw near to God, and He will draw near to you...

It is not our job to try to fight the Devil, but to submit to God, Who created the Devil, and is in charge of the Devil! THIS IS THE BATTLE OF THE AGES! Once that we recognize God as sovereign, we will STOP trying to blame everything on the Devil, realizing that there is a purpose for all of our fiery trials. Satan is not fighting against God, but rather, he is WORKING FOR GOD to accomplish His (God's) purpose, which is to produce overcomers. It is not the DOG ON THE LEASH that we are to be concerned with. Remember...It is the Master of that dog...

THAT CONTROLS THE LEASH!

❖

September 22

THE PURPOSE OF EVIL - PART 14

STRONG DELUSION

According to Martin Zender: "GOD PURPOSELY SENDS DECEPTIONS INTO THE WORLD - even in the form of mistranslated scripture - to separate truth lovers from the lovers of injustice. I'm glad you're here. I will quote you three scriptures to support this disturbing point. Proverbs 25:2…It is the glory of God to conceal a matter, and the glory of kings to investigate a matter…1st Corinthians 11:19…For it must be that there are sects also among you, that those also who are qualified may be becoming apparent…2nd Thessalonians 2:11,12…And therefore **God will be sending them an operation of deception (strong delusion),** for them to believe the falsehood, that all may be judged who do not believe the truth, but delight in injustice…In the last days, GOD HIMSELF will send an operation of deception. This is hard for many to take. They say God would never do such a thing, or anything like it. BUT HE WOULD. HE HAS DONE IT BEFORE. In 1st Kings 22:23, GOD HIMSELF put a deceiving spirit in the mouth of King Ahab's prophets, to cause the king to fall at Ramoth Gilead. God wants people to SEARCH, and He makes it so they have to. HE HIDES TRUTH - or situates it at an oblique angle - and then says, GO FIND IT. Show Me how badly you want it. If you want it, you'll get down on your hands and knees if you have to." (Martin Zender Goes To Hell, Martin Zender)

We must also understand the concept of **darkness** and **light**. **Darkness** is associated with deception, and **light** is associated with truth. God starts everything in **darkness** and then brings in **light** to dispel the **darkness**. This is the story of the Bible. It is able to be seen from the very outset of the purpose and plan of God. Genesis 1:2,3 states…And the earth was without form, and void; and **darkness** was upon the face of the deep. And the Spirit of God moved upon the face of the waters. And God said, Let there be **light**: and there was **light**…

Can we now see that God is saving us, bringing us out of **darkness** into His marvelous **light** (1st Peter 2:9)? God knows that we see the **light** better from a position of **darkness** (deception / delusion), for in **darkness** it is easy to see A BRIGHT **LIGHT**! Everything pertaining to man starts in **darkness** (deception / delusion), but God is bringing us to the **light**…

FOR GOD IS **LIGHT**!

❖

September 23

THE PURPOSE OF EVIL - PART 15

CONCLUSION

According to A. P. Adams: "We have seen that **one of the purposes of evil is to develop in our characters attributes akin to God: pity, mercy, compassion, charity, gentleness,** etc. Now suppose we lived in a world of absolute justice where no one suffered except what they strictly deserved to suffer, where the innocent never suffered, but only the guilty, and they suffered just so much - no more and no less - as was due to their transgression and as would be beneficial to the transgressor. Suppose we lived in such a world as that. At first thought it would seem as though it would be a very nice kind of world; but how could we in such a world develop the godlike attributes above referred to? There would be no room for heavenly compassion and sweet charity and pity in a world of absolute justice. We would not be likely to pity very much a person who we knew was receiving only the punishment due his fault and that in the end would be for his benefit and blessing. Is it not plain that just this **kind** of evil, i.e., the evil of injustice, is needed in order that those crowning attributes of God, the tender and loving qualities of our Father in heaven, may be developed and perfected in His human children?" (The Purpose Of Evil, A. P. Adams)

Evil, for the time being, is a thorn in our side. With that being said, though, evil is to be seen as part of the purpose and plan of God. Evil did not take God by surprise, but rather, GOD CREATED EVIL FOR A PURPOSE! It is used by God to TEACH His creation, bringing mankind to a desired end. Romans 12:21 tells us to NOT BE OVERCOME WITH EVIL, BUT OVERCOME EVIL WITH GOOD...

God, in this present age, is dealing with, selecting out, and **QUALIFYING** a remnant of overcomers. These overcomers, by the Spirit of God, are learning to OVERCOME EVIL WITH GOOD. This is necessary for God to produce overcomers. God has created and placed **OPPOSITION** (evil) in the path of those who are destined to be overcomers in this present age. **THIS OPPOSITION WILL PROVE TO BE THE SALVATION OF THE ENTIRE CREATION!** Romans 8:18 states...the sufferings of this present time are NOT WORTHY to be compared with THE GLORY which shall be revealed in us...This same remnant is to be used to set the entire creation free in the ages to come! We must look at the BIG PICTURE, for God is teaching the creation to OVERCOME EVIL WITH GOOD! Now we can see...

THE PURPOSE OF EVIL!

September 24

THE SOVEREIGNTY OF GOD - PART 1

SOVEREIGNTY EXPLAINED

According to George Addair: "By the Sovereignty of God, we mean the supremacy of God. We mean His Kingship and Headship. It literally means, "the Godhood of God". To declare that God is sovereign is to declare that He is God. It is to declare "That He is the most high, doing according to His will in the army of heaven and among the inhabitants of the earth, so that none can stay His hand or say unto Him, What have You done?" (Daniel 4:35). To say that God is sovereign is to declare that He "is the Almighty, the possessor of all power in heaven and earth, so that none can defeat His counsels, thwart His purpose, or resist His will" (Psalm 115:3). To say that God is sovereign is to declare that He is "The governor among the nations" (Psalm 22:28). He sets up kingdoms, overthrows empires, and determines the course of dynasties as pleases Him best. To say that God is sovereign is to declare that He is "The only potentate, the King of kings, and Lord of Lords" (1 Timothy 6:15)." (The Absolute Sovereignty Of God, George Addair)

According to Webster's Dictionary, the word "sovereign" means: supreme; preeminent; indisputable: sovereign power. The word "sovereignty" means: supreme and independent power and authority.

This is the way that we should view our God. The scriptures declare that God has created all things, orchestrates all things, is before all things, controls all things, and is responsible for all things. That, my friend, IS SOVEREIGN!

According to George Addair: "Such a God is revealed in the pages of the Sacred Scriptures. However, God is not described as such in modern times. The God presented to people in this twentieth century is practically helpless. He is presented as an effeminate being who commands the respect of no really thoughtful person. Even from the pulpit, the preacher presents God as one who should be pitied rather than one to be respected. I heard one preacher, when describing the state of affairs on earth today say, "Poor God!". The message proclaimed in most churches today implies that God has failed because mankind has rejected Him. Few people seem to realize that He is working ALL THINGS according to His own will (Ephesians 1:11)." (The Absolute Sovereignty Of God, George Addair)

Our goal over the next several days will be to prove (from the scriptures) that **GOD IS SOVEREIGN!** He is not the weak and emaciated God that is presented in modern day Christianity, but…

IS IN CONTROL OF <u>ALL</u> THINGS!

September 25

THE SOVEREIGNTY OF GOD - PART 2

THE PURPOSE OF GOD ACCORDING TO ELECTION

Romans 9:10-13 states…And not only this; but when Rebecca also had conceived by one, even by our father Isaac; (*For the children being not yet born, neither having done any good or evil,* **that the purpose of God according to election might stand**, *not of works, but of Him that calls;*) It was said unto her, The elder shall serve the younger. As it is written, Jacob have I loved, but Esau have I hated…

The above mentioned scriptures speak of one of the aspects of God's sovereignty that is little talked about and little understood. It speaks of THE PURPOSE OF GOD ACCORDING TO "ELECTION". The word "election" simply means: to choose, or select for oneself. Does God CHOOSE certain people over other people? Does God harden or soften people's hearts to do or not do certain things? Does God have mercy on some and not on others? Does God choose certain people to be vessels of wrath and others to be vessels of mercy (vessels of dishonor and honor)? YES! YES! YES! YES!

Romans 9:17 tells us that GOD RAISED UP PHARAOH, AND THEN HARDENED HIS HEART, that His (God's) name would be declared throughout all the earth. If there was no Pharaoh, and no slavery of God's people to this Pharaoh, then there would be no need for a mighty deliverance of God's people, which included mighty plagues, and the parting of the Red Sea. Can you see why it was NECESSARY FOR GOD TO HARDEN PHARAOH'S HEART? It was His purpose according to "election".

The scriptures also tell us that the disciples of Christ did not choose Him, but that HE (Jesus) CHOSE THEM (John 15:16). The apostle Paul is also referred to as a CHOSEN VESSEL in Acts 9:15. As a matter of fact, ALL BELIEVERS in this present age are referred to as A CHOSEN GENERATION (1st Peter 2:9), for we have been elected according to the foreknowledge of God the Father (1st Peter 1:2). Ephesians 1:4,5 states…According as **He has chosen us** in Him before the foundation of the world, that we should be holy and without blame before Him in love: Having **predestinated us unto the adoption** of children by Jesus Christ to Himself, according to the good pleasure of His will, …

The next aspect of God's sovereignty that we will attempt to speak of will be the foreknowledge of God. As we recognize God's sovereignty, WE ARE ACTUALLY MAGNIFYING AND GLORIFYING HIM to the extent that His name would be declared throughout all the earth. The more God's sovereignty is understood, the bigger He becomes in our eyes. Remember…

GREAT IS THE LORD, AND GREATLY TO BE PRAISED!

September 26

THE SOVEREIGNTY OF GOD - PART 3

FOREKNOWLEDGE

"Foreknowledge" is a divine attribute of God, whereby God sees all things in the present tense. There is no past, present, or future with God. Neither time nor space mean anything to Him. "A day is as a thousand years and a thousand years is as a day" (2nd Peter 3:8). According to Webster's Dictionary, the word "foreknowledge" means: knowledge of something before it exists or happens. This attribute of God is to be seen in Psalm 139. Psalm 139:1-8 states...O Lord, You have searched me, and known me. You know my downsitting and my uprising, You understand my thought afar off. You know my path and my lying down, and are acquainted with all my ways. For there is not a word in my tongue, but, lo, O LORD, You know it altogether. You have beset me behind and before, and laid Your hand upon me. Such knowledge is too wonderful for me; it is high, I cannot attain unto it. Where shall I go from Your Spirit? or where shall I flee from Your presence? If I ascend up into heaven, You are there: if I make my bed in hell (the grave), behold, You are there...

This divine attribute of God ("foreknowledge") is obviously one of His most AWESOME attributes! SUCH KNOWLEDGE IS TOO WONDERFUL FOR US; IT IS HIGH, WE CANNOT ATTAIN UNTO IT. We must admit that God's "foreknowledge" is something that we can only recognize and talk about, but will not be able to fully comprehend. It is what makes Him Who He is. It is what makes Him GOD ALMIGHTY, knowing the end from the beginning. He knows all our past, present, and future.

Being aware of this divine attribute, we should have confidence in God, for He knows what is ahead. With this in mind, we should consider what this teaches us about God. This attribute ("foreknowledge") brings us to the conclusion that: GOD DOES NOT REACT, BUT RATHER, HE CREATES, CAUSES, AND COMPLETES! Remember...Jesus is the AUTHOR and FINISHER of our faith...The Bible tells us that...Jesus was delivered by the **DETERMINATE COUNSEL AND "FOREKNOWLEDGE" OF GOD** (Acts 2:33)...

In conclusion, we are now able to see that the whole purpose and plan of God is based on His "FOREKNOWLEDGE"! Without "foreknowledge", there would be no Jesus, no creation, no fall, no salvation, and no restoration. Without foreknowledge, GOD WOULD NOT BE GOD!!! But let us be thankful, for our WONDERFUL GOD IS A GOD OF "FOREKNOWLEDGE"! There is none like unto Him. O THE DEPTH OF THE RICHES BOTH OF THE WISDOM AND KNOWLEDGE OF GOD! HOW UNSEARCHABLE ARE HIS JUDGMENTS, AND HIS WAYS...

PAST FINDING OUT (Romans 11:33)!

September 27

THE SOVEREIGNTY OF GOD - PART 4

PREDESTINATION

Romans 8:28-30 states…And we know that all things work together for good to them that love God, to them who are the **called** according to His **purpose**. For whom He did **foreknow**, He also did **predestinate** to be conformed to the image of His Son, that He might be the firstborn among many brethren. Moreover whom He did **predestinate**, them He also **called**: and whom He **called**, them He also **justified**: and whom He **justified**, them He also **glorified**…

Ephesians 1:4,5 states…According as **He has chosen us** in Him before the foundation of the world, that we should be holy and without blame before Him in love: **Having predestinated us unto the adoption** of children by Jesus Christ to Himself, according to the good pleasure of His will…

According to Andrew Telford: "What does the word "Predestination" mean when you look at the etymology of the word itself? "Predestination" is made up of two words. The first part is "pre", which means before, or beforehand. The last part of the word is "destination" which means the climax, end or farthest extent. The little word "pre" has to do with something beforehand. The word "destination" has to do with the farthest extent. We understand by this then, what "Predestination", according to the precise meaning of the word has to do with: something beforehand and something at the farthest end or termination. "Predestination" has nothing to do with anything in between. The time is designated by the word "pre" and the farthest extent is designated by the word "destination." "Predestination" is God doing something beforehand, and doing something about or concerning, or relative to the farthest extent. "Predestination" does not deal with anything in between these two points. We notice in Romans 8:29 the purpose of "Predestination". It is, that we might be conformed to the image of His Son. Now when will that take place? We read in Romans 8:23 that it will take place when the body is redeemed, and that is the time of my <u>adoption</u>. This is the definite purpose of God in "Predestination". He has <u>"predestinated" us unto the Adoption</u>. Keep in mind the definition of the word. "Predestination" is a divine act of God, whereby, God makes that goal which is <u>Adoption</u>, certain for the believer. The purpose of God in "Predestination" then is <u>Adoption</u>, and when we are <u>Adopted</u> we shall be <u>Son-placed</u>. When we are <u>Son-placed</u> we shall be like Him, we shall then be in the image of His Son." (<u>Subjects Of Sovereignty</u>, Andrew Telford)

Our next goal in this study will be to give an explanation of the word…

ADOPTION!

September 28

THE SOVEREIGNTY OF GOD - PART 5

ADOPTION

Romans 8:15,23 states…For you have not received the spirit of bondage again to fear; but you have received the Spirit of adoption, whereby we cry, Abba, Father…And not only they, but ourselves also, which have the firstfruits of the Spirit, even we ourselves groan within ourselves, waiting for the adoption, to wit, the redemption of our body…

According to Andrew Telford: "What does "Adoption" really mean? It does not mean what we usually take it to mean. Neither does it mean the "adopting of a child." "Adoption" in the Bible does not mean the same as the word "Adoption" when used in relation to the legal transaction of receiving into the family as a son or daughter, a child who has been born of other parents. Evidently the translators failed to find a word in the English language that would express to us clearly, the full meaning of the transaction of God Almighty, when God by a divine act, placed a certain destination and position for the believer. The translators have used the word "Adoption" as the only word at their disposal, to express this act of God. "Adoption" means to be "Son-Placed", not "son-made". You are made a Son the moment you are saved by God's grace. Now, as a son there are certain privileges and benefits God by His sovereign acts has provided for those who are saved. No one has been "son-placed" as yet. One time you will be. You belong to the Lord Jesus Christ now, just as much as you ever will. You have not arrived at the goal which God has predestinated you to-which goal is "Adoption" (Ephesians 1:6). In the early days of the Roman Empire when a boy was born into the family, he was cared for by his parents till he was twenty-one years of age. At the age of twenty-one, they took the child and there placed him in the market place before the public. He was "son-placed". From that time on he could sign his own name to legal documents, and went forward with the full authority of a man. This act at the market place did not make him a son; he was a son when he was born into his parents' family. At the age of twenty-one he was "son-placed". "Adoption" is a definite act of God whereby God sets a goal for the believer. What does Paul mean by the "firstfruits of the Spirit"? The "firstfruits" in the life of any believer is pardon, forgiveness, acceptance, security, sanctification. Do you notice that "Adoption" is not mentioned here among the "firstfruits of the Spirit"? "Adoption" belongs among the "last fruits" of the Spirit. Paul tells us that we should have the "firstfruits of the Spirit", groaning within ourselves and waiting for something to take place. What is that something that Paul and the saints in Rome were waiting for? It is called by the Spirit of God in this verse the "Adoption". He then tells us when it will take place --at the redemption of our bodies. This verse gives us two reasons which tell us that the time of "Adoption" is future. The first proof or reason that "Adoption" is still future is that we are waiting for the "Adoption" to wit. It could not have taken place if they were waiting for "Adoption" to happen at some future time. In the closing part of the verse, it tells us that it will take place at the redemption of our bodies. We now have redeemed souls in unredeemed bodies." (<u>Subjects Of Sovereignty</u>, Andrew Telford) This will take place for the overcomers…

AT THE FIRST RESURRECTION!

September 29

THE SOVEREIGNTY OF GOD - PART 6

SOVEREIGNTY VS. FREE WILL

According to John Gavazzoni: "**Everything that occurs, occurs within the sovereign will of God. Nothing is accidental.** All has been foreseen by Him because **all things come to pass by His decision,** so that everything has occurred by Him, **either doing something to make it come to pass, or by deliberately refusing to act so as, by that absence of His action, to trigger certain consequential results.** The Old Testament prophets gave a preview of this principle, saying, to quote just one representatively, *"I will put My Spirit within them and cause them to walk in My statutes"* (Ezek. 36:27). And the New Testament confirms this with such statements as, *"Who works all things after the counsel of His own will"* (Eph. 1:11). **Now some, completely indoctrinated by the dumbed-down notion of "free will",** upon being confronted with what I've just shared, without any depth of thought at all, **would accuse me of making man out to be a mere robot.** But, I ask, if God has a "free will", and brings man into participation with that will, how can freedom be defined as robotic? Freedom by definition, involves not being controlled by another. **The relationship of God's will to us, is not one of making us do something against our will, but by bringing our will into union with His. This is not coercion, this is causation,** and it is causation by the force of love which ultimately **worked by God leaving us to ourselves to do what we would do left to ourselves; which was to crucify His Son, and then to love such enemies back to Himself by the power of forgiving love.**" (Free Will, John Gavazzoni)

In simple terms, man is able to make choices, but our choices can only be made inside the realm of the sovereignty of God. Remember…God asked Jonah to go to Nineveh. Jonah made a choice to go in the opposite direction. GOD, BY HIS SOVEREIGNTY, SENT JONAH ON A FISHING TRIP (speaking of Jonah in the belly of the great fish)! Jonah made another choice. This time his choice was in line with what God wanted him to do. What made the difference? THE FISHING TRIP, OF COURSE! Without the divine intervention of God (having Jonah thrown overboard into the great fish), there would be no choice from Jonah to go to Nineveh. So you would have to say that without the sovereign act of God, Jonah, who was headed in the opposite direction of what God wanted him to do, would not have gone to Nineveh.

According to John Gavazzoni: "**The truth is that the only One in the universe Who has true "free will" is God Himself.** As is true of every good thing, "free will" is something found in God's very nature and **we can only experience "freedom of will" by God causing us to participate in His freedom by causing us to become** *"partakers of the divine nature"* (II Pet. 1:4); and that is His choice not ours. That is, **He causes us to participate in the divine ability to desire something, then foreordain it, predestine it, and make it come to pass.** That's freedom; to be without constraint, without hindrance, without anything that can, in any degree, stop or hinder one's desire. **The scripture is quite clear that God will bring to pass His desire for all men and for the entire cosmos.**" (Free Will, John Gavazzoni)

Think of God's dealings with Pharaoh, Esau, Jonah, and the apostle Paul, just to name a few. It won't take long for you to admit…

THAT GOD IS SOVEREIGN!

September 30

THE SOVEREIGNTY OF GOD - PART 7

THE SOVEREIGN BLINDING OF ISRAEL

Romans 11:25-32 (Today's English Version) states…There is a secret truth, my friends, which I want you to know, for it will keep you from thinking how wise you are. It is that the stubbornness of the people of Israel is not permanent, but will last only until the complete number of Gentiles comes to God. And this is how all Israel will be saved. As the scripture says, "The Savior will come from Zion and remove all wickedness from the descendants of Jacob. I will make this covenant with them when I take away their sins." Because they reject the Good News, the Jews are God's enemies for the sake of you Gentiles. But because of God's choice, they are His friends because of their ancestors. For God does not change His mind about whom He chooses and blesses. As for you Gentiles, you disobeyed God in the past; but now you have received God's mercy because the Jews were disobedient. In the same way, because of the mercy that you have received, the Jews now disobey God, in order that they also may now receive God's mercy. **For God has made all people prisoners of disobedience, so that He might show mercy to them ALL…**

If we are not able to get excited about a passage of scripture such as this, then there is not much that will excite us. This passage is referring to the sovereign act of God, in which He initially blinded the Gentiles and showed mercy to the Jews, and then blinded the Jews to show mercy to the Gentiles. It states that…GOD MADE ALL PEOPLE PRISONERS OF DISOBEDIENCE, SO THAT HE MIGHT SHOW MERCY TO THEM ALL. This sovereign act is to be seen as the wisdom and knowledge of God. It will result in the RECONCILING OF THE WORLD!

Romans 11:11,12 states…I say then, Have they stumbled that they should fall? God forbid: but rather through their fall salvation is come unto the Gentiles, for to provoke them to jealousy. Now if the fall of them be the riches of the world, and the diminishing of them the riches of the Gentiles; how much more their fullness?…(Read also Romans 11:15.)

We must see that God is responsible for this sovereign act. **It is God that gives the spirit of slumber, eyes that can not see, and ears that they should not hear** (Romans 11:8)…God is using this sovereign act to reconcile ALL THINGS AND ALL PEOPLE UNTO HIMSELF.

HE WILL SHOW MERCY TO ALL!

October 1

THE SOVEREIGNTY OF GOD - PART 8

FOR OF HIM, AND THROUGH HIM, AND TO HIM ARE ALL THINGS

According to Dr. Stephen Jones: "The apostle Paul has begun to understand the ways of God, and so he does not hesitate to agree fully with the plan of God in locking both Israel and the world in blindness for a season. Why? Because *out of* Him, and *through* Him, and *into* Him are all things. These words indicate that all things ORIGINATE in God; all things are processed THROUGH Him, and all things are going back INTO Him. This is just another way of saying that in the end, God will be all in all (1 Cor. 15:28). He will not be All in just a few, nor in a tiny remnant, nor will He be limited to all Israel. He will be all IN ALL." (Blindness In Part, Dr. Stephen Jones)

According to Dr. Harold Lovelace: "This verse (Romans 11:36), as much or maybe more than any other verse in the Bible, gives the <u>entire</u> <u>picture</u> in explaining all about God and His creation. Noticing the three prepositions, "of", "through", and "to" and are all related to Him (God) and ALL THINGS. All things are "of" God, all things are "through" God, and all things are "to" (returning to) God. See 1st Corinthians 8:6; 11:12; 15:28; 2nd Corinthians 5:18; Ephesians 4:6; Colossians 1:16-20; and 3:11." (Read And Search God's Plan, Dr. Harold Lovelace)

If this verse of scripture is not a declaration of God's sovereignty, then there are none that declare such. This verse tells us that **God is in control of all things**, including the origin, sustaining, and ending of all things. This is referred to as **THE LAW OF CIRCULARITY**, which in simple terms states: All things must eventually return to their point of origin. There is no such thing as going in a direction away from your point of origin (for ever and ever), never returning to that point of origin. This is a sovereign law of God that includes **the entire creation.**

According to Dr. Stephen Jones: "In other words, "the all" that was inclusive of all creation is also to be reconciled back to God by the blood of the cross. All creation had become God's enemy in need of reconciliation. This is what Paul said in Romans 11, where Israel had become God's enemy through their unbelief, joining the world of enemies in need of God's reconciliation. This was accomplished on the cross, and its purpose shall be fulfilled, for this is the divine plan, and no man can prevent it from happening. Hallelujah!" (Blindness In Part, Dr. Stephen Jones)

Our next effort will be to show more scriptures that declare God as…

ABSOLUTELY SOVEREIGN!

October 2

THE SOVEREIGNTY OF GOD - PART 9

ALL THINGS ARE OF GOD

According to A. P. Adams: "There is no statement in the Bible that is more remarkable and even startling than this. When you think of it seriously, it seems as though Paul was very unguarded and careless in his language. We are apt to think that he ought to have modified and limited it in some way such as, for instance, all *good* things are of God. But no, Paul makes the sweeping, unqualified statement, "all things are of (literally, *out of*) God." Furthermore, so important did Paul consider this truth that he repeats it over and over again. The direct statement is made no less than six times in the writings of the apostle. See Rom. 11:36; I Cor. 8:6, I Cor. 11:12; 2 Cor. 5:18; Eph. 1:11, and Heb. 2:10. Now was the apostle careless and a little too bold in these utterances, or did he mean just what he said, and are they true, taken full strength? I say without hesitation, yes, to the two latter questions. The more we learn of God's works and ways the more we shall understand that in a sense absolutely "*all* things are of God"; or in other words, as it has often been expressed, God *is in everything.*" (<u>We Are God's Workmanship</u>, A. P. Adams)

The question is then, what side of the fence will we be found on? Will we be found on the sovereign side, believing that ALL THINGS ARE OF GOD?...or will we be found on the traditional side, believing that God merely reacts to mankind, and is doing His best to fight off a powerful Devil, trying to save as many people as He can? It is time to recognize our God for WHO HE IS! **HE IS SOVEREIGN!** NOT ONLY IS HE POWERFUL, BUT HE IS ALL-POWERFUL. NOT ONLY IS HE KNOWING, BUT HE IS ALL-KNOWING. NOT ONLY IS HE PRESENT, BUT HE IS ALL-PRESENT. NOT ONLY IS HE LOVING, BUT HE IS ALL-LOVING (HE **IS** LOVE). HE POSSESSES **INDISPUTABLE POWER! HE IS ALMIGHTY!**

Let us stop vomiting out traditional teaching that strips God of His sovereignty. We must be honest and admit that the modern day church is weak in the things of God. This is due to the fact that THEY VIEW THEIR GOD AS A WEAK GOD. They are simply a product of their preaching and teaching. Most Christians have resigned themselves to a belief that God will lose most of humanity to an eternal torture pit. This poor, pathetic, and pitiful teaching has caused many to be blinded to the sovereignty of God. THANK GOD THAT THIS TEACHING (eternal torture) IS NOT TRUE! Not only is it not true, but it is not even close to a proper description of our Father, for...

ALL THINGS ARE OF GOD!

October 3

THE SOVEREIGNTY OF GOD - PART 10

CONCLUSION

According to George Addair: "Almost every person who is familiar with the Bible readily agrees that God possesses a **foreknowledge** of everything that has been, is now, or will ever be. This is confirmed by many passages of the Bible among which are "known unto God are all His works from the beginning" (Acts 15:18); "but all things are open and naked unto the eyes of Him" (Hebrews 4:13). To understand this truth is to realize that nothing happens by mere chance and the course of your life as well as the course of the world is certain because **foreknowledge** indicates that the course is fixed. If it were not fixed it could not be foreknown. And the fact that it is fixed is so vividly revealed in Ephesians 1:11, "Being predestined according to the purpose of Him Who works all things after the counsel of His own will." (The Absolute Sovereignty Of God, George Addair)

Our relationship with God will be greatly enhanced as we come to an understanding that God is sovereign. The fact that God is sovereign is what sets Him apart from anything or anyone else. It is what makes Him God. It is the GODHOOD OF GOD! His **foreknowledge**, **power**, and **love** are the very attributes that declare that HE ALONE IS GOD, AND THAT THERE IS NONE ELSE BESIDE HIM! Not only does He possess **foreknowledge**, **power**, and **love**, but these three attributes are to be seen as UNLIMITED in their demonstration and manifestation of WHO HE IS! HE IS THE GREAT I AM! He has the **knowledge**, **power**, and **love** to carry out to completion (perfection) that which He purposes from the beginning.

If we preach a God Who is lacking in any of these areas, then He is not sovereign. If His power is limited in any way, then He is not sovereign. If His love is limited in any way, then He is not sovereign. Some may ask the question, what does love have to do with sovereignty? It has everything to do with sovereignty. If sovereignty is to be found in the hands of a God Who is not love, then that God would be nothing more than a cruel dictator. But thank God that that is not the case with our God, FOR GOD **IS** LOVE! He is ALL-POWERFUL and ALL-LOVING! He is everything to everyone! He is…

ALL IN ALL!

October 4

PARTAKERS OF THE DIVINE NATURE - PART 1

THE ROOT OF THE PROBLEM

Ephesians 2:3 states…Among whom also we all had our conversation in times past in the lusts of our flesh, fulfilling the desires of the flesh and of the mind; **and were by nature the children of wrath**, even as others…

This verse of scripture gives us an explanation concerning man and the root of his problem. It tells us that…WE ARE BY NATURE THE CHILDREN OF WRATH…**This is the very root of our problem!** Man is born with a nature that is contrary (or against) to God. This nature can be referred to as: the sin nature, the beast nature, or that nature that is anti-Christ (against, or instead of Christ). The word "nature" refers to the intrinsic character of a person or thing. The word "wrath" speaks of intense desire and longing. This tells us that man is born with an intrinsic character that automatically desires and longs to fulfill the desires and lusts of the flesh. **The root of our problem is to be found in the nature that we are born with.** This nature, left up to itself, will ALWAYS be contrary to the things of the Spirit. It will always gravitate to the things of the flesh. This nature will always seek self-promotion and self-exaltation, which is that spirit of anti-Christ (that which is instead of or against Christ). As well, this nature causes us to constantly come short of the glory of God, bringing us into a lifestyle of sin. (The word "sin" means to miss the mark. The mark that is being missed is the very nature of God.) It is not so much that sin is our problem, as much as it is the FALLEN NATURE that we were born with that produces sin in our lives. That is the problem. This fallen (sin) nature could also be referred to as the ADAMIC NATURE, for we did inherit it from Adam.

Genesis 5:3 tells us that Adam lived 130 years, and brought forth a son IN HIS OWN LIKENESS, AFTER HIS IMAGE; AND CALLED HIS NAME SETH…This tells us that Adam brought forth children in his own likeness, passing on his fallen state and fallen condition (nature). This is the reason that we are by nature the children of wrath.

WE MUST **LOOK WITHIN** TO SEE OUR PROBLEMS AND FAILURES, for they are the result of our (inherited) Adamic Nature. It will do us no good to look without, pointing our self-righteous finger at others. We must deal with…

THE ROOT OF THE PROBLEM!

October 5

PARTAKERS OF THE DIVINE NATURE - PART 2

THE MAN OF SIN

After seeing that our fallen nature is the root of our problem, we are then freed up to <u>see</u>, having revealed to us…"THE MAN OF SIN". 2ND Thessalonians 2:3,4 states…Let no man deceive you by any means: for that day shall not come, except there come a falling away first, and **that "man of sin" be revealed**, the son of perdition; Who opposes and exalts himself above all that is called God, or that is worshipped; so that he as God sits in the temple of God, showing himself that he is God…

The key to understanding this passage (2nd Thessalonians 2:3,4) is to LOOK WITHIN YOURSELF, seeing your fallen nature as the "man of sin" that sits in the temple of God. Remember…

The apostle Paul told us that **WE ARE THE TEMPLE OF GOD!** Well…This is where the "man of sin" is said to be found at. This would mean that the terminology "man of sin" is referring to the carnal (fleshly) nature within the temple of God that is opposing the things of God. What is it that opposes the Spirit of God? Well…THE FLESH, OF COURSE! The flesh wars against the Spirit, and the Spirit wars against the flesh.

The most important point for us to see concerning the "man of sin" is this: The "man of sin" in NOT something or someone OUT THERE. He (the "man of sin") is not just one man who will rise on the scene to take over the world. This "man of sin" is **WITHIN US**, even in our members, stemming from our fallen nature. The apostle Paul referred to it in Romans 7:5, when he stated… For when we were in the flesh, the motions of sins, which were by the law, DID WORK IN OUR MEMBERS to bring forth fruit unto death…

After coming to the revelation that **our fallen nature is the root of our problem**, and that the "man of sin" is within us (the temple of God), we are then headed toward one of the most profound revelations in all of the Bible. This revelation will SET US FREE from self, including a lifestyle of pointing the finger at others. We must see that **all of our problems come from within**, that is, they are internal, not external. As long as we keep waiting for some literal "man of sin" to walk on the scene, not discerning that "man of sin" that is within, it will never be revealed to us that the "man of sin" is that CARNAL MIND…

WITHIN US!

October 6

PARTAKERS OF THE DIVINE NATURE - PART 3

<u>O WRETCHED MAN THAT I AM!</u>

Romans 7:23,24 states…But I see another law in my members, warring against the law of my mind, and bringing me into captivity to the law of sin which is in my members. **O wretched man that I am!** who shall deliver me from the body of this death?…

THIS IS ONE OF THE MOST PROFOUND STATEMENTS THAT THE APOSTLE PAUL MADE IN ALL OF HIS WRITINGS! When a person comes to the understanding (revelation) that ALL THEIR PROBLEMS ARE TO BE FOUND WITHIN THEM, it is equivalent to a pregnant woman whose water breaks, for then she knows the baby is sure to come forth. To realize that we are wretched outside of God does not at first sound like good news. After we get over the initial shock of seeing our total depravity (the condition of our hopeless nature), we are then IN POSITION TO RECEIVE OF GOD'S DIVINE NATURE, WHICH GIVES US ALL THINGS THAT PERTAIN TO LIFE AND GODLINESS. It is not until we see ourselves for who we are outside of God that we can see the potential of WHO WE ARE IN CHRIST.

This process of seeing ourselves as wretched is not a pity party or false humility, but rather, we are coming to the place where we are poor in spirit, for Jesus said…Blessed are the poor in spirit: for theirs is the kingdom of heaven…This could also be referred to as the BADGE OF BROKENNESS. It is an awareness of our inherited spiritual condition outside of God. After realizing this (being brought to a realization of this by God), we are now headed in the right direction, which causes us to look unto GOD AS OUR POWER SOURCE. We will begin to see Him as the AUTHOR AND FINISHER OF OUR FAITH. This brings us to a place of total hopelessness in self, but of total victory in Christ. We become totally dependent on the grace of God, **having no confidence in the flesh.**

This is what Jesus was referring to when He explained the process of denying self, taking up our cross, and following Him. As we enter into this process, we will find that death (the carnal mind that is in us) is giving way to the life of Christ, being swallowed up in victory. This will take our attention off of trying to fight the Devil, which is really not our problem, for we are not told (in scripture) to fight the Devil, but rather, we are told to SUBMIT TO GOD. We must lose our life for His name's sake, for then, and only then, will we find life. This is the key to any and all victory in God. (Scriptures used: 2nd Peter 1:3-4, Matthew 5:3, Hebrews 12:2, Philippians 3:3, Matthew 16:24-25, 1st Corinthians 15:54-56, James 4:7.) Now for some hope from…

GOD'S DIVINE POWER!

October 7

PARTAKERS OF THE DIVINE NATURE - PART 4

HIS DIVINE POWER

2nd Peter 1:3 states…According as His divine power has given unto us all things that pertain unto life and godliness, through the knowledge of Him that has called us to glory and virtue…

Are you ready for some HOPE? Are you ready for some GOOD NEWS? Are you ready for a truth from God's Word that will set you free from a life of failure, frustration, and condemnation? We as Christians desire to walk in victory. We desire to be overcomers. We long for the ability and knowledge to walk in the Spirit each and every day. Many set out to serve God, trying to serve Him on zeal alone, but find themselves hitting a brick wall, not being able to apprehend that which they are seeking for. Is it that they just don't want God bad enough? Are they not totally sold out to God?…NO!

Remember…The apostle Paul found himself in the same condition. Romans 7:18 states…For I know that in me (that is, in my flesh,) dwells no good thing: for to will is present with me; but how to perform that which is good I find not…

So…The question is, HOW DO WE OVERCOME? HOW DO WE WALK IN THE SPIRIT? HOW DO WE BECOME LIKE THE SON OF GOD? We must first realize (as we have previously stated) **that this ability (the ability to overcome the flesh) is not to be found in us.** There must be another POWER SOURCE (other than us) that is available to us that will enable us to be who we are called to be. THIS POWER SOURCE IS <u>GOD'S</u> <u>DIVINE</u> <u>POWER</u>! It is SO IMPORTANT that we understand this, for the scriptures tell us that **His divine power has given us all things that pertain unto life and godliness, through the knowledge of God**…If there is something available to us that gives us ALL THINGS that pertain to life and godliness, then we might want to learn of it, taking notice of what it is, even how to receive of it.

An understanding of 2nd Peter chapter one will deliver you from a life of trying to please God in the flesh, for the flesh (your ability) WILL FAIL GOD EVERY TIME! 2ND Peter chapter one is one of THE MOST IMPORTANT PASSAGES of scripture in the entire Bible. If we are able to discover its meaning, then we will be ushered into THE VERY ABUNDANT LIFE THAT JESUS SPOKE OF!

WHAT GREAT AND PRECIOUS PROMISES!

October 8

PARTAKERS OF THE DIVINE NATURE - PART 5

THE KNOWLEDGE OF GOD

In order to be a partaker of something it is imperative that we have a knowledge of what it is that we are to partake of. In this case we are referring to a knowledge of partaking of GOD'S DIVINE NATURE. The word "knowledge" used in 2nd Peter 1:2 comes from the Greek word "epignosis", which means: clear and exact knowledge, expressing a more thorough participation in the object of knowledge on the part of the subject, knowledge which very powerfully influences the form of the religious life, and a knowledge laying claim to personal sympathy and exerting an influence upon the person. In this case (2nd Peter 1:2) it would refer to having an intimate and thorough knowledge of God. This knowledge would be based off of a person's experience in God, which knowledge would influence the life of that person, and which knowledge would result in a manifestation of the CHRIST-LIFE.

Pay close attention to the word "knowledge" in 2nd Peter chapter one. It is used no less than six times. Peter was obviously placing an extreme amount of emphasis on the believer's need for THE KNOWLEDGE OF GOD. As well, Romans chapters six through eight places the same amount of emphasis on the importance of the believer having a thorough knowledge of God. This knowledge (the knowledge of the person and work of the Lord Jesus Christ) is what leads us to be a partaker of God's divine nature.

Without a true and proper knowledge of God, we are doomed to failure and condemnation, being sentenced to the bondage of the traditions and doctrines of men. Hosea 4:6 states…My people are destroyed **for lack of knowledge**…This tells us that a lack of knowledge is what causes us to perish, keeping us in a life of failure, frustration, and condemnation.

The difference between a believer and a non-believer is this: One believes and **knows** about God, and the other does not. THE KNOWLEDGE OF GOD IS WORTH MORE THAN ALL THE

EARTHLY RICHES THAT ONE COULD ACQUIRE! IT IS WORTH WHATEVER IT TAKES TO ACQUIRE IT! It is to be seen as a mighty key in God's Kingdom that unlocks to us an experience that could not otherwise be experienced. The opposite of perishing is to live. Let us seek the knowledge of God...

THAT WE MIGHT LIVE!

October 9

PARTAKERS OF THE DIVINE NATURE - PART 6

SHARERS IN THE VERY NATURE OF GOD

2nd Peter 1:4 states...Whereby are given unto us exceeding great and precious promises: that by these you might be **partakers of the divine nature**, having escaped the corruption that is in the world through lust...

If there are certain key scriptures in the Bible that unlock to us how to be all that God has called us to be in Christ, then this is definitely one of those scriptures, and just might be the most important one. We are told that...WE HAVE BEEN GIVEN EXCEEDING GREAT AND PRECIOUS PROMISES; THAT BY THESE WE MIGHT BE PARTAKERS OF THE DIVINE NATURE. The New Testament In Modern Speech renders this passage as follows: It is by means of these that He has granted us His precious and wondrous promises, in order that through them you may, one and all, BECOME SHARERS IN THE VERY NATURE OF GOD, having completely escaped the corruption which exists in the world through earthly cravings...

WHAT A PRECIOUS AND WONDROUS OPPORTUNITY THAT HAS BEEN MADE AVAILABLE TO US! CAN YOU BELIEVE WHAT HAS JUST BEEN STATED? **WE HAVE BECOME SHARERS IN THE VERY NATURE OF GOD!** This means that we are partakers and participators in all that God is. This is good news. This is VERY GOOD NEWS! This is our hope, and is in fact our only hope! It is the hope that we have been, are being, and will be saved from the nature that we were born with. This is our salvation!

The other aspect of this scripture that should cause us to rejoice is this: This passage speaks of something that GOD HAS ACCOMPLISHED, simply leaving us as sharers in HIS ACCOMPLISHMENT. We are not called upon to do anything, but rather, to receive (and be) that which will enable us to be like Him. We must STOP trying to live for God in the flesh. We will never accomplish godliness in the flesh. In essence, we are to simply take on God's nature, just as one would partake of a meal on a table that has been fully set. This is what it means to labor (be diligent) to enter into God's rest (Hebrews 4:1-11). As we take on, partake of, participate in, and receive of the VERY NATURE OF GOD, we are given one of the most unbelievable promises in all of the Bible. So let us make our calling and election sure, for we are...

SHARERS IN THE VERY NATURE OF GOD!

October 10

PARTAKERS OF THE DIVINE NATURE - PART 7

YOU SHALL NEVER FALL

2ND Peter 1:10 states…Wherefore the rather, brethren, give diligence to make your calling and election sure: for if you do these things, **you shall never fall**…

This is quite an unbelievable promise, but if the Bible is true (which it is), then we must believe it and take it for what it says. This verse is telling us the result of partaking of the divine nature. It tells us of a position in God that gives us the ability to NEVER FALL. The word "fall" in this verse means to stumble. Well…If you are not able to stumble, how can you even fall? This does not mean that we are destined to never make a mistake, but rather, it speaks of a POSITION OF TESTIMONY that is sure and rock solid, and that will never fail. This "position of testimony" is to be found IN CHRIST, Who is the ANOINTED ONE OF GOD. To be IN CHRIST is to be a part of the **NEW CREATION MAN**, having God's divine nature as our power source. The old man is dead and buried! We have been raised with Christ in newness of life. It is the **exchanged life process**.

With these things being said, we are now on a path to CERTAIN VICTORY, having positioned and aligned ourselves with a POWER that will enable us to NEVER STUMBLE. Due to the fact that we have been born with a fallen nature, this becomes VERY EXCITING NEWS to the human race. All we know is a life of stumbling, falling, sin, frustration, futility, vanity, and condemnation. God's divine nature is the ONLY THING that is able to free us from the vicious cycle of constantly coming short of the glory of God, which leads to failure, frustration, and condemnation. As well, God's divine nature liberates us, causing us to be ushered into a new dimension of living, in which we are promised to receive of God's abundant life. This new and living way is the opposite of falling short the glory of God. It introduces us to the potential of never falling. How can we fall as long as we are sharing in the very nature of God? It is impossible to fall when one is walking in the Spirit. God's nature is bringing us to the place where we only do those things that please our Father. After partaking of Who God is, godliness will become a…

BYPRODUCT OF GOD'S DIVINE NATURE!

October 11

PARTAKERS OF THE DIVINE NATURE - PART 8

DOING…A BYPRODUCT OF GOD'S NATURE

2ND Peter 1:5-8,10 states…And beside this, giving all diligence, add to your faith virtue; and to virtue knowledge; And to knowledge temperance; and to temperance patience; and to patience godliness; And to godliness brotherly kindness; and to brotherly kindness charity. For if these things be in you, and abound, they make you that you shall neither be barren nor unfruitful in the knowledge of our Lord Jesus Christ…Wherefore the rather, brethren, give diligence to make your calling and election sure: for if you do these things, you shall never fall…

As one takes a first glance at this passage of scripture it appears that we are being given a list of things that we must do to become like God. In fact, MANY Christians spend a lifetime trying to "work up" or "muster up" enough strength in and of themselves to try to become like God. BUT THIS IS NOT THE CASE!

We must go back to the original statement that Peter made. 2nd Peter 1:4 states…**we have been made partakers of the divine nature**…The statements that Peter makes in verses four through eleven are to be seen in light of his original statement. This means that faith, virtue, knowledge, temperance, patience, godliness, brotherly kindness, and charity are BYPRODUCTS OF PARTAKING OF THE DIVINE NATURE. If you think that you are capable of producing these attributes of God in your life outside of the divine nature, then you will find yourself right back in your original predicament, which is…O WRETCHED MAN THAT I AM!

We must be careful not to get the cart before the horse. MANY think that what they do will produce the divine nature. This is just the opposite of the truth. We must understand that it is the divine nature at work within us that will produce godliness in our lives. This is what James meant when he stated that…faith without works is dead…Did James mean to tell us that works produce faith? NO! His statement (faith without works is dead) simply means that proper faith in the Lord Jesus Christ will produce proper godly works. When Peter mentioned doing certain things which would result in never falling, he was meaning that the doing of these things would be a byproduct of God's divine power and nature. It is God's divine power that stems from His divine nature, producing the fruit of the Spirit in our lives, for…

WE ARE HIS WORKMANSHIP!

October 12

PARTAKERS OF THE DIVINE NATURE - PART 9

A TRIUMPHANT ADMISSION INTO THE ETERNAL KINGDOM

2ND Peter 1:11 (The New Testament In Modern Speech) states…And so a triumphant admission into the eternal Kingdom of our Lord and Savior Jesus Christ will be freely granted to you…

The message of God has always been…THE KINGDOM OF GOD. To partake of God's divine nature is to partake of God's Kingdom. The working of God's nature within us is at the very heart of the true meaning of what His Kingdom is to accomplish. His Kingdom, which is within us, is His rule and reign within our hearts and lives. That which is to rule and reign in us is HIS DIVINE NATURE! In times past we have all been ruled by our fallen nature, but now, through the cross of the Lord Jesus Christ, we have been introduced to a NEW NATURE. This new nature comes in with the Holy Ghost and fire. Its purpose is to **burn up** our old nature, which is to be characterized as wood, hay, and stubble. In essence (spiritually speaking), we are going from wood, hay, and stubble to gold, silver, and precious stones. Gold (in the scriptures) is always a symbol of DEITY, DIVINITY, OR THAT WHICH IS GOD-LIKE. Since God's Kingdom is the Kingdom that is within us, we can now see what it is that causes His Kingdom to grow and flourish from within. IT IS HIS DIVINE NATURE THAT IS AT WORK INSIDE OF US! As His nature becomes our nature, and His power becomes our power, we are sure to find ourselves triumphantly entering into the eternal Kingdom (the Kingdom of the ages).

God's purpose for His creation is that His Kingdom would fill ALL THINGS. Those who press into the Kingdom will no doubt become like their King, understanding that it is their King's nature which enables them to be conformed to His image. Without God's divine nature being stamped into the soulish part of man, there is no way to be given an admission into the eternal Kingdom. This leads us to the conclusion that God's goal for the human race is to triumphantly enter into His Kingdom. His divine nature is simply the means by which we will achieve this goal. Not only will we achieve this goal, but we will become like Him in the process. We will become one with our Father. How could we not become like Him? We are partaking of…

HIS NATURE!

October 13

PARTAKERS OF THE DIVINE NATURE - PART 10

CONCLUSION

In conclusion, we have shown that the root of man's problem stems from his inherited Adamic Nature. We have also stated that all of man's problems are internal, not external. This leaves man in a predicament, causing him to be ruled by his carnal mind. Finally, he is brought to the reality of his condition, which is…O WRETCHED MAN THAT I AM! After coming to this grand and wonderful revelation, we are then driven to the only power source that will enable us to be who God has called us to be in Christ. THIS POWER SOURCE IS THE **DIVINE NATURE**! It is only through the knowledge of God's divine power that we will become sharers (partakers) in His divine nature. This realization then opens us up to the operating table of God, in which we will begin to undergo a spiritual transformation, being conformed into the image of the Son of God. We will find ourselves on a journey, going from the carnal mind to the mind of Christ, from the fallen nature to the divine nature, from the son of perdition to the Son of God, from weakness to power, from condemnation and frustration to victory and satisfaction, from death to life, and from being a part of that which is anti-Christ to becoming the body of Christ.

With this being said, we are now on our way to a state of being in God in which we shall never fall. Our position goes from being IN ADAM to IN CHRIST. This new position in the NEW

CREATION MAN causes us to be one with our Father in purpose and power. We are leaving the realm of religion (denominational death) and entering into the UNLIMITED realm of the eternal Kingdom of God.

Having found a triumphant admission into the eternal Kingdom of our Lord and Savior Jesus Christ, we have aligned ourselves with the purpose of our Heavenly Father, which is…HIS KINGDOM COME. HIS WILL BE DONE IN EARTH, AS IT IS IN HEAVEN.

These promises are to be seen as EXCEEDING GREAT AND PRECIOUS PROMISES. HOW GREAT A SALVATION WE HAVE BEEN GIVEN! How great was our fall, but how great will be our rise in Christ. We are called to soar with eagle's wings FAR ABOVE all principality, and power, and might, and dominion, and every name that is named, not only in this world (age), but also in that which is to come: And God has put all things under our feet, and IN HIM to be the Head over all things, FOR WE ARE HIS CHURCH, HIS BODY, THE FULLNESS OF HIM…

THAT FILLS ALL IN ALL! (Ephesians 1:21-23)

October 14

PHYSICAL DEATH - PART 1

Although the Bible does not say much about physical death, it will be beneficial to at least take into account what it does say. In doing this we will put to rest many false ideas and teachings concerning the state of man after physical death (while awaiting the resurrection). To understand this subject in its proper light we must first be willing to discard any and all ideas about physical death that do not line up with the Holy Scriptures. In order to grasp what happens to a person at physical death we must also understand what man is made up of. In other words, we must see that man is a three-part being made up of **SPIRIT, SOUL, AND BODY.**

1ST Thessalonians 5:23 states…And the very God of peace sanctify you wholly; and *I pray God* your whole **spirit and soul and body** be preserved blameless unto the coming of our Lord Jesus Christ…

According to Dr. Stephen Jones: "When Paul speaks of "you entirely," he lists the three parts of "you." They are spirit, soul, and body. There is a difference between soul and spirit, which men can see if they rightly divide the Word of truth. Heb. 4:12 says that the Word is sharper than any sword and can divide soul and spirit. That alone shows that soul and spirit are two different things. They can be separated. The best way to understand the relationship between spirit, soul, and body is to think of them in terms of their physical counterparts.

Spirit = breath, or wind [Heb. *ruach* = spirit, breath]
Soul = blood (Lev. 17:11) / Body = flesh (self-evident)

The breath gives oxygen to the blood, which is then carried by arteries and capillaries in the body. Even so, the spirit gives life to the soul, which is in the flesh. The relationship between spirit and soul is pictured in the relationship between the breath and the blood. They are different, but it is the spirit that gives life to the soul. It was only when God breathed the breath of life into Adam that he became a living soul. When the breath is removed from a man, his flesh and blood dies. Even so, when God removes the breath of life from a man, *both his body and soul die.* A man's mind, will, and emotion cannot function apart from his flesh (brain). The out-of-body experiences that men often relate to us after being revived from death are not a function of the conscious soul, but of the consciousness of the spirit. As we will see shortly, the spirit and soul each have a separate consciousness." (The Judgments Of The Divine Law, Dr. Stephen Jones)

This study will put to rest the CARNAL IDEAS of men concerning physical death. Most people believe that a person (upon physical death) is either shipped off to an eternal torture pit, or that they are flown to a literal mansion in the sky that exists on a planet called Heaven. We will seek to prove from this study that neither of these two views are correct. In fact, God's dealings with man (as far as reward or punishment are concerned) are not to be administered until the resurrection of the dead, whether it be the first or second resurrection. With this in mind, let us put off the traditions of men concerning this topic, heading boldly into the truth of the matter. In order to do this we must seek for an understanding of...

SPIRIT, SOUL, AND BODY!

October 15

PHYSICAL DEATH - PART 2

BODY, SOUL, AND SPIRIT

Let us now consider what takes place upon physical death concerning man's body, soul, and spirit. Since there is no debate as to what happens to our body upon physical death, we will concentrate most of our effort in explaining what happens to the soul and spirit. We are all fully aware that the body is buried, returning to the earth from whence it came. We have come to call it the GRAVE. Let us now turn our attention to what happens to the soul and spirit.

According to Dr. Stephen Jones: "Death is a return. The body returns to dust, the soul returns to "sleep," and the spirit returns to God. A more metaphysical way of putting it is this: the body goes to the tomb; the soul goes to Hades; the spirit goes to God (heaven). The best example of this in the Bible is Jesus' death. Jesus' body was put in Joseph's tomb (John 19:38-42), His soul went to Hades (Acts 2:31), and His spirit returned to God (Luke 23:46). The soul had no existence prior to God breathing the breath of life into Adam's nostrils, for at that moment, man became a living soul. When that breath is removed, the soul ceases to exist in its conscious state that we call "living." The spirit—that is, man's spirit, as distinct from the Holy Spirit of God—is the part of man that transcends death. Ecclesiastes 12:7 speaks of death, saying, **then the dust will return to the earth as it was, and the spirit will return to God Who gave it.** In the New Testament we find this idea continued in the death of Jesus. Luke 23:46 quotes Psalm 31:5 in giving Jesus' last words:

And Jesus, crying out with a loud voice, said, <u>Father into Your hands I commit My spirit</u>. And having said this, He breathed His last. This detail is recorded in Matthew 27:50 in this way: **And Jesus cried out again with a loud voice, and <u>yielded up His spirit</u>.** So we see that Jesus' spirit did not go either to Joseph's grave with His body, nor did it go to Hades with His soul (Acts 2:27). It went to God Who had given it to Him. The real question is whether or not a person's spirit has a consciousness that is distinct from the consciousness of the soul." (<u>The Judgments Of The Divine Law</u>, Dr. Stephen Jones)

DEATH IS A RETURN!

October 16

PHYSICAL DEATH - PART 3

THE CONSCIOUSNESS OF THE SPIRIT

According to Dr. Stephen Jones: "Man's spirit has a consciousness that is distinct from the consciousness of the soul. The fact that spirit has a conscious mind should not come as a surprise. The Spirit of God (i.e., the Holy Spirit) possesses a conscious mind. God is spirit (John 4:24) and needs no physical brain or soulish mind in order to function consciously. Gen. 6:3 says, "*My Spirit will not always strive with man.*" Such striving would require conscious behavior. Isaiah 11:2 speaks of the Spirit of wisdom, understanding, and knowledge. Such things also require consciousness. In 1 Cor. 2:16 we are admonished to put on the mind of Christ. In Eph. 4:23, 24 "the spirit of your mind" is identified with the "new self" (NASB) or the "new man" (KJV)...**and that you be renewed in <u>the spirit of your mind</u>, and put on the <u>new self</u>, which in the likeness of God has been created in righteousness and holiness of the truth**...It is obviously a spiritual mind and an inner self that has consciousness. Unclean spirits also have a consciousness, as we read many times in the scriptures. For example, Mark 9:26 says of an unclean spirit, "*after crying out and throwing him into terrible convulsions, it came out.*" Man is made in the image of God. Therefore, it seems reasonable to say man's spirit also has a consciousness. Paul tells us in 1 Cor. 2:14 that divine matters cannot be understood with the natural (literally "soulish") mind, but must be understood with the spiritual mind. So what does this mean? Where does the spirit go when it "returns" to God? To answer that, one must stop trying to think carnally. Heaven is not "located" somewhere in or beyond the stars. The spirit does not have to travel anywhere. It does not take a certain amount of time to go from heaven to earth or from earth to heaven. Ezekiel 44:17 speaks of it figuratively as changing clothes. Paul uses the same terminology in 2 Cor. 5:2-4. When Jesus appeared to His disciples after His resurrection, He demonstrated His ability to move from flesh to spirit form in an instant (Luke 24:36). When a person dies, his spirit remains in the realm of spirit, where there is neither time nor distance. It is always in the realm of "I am." It is not "I was" or "I will be." It is not "I am here" or "I am there." All time is one. All space is one. In the spirit, all things simply are. It is only in the earthly realm that we are bound by time and space. To understand spiritual existence, we must think "outside the box." (The Judgments Of The Divine Law, Dr. Stephen Jones)

THE SPIRIT RETURNS TO GOD WHO GAVE IT!

October 17

JESUS, THE PATTERN SON - PART 1

JESUS IS GOD'S GREATEST SIGN

According to Bill Britton: "JESUS is God's greatest sign! In Isaiah 7:14 the prophet cried out, "Therefore the Lord Himself shall give you a sign; Behold a virgin shall conceive, and bear a son, and shall call His name Immanuel." Now, beloved, get your Bibles, for I want to show you that the Sign was not the virgin who brought forth. It was not the swaddling clothes He was wrapped in, nor was the miraculous birth itself the promised Sign, but rather it was the One Who was born and brought into the world in such a manner. He was and still is God's greatest Sign. Now a sign is that which points to something, and this man Jesus, His birth, life, death and resurrection points unerringly to that great thing which God is doing in the earth, His eternal Purpose in Christ Jesus! The angels spoke to the shepherds in the field on that glorious night, "Fear not: for behold, I bring you good tidings of great joy, which shall be to all people. For unto you is born this day in the city of David a Savior, which is Christ the Lord. AND THIS SHALL BE A SIGN UNTO YOU." And then they went on to tell them where to find the child. In Luke, chapter two, that old prophet of God, Simeon, came by the Spirit into the temple and there he found Mary and Joseph with baby Jesus. Here we find hands being laid on Jesus and prophecy going forth over Him at the tender age of six weeks. For Simeon took Him up in his arms and began to prophesy. Hear, my friends, what the Spirit said about Him: "Behold, this child is set for the fall and rising again of many in Israel, and FOR A SIGN which shall be spoken against." (Jesus, The Pattern Son, Bill Britton)

Now that we have established that Jesus is God's greatest sign (a pattern), let us look to Hebrews 2:9-18, which states what He went through for EVERY MAN. In essence, Jesus laid down a PATTERN for all who would follow in His footsteps.

Hebrews 2:9,10,17,18 states...But we see Jesus, Who was made a little lower than the angels for the suffering of death, crowned with glory and honor; that He by the grace of God should taste death for every man. For it became Him, for Whom are all things, and by Whom are all things, in bringing many sons unto glory, to make the Captain of their salvation perfect through sufferings...Wherefore in all things it behooved Him to be made like unto His brethren, that He might be a merciful and faithful high priest in things pertaining to God, to make reconciliation for the sins of the people. For in that He Himself has suffered being tempted, He is able to succor them that are tempted...

As we can see, the Captain of our salvation was perfected through suffering and temptation, for this is...

THE SIGN AND PATTERN FOR ALL OF GOD'S SONS!

October 18

JESUS, THE PATTERN SON - PART 2

THE OPEN HEAVENS

According to Bill Britton: "Remembering now that everything about the life of Jesus is a pattern for His Body, let us look at the order of events that happen when Jesus came to be baptized of John...

1. There had been a prophetic ministry in the land for some time now.
2. In the fullness of time Jesus was ready and came forth to meet His destiny.
3. Jesus, the Pattern, was recognized by the true prophetic ministry as God's Son.
4. Jesus submitted Himself to God's ministry for this hour.
5. In a figure, He died in Jordan's water and rose again to a new realm in God.
6. The heavens were opened unto Him.
7. He saw God the Holy Ghost in a bodily shape.
8. He received an anointing of the Spirit beyond what He had previously had.
9. He heard the voice of God announcing Him as the Son of God.
10. He was led by the Holy Spirit into a wilderness place where He battled Satanic forces hand to hand, face to face, and defeated and overcame Satan.
11. He began a 3-1/2 year ministry of love, life, and power such as the world had never seen, not even from the greatest of the prophets.

Matt. 3:16: "And Jesus, when He was baptized, went up straightway out of the water; and, lo, the heavens were opened unto Him." Mark 1:10: "And straightway coming up out of the water, He saw the heavens opened." Glory to God! Something happened here that began the fulfillment of Jacob's dream of the ladder. You remember that Jacob dreamed as he lay there at Bethel with his head on a stone for a pillow and saw in his dream the heavens opened, and a ladder set up on the earth, and the angels of God ascending and descending on the ladder. Jacob awoke out of his sleep in fear and dread and cried: "How dreadful is this place! This is none other but the house of God, and this is the gate of heaven" (Genesis 28:17). So he changed the name of that place from Luz to Bethel because Bethel signified "HOUSE OF GOD". He had actually seen, in a type, the true house of God, the fullness of the Son of Man in Christ and His people." (Jesus, The Pattern Son, Bill Britton)

After having been called, recognized, and placed as a son of God, we will then have the heavens opened to us (spiritually speaking), being dead to our old life and anointed with the new life of Christ. We are now to be led by the Holy Spirit of God. It is quite interesting where the Spirit first leads us on this journey of SONSHIP. It is not the most desired place, but it does bring about the most desired results. It is…

THE WILDERNESS!

October 19

JESUS, THE PATTERN SON - PART 3

THE WILDERNESS

Matthew 4:1 states…Then was Jesus led up of the Spirit into the wilderness to be tempted of the devil…

After being called, recognized, and declared as a son of God, having the heavens opened to us, we are then **LED UP OF THE SPIRIT INTO THE WILDERNESS TO BE TEMPTED OF THE DEVIL**. Notice that it is THE SPIRIT OF GOD that leads us into a wilderness experience to be tempted of the Devil. We must stop thinking that God is mad at us when we find ourselves in a wilderness experience. GOD IS THE ONE WHO HAS LED US THERE BY HIS SPIRIT! If God leads us into the wilderness to be tempted of the Devil, then there must be a purpose for it, and it must be for our good.

The word "wilderness" means: solitary, lonely, and lonesome. This would mean that God is responsible for placing us in lonely circumstances in our lives. Many times we find ourselves all alone in what we are thinking, doing, or saying. We begin to feel the pressure of satanic forces coming against us to tempt us to go outside of the will of God. This is Satan (the prince of the power of the air) coming against our mind to try us, putting us to the test. Even though we do not enjoy our seasons of wilderness in life, we will come to understand that they are necessary, and even for our good. The wilderness is what brings us in contact with FIERY TRIALS. This causes us to go from glory to glory, growing up into a fully mature son of God. WE ARE GROWING UP IN GOD! WE ARE PUTTING ON THE LORD JESUS CHRIST! WE ARE LEARNING TO PARTAKE OF THE DIVINE NATURE! WE ARE HAVING HIS LAWS WRITTEN ON OUR HEARTS! WE ARE LEARNING THAT GOD IS SOVEREIGN! WE ARE LEARNING TO ACCESS HEAVENLY PLACES IN CHRIST JESUS! WE ARE LEARNING TO CAST DOWN IMAGINATIONS, AND EVERY HIGH THING THAT EXALTS ITSELF AGAINST THE KNOWLEDGE OF GOD, BRINGING INTO CAPTIVITY EVERY THOUGHT TO THE OBEDIENCE OF CHRIST; (2nd Corinthians 10:5)…

We must see that it is God Who places us in these experiences, for without going through the wilderness there is no possible way for us to be an overcomer. How can we overcome if there is nothing to overcome? The purpose of the wilderness is to teach us to endure temptation, suffering, and fiery trials. It is in and through the wilderness experience that we are able to become like the Son of God. Every time we leave the wilderness, we leave…

IN THE POWER OF THE SPIRIT!

October 20

JESUS, THE PATTERN SON - PART 4

ENDURING TEMPTATION

James 1:2-4 states…My brethren, count it all joy when you fall into divers temptations; Knowing this, that the trying of your faith works patience. But let patience have her perfect work, that you may be perfect and entire, wanting nothing…

James 1:12 states…Blessed is the man that endures temptation: for when he is tried, he shall receive the crown of life, which the Lord has promised to them that love Him…

1st Peter 4:12,13 states…Beloved, think it not strange concerning the fiery trial which is to try you, as though some strange thing happened unto you: But rejoice, inasmuch as you are partakers of Christ's sufferings; that, when His glory shall be revealed, you may be glad also with exceeding joy…

The reason that MOST CHRISTIANS remain as spiritual babes in Christ is due to the fact that they do not apply these scripture passages to their lives. Scripture passages such as these teach us that God has us in a process. This process is one in which we are becoming a (fully mature) son of God. Those that do not see that they are in a process (sonship) will find themselves continually fighting against the very will of God, not understanding that the things they are going through are for their benefit. Remember…The Son of God was tempted, went through fiery trials, and suffered. As well, the sons of God must be tempted, go through fiery trials, and suffer as a Christian (1st Peter 4:16). IT IS THE PATTERN THAT WAS LAID DOWN BY THE PATTERN SON. If you were to list out the recipe for the making of a son of God, it would include temptation, fiery trials, and suffering as a Christian.

The word "temptations" that is used in James 1:12 means <u>trials</u>. Surely we know that Jesus was tempted in all points as we are, yet without sin (Hebrews 4:15). So how could we be conformed to the image of the Son of God without going through the same? It is not that we ask for, wait for, or enjoy our temptations, fiery trials, and sufferings, but we must see why they are necessary when they do come our way. We must also see that they are for a specific purpose. THEY ARE FOR A PURPOSE! The purpose is that we are to be conformed to the image of the Son of God, THE PATTERN SON!

The apostle Paul understood this to a degree that most do not. Romans 5:3-5 states…And not only so, but **we glory in tribulations** also: knowing that tribulation works patience; And patience, experience; and experience, hope: And hope makes not ashamed; because the love of God is shed abroad in our hearts by the Holy Ghost which is given unto us…

BLESSED IS THE MAN THAT ENDURES TEMPTATION!

October 21

JESUS, THE PATTERN SON - PART 5

WE SHALL ALSO REIGN WITH HIM

2nd Timothy 2:11,12 states…It is a faithful saying: For if we be dead with Him, we shall also live with Him: If we suffer, we shall also reign with Him: if we deny Him, He also will deny us…

The work of the Lord Jesus Christ (The Pattern Son of God) is to bring man to the place that God has purposed from the very beginning. This is explained to us in Genesis 1:26, which states…And God said, Let Us make man in Our image, after Our likeness: AND LET THEM HAVE DOMINION…The word "dominion" obviously speaks of ruling and reigning, for one who reigns does indeed have dominion over that which he reigns. This *process of sonship*, which we currently find ourselves in, is that process which is bringing us from death to life, teaching us how to rule and reign with Christ. This is a threefold process that includes our spirit, soul, and body. Our spirit has been saved, our soul (mind, will, and emotions) is being saved, and our body is yet to be saved at the resurrection. We are learning to reign with Him one step at a time. We are currently learning to reign over our Adamic Nature by partaking of God's divine nature. With this being said though, this is not the fullness of our reigning experience with God. The fullness is to be realized at the ADOPTION, **THE REDEMPTION OF OUR BODIES.** This is what Paul referred to when he spoke of the manifestation of the sons of God, at which time we (the overcomers) shall be given power over the nations TO RULE AND REIGN OVER THEM WITH A ROD OF IRON!

At this present time we are in training. We are going through temptations, fiery trials, sufferings, and tribulations. These things must take place in order for God to qualify His people for the first resurrection. This (the first resurrection) is the time at which we shall receive the redemption of our body. This is the TRUE PROMISED LAND (our glorified bodies) that we have so long awaited to inherit. This process is to be seen in type and shadow in the Old Testament, in which God delivered His chosen people from Egyptian bondage in three phases (out of Egypt, through the wilderness, and into the Promised Land). It is also to be seen in the Feasts of Israel (Passover, Pentecost, and Tabernacles). These types and shadows apply to individuals as well as the entire creation. This is the purpose of God for His creation. It is for us to reign with Him. IT IS TO HAVE DOMINION!

WE SHALL REIGN WITH HIM!

October 22

JESUS, THE PATTERN SON - PART 6

DEATH TO SELF

Matthew 26:38,39 states…Then said He unto them, My soul is exceeding sorrowful, even unto death: tarry here, and watch with Me. And He went a little farther, and fell on His face, and prayed, saying, O My Father, if it be possible, let this cup pass from Me: nevertheless not as I will, but as You will…

The most important thing that Jesus taught us (concerning our sonship process) was that there must be a death to the self-life. This is what enabled Him to do only those things that pleased the Father. The problem of mankind has always been…THE SELF-LIFE! Remember…It is the soulish part of man that is in need of sanctification. Well…This involves a death to our ways, causing us to embrace God's ways. The Father is bringing us to the place where our life clearly says…NOT AS I WILL, BUT AS YOU WILL!

This death to self (the soulish part of man) is what enables the Spirit of God to flow unhindered through man, causing his mind, will, and emotions to be conformed to the image of the Son of God. As we have already stated, this process is called sanctification, and is to be found at work in all of God's sons. Without the death of self there is no way to experience the resurrection life of the Lord Jesus Christ. It is not possible to have a resurrection without a death first. This is why it is so important for us to understand what Jesus was teaching when He stated…NOT AS I WILL, BUT AS YOU WILL! He was laying down the pattern for all who would follow in His footsteps. It is the pattern which acknowledges that the Father's will is greater than ours. This was at the very heart of the Lord's Prayer, which states…YOUR KINGDOM COME! YOUR WILL BE DONE!

It is those who understand this principle in God that will grow in grace and in the knowledge of the Lord. If self is not recognized for what it is and dealt with, it will prevail, causing the Spirit of God to be quenched in our lives. On the other hand, if self is recognized for what it is and dealt with, then we have tapped into THE VERY KINGDOM OF GOD! How is it that so many Christians do not see this aspect of the ministry of the Pattern Son of God, AND THAT IT APPLIES TO ALL OF GOD'S SONS? Blessed is the person who is able to see that their greatest enemy is to be found when they look in the mirror. It is this person that will experience all that the Father is and has to give. It is this person who understands the person, work, and ministry of…

THE PATTERN SON OF GOD!

❖

October 23

JESUS, THE PATTERN SON - PART 7

YOU ARE THE CHRIST

Matthew 16:15,16 states…He said unto them, But whom say you that I am? And Simon Peter answered and said, You are the Christ, the Son of the living God…

Many people are able to recognize Jesus as the Christ, but do not see that He laid down a pattern for us to be a part of the Christ as well. Jesus, Who is the Christ, opened the door for us to become a part of the Christ. He is the Head and we are His body. WE ARE THE BODY OF CHRIST! The reason that many people do not understand this simple point is due to the fact that many do not grasp **THAT "CHRIST" IS NOT JUST MADE UP OF JESUS, BUT IS A MANY MEMBERED MAN, INCLUDING HIS BODY!**

1st Corinthians 12:12-14 states…For as the body is one, and has many members, and all the members of that one body, being many, are one body: **so also is Christ.** For by one Spirit are we all baptized into one body, whether we be Jews or Gentiles, whether we be bond or free; and have been all made to drink into one Spirit. For the body is not one member, but many…

This revelation will set your soul on fire to serve God! When a person realizes that he is a part of the Christ, the Savior of the world, it is all the motivation you will ever need to press into the high calling of God. In essence, Jesus is THE CHRIST, and we are HIS CHRIST. Remember… "Christ" is a many membered man (body) with the Lord Jesus as the Head. The Head needs the body, and the body needs the Head. THEY ARE ONE!

The word "Christ" means **Anointed One or Messiah**. With this in mind, let us look to Psalm two, which does speak of the Anointed and what He is to accomplish. Remember…The Anointed One is a many membered man (body). Psalm 2:2,7-9 states…The kings of the earth set themselves, and the rulers take counsel together, against the LORD, and against His Anointed…I will declare the decree: the LORD has said unto Me, You are My Son; this day have I begotten You. Ask of Me, and I shall give You the heathen for Your inheritance, and the uttermost parts of the earth for Your possession. You shall break them with a rod of iron; You shall dash them in pieces like a potter's vessel…This same scripture verse is repeated in Revelation 2:26, and is said to include all the overcomers, showing that the Christ is a many membered man (body). It is also stated in Revelation 11:15 that the kingdoms of this world are become the kingdoms of our Lord (Jesus), and of…

HIS CHRIST!

October 24

JESUS, THE PATTERN SON - PART 8

CONCLUSION

It has been our goal in this study to show that JESUS IS GOD'S GREATEST SIGN. He is a pattern for all who would follow in His footsteps. He was made a little lower than the angels (Elohim), for the suffering of death, crowned with glory and honor, that He by the grace of God should taste death for every man (Hebrews 2:9)…The Captain of our salvation was made perfect through sufferings in order that He might bring many sons unto glory (Hebrews 2:10)…It was for this purpose that Jesus went through all that He did. He laid down His life that He might be the Savior of the world, taking away the sin of the world. In doing so, He became a pattern (sign) as the only way to the Father.

The mistake that is so commonly made concerning the life and ministry of Jesus Christ is that we do not apply His life, ministry, sufferings, temptations, trials, death, and resurrection to our own life. WE MUST SEE OURSELVES AS PART OF THE CHRIST, WHO IS THE IMAGE OF THE INVISIBLE GOD, THE FIRSTBORN OF EVERY CREATURE (Colossians 1:15)…We must see that our life is to be patterned after His life. Philippians 3:10-14 states…That I may know Him, and the power of His resurrection, and the fellowship of His sufferings, being made conformable unto His death; If by any means I might attain unto the resurrection of the dead. Not as though I had already attained, either were already perfect: but I follow after, if that I may apprehend that for which also I am apprehended of Christ Jesus. Brethren, I count not myself to have apprehended: but this one thing I do, forgetting those things which are behind, and reaching forth unto those things which are before, I press toward the mark for the prize of the high calling of God in Christ Jesus…

The apostle Paul obviously understood that Jesus had laid down a pattern in which we were to identify with His death, burial, and resurrection. This process of being conformed to the image of the Pattern Son includes the transformation of our spirit, soul, and finally, our bodies, for Paul stated that Jesus Christ would change our vile bodies, that they may be fashioned like unto His glorious body (Philippians 3:21)…We are to realize that there is no stopping place in God. We have not fully apprehended or attained, but WE PRESS INTO THE HIGH CALLING OF OUR GOD! We press into this glorious process of SONSHIP! We are destined to become like…

THE PATTERN SON!

October 25

TEN DANGEROUS POSSESSIONS
(GROWING UP IN GOD)

#1 - ZEAL WITHOUT KNOWLEDGE

According to Bill Britton: "For a man to possess such God-given gifts as knowledge, ability, talent, authority, or riches, would seem to be a great thing. But sad to say, **these things can become dangerous** and even destructive unless accompanied by that which puts it into force for the good of God's Kingdom." (Ten Dangerous Possessions, Bill Britton)

The apostle Paul told us in Philippians 3:6 that his zeal only resulted in persecuting the true church, and as well, he told us in Romans 10:1,2 that it is possible to possess a zeal of God, BUT NOT ACCORDING TO KNOWLEDGE. The word "zeal" speaks of an earnest desire to do something. This "earnest desire" to do something for the Kingdom of God is good, but left alone, not being joined to knowledge, it becomes destructive and hinders our witness for God. UNFORTUNATELY, MANY CHRISTIANS TURN OFF MORE PEOPLE TO THE LOVE OF GOD THAN THEY DRAW TO THE LOVE OF GOD. Their earnest desire to "save souls" is not coupled with the knowledge of God, doing more harm than good. The apostle Paul, before his conversion, went about breathing out threatenings and slaughter against the disciples of the Lord (Acts 9:1). He did this as a result of acting solely on a zeal for God, BUT NOT ACCORDING TO KNOWLEDGE.

Proverbs 2:1-5 tells us of the importance of finding the knowledge of God. It states…My son, if you will receive My words, and hide My commandments with you; So that you incline your ear unto wisdom, and apply your heart to understanding; Yes, if you cry after knowledge, and lift up your voice for understanding; If you seek her as silver, and search for her as for hid treasures; Then shall you understand the fear of the LORD, and find the knowledge of God…

Once that knowledge comes alongside of zeal, then zeal becomes a powerful force in the Kingdom of God that can turn the world upside down. Knowledge is what guides zeal in the right direction, making it (zeal) a good thing rather than a destructive thing. Knowledge becomes a governor to zeal, not allowing it to get out of control or to be used in a destructive manner. If you are zealous for the things of God, by all means, DO NOT LOSE YOUR ZEAL, but please **study** to show yourself approved unto God. You must acquire…

THE KNOWLEDGE OF GOD!

October 26

TEN DANGEROUS POSSESSIONS
(GROWING UP IN GOD)

#2 - KNOWLEDGE WITHOUT WISDOM

After seeing our need for knowledge (the knowledge of God), we must then see our need for wisdom, for knowledge becomes a dangerous possession when it is not bridled by wisdom. The apostle Paul told us in 1st Corinthians 8:1,2 that…we know that we all have knowledge. Knowledge puffs up (causes one to be puffed up in pride), but charity (love) edifies. And if any man think he knows any thing, he knows nothing yet as he ought to know…With this being said, we can see that man finds himself in a maturing process of GROWING UP IN GOD. Each step of the journey is to lead us to another level in God. To stop at any one of these levels is to not completely grow into all that God has for you.

Knowledge without wisdom becomes a dangerous possession, causing people to be elevated into thinking more highly of themselves than they ought to. Many people go about spewing out their knowledge to everyone, hoping that others will recognize how smart they are. They try as much as possible to use big words that neither they nor their listeners understand. They lean on intellect rather than the Holy Spirit, always using an abundance of words, hoping to confuse the listener while maintaining the upper hand in the conversation.

Proverbs 17:27,28 states…He that has knowledge spares his words: and a man of understanding is of an excellent spirit. Even a fool, when he holds his peace, is counted wise: and he that shuts his lips is esteemed a man of understanding (WISDOM…i.e., A WISE MAN)…What a beautiful scripture! This shows that knowledge, when it is accompanied by wisdom, becomes very beneficial and fruitful in the Kingdom of God. But knowledge without wisdom becomes dangerous, hurtful, and begins to STINK with the smell of self-righteousness.

WISDOM is that godly attribute that knows how to, when to, and in what manner to distribute knowledge. Knowledge that is spoken in love (at the right time) is more precious than all that this world has to offer. So…Let us GROW UP IN GOD, praying for zeal, knowledge, and wisdom to be added to our Christian walk. As this takes place, we will find ourselves growing up into the son of God that we are called to be. We will find that people will be drawn to us to see what it is in our life that causes us to walk in such zeal, knowledge, and…

WISDOM!

October 27

TEN DANGEROUS POSSESSIONS
(GROWING UP IN GOD)

#3 - ABILITY WITHOUT CHARACTER

According to Bill Britton: "Ability is a wonderful possession, but without godly character behind it, it is dangerous and destructive both to yourself and others. Seemingly everyone does not have great ability, but there is no excuse for not having a Christian character. Anyone, with the help of the Holy Spirit, can develop a Christ-like nature and character. No matter how much or how little ability you have, you do not have to be corrupt, deceitful, dishonest, or greedy. God is more interested in you being like Jesus in character, rather than you having His power and authority." (Ten Dangerous Possessions, Bill Britton)

The word "character" means: the features and traits that form the individual nature of a person or thing. The character and nature that we are speaking of is (of course) the character and nature of God. This character (through partaking of God's divine nature) is to be written on our hearts. God gives men and women ability to do certain things, giving some tremendous ability, that is, above and beyond the ability of others. It is very important that we realize that to whom much is given, MUCH IS REQUIRED! With this God-given ability comes a calling. THIS CALLING INVOLVES US BEING CONFORMED TO THE CHARACTER AND NATURE OF GOD! Without the character (nature) of God in our lives, ability becomes a dangerous possession that will be used for self-promotion, corruption, deceitfulness, dishonesty, and greed. THERE ARE SO MANY PEOPLE WITH SO MUCH ABILITY, HAVING SO LITTLE OF THE CHARACTER OF GOD IN THEIR LIVES!!!

The Bible refers to a person not having the character of God as a WORKER OF INIQUITY. This is to be found in Matthew 7:22,23. A "worker of iniquity" refers to a lawless person, speaking of lawlessness, and refers to people who do not have God's laws written on their hearts. The people spoken of in this passage possessed tremendous ability, being able to prophesy, cast out demons, and do many wonderful works in the name of the Lord, but did not possess the character (nature) of God. They did not experientially know God. These people will depart into judgment for the purpose of correction. The purpose of the correction will be to have the character of God applied to their heart and life.

As for the true servants of God, WE ARE CURRENTLY IN THE PROCESS OF HAVING THE DIVINE CHARACTER (NATURE) WRITTEN ON OUR HEARTS. May we be diligent to pray for godly character, for ability without character is…

A DANGEROUS POSSESSION!

October 28

TEN DANGEROUS POSSESSIONS
(GROWING UP IN GOD)

#4 - RESPONSIBILITY WITHOUT FAITHFULNESS

According to Bill Britton: "Many are crying to God daily to give them a ministry, a job, a responsibility in the Kingdom. And Paul told Timothy that if any man desired the office of a bishop, he desired a good work. But he went on to say that such a one should be proved, tested and tried, to see that he was faithful in that which God gave him. For if a man is not faithful to his own family, how can he be faithful to the church of the living God? And if he cannot rule in the temporal relationships in his earthly home, how can he rule in the eternal glory of God's house? If he is faithful in that which is small, then he will be faithful in the greater things. It is a great thing to have a large responsibility in God's house. But it is a dangerous thing to have, unless you have a spirit of being faithful." (<u>Ten Dangerous Possessions</u>, Bill Britton)

There is much preaching today on faith, but very little preaching on faithfulness. This is talked about by Jesus in Luke 19:11-27 where He teaches a parable about the good and wicked servant. The good servant, who is rewarded and given authority over all that belongs to his Lord, is that servant who has been FAITHFUL in that which is small. The wicked servant is that servant who was entrusted with that which belonged to his Lord (given responsibility), but did nothing with it, and was not faithful to bring forth the desired fruit which his Lord required.

The very reason that the Lord gives us responsibility is for the purpose of teaching us faithfulness. A person who is faithful is unwavering and dedicated, being diligent in what God has called him to do. Without faithfulness it is impossible to experience the Father in His fullness. Man is only able to partake of the Father in small doses. This happens little by little, day by day, causing us to be changed from glory to glory. We can not handle all of our Father's power and love at one time. It requires for us to be faithful, receiving our daily bread one day at a time. In an age of everything being handed to us on a silver platter, it is difficult to learn this principle in God. Nevertheless, those who take responsibility and add to it faithfulness will be the ones to rule and reign with Christ. How we long to hear these words from our Lord...WELL DONE MY GOOD AND **FAITHFUL** SERVANT...

ENTER INTO THE JOY OF THE LORD!

October 29

TEN DANGEROUS POSSESSIONS
(GROWING UP IN GOD)

#5 - GIFTS WITHOUT LOVE

According to Bill Britton: "In chapter 13 of 1st Corinthians we hear Paul saying that it is possible to have gifts of the Spirit, such as tongues, prophecy, faith, and knowledge and still not profit from their use, because we do not have the divine motivation of "agape" love. Without love, the gifts are useless, meaningless, and even dangerous. Used in love and humility, the gifts are a means of communication with heaven, a mighty weapon against the forces of hell. They strengthen, edify, and build up the church, bringing glory to God. But God have mercy on that one who uses a gift from God to bring fame and fortune to himself, to build himself a kingdom, or to attack or mislead God's dear children." (Ten Dangerous Possessions, Bill Britton)

1st Corinthians chapter 13 is probably one of the most important (if not the most important) passages of scripture in the entire Bible. It teaches us that the most important attribute of our Heavenly Father is LOVE. Remember...**GOD IS LOVE!** To operate in the gifts of the Spirit without love is to become as sounding brass or a tinkling cymbal. The *gifts* of the Spirit without the *fruit* of the Spirit WILL PROFIT US NOTHING. This was the new commandment that Jesus came to give us.

John 13:34,35 states...A new commandment I give unto you, That you love one another; as I have loved you, that you also love one another. By this shall all men know that you are My disciples, if you have love one to another...Notice the importance of this statement that is made by Jesus. BY LOVE shall all men know that we are the disciples of the Lord Jesus Christ. Thank God for the gifts of the Spirit that the Father bestows on us, but the gifts of the Spirit cannot bring us to full maturity in God. In order to mature and grow up in God we must learn to receive and partake of God's great love. For whether there shall be prophecies, they shall fail; whether there be tongues, they shall cease; whether there be knowledge, it shall vanish away, **BUT LOVE NEVER FAILS** (1st Corinthians 13:8)...

Let us cherish the gifts of the Spirit that have been given to us, but let us add to these gifts of the Spirit the fruit of the Spirit, for this is the more excellent way that the apostle Paul spoke of. It is by this more excellent way that men shall come to know and see that we are the true disciples of the Lord Jesus Christ. Now abides faith, hope, love, these three...

BUT THE GREATEST OF THESE IS LOVE!
(1ST Corinthians 13:13)

October 30

TEN DANGEROUS POSSESSIONS
(GROWING UP IN GOD)

#6 - FELLOWSHIP WITHOUT LOYALTY

Hebrews 10:24,25 states…And let us consider one another to provoke unto love and to good works: Not forsaking the assembling of ourselves together, as the manner of some is; but exhorting one another: and so much the more, as you see the day approaching…

There are three main reasons why that we should assemble together with other believers in Christ. They are: fellowship, worship, and instruction in the things of the Lord. As the Lord brings people into our lives to fellowship with, we will begin to create a tie and bond with these people. These people become important to our growth in the Lord, just as we become important to their growth in the Lord. We are members of the same body, working and walking together to achieve a common goal. We must recognize that we are members of the body of Christ.

This fellowship is glorious, wonderful, and strengthens us tremendously, but this same fellowship becomes dangerous when loyalty is not involved. After being introduced to like-minded people that we know that the Lord has brought into our lives, we then become responsible to remain loyal to them. This does not mean that we must agree with every word they say, having the exact same vision in God that they have, but it does mean that we are to remain in contact with them, love them, pray for them, associate with them, and continue to assemble ourselves with them (if at all possible). The idea of loyalty teaches us one very important thing. IT TEACHES US NOT TO ISOLATE OURSELVES!

Those who isolate themselves from others are sure to go downhill spiritually. Isolation is one of the great traps that many people fall into. If we think that we can make it on our own, that is, without the other members of the body of Christ, then we are proving by our behavior that we do not understand the principle of loyalty as far as fellowship is concerned. It is so very important that we understand this, for what our Lord is doing involves and requires a body of believers who are loyal to each other and their Lord. Think of your physical body. Can you imagine if your brain was not loyal to send the signal for your hand to move, or if your hand was not loyal to receive the signal from the brain and move accordingly? If this was the case, YOUR BODY WOULD NOT FUNCTION PROPERLY. In the same sense, when we are not loyal in our fellowship the body of Christ does not function properly, and that makes for a weak body. Let us be…

LOYAL IN OUR FELLOWSHIP!

❖

October 31

TEN DANGEROUS POSSESSIONS
(GROWING UP IN GOD)

#7 - TALENT WITHOUT CONSECRATION

Those who are talented in areas of their lives are usually the first ones to know it, for a very talented person does not need to be told that he or she is talented. This talent, whatever it may be, is sure to be a blessing to all. But a person's talent can become a dangerous thing if their talent is not consecrated to God. If a person does not recognize that their talent comes from the Father, then they will fall prey to the clutching grip of this world, for the world will surely recognize their talent, looking for a way to market it for the purpose of making money. The Bible tells us that every good gift and every perfect gift is from above, and comes down from the Father of lights, with Whom is no variableness, neither shadow of turning (James 1:17)…If this is not recognized, then we will take credit for our talent, turning it over to the world for worldly gain, becoming a lover of this world. 1st John 2:15 states…Love not the world, neither the things that are in the world. If any man love the world, the love of the Father is not in him…

How many people have there been down through history who were given talents by God to be used for the Kingdom of God, but used them instead for the purpose of worldly gain alone? The very reason that God blesses us with particular talents is that we might recognize that He gave us the talent, be thankful for the talent, consecrate the talent back to Him for His use, and then use the talent to glorify Him and His Kingdom in this earth.

It is a sad thing to see a person take his God-given talent and give it over totally to the world for the purpose of becoming famous or rich. Please do not think that I am saying that it is wrong to be famous or rich, for it is not. The point that we are discussing is the consecration and dedication of one's talent to the Lord. If the Lord chooses to make you rich as a result of your talent, then that is His business, but do not use your talent to seek for worldly gain alone. USE IT TO GLORIFY GOD! Do not sell your God-given talent out to the world, but rather, consecrate it and dedicate it back to the One Who gave it to you. You must view it as a gift that came from above, and came down from the…

FATHER OF LIGHTS!

November 1

TEN DANGEROUS POSSESSIONS
(GROWING UP IN GOD)

#8 - AUTHORITY WITHOUT COMPASSION

According to Bill Britton: "It is absolutely necessary to have government, even in the things of God. Therefore, someone must be given authority by the Spirit. But authority is dangerous, unless the person with it has a heart full of compassion for others. Look at Saul, the king that Israel chose to serve over them. God told them what kind of man he would be, one that would make slaves of them, and would think only of himself. He used his power without mercy, and would even have killed his own son had not the people restrained him. Being David's king, he had much authority in David's life, even chose his wife and the place he should live. David was a blessing to the king with his harp. But Saul had no compassion for others. And his power and authority was a dangerous possession. It caused his downfall, the death of Jonathan, and would have destroyed David had not God protected him." (Ten Dangerous Possessions, Bill Britton)

It is extremely important that we let God work into us HIS COMPASSION AND LOVE FOR OTHERS! Those who will rule the nations in the coming age will be those who have had the character and nature of their Heavenly Father written upon their hearts. Our Heavenly Father is not going to put people into positions of authority that have not learned compassion. Jesus (in Matthew 9:36) saw the multitudes and was MOVED WITH COMPASSION FOR THEM, because they fainted, and were scattered abroad, as sheep having no shepherd…As we can see, Jesus came to exercise authority over the multitudes, but He did it BEING MOVED WITH COMPASSION. As well, the story of Joseph tells us of him (Joseph) being elevated to a place of authority and leadership, but we also see that Joseph forgave, loved, and had compassion on his brothers who sold him as a slave into Egyptian bondage.

According to Bill Britton: "Every man has authority in some area of his life. A man who is a husband and father has an authority delegated to him in his home. He may be on the bottom of the heap on his job, or at church, but at home he has authority. Happy is the home where this authority is accompanied by compassion and a love for his family. There are men who are mousy and submissive in the world, yet are brutal to their children at home, or a dictator over their wife. Such a man needs help and deliverance. The only place he has authority, he has no compassion. God could not trust such a one to rule over the nations. Rulers need compassion and love for others." (Ten Dangerous Possessions, Bill Britton)

Let us be…

MOVED WITH COMPASSION!

November 2

TEN DANGEROUS POSSESSIONS
(GROWING UP IN GOD)

#9 - RICHES WITHOUT SHARING

According to Bill Britton: "The power to get wealth is in the hand of the Lord. The Bible warns us much about being greedy of filthy lucre. It tells us to withdraw ourselves from those who suppose that gain is godliness (that is, having plenty is a sign of holiness, life, and the favor of God). We read that the love of money is the root of all evil, and that coveting after money will pierce us through with many sorrows. They that will be rich fall into temptations and a snare. All this makes it sound like money is a bad thing. Yet it seems that everyone continues to want more of it. Having riches is not bad, if you know how to use them to the glory of God. But a covetous or greedy spirit will not allow you to share your riches with others. And riches can be a dangerous possession unless there is sharing according to the direction of the Spirit." (Ten Dangerous Possessions, Bill Britton)

The apostle Paul taught on the importance of giving in 2nd Corinthians 9:6 when he said… He which sows sparingly shall reap also sparingly; and he which sows bountifully shall reap also bountifully. Every man according as he purposes in his heart, so let him give; not grudgingly, or of necessity; for God loves a cheerful giver…As well, Romans 12:8 tells us that there is a ministry of giving. What is this ministry of giving? It is an attitude of being willing and ready to give of your riches, doing the best you can at all times, being led by the Spirit of God as to where to direct your giving. This is to be done in love with a cheerful heart and not with a grudging attitude as though you were paying money to a bill collector.

The book of James speaks very strongly concerning those that heap treasure for themselves for selfish reasons. James 5:1-3 states…Go to now, you rich men, weep and howl for your miseries that shall come upon you. Your riches are corrupted, and your garments are moth-eaten. Your gold and silver is cankered; and the rust of them shall be a witness against you, and shall eat your flesh as it were fire. You have heaped treasure together for the last days…

It is quite obvious that the Lord is NOT PLEASED WITH A SELFISH ATTITUDE AS FAR AS RICHES ARE CONCERNED. He is not pleased with those who heap treasure together with no intention of sharing their riches with others. The very reason that the Lord gives certain people power to get wealth is that they will share their riches with others. Let us be careful to remember that…

THE LOVE OF MONEY IS THE ROOT OF ALL EVIL!

November 3

TEN DANGEROUS POSSESSIONS
(GROWING UP IN GOD)

#10 LIFE WITHOUT JESUS

According to Bill Britton: "Can life really be a dangerous possession? Yes, dear ones, all that we have said previously can be summarized in these words…life without Jesus, a meaningless, tasteless, useless, and even dangerous possession. To make life worthwhile, we must have the nature of Jesus in us. To the extent that we allow Him to come within, to that extent we enjoy the benefits of a full, happy, and fruitful life. Life without Jesus is a struggle for an existence with no eternal quality or divine benefits. To find the excitement of a life full of the thrills of real happiness and the delicious taste of lasting joy, you must have Jesus within. There is no other way." (Ten Dangerous Possessions, Bill Britton)

We must see that the very reason that Jesus came to this earth was to bring us from a condition of death to life. This means that we are being brought from the carnal mind (death) to the mind of Christ (life). A life that is lived in the carnal mind is no life at all, but is actually death, FOR TO BE CARNALLY MINDED IS DEATH! True life can only be experienced in and through Christ, FOR HE IS LIFE! God is bringing us to the place where we can say, along with the apostle Paul…I AM CRUCIFIED WITH CHRIST: NEVERTHELESS I LIVE; YET NOT I, BUT CHRIST LIVES IN ME: AND THE LIFE WHICH I NOW LIVE IN THE FLESH I LIVE BY THE FAITH OF THE SON OF GOD, WHO LOVED ME, AND GAVE HIMSELF FOR ME. I DO NOT FRUSTRATE THE GRACE OF GOD: FOR IF RIGHTEOUSNESS COME BY THE LAW, THEN CHRIST IS DEAD IN VAIN (Galatians 2:20)…

Without the Galatians 2:20 experience being applied to our lives, we really have no life at all, but we are actually walking in death (the carnal mind). In essence, our life (or the lack thereof) becomes a dangerous possession, in that we constantly bring forth death (carnality) instead of bringing forth life (Christ) to those around us. How our Heavenly Father longs for us to lose our life for His name's sake, for when this is done we have actually found the true source of life, which is Jesus Christ! Without a death to the self-life we are doomed to frustrate the grace of God over and over again. But when the life we live becomes the life that is lived by the very faith of the Son of God, the true life in Christ (that we possess) becomes a wonderful and glorious possession! This possession becomes the very thing that is used to set us free, including the entire creation. It is His…

ABUNDANT LIFE!

November 4

FREQUENTLY ASKED QUESTIONS ABOUT THE SALVATION OF ALL MEN - #1

According to Charles Slagle:

Question:

"This teaching cancels out any necessity for Calvary. What would be the point of Christ dying on the cross if God plans to save everyone anyway?

Answer:

That's like asking, "What's the point of having a hospital that has discovered the cure for all diseases?" Just because Calvary will prove itself to be 100% successful does not render Christ's sacrifice unnecessary. If a rescue team saved all the passengers on a sinking ship, would that prove their mission to be futile? The unscriptural dogma that only some will be saved undermines the atonement. It renders our Lord's work as mostly a failure. Some (Calv-Arminians?) believe that most people will be saved. This renders Christ's atonement *almost* successful!" (Question and answer by Charles Slagle)

Not only does the teaching of eternal torture make a mockery of the cross of Christ, but it also would make His sacrifice an absolute failure. The scriptures tell us that the Father sent the Son to be the Savior of the world (1st John 4:14). The question is, did He succeed or fail? Is He the potential Savior of the world or the actual Savior of the world? The very reason that Christ died on the cross was TO TAKE AWAY THE SIN OF THE WORLD. As a result of His sacrifice there was purchased a universal salvation for the entire human race. Jesus reversed the curse of Adam that was upon us, bringing salvation, blessing, forgiveness, and grace (READ ROMANS CHAPTER 5).

The other aspect of the cross that many do not understand is that Jesus did not die to save us from eternal torture, but He died to save us from SIN AND ITS CONSEQUENCES! Remember… The wages of sin is DEATH (not eternal torture). So…Jesus came to save us from SIN AND DEATH. Well…What is sin? What is death? The word "sin" means TO MISS THE MARK. Romans 8:6 tells us that…TO BE CARNALLY MINDED IS DEATH. So… "Sin" is a missing of the mark of the very nature of God, and "death" is first and foremost the spiritual condition of being in the carnal mind, as well as physical death.

As God gives us eyes to see, we will grasp that **He has already reconciled the world to Himself** (2nd Corinthians 5:18-21). What is now left is for men to be awakened to what the Father has already accomplished. This will happen to every man in his own order (1st Corinthians 15:22-28), continuing into the ages to come (Ephesians 2:7), until our God is all in all (1st Corinthians 15:28)!!! This is why the Son of God poured out His life. He came…

TO SAVE US ALL!

November 5

FREQUENTLY ASKED QUESTIONS ABOUT THE SALVATION OF ALL MEN - #2

According to Thomas B. Thayer:

Question:

"Don't we need hell to keep people moral?"

Answer:

The belief of future endless torments does not restrain nor prevent men from the indulgence of their criminal passions. Those believing are no better, in character or conduct, *because* they believe it. The hell of the Burmans is as horrible as imagination or invention can make it; and yet they are notoriously corrupt, licentious, bloody-minded - the greatest thieves, liars and cheats in the world. The disbelief of endless torments does not make man immoral or wicked." (The Origin And History Of The Doctrine Of Endless Punishment, Thomas B. Thayer)

There will always be those who insist that…Without dangling people over the flames of an eternal hell, that those people will not turn to God for salvation. Such has been the belief of Evangelical Christianity for many centuries now. While it is true that many experience their conversion after hearing a preacher scare them to death about being tortured forever, the person has come to the Lord for the wrong reason, and is being motivated to serve God out of a fear of eternal hell, rather than the true motivation for serving the Lord, which is LOVE. **FEAR OF ETERNAL TORTURE IS NEVER A PROPER MOTIVE FOR ONE TO BEGIN A RELATIONSHIP WITH THE LORD!!!** 1st John 4:18,19 states…There is no fear in love; but perfect love casts out fear: because fear has torment. He that fears is not made perfect in love. **We love Him, because He first loved us**…

There are many that would make the statements…We need the threat of eternal torture to bring us to God…&…We need the threat of eternal torture to keep us right with God. This would be the same as saying that a bride needs the threat of never-ending torture to marry and to stay married to her husband. While it is possible that a marriage could be started and sustained based off of this premise, the marriage would be based on fear (not on love), WHICH IS A WRONG MOTIVE!

The large majority of those in Christianity are serving God because they are afraid of what will happen to them if they don't. This way of thinking does not keep people moral in the eyes of God, for it is not true morality. IT IS NOTHING MORE THAN SELF-RIGHTEOUSNESS MOTIVATED BY FEAR OF ETERNAL TORTURE! As well, let us look down through history. The "so-called" gospel of eternal torture has not caused the masses and the nations of the world to turn to God. THEY KNOW WHAT CHRISTIANITY PREACHES, BUT YET THE NATIONS ARE NOT COMPELLED TO TURN TO GOD AFTER HEARING THE MESSAGE OF ETERNAL TORTURE IN HELL. The good news is…THE TEACHING OF ETERNAL TORTURE IS A LIE! While it may momentarily scare some into serving God, it can never, never, never produce the fruit of the Spirit, which is…

LOVE!

November 6

FREQUENTLY ASKED QUESTIONS ABOUT THE SALVATION OF ALL MEN - #3

According to Charles Slagle:

Question:

"Why live a good life if all will be saved? (Why are we serving God?)

Answer:

Why live a good life if God plans to save everyone in the end -- no matter what they have done? It's amazing how often folks ask that question without giving more thought to it before they voice it. My first response to people who pose that question is another question: "Are you saying the only reason you don't cheat on your spouse, abuse your children, or steal from your neighbors is because you're afraid of going to hell?" Hmmm... Awkward question, that one... It usually brings a blush to folks who insist that people need to be threatened with never-ending punishment to give them "incentive" to seek the Lord, to live morally and ethically, and to love their neighbors as they love themselves. Why do those who advocate the dogma of endless hell find my question embarrassing? It is because they have a conscience, that's why. The human conscience knows that right is right, because it is right. So we find it shameful to suggest that the only reason we would do right by others is to avoid being trashed and burned forever." (Question and answer by Charles Slagle)

If a person is seriously asking this question it shows that the only reason they are serving God is because they are afraid of eternal torture. We must all be truthful with ourselves to see whether or not that we are in the faith. We must ask ourselves...WHY ARE WE SERVING GOD? WHAT IS IT THAT MOTIVATES US TO SERVE HIM? Is it fear or love? If it is fear, then we have become as sounding brass, or a tinkling cymbal. 1ˢᵗ Corinthians 13:3 states...And though I bestow all my goods to feed the poor, and though I give my body to be burned, and have not love, IT PROFITS ME NOTHING...

So...Why should we serve God? WE SHOULD SERVE HIM BECAUSE HE FIRST SERVED US! WE SHOULD LOVE HIM BECAUSE HE FIRST LOVED US! **O THAT MEN WOULD BE ABLE TO GRASP THAT <u>GOD</u> IS LOVE!!!** Micah 7:18,19 states...Who is a God like unto You, that pardons iniquity, and passes by the transgression of the remnant of His heritage? He retains not His anger for ever, because He delights in mercy. He will turn again, He will have compassion upon us; He will subdue our iniquities; and You will cast all their sins into the depths of the sea... To understand a scripture like this is to understand the character and nature of God. As you see your Father in this light...

YOU WILL WANT TO SERVE HIM!

FREQUENTLY ASKED QUESTIONS ABOUT THE SALVATION OF ALL MEN - #4

According to Charles Slagle:

Question:

"This may be the truth. Even so, the restoration of all things could be dangerous teaching for unstable people who would interpret it as license to sin.

Answer:

People looking for excuses to sin will always find them under any belief-system. Regarding the salvation of all mankind, Paul said, "These things prescribe and teach" (1 Tim. 4:9-11). Understanding God's true character and plan for His creation lays a healthy foundation for authentic righteousness that comes from whole-hearted trust and love toward the Lord. The greatest commandment of all is that we love Him with *all* our being. How can we totally trust and love our Creator, and at the same time be totally convinced that His commitment to *us* is conditional?" (Question and answer by Charles Slagle)

What is truly at stake concerning the restoration of all things is whether it is true or not. If it is true, then there is no way that it can be harmful to tell others about it. It should be taught and preached to the world. IT IS GOOD NEWS! There are millions of people right now who are living in rebellion to the will of God. These people who are living in rebellion are doing so despite being told that if they do not get right that God is going to torture them forever. Those who are looking for a way to live in rebellion to God are going to do so no matter what they are taught about God. Please believe me, GOD IS GOING TO CORRECT THESE PEOPLE IN THE AGES TO COME! Their wood, hay, and stubble will not go unnoticed before God. His consuming fire will burn up any and all carnality that is within us, whether now or in the ages to come.

As we have stated, those looking for excuses to sin will always find them under any belief-system. But it is our job to teach the truth of God. It is our duty to proclaim the true gospel of salvation, forgiveness, restoration, and reconciliation. 1st Timothy 4:9-11 states…This is a faithful saying and worthy of all acceptance. For therefore we both labor and suffer reproach, because we trust in the living **God, Who is the Savior of all men**, specially of those that believe. **These things command and teach…**We are told by the apostle Paul to COMMAND AND TEACH THAT GOD IS THE SAVIOR OF ALL MEN. As we do this, we will be pleasantly surprised to see how many more people will be drawn to the saving knowledge of the Lord Jesus Christ.

COMMAND AND TEACH THESE THINGS!

November 8

FREQUENTLY ASKED QUESTIONS ABOUT THE SALVATION OF ALL MEN - #5

Question:

If the teaching of the salvation of all men is true, then why are there so few people who understand it?

Answer:

To the surprise of many people, there are more people who believe and understand the salvation of all men than you would think. (Compared to the number of people who believe and teach eternal torture though, it is few.)

As you do a study of early church history (from the apostle Paul until the Dark Ages/about 500 A.D.), you will find that most of those in Christendom (including the teachers) did not believe or teach eternal torture. The majority of Christians believed and taught the ultimate salvation of all men in the ages to come. This can be easily researched and seen to be true. This can be confirmed by studying the writings of Origen and those who followed in his footsteps. Augustine, who flourished between 400 A.D.- 430 A.D., was the first to argue that "aionios" signified strictly endlessness as it referred to the punishment of unbelievers and the wicked.

According to Dr. Harold Lovelace: "The great truth of the salvation of all creation by God was denounced by the Fifth General Council of the Catholic Church held in Constantinople from May 4, A.D. 553 until June 2, A.D. 553. The Dark Ages, as they are known, came upon the world for about 1,000 years, and this great truth was hidden." (<u>Read And Search God's Plan</u>, Dr. Harold Lovelace)

It is very helpful to know this information which we have just stated, but this is still not the heart of the matter. That which is at stake concerning the salvation of all men is simply… WHETHER OR NOT IT IS TRUE! THAT IS ALL THAT MATTERS! **HOW MANY PEOPLE BELIEVE SOMETHING HAS ABSOLUTELY NOTHING TO DO WITH WHETHER OR NOT IT IS TRUE!** If the majority of people believe that two plus two does not equal four, that still does not cancel out the fact that two plus two equals four. People would rather "go with the flow", "not rock the boat", believe everything their pastor tells them (never researching it for themselves), and continue to "play church", remaining a form of godliness that denies the power of God.

FORGET ABOUT WHO BELIEVES WHAT! DO WHAT THE BIBLE TELLS YOU TO DO! **STUDY TO SHOW YOURSELF APPROVED UNTO GOD!!!** Come to the Father in prayer, asking Him to show you the truth. Do not ask Him to show you what YOU WANT TO SEE, but rather, ask Him to show you THE TRUTH! It is only in knowing the truth that we can be…

MADE FREE!

November 9

FREQUENTLY ASKED QUESTIONS ABOUT THE SALVATION OF ALL MEN - #6

Question:

Does the reconciliation of all things include the powers of darkness?

Answer:

YES...OF COURSE IT DOES! It is the reconciliation of ALL THINGS!

Colossians 1:16-20 is an incredible passage of scripture that explains to us in great detail that there is to be a reconciliation of all things. This reconciliation of all things is a direct result of the cross of the Lord Jesus Christ. WOW...That is a powerful cross! Thank God for the cross (the atonement) of the Lord Jesus Christ! Colossians 1:16-20 states...**For by Him were all things created**, that are in heaven, and that are in earth, visible and invisible, whether they be thrones, or dominions, or principalities, or powers: all things were created by Him, and for Him: And He is before all things, and by Him all things consist. And He is the head of the body, the church: Who is the beginning, the firstborn from the dead; that in all things He might have the preeminence. For it pleased the Father that in Him should all fullness dwell; And, **having made peace through the blood of His cross, by Him to reconcile all things unto Himself**; by Him, I say, whether they be things in earth, or things in heaven...As well, Ephesians 3:9-11 sheds light on this subject. It states...And to make all men see what is the fellowship of the mystery, which from the beginning of the world has been hid in **God, Who created all things by Jesus Christ**: To the intent that now unto **the principalities and powers in heavenly places might be known by the church the manifold wisdom of God**, According to the eternal purpose which He purposed in Christ Jesus our Lord...

Many people have no understanding at all that GOD IS SOVEREIGN, and that God is responsible for having created ALL THINGS, INCLUDING SATAN AND THE POWERS OF DARKNESS. In our daily Christian walk we find ourselves fighting against principalities, powers, rulers of the darkness of this world, and spiritual wickedness in high places. Well...THE SCRIPTURES HAVE JUST TOLD US THAT GOD IS RESPONSIBLE FOR HAVING CREATED THESE FORCES OF DARKNESS. In fact, Ephesians 3:9-11 tells us that the powers of darkness are the MANIFOLD WISDOM OF GOD. Principalities and powers are created and used by God, according to the eternal purpose (the purpose of the ages) which He purposed in Christ Jesus. They are used to shape and mold the sons and daughters of God into the very image of God. HOW CAN THIS BE?

In order for God to bring about His purpose of the ages there had to be **opposition** and obstacles for His children to overcome. God created the powers of darkness (including Satan - the prince of the power of the air - the spirit that now works in the children of disobedience), giving His children something to overcome. We must understand that God wanted overcomers. In order for there to be overcomers there had to be something to overcome. So...God made sure to it that there would be things to overcome. When the purpose of God is completed (at the end of the ages) there will be no more need for the powers of darkness, at which time these powers, WHICH GOD CREATED...

SHALL BE RECONCILED UNTO HIM!

November 10

FREQUENTLY ASKED QUESTIONS ABOUT THE SALVATION OF ALL MEN - #7

According to John Gavazzoni:

Question:

"Is God going to force people to be saved?

Answer:

The relationship of God's will to us, is not one of making us do something against our will, but by bringing our will into union with His. This is not coercion, this is causation, and it is causation by the force of love which ultimately worked by God leaving us to ourselves to do what we would do left to ourselves; which was to crucify His Son, and then to love such enemies back to Himself by the power of forgiving love." (Answer from: <u>Free Will</u>, John Gavazzoni)

We MUST understand our salvation experience in the light of God's sovereignty. WE DON'T JUST WAKE UP ONE FINE MORNING AND DECIDE TO BEGIN A RELATIONSHIP WITH THE LORD. The Bible tells us that the Spirit of God must first DRAW us. John 6:44 states…No man can come to Me (Jesus is speaking), except the Father which has sent Me **draw** him: and I will raise him up at the last day…Let us not take these words lightly, for they testify that a person can not even come to God unless God, by His Spirit, draws that person. This blows to pieces the idea that we are responsible to just wake up one morning and *choose* to serve the Lord. It is IMPOSSIBLE to come to God unless HE FIRST DRAWS YOU!

John 12:32,33 states…And I, if I be lifted up from the earth, **will draw all men unto Me.** This He said, signifying what death He should die…It is imperative that we seek to understand this statement from the Lord Jesus. It testifies that God is sovereign. Unfortunately, there are very few people that understand what Jesus was actually saying. The word "draw" that is found in this scripture verse (John 12:32) means to DRAG. God is lovingly dragging us to Himself in the same way that a man in love would continue pursuing the woman that he was madly in love with. You must come to the realization that **our Heavenly Father will not be denied. He will draw (drag) ALL MEN unto Himself.** This will not be fully accomplished in this present age, but will continue in the ages to come until EVERY KNEE BOWS AND EVERY TONGUE CONFESSES THAT JESUS CHRIST IS LORD (Philippians 2:10,11)! We should be excited to know that our Father WILL STOP AT NOTHING to reveal His love to us, for He has promised to…

DRAW (DRAG) ALL MEN!

November 11

FREQUENTLY ASKED QUESTIONS ABOUT THE SALVATION OF ALL MEN - #8

Question:

Why should we preach the gospel now if God is going to have all men to be saved in the end?

Answer:

This is a very ridiculous question, but nevertheless, many people continue to ask it in light of the salvation of all men. Our answer is to be found from Romans 10:14,15. We must understand that the preaching (and teaching) of the gospel is the means by which God AWAKENS the human race to what He has ALREADY ACCOMPLISHED in Christ. This is taking place and will continue to take place in the ages to come.

Romans 10:14,15 states…How then shall they call on Him in Whom they have not believed? and how shall they believe in Him of Whom they have not heard? and how shall they hear without a preacher? And how shall they preach, except they be sent? as it is written, How beautiful are the feet of them that preach the gospel of peace, and bring glad tidings of good things!…Let us also consider what 2nd Corinthians 5:18 tells us. It states…And all things are of God, Who has reconciled us to Himself by Jesus Christ, and has given to us the ministry of reconciliation…

What beautiful passages of scripture! They both testify to the fact that we have been called to preach and minister the salvation and reconciliation of our great God. We must first take into account that God has already (past tense) reconciled the world unto Himself. This means that ALL PEOPLE have been reconciled to God by Jesus Christ (whether they know it or not). Even with this having been accomplished, mankind is still called upon (by God) to recognize, repent, and respond to what God has made available. We don't preach to "get people saved", but rather, we preach to AWAKEN THEM to the fact that God has already saved and forgiven them. THIS IS GOOD NEWS! THIS IS THE GOSPEL! We must stop thinking that our preaching, altar calls, and formulas (the sinner's prayer) is what saves a person. In essence, they are already reconciled, but they just don't know it yet. With this being said though, man is still accountable (to God) to repent and respond in faith to the message of reconciliation, which then leads us through the salvation process of our spirit, soul, and body.

We are called upon to preach the gospel for the purpose of awakening the human race to the fact (GOOD NEWS) that they have been reconciled to God by the death of His Son Jesus Christ. How can a person know that they have been reconciled to God unless someone tells them? This is God's method of causing all men to come to the saving knowledge of the Lord Jesus Christ, WHETHER NOW, **OR IN THE AGES TO COME!** So…Let us…

PREACH THE GOOD NEWS!

FREQUENTLY ASKED QUESTIONS ABOUT THE SALVATION OF ALL MEN - #9

Question:

If the salvation of all men is God's ultimate purpose for the human race, then why is it so difficult for so many people to understand?

Answer:

Our answer is to be found in the understanding of Proverbs 25:2. As well, the organized church (Babylon) has done a great job of misrepresenting the true God. This has caused many to believe the lie of eternal torture. People are comfortable with the status quo message that is supported by the religious leaders of Evangelical Christianity. They assume that it (the false message of eternal torture) must be right because the majority of Christians believe and teach it.

The salvation of all men is plain to see when we are not under the influence of the carnal mind, the traditions and doctrines of men, the power of the organized church, and the negative influence of family and friends who have been seduced by all the things that we just mentioned. With this being said though, the main reason that many do not see the deep things of God is to be found in the understanding of Proverbs 25:2. It states…It is the glory of God to conceal a thing: but the honor of kings is to search out a matter…

It is imperative that we understand God's dealings with man. GOD PURPOSELY HIDES THE TRUTH UNDER THE TRADITIONS AND DOCTRINES OF MEN SO THAT WE WILL SEARCH FOR IT! This verse (Proverbs 25:2) also tells us that God is glorified in the fact that He hides the truth and that we will then search for it. The truth of the salvation of all men (along with all other truth) must be revealed to a person by the Spirit of God. This takes place as we begin to search out the matter.

Ephesians 1:9,10 sheds even more light on this particular subject. It states (The Emphasized Bible)…making known to us **the sacred secret of His will**, according to His good pleasure which He purposed in Him, - For an administration of the fullness of the seasons, to reunite for Himself (under one Head) the all things in the Christ, the things upon the heavens, and the things upon the earth, in Him…This verse tells us that the reconciliation of all things is a **<u>SACRED</u> <u>SECRET</u> THAT MUST BE MADE KNOWN TO US!!!** If God has a SACRED SECRET, then that tells us that He has concealed something that we must search out.

In conclusion, we must see that the act of God concealing something (such as the truth of the salvation of all men) is the very GLORY OF GOD! God is actually glorified by the fact that His purpose of the ages is concealed. Because it is concealed, it causes us to search out the matter, laying down our lives in pursuit of the MYSTERIES OF THE KINGDOM OF GOD! It results in God being revealed to us and glorified in all the earth. May the Heavenly Father reveal to you…

HIS SACRED SECRET!

November 13

FREQUENTLY ASKED QUESTIONS ABOUT THE SALVATION OF ALL MEN - #10

Question:

As far as the teaching of the salvation of all men is concerned, what if we are wrong?

Answer:

When a person is ready to seek the Lord with all his heart, dropping all personal agendas, he will see that the scriptures proclaim this great truth. IT IS UNDENIABLE! But for the sake of argument, let us suppose that this teaching is wrong. What is it that those who believe it would be found guilty of? Generally speaking, we would be found guilty of two main things, which are:

1. BELIEVING THAT GOD IS ALL-LOVING
2. BELIEVING THAT GOD IS ALL-POWERFUL

As well, we would be found guilty of believing that God actually had a purpose and plan for the entire creation that makes sense. Some other things we would be guilty of are:

1. Believing what the scriptures actually teach...
2. Reading the scriptures...
3. Studying the scriptures in their original Hebrew and Greek...
4. Studying the word meanings of the English words "hell", "for ever", "eternal", and "everlasting"...
5. Challenging the present teachings of the organized church...
6. Studying church history...
7. Believing that God is sovereign...
8. Believing that God is love...
9. Believing that the cross of Jesus Christ was a total and complete universal victory for the entire human race...
10. Loving and forgiving all people...

When a person comes to the understanding that God is ALL-LOVING and ALL-POWERFUL, the ridiculous teachings of men (such as eternal torture) no longer deceive us. We know the heart of our Heavenly Father. We know that He is ABLE and WILLING to SAVE ALL! This is Who He is. **HE IS THE SAVIOR OF THE WORLD!!!** Do not the scriptures testify of this? Does not your heart cry out that this is so? The only thing that stops people from hearing the voice of God in their heart concerning this matter is the negative power of the traditions and doctrines of men, and those who are under the spell of organized religion.

Once a person is set free from the bondage of the organized church, he is truly SET FREE from the most powerfully negative force that is known to the human race. There is nothing more wicked than the Pharisee (religious) spirit. It always produces self-righteousness and stinks in the nostrils of God. There is one more question that must be asked concerning the salvation of all men in the ages to come. That question is...

WHAT IF WE ARE RIGHT?

November 14

THE PURPOSE OF THE LAW - PART 1

According to Randy Bonacorso: "If there is one single topic in the Bible that remains shrouded in confusion, it would be understanding the purpose of the law. We are of course speaking of the law of Moses and all that is contained therein. There is so much confusion on this topic that one hardly knows where to begin. There are those who say that the law has no more purpose in our lives in this day and age, paying absolutely no attention to it at all. Then there are those who are still under the bondage of trying to keep the law, living a life of condemnation, frustration, hypocrisy, self-righteousness, and failure. Still yet, there are those who want to play both sides of the fence, trying to keep certain laws while totally ignoring and disregarding others. ARE YOU CONFUSED YET? MOST OF THE CHURCH IS! Let us look to the scriptures for solid and concrete answers to this perplexing problem. 1st Timothy 1:8,9 states…But we know that the law is good, if a man use it lawfully; Knowing this, that the law is not made for a righteous man, but for the lawless and disobedient…The definition of sin is clearly spelled out and defies complication. John's first epistle defines sin as "transgression of the law" (3:4). Paul writes in Romans 3:20, "By the law is the knowledge of sin." In Romans 5:13 he says, "For until the law sin was in the world: but sin is not imputed when there is no law." Finally, he puts it as simply as possible: "For where no law is, there is no transgression" (Romans 4:15)." (The Gospel Of Maturity, Randy Bonacorso)

With a little bit of research we can already begin to see that there is a purpose for the law, and that this purpose is very specific. The very first and foremost purpose of the law is to bring us to the knowledge of sin. It is so important that we understand this primary purpose of the law. Many people use the law unlawfully, using it as a means to acquire righteousness with God, making themselves feel superior to others. THERE IS NO BONDAGE LIKE THE BONDAGE THAT ACCOMPANIES A PERSON WHO IS TRYING TO ACQUIRE THE RIGHTEOUSNESS OF GOD BY THE KEEPING OF THE LAW. THE VERY PURPOSE OF THE LAW IS TO SHOW MAN THAT HE IS NOT ABLE TO KEEP IT (THE LAW) IN AND OF HIMSELF. The law is a mirror in which we see ourselves for who we really are. It shows us the condition of our condition. This is explained to us in Romans chapter three. We are told that the law is the very thing that reveals to us our sinful condition. This is a very important step in our salvation process, for it brings to our attention…

THE KNOWLEDGE OF SIN!

THE GLORY OF GOD & THE HONOR OF KINGS

November 15

THE PURPOSE OF THE LAW - PART 2

THAT EVERY MOUTH MAY BE STOPPED

Romans 3:10,11,19,20 states…As it is written, There is **none** righteous, no, not one: There is **none** that understands, there is **none** that seeks after God…Now we know that what things soever the law says, it says to them who are under the law: **that every mouth may be stopped, and all the world may become guilty before God**. Therefore by the deeds of the law there shall no flesh be justified in His sight: for by the law is the knowledge of sin…

In spite of what this passage of scripture has to say, many continue to use the law unlawfully. Instead of applying this passage to themselves by having their mouths stopped and being convinced of their guilt, they use the law to run their mouths, pointing their fingers at others who do not measure up. The whole point of this passage of scripture is to proclaim THAT THERE IS NO ONE WHO MEASURES UP TO THE RIGHTEOUSNESS OF GOD. WE ARE ALL IN THE SAME BOAT! Some pride themselves on how much of the law that they keep, but we must keep in mind that to break just one part of the law makes us guilty of breaking the entire law (James 2:10). There are those who always condemn certain people for doing certain things, but do not realize that in doing so that they are using the law unlawfully. While we may not do the thing that we are condemning others for, there are surely areas in our life which we do not measure up to the law of God. In essence, we become guilty of doing the very same thing that we are condemning that person of doing, for all have broken God's law in some area. Remember…For whosoever shall keep the whole law, and yet offend in one point, HE IS GUILTY OF ALL (James 2:10)…

All of this sure sounds very discouraging, doesn't it? It is very discouraging UNTIL THAT WE SEE THE PURPOSE OF THE LAW. If you think that by the keeping of the law you will attain to the righteousness of God, you will live a very frustrated life. As well, you will be seen by others as just another Pharisee. But if you see the law for what it is, then the law becomes very beneficial to your salvation experience and growth in God. It is, as we have stated, a mirror that causes a person to see their inadequacy, unrighteousness, sin nature, failure to measure up to God, fallen condition, and the fruit of their self-life.

The law definitely has a purpose. It is designed to show mankind that we are not capable of keeping it, pointing to something greater. That something greater is what we so desperately need. It is the…

GRACE OF GOD!

❖

November 16

THE PURPOSE OF THE LAW - PART 3

THE LAW WAS OUR SCHOOLMASTER

Galatians 3:24,25 states…Wherefore the law was our schoolmaster to bring us unto Christ, that we might be justified by faith. But after that faith is come, we are no longer under a schoolmaster… This same thought is to be seen in John 1:17. It states…For the law was given by Moses, but grace and truth came by Jesus Christ…

The word "schoolmaster" means a child guardian. The idea is that the child guardian brings the child unto the teacher. The very purpose of the law is to bring us to something greater. This something greater is Jesus Christ Himself. We are being brought from law to grace. The guardian (the law) is bringing us to the teacher (grace). We are to see the grace of God as our teacher. So…This makes the law VERY IMPORTANT!

The law has a definite purpose. Its purpose is to show us that we are bankrupt (spiritually speaking), and that we are powerless to achieve the righteousness of God outside of His grace. THE LAW ACTUALLY DRIVES US INTO THE ARMS OF THE GRACE OF GOD. It is an instrument designed to bring us to something better and greater. It is impossible to walk this Christian walk without the grace of God.

The "grace" of God is His unmerited favor toward man in Christ, but let us not stop there, FOR IT IS SO MUCH MORE THAN THAT. The "grace" of God is actually speaking of the very nature of God that emanates through a person to enable them to overcome all things. It could be said that…Going from law to grace is the same as going from our nature to His nature. The next logical question would be, how is it that we access this grace (nature) of God?

Ephesians 2:8,9 states…**For by grace are you saved through <u>faith</u>**; and that not of yourselves: it is the gift of God: Not of works, lest any man should boast…Not only are we brought from law to grace (from our nature to His nature), but we are also being brought from works to faith. Now we can see how important the law is when it is used lawfully. It is the very thing that is pushing us forward into the grace of God. It is actually designed by God for this specific reason. Remember… The letter of the law kills, but it is the Spirit of God that brings life (2ⁿᵈ Corinthians 3:6). When we realize this, recognizing the law as our schoolmaster, WE HAVE TAPPED INTO THE VERY GRACE OF GOD. WE ARE NO LONGER FRUSTRATING THE GRACE OF GOD! We thank God for the law that came by Moses, for it is good. But we thank God even more for grace and truth that came by Jesus Christ…

FOR IT IS A BETTER COVENANT!

November 17

THE PURPOSE OF THE LAW - PART 4

I WILL PUT MY LAW IN THEIR INWARD PARTS

Jeremiah 31:31-33 speaks to us concerning the purpose of the law. It states…Behold, the days come, says the LORD, that I will make a new covenant with the house of Israel, and with the house of Judah: Not according to the covenant that I made with their fathers in the day that I took them by the hand to bring them out of the land of Egypt; which My covenant they brake, although I was an husband unto them, says the LORD: But this shall be the covenant that I will make with the house of Israel; After those days, says the LORD, **I will put My law in their inward parts, and write it in their hearts**; and will be their God, and they shall be My people…

This passage of scripture gives us great insight into the purpose of the law. It tells us that the original covenant (the law) that God gave mankind (Israel) was a stepping stone to a better covenant. God knew full well that no one would be able to keep or fulfill His first covenant (except for the Son of God). The very purpose of the first covenant was to show man that he was inadequate in and of himself to achieve godliness. The first covenant was on the shoulders of mankind to perform that which God had commanded. The result was, is, and always will be failure. After that is established in your life (a realization that you can not keep the law), then the letter of the law has served its purpose, making you ready for the next step in God. The next step is to have the SPIRIT OF THE LAW WRITTEN ON YOUR HEART! This is the better covenant! This is why Jesus died. He did not come to do away with the law, BUT TO FULFILL IT!

Colossians 2:13,14 states…And you, being dead in your sins and the uncircumcision of your flesh, has He quickened together with Him, having forgiven you all trespasses; Blotting out the handwriting of ordinances that was against us, which was contrary to us, and took it out of the way, nailing it to His cross…As a result of what Jesus accomplished we are no longer held captive by the letter of the law, but we are now introduced to a better covenant. This better covenant involves God doing in us what we could not do for ourselves. GOD HAS PROMISED TO WRITE HIS LAWS IN OUR INWARD PART (HEARTS)! This is accomplished by grace through faith. In essence, the spirit of the law is being written on our hearts. It could also be said that the spirit of the law is GOD'S DIVINE NATURE. So…We can see that we are no longer under the letter of the law, but we have made the transition into…

THE SPIRIT OF THE LAW!

November 18

THE PURPOSE OF THE LAW - PART 5

CONCLUSION

According to Dr. Stephen Jones: "We know from Rom. 3:23 that "all have sinned." Therefore, every man is a debtor in the eyes of the law. It is the law that has put us all into slavery because of our sin. But we have a Redeemer, Jesus Christ, Who came and paid the full penalty for our sins. Once the debt has been paid, we have been set free from the slavery imposed upon us by the law. We are now under grace. Does this mean, then, that we are now free to sin at will? Are we now free to *"sin that grace may abound*?" (Rom. 6:1) Of course not. Grace is not a license to sin. Sin is lawlessness. The law was not put away; the law was upheld. Jesus could have set us free by putting away His law, for this would have legalized sin. But He did not. He upheld the law and paid its full price. One of the most misunderstood verses of all time is found in Rom. 6:14, 15, where Paul wrote, **For sin shall not be master over you, for you are not under law, but under grace. What then? Shall we sin because we are not under law but under grace? May it never be!** Many people take Rom. 6:14 and interpret it to contradict Jesus, Paul, and John, saying that this means the law was put away. Paul says in Rom. 3:31, **Do we then nullify the law through faith? May it never be! On the contrary, we establish the law.** It is not right to pit Rom. 6:14 against Rom. 3:31. If they seem to be contradictory, it is because we do not understand Paul's writing. It is our hope that this will give the reader a better understanding of Paul's writings, so that we do not use him as an excuse to violate the law of Christ as given to Moses. One's obedience to the law cannot be used to justify any man. Learning obedience is the process of sanctification, not justification. Jesus came as our Redeemer, so that we are redeemed from the slavery caused by sin. In paying the debt that the law demanded for sin, He sustained the law, bearing witness of its righteous standard. We who have been set free from the law are now free to be obedient to our Redeemer, as the law says in Lev. 25:53. Now that we have been set free from the taskmaster of sin (lawlessness), we have been set free to be bondservants of Jesus Christ, our Redeemer." (The Purpose Of Law And Grace, Dr. Stephen Jones)

May we realize that we have been set free from having to perform the letter of the law, but that we are now made partakers of having the spirit of the law…

WRITTEN ON OUR HEARTS BY GRACE!

November 19

LEADING MEN TO REPENTANCE

Have you considered that all men need to repent? We have all sinned and come short of the glory of God (Romans 3:23). The word "repent" comes from a Greek word "metanoia", which means: a real change of mind and attitude toward sin itself and the cause of it (not merely the consequences of it), which affects the life and not merely a single act.

God desires all men to repent. As well, we should desire that all men would repent. When someone repents, in essence, **they turn from sin and turn to God**. Have you considered what causes men to repent? Have you considered how to lead men to repentance? Romans 2:4 tells us that…THE GOODNESS OF GOD LEADS MEN TO REPENTANCE…**What an interesting scripture!**

Why is it then that most preachers use *fear* to try to lead men to repentance? They especially use *fear of eternal torture in hell* as a means to try to "get people saved". It is very sad that the true message of the goodness of God has been reduced by the traditions of men into…*repent…or God will torture you forever…*

The message of eternal torture has never been (nor ever will be) the true gospel. It came from the Dark Ages, more specifically, the Catholic Church. Let God show you His love, goodness, grace, and mercy for the whole creation. THIS IS THE ONLY THING THAT CAUSES PEOPLE TO TURN TO GOD FOR THE RIGHT REASON (with the right motive in their heart)! All else is wood, hay, and stubble.

1st John 4:18 states…There is no fear in love; but perfect love casts out fear: because fear has torment. He that fears is not made perfect in love…Tell men about God's love, goodness, grace, and His mercy. This is what will lead them to true repentance. You must also understand that His wrath, judgment, vengeance, and punishment are all a part of His love. THEY ARE FOR THE PURPOSE OF CORRECTION! Let us STOP using fear (especially fear of hell) to motivate people to repent and serve God. That message (eternal torture…which is not true) does not give a person a true foundation to start a relationship with the Lord! Remember…

THE GOODNESS OF GOD LEADS MEN TO REPENTANCE!

November 20

BORN AGAIN…WHAT DOES IT MEAN?

Take some time right now to read John 3:3…Don't read it with your mind already made up! It would do you good to take a fresh look at this scripture! Many people read scriptures with their minds already made up, not even stopping to consider if they really understand what is being said.

No…It does not say…you must be born again to go to heaven. LOOK AT WHAT IT SAYS… Except a man be born again, **HE CANNOT SEE THE KINGDOM OF GOD**.

The words "born again" mean: born (begotten) from above. The word "see" means: not the mere act of looking, but the actual PERCEPTION of the object. It means to perceive, grasp, or understand with the mind. John 3:3 could be more clearly stated as…Except a man be born again / begotten from above (have a spiritual awakening from God, being awakened out of the carnal mind to the mind of Christ), he cannot see (perceive, understand, or grasp with his mind) the Kingdom of God (the rule / reign of God from within…righteousness, peace, and joy in the Holy Spirit).

THIS SCRIPTURE IS NOT ABOUT GOING TO HEAVEN OR HELL! IT IS NOT ABOUT GOING TO AN ALTAR IN A CHURCH TO SAY A SINNER'S PRAYER! **IT IS ABOUT BEING AWAKENED BY THE SPIRIT OF GOD TO UNDERSTAND HIS KINGDOM!!! WAKE UP AND SMELL THE COFFEE!** God is interested in you understanding His Kingdom. Furthermore, the born again experience is a lifelong process, not just a one time thing you do at an altar in a church building. Don't you want to see (perceive) His Kingdom? All that most people see is a religion or a particular denomination. Ask God to cause you to see (perceive) His Kingdom that is available to you in the here-and-now. He will awaken you to a glorious and marvelous Kingdom (that is in you…Christ, the hope of glory), awaiting to be experienced.

THINK ABOUT IT!

November 21

THE FOUR MOST POWERFUL FORCES

Here are what I believe to be the four most powerful forces:

1. THE TRADITIONS AND DOCTRINES OF MEN
2. KNOWING THE TRUTH OF GOD'S WORD
3. UNITY IN CHRIST
4. THE LOVE OF GOD

#1. The traditions and doctrines of men are so powerful that they (if believed) make the Word of God of none effect (Matthew 15:6-9 / Mark 7:7-13).

#2. The truth of God's Word (after it has been revealed to you) is so powerful that it is the only thing that can set you free from the traditions and doctrines of men (John 8:32).

#3. Unity in Christ (those who are in one mind and one accord) is so powerful that it only took twelve apostles to turn the world upside down (Acts 17:6).

#4. The love of God (which is more powerful that anything that we have just mentioned) is so powerful that it is the only thing that NEVER FAILS (1ST Corinthians 13:8).

Meditate on these forces and respect them for their power, understanding the part they play in the Kingdom of God. Remember…ALL POWER IS OF GOD (Romans 13:1)! It is God Who sends strong delusion, and it is God Who has the power to reveal His truth, causing someone to come out of the traditions and doctrines of men. It is God Who enables His people to come together in unity, and it is God (Who is love) Who has the power to love the human race back to Himself, every man in his own order!

AMEN!

November 22

WHAT IS ETERNAL LIFE?

John 17:3 states…And this is life eternal, that they might know You the only true God, and Jesus Christ, Whom You have sent…

What better definition can we get concerning the meaning of eternal life! This definition comes straight from the mouth of the Lord Jesus Christ. The word "eternal" (which describes the kind of life mentioned here) comes from the Greek word "aionios", which means: age-lasting, age-abiding, or of the ages. It could be said that this life is the LIFE OF THE AGES.

God's plan is a plan of ages, in which the life of the ages is available to us. This is God's life inserted into the ages of time. God has no beginning and no ending. This is the true definition of that which is eternal. He created time and framed the ages to make man in His image. The ages have a beginning and an ending. To have God's life in His plan of the ages is to have *the life of the ages*. This life has nothing to do with time, but is God's life received and inserted into the ages of time. Remember…The word "eternal" speaks of something that has no beginning and no ending. **Eternal life is a quality of life, not a quantity or length of time.**

When the last enemy (which is death) is destroyed, there will be nothing left but life. True eternity is timelessness. So…Remember that this life of the ages is the quality of the Christ-life. What is the life of the ages? Jesus plainly told us that it is KNOWING GOD AND THE ONE HE SENT! The life of the ages is to KNOW GOD! Eternal life is not salvation from an eternal torture pit in hell, but rather, it is…

KNOWING GOD!

November 23

THE MANIFESTATION OF THE SONS OF GOD

Romans 8:19-22 states…For the earnest expectation of the creature waits for the manifestation of the sons of God. For the creature was made subject to vanity, not willingly, but by reason of Him Who has subjected the same in hope, Because the creature itself also shall be delivered from the bondage of corruption into the glorious liberty of the children of God. For we know that the whole creation groans and travails in pain together until now…

This is one of the most amazing and informative scripture passages in the Bible. Have you considered these verses? Are you aware of what is being said? Do you know what its implications are? To understand this passage of scripture is to understand the purpose and plan of God for the ENTIRE CREATION! Let us look at the key words in this passage.

The key words are: earnest expectation, creature, manifestation of the sons of God, creature, vanity (not willingly), in hope, creature…delivered, the children of God, and whole creation. These key words paint a beautiful picture of the purpose and plan of God. This passage implies that God is responsible for putting the whole creation into vanity (futility / failure), and that He did it in hope. It goes on to tell us that the creation is ANXIOUSLY LOOKING WITH AN OUTSTRETCHED HEAD FOR THE MANIFESTATION OF THE SONS OF GOD. The creation is awaiting the hope that all (the entire creation) will be made alive in Christ, every man in his own order (1st Corinthians 15:22,23). We are told that God's people (the overcomers) will play a part in the deliverance of the entire creation, for it is the manifestation of the sons of God that is said to set the creation free! This is speaking of the fullness of God that is to be manifested through His sons (and daughters) for all the world to see. It is actually a manifestation of the Son of God through the sons of God, for we are His body. At this time the sons of God will be given their glorified bodies. It is an appointed time that is in the hand of the Father. This (the manifestation of the sons of God) is to be seen as the fulfillment of the FEAST OF TABERNACLES. IT IS THE FIRST RESURRECTION! Romans 8:19-22 tells us that the purpose of this manifestation is for DELIVERANCE! God's sons are going to deliver the creation from the government of man, bringing the nations into the government of God. **It is going to be glorious, wonderful, amazing, unspeakable, and astounding!!! The sons of God will continue to be used in the ages to come, bringing all people to a saving knowledge of the Lord Jesus Christ. ALL SHALL BE MADE ALIVE IN CHRIST!**

The hope of the whole creation hinges on the manifestation of the sons of God. This is (of course) a direct result of the saving work (the cross and resurrection) of the Lord Jesus Christ. The work of the Lord Jesus Christ GUARANTEES that there shall be a manifestation of the sons of God. Remember…The only reason there shall be a manifestation of the sons of God is because there was a manifestation of the Son of God. TO GOD BE THE GLORY!

The creation is on its "tip toes" anxiously awaiting this great event. Don't you want to be a part of it? We must realize that this is what God is preparing us for. Remember…The sufferings of this present time are not worthy to be compared with the glory which shall be revealed…

IN US!

November 24

ANTICHRIST

According to Ray Knight: "Tradition has taught for years that an Antichrist will arise and sit himself in a temple in Jerusalem and declare that he is god. If that wasn't enough, great theologians have declared that any despot in the world is the Antichrist . . . we've had Hitler, Kissinger, Stalin, etc., not forgetting every Pope in his day! Again, when one looks at the Word of God, one will see that there is a difference.

ANTICHRIST means INSTEAD OF CHRIST — The Greek word is *ANTICHRISTOS* 500 . . . *anti* 473 = **instead of**, substitution; *CHRISTOS* 5547 = the anointed One. . . from *CHRIO* 5548 = to smear with oil. So the meaning of the word translated as *'antichrist'* . . . it is primarily what is put **instead of** the anointing by the Anointed One . . . Christ. 'Anti', in our everyday language, means something that is *against* something. This is the effect every time a substitution is made for the true anointing. Many replacements for the anointing have been made and are being made by the church." (<u>Antichrist</u>, Ray Knight)

1st John 2:18-22 states…Little children, **it is the last time**: and as you have heard that antichrist shall come, **even now are there <u>many</u> antichrist<u>s</u>**; whereby we know that it is the last time. **They** went out from us, but **they** were not of us; for if **they** had been of us, **they** would no doubt have continued with us: but **they** went out, that **they** might be made manifest that **they** were not all of us. But you have an unction from the Holy One, and you know all things. I have not written unto you because you know not the truth, but because you know it, and that no lie is of the truth. Who is a liar but he that denies that Jesus is the Christ? **He is antichrist, that denies the Father and the Son**…1st John 4:3 states…And every spirit that confesses not that Jesus Christ is come in the flesh is not of God: and **this is that spirit of antichrist**, whereof you have heard that it should come; **and even now already is it in the world**…2nd John 1:7 states…For **<u>many</u> deceiver<u>s</u>** are entered into the world, who confess not that Jesus Christ is come in the flesh. **This is a deceiver and an antichrist**…2nd Thessalonians 2:3,4 states…Let no man deceive you by any means: for that day shall not come, except there come a falling away first, and that man of sin be revealed, the son of perdition; Who opposes and exalts himself above all that is called God, or that is worshipped; so that he as God sits in the temple of God, showing himself that he is God…

Are you ready for a revelation? THE MAN OF SIN IS INSIDE OF YOU! YOU ARE THE TEMPLE THAT IS BEING TALKED ABOUT IN 2ND THESSALONIANS! Remember…Your body is the temple of the Holy Spirit (1st Corinthians 6:19). STOP LOOKING TO JERUSALEM OR SOMEWHERE OVER IN THE MIDDLE EAST! YOU ARE THE TEMPLE OF GOD! LOOK TO YOURSELF! LOOK IN THE MIRROR! YOU HAVE JUST DISCOVERED THE ANTICHRIST!!!

Let the Lord consume the man of sin (the spirit of antichrist) inside of you with the brightness of His coming (presence). STOP LOOKING TO SOMETHING EXTERNAL!

LOOK TO YOURSELF!

November 25

IF I BE LIFTED UP

John 12:32,33 states…And I, if I be lifted up from the earth, will draw all men unto Me. This He said, signifying what death He should die…

What part of this passage do we not understand? Was Jesus lifted up from the earth?…YES! Will Jesus draw all men unto Himself?…YES!

As we have stated in previous teachings, the word "draw" that is used in verse 22 comes from the Greek word "helkuo". It means to draw with love, but it can also mean to <u>DRAG WITH FORCE</u>! Jesus clearly stated…that if I am lifted up from the earth (speaking of His death on the cross), I WILL DRAW ALL MEN UNTO ME…HOW PLAIN CAN IT BE! JESUS WILL DRAW ALL MEN UNTO HIMSELF! BELIEVE IT! PROCLAIM IT!

This declares that the cross of the Lord Jesus Christ was an absolute universal victory!!! He really is…THE SAVIOR OF THE WORLD! You can voluntarily come to the love of Jesus, or He will *drag* you in to know His love. He loves each and every one of us SO MUCH! He will stop at nothing! HE WILL HAVE ALL MEN TO COME TO HIS LOVE AND FORGIVENESS!

Did your parents ever *drag* you into something that you did not want to do? Well…Sure they have. As we get older we realize that the things that our parents *made us do* were for our benefit. We have all learned valuable lessons from things in life that we did not want to do. Why would your parents *drag* you into something that you did not want to do? BECAUSE THEY LOVE YOU! BECAUSE THEY WANT YOU TO LEARN! BECAUSE THEY KNOW WHAT IS BEST FOR YOU! BECAUSE WE NEED TO BE CORRECTED! In the same sense, God is going to draw all men unto Himself.

God will not allow His love to be defeated by any person! HIS LOVE WILL CONQUER ALL! He was lifted up from the earth. He will draw all men unto Himself! Jesus is a ransom for all, to be testified in *due time…*

HALLELUJAH!

November 26

THE MARK OF THE BEAST

Revelation 13:16-18 states…And he causes all, both small and great, rich and poor, free and bond, to receive a mark in their right hand, or in their foreheads: And that no man might buy or sell, save he that had the mark, or the name of the beast, or the number of his name. Here is wisdom. Let him that has understanding count the number of the beast: for it is the number of a man; and his number is Six hundred threescore and six…

Many people down through history have come up with a bunch of crazy ideas about this passage of scripture. They lean on intellect and the natural mind to try to discern the things of God. This causes people to *literalize* things that are to be understood spiritually.

It is not a matter of taking the mark of the beast, but rather, it is an issue of getting rid of the mark (of the beast) that we already have, for we were born with the mark of the beast. WE HAVE THE MARK! It is not a literal mark, but a spiritual one. We are marked from birth with the beast nature (or Adamic Nature) that we inherited from Adam. In essence, it is the name of the beast that we have. The word "name" means **nature**. So…As we have stated, WE HAVE THE NATURE OF THE BEAST! Ephesians 2:3 states… we are by **nature** the children of wrath…Ecclesiastes 3:18 states…I said in my heart concerning the estate of the sons of men, that God might manifest them, **and that they might see that they themselves are <u>beasts</u>**…

We must realize that we are marked with the beast nature in our right hand and forehead. The words "right hand" speak of everything we do. The word "forehead" speaks of our mindset (the carnal mind), including everything we think and say…As we can see, it is our whole being that is marked with this fallen nature.

So…What is the solution? How do we get rid of (overcome) this mark? The answer is to be found in Revelation 14:1. It states…And I looked, and, lo, a Lamb stood on the mount Sion, and with Him an hundred forty and four thousand, **having His Father's name written in their foreheads**…Can you grasp the spiritual implications of this? We must have the Father's name written on our forehead!

The solution to the mark of the beast is to be found in pressing toward the MARK for the prize of the high calling of God in Christ Jesus (Philippians 3:14). It is the mind of Christ that we need to replace the carnal mind. As well, it is the divine nature of our Heavenly Father that we need to replace our beast nature. The number six is the number of man and his achievements. With this being said, we can now see the significance of the number 666. It speaks of the full manifestation of the carnality of man. Can we see that God is bringing us from the carnal mind to the mind of Christ? This is our salvation process! Thank God that we are being delivered from the…

MARK OF THE BEAST!

November 27

TORMENTED IN THE PRESENCE OF THE LAMB

Revelation 14:10 states…and he shall be tormented with fire and brimstone in the presence of the holy angels, and in the presence of the Lamb…

This is quite an interesting scripture. Let us look at some of the key words in this verse and their meanings. The words "fire and brimstone" clearly speak of DIVINE PURIFICATION. This fire (which is a spiritual fire) is the fire of God Himself. Its purpose is to consume wood, hay, and stubble (the carnality in man). Remember…GOD IS A CONSUMING FIRE!

According to Louis Abbott: "There is an interesting rock used in Biblical days to test the quality of precious metals called a touchstone. It is quite unfortunate that most translations following the King James tradition have hidden the Biblical references to this stone from us. The King James Bible Concordances have also hidden its meaning. Using the Strong's or Young's Concordances, when looking up the English word "torment," we discover that the noun for one of these Greek words is basanoj "basanos," Strong's number 931. Strong's number 928 "torture," and 929 "torment" are derivatives of this noun, "basanos," which Strong's Concordance says is a "touchstone." Webster's Collegiate Dictionary 5th Edition, tells us that a touchstone is "1. A black siliceous stone allied to flint;-used to test the purity of gold and silver by the streak left on the stone when rubbed by the metal. 2. Any test or criterion by which to try a thing's quality." Those of us who dig deep enough will discover why the early believers did not see the lake of fire as a place of "eternal torment." They knew that the wording in this passage referred to a place of divine testing and not a place of "eternal torment." The Greek word for "sulfur" is qeiou "theeion" which is akin to "theos," which means god. Sulfur (brimstone) was used to purify temples in ancient days. It was also used for healing purposes. The fact that this passage of scripture speaks of "day and night" proves that "aionas ton aionon" in this passage should not have been translated "forever and ever." Divine fire will test the works of men and angels." (<u>An Analytical Study Of Words</u>, Louis Abbott)

We are now able to see that the word "torment" means testing. (A stone used to test the purity of gold.) Remember…Gold is symbolic of divinity, or that which is divine (God-like). The words "tormented" and "lake of fire and brimstone" clearly speak of a severe time of testing. This testing is for the purpose of purifying the person. The goal of God is to burn up the carnal nature in man, bringing him to the place where he is possessed by the divine nature. Notice where the testing is taking place. IN THE PRESENCE OF THE LAMB! THE VERY PRESENCE OF GOD IS A PURIFYING LAKE OF FIRE! This torment (severe testing), although severe, is not to torture the person forever, but rather, it is to correct, purify, and restore the person. It is to bring them to the place where they can embrace…

THE PRESENCE OF THE LAMB!

November 28

WHY DID JESUS DIE? / THE ATONEMENT

Romans 5:11 states…we also joy in God through our Lord Jesus Christ, by Whom we have now received the **atonement**…

The word "atonement" means: the reconciliation of humankind to God through Christ. The word "reconciliation" means: to restore to a friendly or peaceable state, at one in harmony, *at onement*, unity, and to make amends for wrong or injury. Here is a list from A. P. Adams that addresses the atonement. It addresses the question…Why did Jesus die?

According to A. P. Adams:

1. The atonement was not to satisfy God's Justice, but to reveal His Love.
2. The justice of God is not against the sinner, demanding his condemnation, but for him, insuring his salvation.
3. God is not in contrast with, much less in opposition to Christ in the atonement, but in perfect harmony and accord.
4. The atonement is not the exclusive work of Christ in order to reconcile God unto the world, but it is the work of "God in Christ" to reconcile the world unto Himself.
5. Christ does not have to plead with God in order to make Him willing to pardon the sinner, but God, by His ministers, "beseeches" (II Cor. 5:20) the sinner to make them willing to be pardoned.

6. Hence the atonement is not to propitiate God, but man; not to make God favorably disposed toward man, but to make His already existing favor known to man.

7. Christ did not die as our substitute, but as our companion and associate; not instead of man, but with him and for him.

8. Christ did not die to save us from the penalty of sin, but from sin itself.

9. Christ did not die that we might not die, but to deliver us out of a death in which we were already involved.

10. The sinner is not redeemed because he repents, but he is called upon to repent because he has been redeemed.

11. The atonement is not the cause of God's love to man, giving rise to that love, but the effect, flowing out of that love.

12. The final outcome of the atoning scheme is not a partial success, but a perfect, absolute, and universal triumph! (The Atonement, A. P. Adams)

Each one of these lofty statements carries with it a tremendous thought worthy of much meditation. As you <u>dig deep</u> (past the traditions of men) you will find every statement to be 100% correct. This is what the Bible teaches about the death of the Lord Jesus Christ. We are indebted to such a great man of God as A. P. Adams! He, in spite of having to go against the traditional teaching of his day, spoke the truth concerning the atonement. Read over each one of these statements again carefully, studying each one for the truth that it contains.

ENJOY YOUR SEARCH!

November 29

THE UNPARDONABLE SIN "<u>?</u>"

Mark 3:29 states…But he that shall blaspheme against the Holy Ghost has never forgiveness, but is in danger of eternal damnation…

According to Gary Amirault: "We have all heard of the term "the unpardonable sin." You will not find this term in the Bible, at least not in the Greek text. Some Bibles, such as the New Open Bible New American Standard puts headers into the text such as "Scribes Commit the Unpardonable Sin." These headers are not in the Greek text. They have been added by the editors of that particular translation. This is one reason why so-called "study Bibles" often are a detriment rather than a help. The Scofield Reference Bible was among the first to use such techniques. The Pre-trib Rapture teaching was greatly aided by these kinds of additions into Bibles such as Scofields. They clearly "add to the Word of God" as do most "study Bibles." (The Power Of Life And Death In A Greek Four Letter Word - Aion, Gary Amirault)

Let us take a look at what this passage is actually saying. The correct translation of this passage should read as follows: But whoever may speak evil in regard to the Holy Spirit has not forgiveness - to the age, but is in danger of age-during judgment; (Young's Literal Translation)…

Yes…This scripture definitely speaks of judgment and correction (because the Pharisees said that Jesus performed miracles by the power of Satan), but the judgment is not eternal, but age-during (of the ages, or…within the ages of time). The Greek word "aionios" should always be translated age-during (or…of the ages), but not eternal or everlasting. So…All of God's dealings with man are to be seen as within the ages of time ("aionios"). Having a knowledge of this helps us to be able to discard silly teachings such as eternal torture. God is not going to eternally torment any of His creation. He is a loving Father Who wants to correct (judge), not torture. After understanding that God's plan is a plan of ages, you can then see how that age-during judgment fits within His plan of the ages, but does not go beyond the ages.

Yes…There is a consequence for sin, but thank God that our Heavenly Father seeks to correct for the purpose of restoration, rather than subjecting someone to vindictive and endless torture. This (endless torture) could never serve any redeeming purpose!

THERE IS NO SUCH THING AS AN UNPARDONABLE SIN. REMEMBER…LOVE NEVER FAILS!

November 30

THE RAPTURE "?"

Many Christians believe in a *rapture* of the church. They teach that the body of Christ will be physically caught up into the clouds to meet the Lord in the air (literally). Let us examine this teaching to find out if it is truth or tradition. Let us also examine the scripture that is used for this doctrine to see if it is being rightly divided. We will now turn our attention to the words of J. Preston Eby…

According to J. Preston Eby: "It wasn't until the early or mid 1800's that there was any significant group of believers around the world that looked for a "rapture" of the church prior to a seven-year tribulation period. It may come as a shock to some who read these lines, but it is a fact nonetheless, that the "rapture" teaching was NOT taught by the early church, it was NOT taught by the church of the first centuries, it was NOT taught by the Reformers, IT WAS NOT TAUGHT BY ANYONE (except a couple Roman Catholic theologians) UNTIL ABOUT THE YEAR 1830! It began as a Roman Catholic invention! The Jesuit priest Ribera's writings influenced the Jesuit priest Lacunza, Lacunza influenced Irving, Irving influenced Darby, Darby influenced Scofield, Scofield and Darby influenced D. L. Moody, and Moody influenced the early PENTECOSTAL MOVEMENT. How? you ask. The Assemblies of God is today by far the largest Pentecostal denomination in the world. When the Pentecostal movement began at the turn of the century and the Assemblies of God held their first General Council in 1914 in Hot Springs, Arkansas they were a small movement and didn't have their own Publishing House. They needed Sunday School and study materials for their churches - so where do you suppose they got it? They bought it from Moody Press and had their own cover stitched on it! So what do you think the Assemblies of God people believed? They believed what Moody Bible Institute taught! This had its impact on Pentecostal theology, because in the early years there were practically NO PREMILLENIALISTS IN THE PENTECOSTAL MOVEMENT! Most of the ministers in those early days came from Presbyterian, Methodist, or other historic denominations - men who, being baptized in the Holy Spirit and leaving their denominations, joined themselves to the Assemblies of God or one of the other emerging Pentecostal denominations. That is how the Pentecostal movement became influenced and saturated with the "Secret Rapture" doctrine - by a direct chain right back to the Roman Catholic Church! And now, my friend - you know the REST OF THE STORY! "Rapture" is not a biblical word. Let all of God's people stop speaking of the "rapture." The word "rapture" is not in the scripture and is at best very misleading. If instead of the "rapture" we speak of being caught up in the spirit (Acts 8:39; II Cor. 12:2-4; Rev. 4:1-2), translated into the Kingdom (Col. 1:13), raised up into the heavenlies with Christ (Eph. 2:5-6), and caught up into the throne, the spiritual dimension of the Christ's authority, power and glory (Rev. 4:1-2; Rev. 3:21; Rev. 12:5) we will rid ourselves of much confusion and carnal delusion, and we will have a much better understanding of present spiritual realities and the immediate program of God." (Looking For His Appearing, J. Preston Eby)

Let us look at the scripture that many misinterpret and turn into a *rapture doctrine*. 1st Thessalonians 4:17 states…Then we which are alive and remain shall be caught up together with them in the clouds, to meet the Lord in the air: and so shall we ever be with the Lord…The word "rapture" is not to be found in the Bible, but it is in the dictionary. It means: a strong feeling that absorbs the mind; very great joy, lifted high in mind and spirit. It is not so much a physical catching up, but it is a spiritual catching up. The word "clouds" in 1st Thessalonians speaks of PEOPLE, not literal clouds that are in the sky. Remember…The apostle Paul referred to God's people as a GREAT **CLOUD** OF WITNESSES (Hebrews 12:1). The word "air" speaks of a place or seat of authority. Satan, at this present time, is the PRINCE OF THE POWER OF THE **AIR.** 1st Thessalonians 4:17 speaks of the **RESURRECTION**, not a *rapture*. The sons and daughters of God (the overcomers) shall come forth (at the first resurrection) with glorified bodies. They will be elevated to the place and position of THE PRINCE OF THE POWER OF THE AIR, bringing down the principalities and powers that are now in position as the prince of the power of the air. Those who have gone to be with the Lord are COMING (not going) with their glorified bodies. Then those which are alive and remain shall be caught up (put on immortality) together with them in the clouds (speaking of the great cloud of witnesses…God's people) to meet the Lord in the air (the place and position of authority that He occupies): and so shall we ever be with the Lord (we shall ever remain in complete and total oneness with Him)…

As well, it is correct to say that there is a spiritual catching up of the body of Christ going on at this present time. Remember…God has quickened us together with Christ, and has raised us up together, AND MADE US TO SIT TOGETHER IN HEAVENLY PLACES IN CHRIST JESUS (Ephesians 2:5,6)…

COMFORT ONE ANOTHER WITH THESE WORDS!

December 1

JESUS PREACHED TO THE DEAD

1ST Peter 3:18-20 states…For Christ also has once suffered for sins, the just for the unjust, that He might bring us to God, being put to death in the flesh, but quickened by the Spirit: By which also He went and preached unto the spirits in prison; Which sometime were disobedient, when once the longsuffering of God waited in the days of Noah, while the ark was a preparing, wherein few, that is, eight souls were saved by water…1st Peter 4:6 states…For this cause was the gospel preached also to them that are dead, that they might be judged according to men in the flesh, but live according to God in the spirit…Psalm 68:18 states…You have ascended on high, You have led captivity captive: You have received gifts for men; yes, **for the rebellious also**, that the LORD God might dwell among them…

According to J. Preston Eby: "It was for this very reason that Jesus Christ, after His death and resurrection, went to PREACH to the spirits in prison, the spirits of the men who had been *disobedient* in the days of Noah. To them He carried the WORD OF RECONCILIATION, showing not only that Christ had died for their sins, but that He was risen for their justification. If perchance our minds are numbed with the glory of such a thought, let us consider the words from Weymouth translation. "Christ also once for all died for sins, the innocent One for the guilty many, *in order to bring us to God*. He was put to death in the flesh, but made alive in (by) the Spirit, IN (BY) WHICH HE ALSO WENT AND P-R-E-A-C-H-E-D TO THE SPIRITS THAT WERE IN PRISON, who in former times had been *disobedient*, when God's long-suffering patiently waited in the days of Noah during the building of the ark, in which a few persons - eight in number - were brought safely through the water" (I Pet. 3:18-20). Despite the crafty and deceptive efforts of some to twist and explain away the plain meaning of this passage, it reveals that Jesus, after His death and resurrection, went and preached, not to men in the flesh, but to SPIRITS in prison; not to angels, not to Abraham, Isaac, and Jacob or any of the other Old Testament saints; but to those men who had been DISOBEDIENT to the preaching of Noah in the days preceding the flood. And what did He preach to these long-departed spirits? Well, I Pet. 4:6 certainly answers this question! This passage is only a few verses further on from the one under consideration, and as Peter continues speaking of the same subject we are informed, "For this cause was *the Gospel* preached also *to them that are dead*, that they might be judged according to men in the flesh, but *live according to God in the spirit.*" The message is clear - though these were dead, and lived on in the spirit, but not in the flesh, THE GOSPEL WAS PREACHED unto them that they might be judged, or dealt with, the same as men who were alive in the flesh. Please notice, precious friend of mine, it was not doom or gloom or judgment that was preached to these, but THE GOSPEL, the GOOD NEWS WHICH IS THE POWER OF GOD UNTO SALVATION was PREACHED even to these spirits in prison, the disobedient ones! And what was the result of such a wonderful mission? "Wherefore He says, When He ascended up on high, He LED CAPTIVITY CAPTIVE ... now He that ascended, what is it but that He also descended first into the lower parts of the earth? He that descended is the same also that ascended up far above all heavens, that HE MIGHT FILL ALL THINGS" (Eph. 4:8-10). Some suppose this leading "captivity captive" refers to the Lord at His ascension leading the Old Testament saints out of Paradise into the more immediate presence of God. The phrase is a quotation from the Old Testament, and in the two places where it occurs, on both occasions it plainly refers to the leading captive of FOES. In Judges 5:12, in the song of Deborah as she was leading the strains of a victory song after subduing the armies of Sisera, we read of her prophesying to Barak, singing, "Arise, Barak, and lead your captivity captive, you son of Abinoam." What was she speaking of? Barak went out against the armies of Sisera - he captured of the enemy, taking dominion over them with the sword - and any that were captured alive were led back captive to his own land, thus he "led that captivity captive," parading back victoriously. Who were the captives? The armies whom he had conquered! So also in the passage from which the phrase is quoted in Eph. 4:8-10. The quotation is from Ps. 68:18 where we read, "You have ascended on high, You have led captivity captive: You have received gifts for men; yea, FOR THE REBELLIOUS ALSO, THAT THE LORD GOD MIGHT DWELL AMONG THEM!" There is every suggestion here that the captives thus led were not the righteous but the unrighteous, for they are described as "rebellious." And Christ will dwell among the rebellious! What a word! What a work!" (Hell, J. Preston Eby)

Remember…NOTHING CAN SEPARATE US FROM THE LOVE OF GOD…

NOT EVEN DEATH!

December 2

THE COUNSEL OF MEN OR GOD

Acts 5:34-39 states…Then stood there up one in the council, a Pharisee, named Gamaliel, a doctor of the law, had in reputation among all the people, and commanded to put the apostles forth a little space; And said unto them, You men of Israel, take heed to yourselves what you intend to do as touching these men. For before these days rose up Theudas, boasting himself to be somebody; to whom a number of men, about four hundred, joined themselves: who was slain; and all, as many as obeyed him, were scattered, and brought to naught. After this man rose up Judas of Galilee in the days of the taxing, and drew away much people after him: he also perished; and all, even as many as obeyed him, were dispersed. And now I say unto you, Refrain from these men, and let them alone: for if this counsel or this work be of men, it will come to naught: But if it be of God, you cannot overthrow it; lest haply you be found even to fight against God…

It would do all of us good to meditate on this passage of scripture from time to time. It says one simple thing…RELAX! You don't have to try to prove God or His revelation truth to anyone. Truth can stand on its own. All it needs is a little time and it (truth) will manifest itself. A lie will come to naught, but truth cannot be overthrown. Kick back and relax, watch, and pray. THE TRUTH WILL RISE TO THE TOP! YOU DO NOT HAVE TO TRY TO FORCE IT ON PEOPLE! It does not matter whether someone believes you or not. TRUTH IS TRUTH! Let the day declare it. Let the God Who answers by fire be God!

It is not your responsibility to try to force someone to believe something that they do not believe yet. Religion (man's ideas about God) is known for trying to force itself on people, using fear to persuade people to believe whatever that particular religion or denomination believes. GET AWAY FROM THAT MINDSET! GOD IS NOT LIKE THAT. He is patient with all of us. Just wait and watch. If it is of men, it will fail. If it is of God, YOU CANNOT OVERTHROW IT! We are far too quick to judge things, not waiting to see whether or not it is of God or men. STUDY, WAIT, WATCH, AND PRAY. Remember…If it is of God…

YOU CANNOT OVERTHROW IT!

December 3

THE SERVANT OF THE LORD

2ND Timothy 2:24,25 states…And the servant of the Lord must not strive; but be gentle unto all men, apt to teach, patient, In meekness instructing those that oppose themselves; if God peradventure will give them repentance to the acknowledging of the truth…

This passage of scripture gives us the definition of a true servant. It says that a true servant of the Lord must…

1. NOT STRIVE (fight)
2. BE GENTLE (placid, mild, easy, compliant)
3. BE APT TO TEACH (communicate by teaching)
4. BE PATIENT (to endure evil)
5. HAVE MEEKNESS (not weakness, but controlled strength)
6. BE INSTRUCTING (to train, chastise, chasten)

We must seek the face of God for these qualities. These qualities are part of God's divine nature that He will impart to us as we partake of Who He is. Notice the behavior that should accompany the servant of the Lord. It is a laying down of our lives, which results in us being a demonstration of the life of Christ. Most Christians pride themselves on their ability to debate, argue, and cram the gospel down the throats of their listeners. They never seem to realize that they are pushing people away. WE MUST LEARN HOW TO PRESENT THE REAL JESUS AND HIS TRUE GOSPEL TO THE WORLD! It is not so much what we say, but it is how we present and say what it is we are speaking.

Do not be conformed to the organized church and its methods of using fear, debating, force, impatience, pride (ego), and the traditions of men to reach people. BE A SERVANT OF THE LORD! As these attributes are developed in you, you will be able to lead people into the truth of God and into true repentance. What we need are more servants, not "hotshot" preachers out of Bible college who want to prove to the world how great they are. LET GOD CRUSH YOU!

BE A SERVANT!

December 4

WE ARE GOD'S WORKMANSHIP

Ephesians 2:10 states…For we are His workmanship, created in Christ Jesus unto good works, which God has before ordained that we should walk in them…

Let us grasp this great truth, for this is the purpose and plan of God. This truth is the theme of the entire Bible. Ephesians 2:10 is in harmony with Genesis 1:26, which states…And God said, Let Us make man in Our image, after Our likeness: and let them have dominion over the fish of the sea, and over the fowl of the air, and over the cattle, and over all the earth, and over every creeping thing that creeps upon the earth…

This is the very reason that God subjected the creation to vanity, not willingly. As a result of this, God is the potter, and we are His clay. WE ARE HIS WORKMANSHIP! He lowered us into this realm that He might work on us, causing us to learn of Him. The result is…OUR LATTER END WILL BE GREATER THAN OUR FORMER!

The word "workmanship" means handiwork. You must see yourself as the handiwork of God. HE IS WORKING ON YOU AND IT IS A PROCESS! It is called **salvation**. Why is He working on you? So that you might become like Him. For what? So that you might have dominion. For what? TO SET THE CREATION FREE! For what? So that God will become ALL IN ALL! This is the end goal of God…THAT HE MAY BE ALL IN ALL (1ˢᵗ Corinthians 15:22-28).

Most Christians are involved in "trying to do a work for God" rather than realizing that they are God's workmanship. You must come to the sobering fact that you cannot *do a work for God*! There is nothing that we can do for Him. HE HAS ALREADY ESTABLISHED HIS PLAN OF THE AGES. WE MUST GET IN WHAT HE IS DOING! Get in the flow of what God is doing, which is to allow Him to work on you, changing your nature from Adam to Christ. Many people are so busy trying to *work for God*, looking for a position in "full-time ministry", that they are not even walking with God. Read the story of Cain and Abel. Cain offered God the work of his hands rather than letting God work on him. The Kingdom of God is not what work that you have accomplished for Him, but rather, it is allowing Him to work His righteousness, peace, and joy into your heart and life. Remember…As the clay is in the potter's hand…

SO ARE WE IN HIS HAND!

December 5

JOB

Job 1:8 states…The Lord said unto Satan, Have you considered My servant Job…Well…Have YOU considered the story of Job? There is much that we can learn from his story. This story shows us Who God is and who man is. It also shows us who Satan is. It gives us a sneak peek into the spirit world.

The story of Job could be looked at as a parable of God's dealings with the whole creation. We must see ourselves as Job. We must also see that God is the One Who initiated the testing of Job. Finally, we must see that the testing of Job was for a specific purpose. It was to cause his latter end to be greater than his former.

Notice Who was responsible for bringing all the evil upon Job. IT WAS THE LORD HIMSELF! THE LORD SAID UNTO SATAN, HAVE YOU CONSIDERED MY SERVANT JOB…As well, read Job 42:11. It speaks of…**ALL THE EVIL THAT THE LORD HAD BROUGHT UPON JOB…**It is imperative that we understand that GOD IS IN CONTROL OF EVERYTHING! GOD CREATED GOOD AND EVIL (AND IS IN CHARGE OF IT)! Most Christians think that God is fighting against Satan, not realizing that God created evil for a purpose. Once you understand that God is sovereign, you will mature tremendously in the Kingdom of God. We must grasp and understand that the story of Job parallels the story of the entire creation. The Lord has subjected the creation to vanity, exposing it to good and evil. This is done for the purpose of dealing with us. God uses good and evil to cause us to learn of Him. As well, He uses good and evil to chastise and correct us. The Lord has turned Satan loose on us, bringing evil on us. WHY? The answer is to be found in Job 42:1-12.

Job 42:1-12 states…Then Job answered the LORD, and said, I know that You can do every thing, and that no thought can be withheld from You. Who is he that hides counsel without knowledge? therefore have I uttered that I understood not; things too wonderful for me, which I knew not. Hear, I beseech You, and I will speak: I will demand of You, and declare Yourself unto me. **I have heard of You by the hearing of the ear: but now my eye sees You. Wherefore I abhor myself, and repent in dust and ashes.** And it was so, that after the LORD had spoken these words unto Job, the LORD said to Eliphaz the Temanite, My wrath is kindled against you, and against your two friends: for you have not spoken of Me the thing that is right, as My servant Job has. Therefore take unto you now seven bullocks and seven rams, and go to My servant Job, and offer up for yourselves a burnt offering; and My servant Job shall pray for you: for him will I accept: lest I deal with you after your folly, in that you have not spoken of Me the thing which is right, like My servant Job. So Eliphaz the Temanite and Bildad the Shuhite and Zophar the Naamathite went, and did according as the LORD commanded them: the LORD also accepted Job. And the LORD turned the captivity of Job, when he prayed for his friends: also **the LORD gave Job twice as much as he had before.** Then came there unto him all his brethren, and all his sisters, and all they that had been of his acquaintance before, and did eat bread with him in his house: **and they bemoaned him, and comforted him over all the evil that the LORD had brought upon him**: every man also gave him a piece of money, and every one an earring of gold. **So the LORD blessed the latter end of Job more than his beginning**: for he had fourteen thousand sheep, and six thousand camels, and a thousand yoke of oxen, and a thousand she asses…

As we can see, the goal of God for the creation is to cause it to SEE (UNDERSTAND) HIM! God is not "out to get us", but rather, He is using good and evil to bring us to a higher place in Him. The latter end of the creation (every person and everything) shall be greater than its beginning.

TO GOD BE THE GLORY!

December 6

FIRE - PART 1

FIRE: *heat and light evolved by ignition and combustion; intensity of feeling; ardor; spirit; severe trial and affliction.* (Webster)

According to Gary Amirault: "Let us see what the scriptures say about this fire which is both heat and light. Heb. 12:28,29 says, "Wherefore we receiving a Kingdom which cannot be moved, let us have grace whereby we may serve God acceptably with reverence and godly fear; **for our God is a consuming fire**. Now a consuming fire is one that consumes or burns up something. And that is what our God is. Don't forget it. Then is it any wonder that when He appears in His mighty messengers (myriads of Himself) He comes with consuming fire to destroy all flesh (carnality within us)? These mighty messengers of Himself are a part of that same fire. Heb. 1:7 says, "And of the angels He says, 'Who makes His ministers a flame of fire.'" The original Greek renders it this way: "And with respect to the angels, indeed He says, 'It is He Who makes His angels winds, and His ministering servants a flame of fire.'" (ed. note: I again corrected the English to the correct words of Benjamin Wilson, author of this Greek text. Another note, there is no "Original Greek.") David said of God, "Who makes His angels spirits; His ministers a flaming fire." Ps.104:4. Now we see that God Himself is a consuming fire, and His ministers are also like a fire. Let us now see what He says about the very Word He speaks. "Is not My Word like as a fire? says the Lord." Jer. 23:29. Again He says, "Wherefore thus says the Lord God of hosts, because you speak this word, behold, I will make MY WORDS IN YOUR MOUTH FIRE, and this people wood, and it shall devour them." Jer. 5:14. God is fire; His ministers are fire, and His Word is fire! With all this fire there must be something that needs to be burned before God can have a people after His own nature and likeness." (His Coming In Flaming Fire, Gary Amirault)

How refreshing it is to let the Bible define fire for us. It is much better than listening to man's ideas about what they think it means or represents. Our next effort will be to turn our attention to the difference between natural and spiritual fire, for there is a difference. Once we understand the spiritual fire of God we will no longer be afraid of God's fire, but we will welcome it, for it is the very thing that...

MAKES US IN HIS IMAGE!

December 7

FIRE - PART 2

FIRE: NATURAL AND SPIRITUAL

According to Dr. Harold Lovelace: "Check again in your Concordance, and you will find that the verses that read "Holy Ghost and fire", "hell fire", "unquenchable fire", "ministers a flame of fire", "fiery indignation", "God is a consuming fire", "lake of fire and brimstone" and "the overcomers stand on a sea of glass mingled with fire". These terms are all from the same Greek word #4442, "pur". **Therefore it is the same fire in all these places.** Now notice that in Mark 14:54 when Peter warmed himself by a fire, it is a different Greek word." (<u>Read And Search God's Plan</u>, Dr. Harold Lovelace)

This proves that the Bible makes a clear distinction between natural and spiritual fire. When the Bible speaks of God applying fire to the lives of people, whether now or in future ages to come, it is referring to a spiritual fire. This is speaking of God Himself, Who is a consuming fire! For example, when Peter spoke of going through fiery trials in 1st Peter 1:7 and 1st Peter 4:12 he was obviously teaching us about having the spiritual fire of God applied to our lives. It is common sense to know that when a person goes through a fiery trial that he or she is not literally on fire. As well, 1st Corinthians 3:13 tells us that God's fire shall try the believers work of what sort it is. Once again, this fire is the (spiritual) consuming fire of God Himself. God does not need to or want to burn anyone in literal (natural) fire for the purpose of torturing them. THAT WOULD BE INSANE! As a matter of fact, IT HAS NEVER ENTERED HIS MIND! At a point in Israel's history, they burned their children, making them pass through the fire unto the false god Molech. The scripture goes on to say that God did not command them to do that, NEITHER DID IT EVEN COME INTO HIS MIND, THAT THEY SHOULD DO THIS ABOMINATION, TO CAUSE JUDAH TO SIN (Jeremiah 32:35). This is concrete evidence that God is not interested in burning people in literal (natural) fire.

Our next effort will be to look at the purpose of this spiritual fire in our lives. If God is a consuming fire, and the Bible speaks so much about fire, then there is obviously something in man that needs to be burned before God can have a people after His own nature and likeness. It is actually impossible for man to become like God without going through His consuming fire. If God is a consuming fire, and His goal is to make us like He is, then we must go through the fire!

FOR OUR GOD IS A CONSUMING FIRE!

December 8

FIRE - PART 3

THE PURPOSE OF FIRE

According to J. Preston Eby: "The word "BURN" means combustion, or to consume. To "consume" does not mean to annihilate, for there is no such thing as annihilation in the absolute sense. When fire consumes a log in your fireplace it does not destroy any of the elements within the log, it merely *changes their form*. "Combustion" is the process by which chemicals combine to form new chemicals. For example: a tree might be cut down, sawed into fire wood, and burned. When the wood is burning the heat causes the chemicals of which the wood is composed to vaporize, mixing with the oxygen in the air to form new chemicals, including water and the gas carbon dioxide. So what was formerly a tree is no longer identified as the form of a tree, but the substance thereof is now simply CHANGED into a DIFFERENT FORM and exists in its new form within the atmosphere as water, carbon dioxide, etc. Thus, to "burn", means to CHANGE. Furthermore, it is interesting to note that fire does not burn down; it always burns up; it seeks the highest level. And all that it consumes "goes up in smoke," to exist in a new form in a higher dimension. Even if you take a pan of water and place it over a fire, before long the water will take on the property of the fire and will begin to go up in steam. To "burn" means to CHANGE, and the change is always UPWARD in its motion. "FIRE" is the heat and light that you feel and see when something burns. It takes heat to start a fire, but once the fire is started it produces heat that keeps the process going. Thus, fire is really HEAT and LIGHT." (The Lake Of Fire, J. Preston Eby)

With this in mind, we are now able to see the purpose of God's consuming fire in our lives. This spiritual fire (that comes from God) is for the purpose of consuming and destroying the man of sin that is within us. God's fire works (within us) to consume our wood, hay, and stubble. He burns up our old nature (the propensity within us to sin) by the brightness of His coming (presence). In turn, HIS FIRE CHANGES US FROM ONE FORM TO ANOTHER. The more we begin to understand the purpose of God's fire, the less we fear it. It is absolutely necessary for every person to go through GOD'S CONSUMING AND PURIFYING LAKE OF FIRE, for in the fire we are CHANGED from glory to glory. We are changed into…

THE IMAGE OF GOD!

December 9

FIRE - PART 4

THE FIERY LAW

According to Dr. Stephen Jones: "In the case of the Great White Throne in Daniel and Revelation, God judges all men according to His own law. The "fire" that proceeds from the throne is the judgment of the divine law according to their works. A common view is that this "fire" is literal and that it will last forever on the grounds that the people will be immortal and fireproof, but will be able to experience pain. Others say that the fire is literal, but that it will simply "burn up" (annihilate) the sinners. In both of these views, God metes out punishment, but *justice* itself is not done. Our view is taken from the divine law itself, for this is how God defines justice. Nowhere does one find in the divine law a provision for burning anyone *alive* for ANY sin. The only use of fire found in the law is where a dead body might be burned (cremated) for the purpose of preventing an honorable burial. In Daniel 7, we see that the fire comes from the throne, which is a universal symbol of law and authority to judge the people. Deuteronomy 33:2, 3 (KJV) says, **And he said, The Lord came from Sinai, and rose up from Seir unto Paran, and He came with ten thousands of saints; <u>from His right hand went a fiery law</u>** [Heb. *"esh dath"*] **for them,** Yea, He

loved the people; <u>all His saints are in Your hand</u>; and they sat down at Your feet; every one shall receive of Your words. Note that it is not merely the law, but a "fiery law." *"Esh"* is the Hebrew word for fire, and *"dath"* means decree, command, or law. Take special note also that this law is said to come from His right hand—and then it says that *"all His saints are in His hand."* As we will show later, His saints are the ones called to administer the law, because they are the ones in whose hearts the divine law is written. That is why both the law and His saints are identified as being in the hand of God. But for now it is enough to see that the law itself is characterized as FIRE." (<u>The Judgments Of The Divine Law</u>, Dr. Stephen Jones)

When we speak of the law, we are of course speaking of the spirit of the law that is being written on our hearts. This is being accomplished as we learn to partake of God's divine nature. The letter of the law was kept and fulfilled alone by the Lord Jesus Christ. God's law is now applied by His Holy Spirit to our hearts and lives. This is what is taking place in the believer's life. This is what it means to be baptized with the...

HOLY GHOST AND FIRE (THE FIERY LAW)!

December 10

FIRE - PART 5

UNQUENCHABLE FIRE

According to Lloyd Ellefson: "In Mark 9:43-44, Jesus states, "...than having your two hands, to go into Gehenna, into the unquenchable fire, where their worm does not die, and the fire is not quenched." An unquenchable fire is not an eternal fire; it is a fire which cannot be put out. It will continue to burn until it has accomplished its purpose. This fire will do the work it was sent to do! Jer. 17:27 says that God will kindle a fire in the gates of Jerusalem which will devour the palaces and it shall not be quenched. However, we know it is not burning in Jerusalem at the present time. It has done its work." (<u>Fire: Natural And Spiritual</u>, Lloyd Ellefson)

According to Otis Skinner: "*Unquenchable fire*. This term is thus used by Jeremiah -- But if you will not hearken unto me, ... then will I kindle a fire in the gates thereof, and it shall devour the palaces of Jerusalem, and it shall not be quenched." -- (Jer. 17:27) Here we have the phrase -- *not be quenched*. But the fire to which it refers ceased to burn when the temple at Jerusalem was consumed. The term, therefore, does not imply endless burning. *Worm dies not*. Isaiah thus uses this expression -- "And they shall go forth and look upon the carcasses of the men that have transgressed against me; for their worm shall not die, neither shall their fire be quenched; and they shall be an abhorring unto all flesh." -- (Isa. 66:24) Here the prophet alludes to the worms which preyed upon the dead carcasses, that were left unburied in the Valley of Hinnom, when Jerusalem was destroyed. Those worms were not more than any of our own day; and were said to die not, because worms were always preying there. The expression, therefore, does not denote endless suffering." (<u>The Doctrine Of Endless Misery Not Taught In The Bible</u>, Otis Skinner)

As we can see, "unquenchable fire" (whether in the natural or the spiritual) does not denote endless fire, but rather, it speaks of a fire which CANNOT BE PUT OUT "UNTIL" IT HAS ACCOMPLISHED ITS PURPOSE! This is the consuming fire of God. His fire is UNQUENCHABLE. The next time you find yourself in the midst of a fiery trial, please understand that your trial is the very unquenchable fire of Almighty God. It cannot and will not be put out "until" it has served its purifying purpose. Thank God for His...

UNQUENCHABLE FIRE!

December 11

FIRE - PART 6

THE LAKE OF FIRE

According to J. Preston Eby: "In my study of the lake that burns with fire and brimstone I was very much helped and impressed by the understanding given by Charles Pridgeon and I would like to quote from his scholarly work on the subject of "BRIMSTONE". He says: "The Lake of Fire and Brimstone signifies a fire burning with brimstone; the word 'brimstone' or 'sulphur' defines the character of the fire. The Greek word "THEION" translated 'brimstone' is exactly the same word "THEION" which means 'divine.' Sulphur was sacred to the deity among the ancient Greeks; and was used to fumigate, to purify, and to cleanse and consecrate to the deity; for this purpose they burned it in their incense. In Homer's *Iliad* (16:228), one is spoken of as purifying a goblet with fire and brimstone. The verb derived from "THEION" is "THEIOO", which means to hallow, to make divine, or to dedicate to a god (See Liddell and Scott *Greek-English Lexicon*, 1897 Edition). **To any Greek, or any trained in the Greek language, a 'lake of fire and brimstone' would mean a 'lake of divine purification.'** The idea of judgment need not be excluded. Divine purification and divine consecration are the plain meaning in ancient Greek. In the ordinary explanation, this fundamental meaning of the word is entirely left out, and nothing but eternal torment is associated with it" -end quote. I realize that the above thoughts define the subject very briefly, but let us summarize the meanings thus: "BURN" means combustion; to change the form of. "FIRE" means heat and light. "BRIMSTONE" means divine. Putting these three together can we not see that the lake burning with fire and brimstone is, actually, **DIVINE HEAT AND LIGHT PRODUCING A CHANGE!** Is such a process eternal? All the laws of nature shout that it is not! More than 2500 years ago the Holy Spirit warned the wicked inhabitants of Jerusalem that God would kindle a fire at Jerusalem's gates which would devour her palaces. "But if you will not hearken unto Me... then will I kindle a fire in the gates thereof, and it shall devour the palaces of Jerusalem, and it shall *not he quenched*" (Jer. 17:27). Did not God say this fire "shall NOT BE QUENCHED?" This prophecy was fulfilled and the fire did occur a few years later and it did destroy all the houses of Jerusalem (Jer. 52:13). Since God said no person or thing would "quench" this fire, did that mean that it would *burn for ever*? Since it accomplished the work it was sent to do, and since it is NOT BURNING TODAY, it obviously went out *by itself* after accomplishing its purpose! **Unquenchable fire is not eternal fire - it is simply fire that cannot be put out until it has consumed or changed everything it is possible for it to change! It then simply goes out, for there is nothing more to burn.** Yet I hear the preachers ranting and raving about poor souls being cast into hell fire where "their worm dies not, and the fire is not quenched" and this, we are told, means eternal, unending torment. How foolish, illogical, and *deceptive*! Such a view contradicts the plain meaning of the term "unquenchable" and its use in the Word of God. Suppose a few filthy, vile men and a few immoral women from some house of prostitution were *forced to sit* in the midst of a large congregation of singing, shouting, worshipping saints. *This certainly would be torment to most of them.* They would be tortured in the flames of the blazing glory of God in that place! If they were not held in their seats *by force*, most of them would rush out of there. I have been in meetings where I witnessed three responses to the glorious manifestation of the Lord's presence. First, the saints who loved the Lord rejoiced and adoringly worshipped. Some who were not Christians, but whose hearts were tender toward the Lord, came under deep conviction and, weeping and broken, gave themselves into the loving hands of Jesus. But others, filled with self, haters of righteousness, I have seen jump up and literally *run* out of a meeting - TORMENTED IN THE PRESENCE OF THE LAMB! Sure, they would rush, even run to get away from the convicting power of the Holy Ghost! I have seen it, and so have you. **To the unsaved, HIS GLORY is a LAKE OF FIRE AND BRIMSTONE - divine, cleansing, purging, purifying, consuming fire!** In ages yet unborn God shall expose ALL MEN to the sweet abiding presence of the Lamb. They will come under such severe processings, under such profound conviction that they will be tormented and have no rest day or night until they finally yield. And when they do, many fountains of tears will flow with weeping, praying, and calling upon the Lord." (The Lake Of Fire, J. Preston Eby)

As we can see, the words "lake of fire and brimstone" mean: DIVINE PURIFICATION! Daniel saw it as a stream and John saw it as a lake. Can we now see that the words "lake of fire and brimstone" are to be understood symbolically, portraying a spiritual fire that is by nature corrective, and for the purpose of purification? This lake of fire speaks of God Himself and His ministers, for our God IS a consuming fire, making His ministers a flaming fire (Hebrews 12:29 and Psalm 104:4).

This experience of purification is to be for a period of time. IT IS NOT FOREVER! This can be discovered by studying the words "olam", "aion", and "aionios", which words do show that God's judgments are "of the ages", but not to continue past the ages, for the ages shall come to an end, and God shall be ALL IN ALL! -OUR GOD IS A CONSUMING FIRE!-

THANK GOD FOR HIS GLORIOUS LAKE OF FIRE!

December 12

FIRE - PART 7

HIS MINISTERS A FLAMING FIRE

Psalm 104:4 states…Who makes His angels spirits; **His ministers a flaming fire**…

What beautiful words! The Lord describes His ministers as FLAMING FIRE! What a privilege it is to be referred to as flaming fire, for God Himself is referred to as a CONSUMING FIRE. The words "flaming fire" tell us that His ministers are becoming a part of the very consuming fire that HE IS. Remember…God is a consuming fire, His Word (law) is fire, AND HIS MINISTERS ARE A FLAMING FIRE!

Let us realize the importance of what this means. This signifies that His ministers are to play a part in BURNING UP the works of the flesh and delivering the entire creation. In essence, we become a part of His consuming fire. God's fiery love will flow through us for the purpose of reconciliation, judgment, and correction. This can be seen in 2nd Thessalonians 1:7-10. It states (The Emphasized Bible)…And, unto you that are afflicted, release, with us, - by the revealing of the Lord Jesus from heaven, with **His messengers of power, In a fiery flame**; holding forth vengeance - against them that refuse to know God, and them who decline to hearken unto the glad-message of our Lord Jesus, Who, indeed, a penalty, shall pay - age-abiding destruction from the face of the Lord and from the glory of His might - **When He shall come, to be made all-glorious in His saints**, and to be marveled at in all who believed, - because our witness unto you was believed, - in that day…

This tells us that it is God's goal to be revealed to the earth in FLAMING FIRE IN HIS SAINTS! The saints of God will actually be the ones to show forth the nature of Almighty God. His ministers will be as flames of fire, BURNING UP the powers of darkness, the works of the flesh, and the confusion of the organized church. They shall (through judgment) release the nations from the carnal mind, which has held them captive for so long. As well, they will execute judgment upon all, taking vengeance on them that know not God. This judgment and vengeance will be for the purpose of correction, not eternal banishment. Although this sounds bad to the carnal mind, as though God is mad at the world, IT IS ACTUALLY WHAT THE ENTIRE CREATION IS GROANING FOR! The apostle Paul referred to this event as the MANIFESTATION OF THE SONS OF GOD! Because the creation itself also shall be DELIVERED from the bondage of corruption into the glorious liberty of the…

CHILDREN OF GOD (HIS FLAMES OF FIRE)!

December 13

THE TWO LIONS

The Bible teaches us that we are being pursued. Not only are we being pursued, but we are being pursued by a lion. In fact, we are being pursued by TWO LIONS. There is obviously no way to escape. Let us look at these two lions and try to pinpoint the purpose of each one.

1st Peter 5:8 states…Be sober, be vigilant; because your adversary **the devil, as a roaring lion**, walks about, seeking whom he may devour…Revelation 5:5 states…And one of the elders said unto me, Weep not: behold, **the Lion of the tribe of Judah, the Root of David**, has prevailed to open the book, and to loose the seven seals thereof…So…There you have it. There are two lions in pursuit of us. They are: THE ROARING LION (THE DEVIL) AND THE LION OF THE TRIBE OF JUDAH (JESUS).

It is said of the roaring lion that he comes to devour. It is said of the Lion of the tribe of Judah that He has prevailed. Matthew 13:3,4 states…And He spoke many things unto them in parables, saying, Behold, a sower went forth to sow; And when he sowed, some seeds fell by the way side, and the fowls came and **devoured** them up…Matthew 13:19 states…When any one hears the word of the kingdom, and understands it not, then comes **the wicked one, and catches away that which was sown in his heart**. This is he which received seed by the way side…John 10:10 states…The thief comes not, but for to steal, and to kill, and to destroy: I am come that they might have life, and that they might have it more abundantly…

So as we can see, the roaring lion comes to devour the life of God, and the Lion of the tribe of Judah comes to bring us into the abundant life of God. So…GOD HAS TRAPPED US BETWEEN TWO LIONS! As we come to an understanding of the purpose of evil, and that God created all things, we will see that the roaring lion is part of God's purpose. THE ROARING LION IS THE VERY THING THAT DRIVES US INTO THE HANDS OF THE LION OF THE TRIBE OF JUDAH! No matter what man does he will come face to face with one of these two lions. One devours life and the other gives life. That which the roaring lion comes to devour is the carnality within man. That is his meat. When we learn not to depend on the carnal mind, we have passed from death to life. Hence, IT IS THE ROARING LION THAT CAUSES US TO SEE OUR NEED FOR THE LION OF THE TRIBE OF JUDAH.

IN HIM (JESUS) WE PREVAIL!

December 14

THE FEASTS OF THE LORD - PART 1

According to Dr. Stephen Jones: "When God led Israel out of Egypt into the wilderness and into the Promised Land, He instituted various holidays, or "feast days" to commemorate important events. The three main feast days are Passover, Pentecost, and Tabernacles. Passover commemorates Israel's departure from Egypt; Pentecost commemorates the day God descended upon Mt. Sinai to give Israel the Law; Tabernacles commemorates the time Israel was supposed to cross the Jordan and enter the Promised Land. It is very important that Christians study these feast days in detail, because they reveal the plan of God for the entire earth on a grand scale. They also reveal the plan of salvation on the individual level. The story written by Moses is not only history, but also is a great allegorical novel by which we can know the mind of God." (<u>The Barley Overcomers</u>, Dr. Stephen Jones)

It will be our goal in this short study to show that these GREAT FEASTS OF THE LORD symbolize and point to something FAR GREATER than just the feast itself. Exodus 23:14-17 states...Three times you shall keep a feast unto Me in the year. You shall keep the feast of unleavened bread: (you shall eat unleavened bread seven days, as I commanded you, in the time appointed of the month Abib; for in it you came out from Egypt: and none shall appear before Me empty:) And the feast of harvest, the firstfruits of your labors, which you have sown in the field: and the feast of ingathering, which is in the end of the year, when you have gathered in your labors out of the field. Three times in the year all your males shall appear before the LORD God...

There are actually seven feasts that the people of Israel celebrated. They are to be found in Leviticus 23:1-37. They are: THE FEAST OF THE SABBATH, THE FEAST OF UNLEAVENED BREAD (PASSOVER), THE FEAST OF FIRSTFRUITS, THE FEAST OF WEEKS (PENTECOST), THE FEAST OF TRUMPETS, THE FEAST (DAY) OF ATONEMENT, AND THE FEAST OF TABERNACLES.

Each one of these feasts represents and symbolizes the **process** of salvation that God brings the individual through, as well as the entire creation. For the time being we will focus our attention on the three main feasts, which are PASSOVER, PENTECOST, AND TABERNACLES. These three great feasts portray the salvation of our spirit, soul, and body on the individual level, and also represent the entire creation coming to God in three harvests, which are to be described as: 1. A remnant in this age...2. The nations in the coming age...3. The rest of the creation (including all things) in the Age of the Ages (the dispensation of the fullness of times)...

THESE ARE GOD'S THREE GREAT LOVE FEASTS!

December 15

THE FEASTS OF THE LORD - PART 2

PASSOVER

According to Dr. Stephen Jones: "On the personal level, the story of Israel in the wilderness gives us the three steps toward full salvation. Step one is revealed by the Feast of Passover. When a man's faith is placed in God through Christ, the "Lamb of God," he is said to become a Christian. He is "justified" by faith in the blood of the Lamb (Christ). This is why Jesus had to die on the cross at the Feast of Passover. He was the true Passover Lamb." (The Barley Overcomers, Dr. Stephen Jones)

According to Easton's Bible Dictionary: "Passover: The name given to the chief of the three great historical annual festivals of the Jews. It was kept in remembrance of the Lord's passing over the houses of the Israelites (Exo 12:13) when the first born of all the Egyptians were destroyed. It is called also the "Feast of Unleavened Bread" (Exo 23:15; Mar 14:1; Act 12:3), because during its celebration no leavened bread was to be eaten or even kept in the household (Exo 12:15). The word afterwards came to denote the lamb that was slain at the feast (Mar 14:12; Col 5:7). A detailed account of the institution of this feast is given in Ex. 12 and 13. It was afterwards incorporated in the ceremonial law (Lev 23:4) as one of the great festivals of the nation. In after times many changes seem to have taken place as to the mode of its celebration as compared with its first celebration (Compare Deu 16:2, Deu 16:5, Deu 16:6; 2ⁿᵈ Chr 30:16; Lev 23:10; Num 9:10, Num 9:11; Num 28:16). Again, the use of wine (Luk 22:17, Luk 22:20), of sauce with the bitter herbs (Joh 13:26), and the service of praise were introduced. There is recorded only one celebration of this feast between the Exodus and the entrance into Canaan, namely, that mentioned in Num 9:5. (See JOSIAH.) It was primarily a commemorative ordinance, reminding the children of Israel of their deliverance out of Egypt; but it was, no doubt, also a type of the great deliverance wrought by the Messiah for all his people from the doom of death on account of sin, and from the bondage of sin itself, a worse than Egyptian bondage (Col 5:7; Joh 1:29; Joh 19:32; 1ˢᵗ Pet 1:19; Gal 4:4, Gal 4:5)." (Easton's Bible Dictionary)

As was stated, this great Feast of Passover has a spiritual meaning for us today. It represents the first step in our salvation process. This feast is applied to our lives when we place our faith in God through Christ, "the LAMB of God". It speaks of our CALLING ON THE NAME OF THE LORD, BECOMING A CHRISTIAN, THE SALVATION OF OUR SPIRIT, AND OF OUR JUSTIFICATION.

According to Dr. Stephen Jones: "Most Christians are aware that there is more to the Christian life than justification. Just as Israel had a long way to go before entering the Promised Land, so also the justified Christian has a long way to go before attaining to the full promise of God. And yet, the Christian life is too often explained purely as a New Testament teaching, without tying it to the foundation of the Old Testament which God carefully established in His dealings with Israel. For this reason, some teach that once they are justified by faith, there is very little more to do except to try to get others saved. This is comparable to an Israelite coming out of Egypt, and then remaining on the shores of the Red Sea trying to coax more people to come out of Egypt. While one should indeed witness to people, Christians must see that their justification does not mean that they are already in the Promised Land." (The Barley Overcomers, Dr. Stephen Jones)

With this in mind, let us be thankful for the Feast of Passover, but let us not stop there. Let us go on to the…

FEAST OF PENTECOST!

December 16

THE FEASTS OF THE LORD - PART 3

PENTECOST

According to Dr. Stephen Jones: "One must go beyond Egypt and beyond the Red Sea (baptism) to Sinai, where Pentecost is experienced. This is the place of the infilling of the Holy Spirit. It is the place where we learn obedience and where the Law of God is written on our hearts. It is the place where we come to know God not only as Savior, but also as a King to be obeyed. Unfortunately, many who claim a Pentecostal experience seem to treat it purely as a New Testament phenomenon, not knowing that this feast has its roots in the giving of the Law at Mt. Sinai. As a result, many who deem themselves Pentecostal by experience think they have been given a license to be lawless and can violate any of the divine laws with immunity, so long as their lawlessness is done in "love." They often taught that love somehow replaced the law of God, instead of seeing that love is defined by the law and is therein expressed." (The Barley Overcomers, Dr. Stephen Jones)

According to Easton's Bible Dictionary: "Pentecost: i.e., "fiftieth", found only in the New Testament (Acts 2:1; 20:16; 1 Cor. 16:8). The festival so named is first spoken of in Ex. 23:16 as "the Feast of Harvest," and again in Ex. 34:22 as "the Day of the Firstfruits" (Num. 28:26). From the sixteenth of the month of Nisan (the second day of the Passover), seven complete weeks, i.e., forty-nine days, were to be reckoned, and this feast was held on the fiftieth day. The manner in which it was to be kept is described in Lev. 23:15-19; Num. 28:27-29. Besides the sacrifices prescribed for the occasion, every one was to bring to the Lord his "tribute of a free-will offering" (Deut. 16:9-11). The purpose of this feast was to commemorate the completion of the grain harvest. Its distinguishing feature was the offering of "two leavened loaves" made from the new corn of the completed harvest, which, with two lambs, were waved before the Lord as a thank offering. The day of Pentecost is noted in the Christian Church as the day on which the Spirit descended upon the apostles, and on which, under Peter's preaching, so many thousands were converted in Jerusalem (Acts 2)." (Easton's Bible Dictionary)

According to Dr. Stephen Jones: "What good is one's Pentecostal experience if the Christian refuses to be led by the Spirit and learn obedience? What good is the Pentecostal experience if the Christian refuses to have the law of God written on his heart? Jesus says that if the Christian remains lawless, He will tell them in the end, "Depart from Me." There will probably be many surprised Christians in that day. This does not mean that those Christians will lose their salvation. But they will indeed lose the blessing of the first resurrection and will have to await the second at the Great White Throne. Furthermore, many who have truly gone beyond the Red Sea and have experienced Pentecost are told that they have attained the "full gospel." This view is comparable to Israel refusing to move away from Mt. Sinai to go to the Promised Land. There is really no *full gospel* until one goes beyond Pentecost and learns the principles of the Feast of Tabernacles." (The Barley Overcomers, Dr. Stephen Jones)

Let us realize the importance of the personal…

APPLICATION OF PENTECOST!

December 17

THE FEASTS OF THE LORD - PART 4

TABERNACLES

According to Easton's Bible Dictionary: "**Tabernacles, Feast of:** the third of the great annual festivals of the Jews (Lev. 23:33-43). It is also called the "Feast of Ingathering" (Ex. 23:16; Deut. 16:13). It was celebrated immediately after the harvest, in the month Tisri, and the celebration lasted for eight days (Lev. 23:33-43). During that period the people left their homes and lived in booths formed of the branches of trees. The sacrifices offered at this time are mentioned in Num. 29:13-38. It was at the time of this feast that Solomon's temple was dedicated (1 Kings 8:2). Mention is made of it after the return from the Captivity. This feast was designed (1) to be a memorial of the wilderness wanderings, when the people dwelt in booths (Lev. 23:43), and (2) to be a harvest thanksgiving (Neh. 8:9-18). The Jews, at a later time, introduced two appendages to the original festival, viz., (1) that of drawing water from the Pool of Siloam, and pouring it upon the altar (John 7:2, 37), as a memorial of the water from the rock in Horeb; and (2) of lighting the lamps at night, a memorial of the pillar of fire by night during their wanderings. "The Feast of Tabernacles, the harvest festival of the Jewish Church, was the most popular and important festival after the Captivity. At Jerusalem it was a gala day. It was to the autumn pilgrims, who arrived on the 14th (of the month Tisri, the feast beginning on the 15th) day, like entrance into a silvan city. Roofs and courtyards, streets and squares, roads and gardens, were green with boughs of citron and myrtle, palm and willow. The booths recalled the pilgrimage through the wilderness. The ingathering of fruits prophesied of the spiritual harvest." Valling's Jesus Christ, p. 133." (Easton's Bible Dictionary)

According to Dr. Stephen Jones: "After giving the Law to Israel, God sent them to Kadesh-Barnea, where they sent twelve men to "spy out the land." When they returned, the spies unanimously agreed that it was a good land to inherit. However, ten of them brought a message of fear, insisting that they would be unable to conquer the land. Caleb and Joshua, on the other hand, had faith that God would give them the land and urged the people to cross the Jordan as God had commanded.

The people then wanted to stone them! Caleb and Joshua escaped being stoned only because the glory of God frightened the people. That "decision day" was the 50th Jubilee from Adam. (See our book, Secrets of Time.) It should have been a day of rejoicing and gladness, a day of blowing the trumpet as the signal for every man to come into his inheritance (Lev. 25:13). Because they refused to enter the land, having no faith, this day came to be commemorated as the Day of Atonement, a day of mourning, fasting, and repentance. If Israel had followed the recommendation of Caleb and Joshua, they would have actually entered Canaan five days later on the first day of Tabernacles. This festival was a seven-day period representing the time of the conquest of Canaan. (When Israel did finally cross the Jordan 38 years later, it took six years to subdue the Canaanites; in the seventh year the land was divided up among all the tribes and families of Israel. In other words, it was seven years from the Jordan Crossing to the Inheritance.)

A detailed study of the feasts leading up to the Feast of Tabernacles can be found in our longer book, The Laws of the Second Coming. Studying these things shows that there is more to salvation than just the spring Feasts of Passover and Pentecost. The fall feasts deal with the final perfection of man. It is meant to portray man's true inheritance in the land.

The Promised Land: The Promised Land is NOT in heaven, but on earth. Canaan was a land filled with "giants" and "enemies" of God who had to be conquered and destroyed. It is common knowledge in many circles that these "giants" represent the carnal tendencies of our own flesh, which we are called to subdue and conquer. This is absolutely correct, but the obvious lesson is often missed. *Our bodies are our inheritance.* Like Canaan, our bodies are presently inhabited with lawless and ungodly desires that rule us. This has been the case ever since Adam, whose sin sold us all into bondage. God had formed Adam from the dust of the ground. His flesh was made of earth (Heb. adama), and hence he was named after the ground from which he came. This glorified flesh was his inheritance. But through sin, Adam incurred a "debt" that he could not pay. So he was sold into bondage to the earth (Gen. 3:17-23) until such time as a near Kinsman would come to redeem him. Adam lost the wonderful, glorified body which had been clothed in the light of God. After his sin, he was naked and ashamed, and God clothed them with coats of skins (Gen. 3:21). The whole idea behind God's plan of salvation is to reverse the effects of Adam's sin upon creation. The law and the prophets from Genesis to Revelation show us how man is redeemed and how he regains the glorified, immortal body that is his lost inheritance. The feast days inform us of the three steps toward receiving this full inheritance: justification, sanctification, and glorification. We are justified in our spirit, sanctified in our soul, and glorified in our body. The first major pattern of this process of full salvation is found in Israel's wilderness journey under Moses. At Passover, Israel became "the church in the wilderness" (Acts 7:38), for they were justified by faith. At Pentecost, Israel was given the Holy Spirit. However, they refused to hear His voice, so they were led, not by the internal witness of the Holy Spirit, but by an external pillar of cloud and fire. Even so, they had opportunity to learn obedience. Then if Israel had gone into the Promised Land on the 50th Jubilee, as Caleb and Joshua had recommended, they would have regained the inheritance that had been lost in Adam. That is, they would have been fully glorified, fully changed into His glory as they passed by the ark. They would have exchanged their coats of skins for the "*house which is from heaven*" (2 Cor. 5:2), as Paul put it. They would have been released at that Jubilee from the house of bondage, and every one of them would have returned to his inheritance. They would have inherited far more than a mere piece of real estate in Canaan. But this was not to be, for this was only a pattern. It was not possible for them to inherit the glorified body that side of the cross. Ultimately, they had to settle for a parcel of ground, rather than true and ultimate inheritance. Israel's story tells us that our inheritance is not to be received in heaven as a spirit, but on earth in a glorified body. Our hope, the "Promised Land," is not to forsake the earth and go to heaven, but is "the redemption of our body" (Rom. 8:23). It is to receive the type of body that Jesus had after His resurrection. It is a body that is immortal and glorified. It is a body that has authority in both heaven and in earth, because it has the genes from both realms, even as Jesus Himself did." (The Barley Overcomers, Dr. Stephen Jones)

GLORY TO GOD!

December 18

THE FEASTS OF THE LORD - PART 5

CONCLUSION

In conclusion, it is imperative that we understand that the feasts of the Lord symbolize the GREAT SALVATION PROCESS as it pertains to individuals and the human race as a whole. In order for God to be all in all (everything to everyone) it is necessary for all to come to the saving knowledge of Who He is and what He has accomplished. This is our salvation. Remember...It is to be carried out in three phases. The failure of many Christians to see that salvation is a process is surely due to those in leadership positions in the body of Christ (for many ministers do not understand or preach that salvation is a process). Instead, they teach God's people to come to an altar to say a "sinner's prayer", after which they are told that they are completely saved, being (at that moment) in full possession of their salvation. All they have to do now is wait until they die and "fly away" to their mansion in the sky (in the sweet by-and-by), unless they happen to get "raptured" first. This type of teaching continually produces spiritual infants who never graduate to the meat of God's Word, but continually stay on the milk of the Word.

The apostle Paul encountered this very thing, which is recorded in 1st Corinthians 3:1-3. It states...And I, brethren, could not speak unto you as unto spiritual, but as unto carnal, even as unto babes in Christ. I have fed you with milk, and not with meat: for hitherto you were not able to bear it, neither yet now are you able. For you are yet carnal: for whereas there is among you envying, and strife, and divisions, are you not carnal, and walk as men?...

To the degree that we do not understand the spiritual implications of the feasts of the Lord, to that degree will we remain in spiritual immaturity, not going into the fullness of God. Many Christians are content to remain in a thirtyfold (Passover) experience with God, but there are some with ears to hear that crave to press into the sixtyfold (Pentecost) and the hundredfold (Tabernacles). The scriptures also speak of these three standings in God in 1st John 2:13. It speaks of:

1. LITTLE CHILDREN
2. YOUNG MEN
3. FATHERS

1st Corinthians 4:15 states…For though you have ten thousand instructors in Christ, yet have you not many fathers: for in Christ Jesus I have begotten you through the gospel…Unfortunately, there are not many in Christendom who can be classified as spiritual fathers, but thank God for the few we have. Those who are fathers most certainly understand the implications of…

THE FEASTS OF THE LORD!

December 19

WISE AS A SERPENT

Matthew 10:16 states…Behold, I send you forth as sheep in the midst of wolves: be therefore wise as serpents, and harmless as doves…

Those who are truly sent to preach the gospel are characterized as sheep going forth in the midst of wolves. As well, we are told to be wise as serpents, and harmless as doves. Let us consider this metaphoric statement that comes from the lips of Jesus. Jesus speaks of: SHEEP, WOLVES, SERPENTS, AND DOVES.

The servants of the Lord who are truly sent forth with the message of truth in their mouths are characterized as sheep. They are to be seen as such, for they are to go forth in meekness, being willing to lay down their lives for the cause of Christ. This can be seen from 2nd Timothy 2:24,25 as the apostle addresses Timothy. It states…And the servant of the Lord must not strive; but be gentle unto all men, apt to teach, patient, In meekness instructing those that oppose themselves; if God peradventure will give them repentance to the acknowledging of the truth…

As we go forth as sheep, we will find ourselves in the midst of ravenous, religious, and self-righteous wolves. These "wolves" are Christians who are ever learning, but never coming to the knowledge of the truth. They point their fingers at others, constantly quoting scriptures to bring condemnation, having absolutely no idea of the true meaning of the scriptures that they quote. These are the very people that we must approach in meekness and in wisdom.

As we look at the times in scripture that Jesus found Himself dealing with the religious hypocrites of His day, we will see and understand why He told us to be wise as serpents. Jesus referred to the Pharisees, Sadducees, and scribes as SERPENTS. In order to deal with a serpent we must be as wise as that serpent. The only difference is that we are to be as harmless as a dove. Those who would be considered Pharisees in this day and age are no different. They mean to harm the people they are attacking with their venom of self-righteousness. They seek to make others look foolish, while they themselves look to gain the praises of men, especially in public.

On the other hand, the true servant of God is meek, being just as wise as the serpent that he is dealing with. He means the serpent no harm. His only true goal is to correct the serpent in love.

THAT IS THE TRUE LOVE OF GOD!

December 20

WISE WITH YOUR PEARLS

Matthew 7:6 states…Give not that which is holy unto the dogs, neither cast your pearls before swine, lest they trample them under their feet, and turn again and rend you…

When sharing with people the mystery of the gospel it is absolutely critical that we strive to be led by the Spirit. Those who truly have insight into the purpose and plan of God must use wisdom in their dealings with others. If God has entrusted you with a knowledge of the mysteries of His Kingdom, then you must learn how and when to distribute these mysteries. To have the SPIRIT OF WISDOM AND REVELATION IN THE KNOWLEDGE OF GOD is to be spiritually rich! How a person handles these riches is of extreme importance. We must discern when it is time to speak and when it is time to be silent.

1st Corinthians 4:12 states…Let a man so account of us, as of the ministers of Christ, and stewards of the mysteries of God. Moreover it is required in stewards, that a man be found faithful…So…As we can see, we have been given mysteries from God. These mysteries are holy and should be likened unto pearls or riches. There are some people who are ready to receive of these mysteries. OTHERS ARE NOT! We must (by the Spirit) discern where someone is at in the Lord, for there are definitely times and situations to hold back certain information from certain people. The person may not be ready for strong meat. In this situation, it would be the same as casting your pearls before swine, or taking that which is holy and giving it to the dogs. This is why the servant of the Lord must not strive; but be gentle unto all men, apt to teach, patient, in meekness instructing those that oppose themselves…

With all this in mind, this in no way means that we should be afraid to speak forth the message of the Kingdom of God, or that it is wrong to speak things that we know will be controversial to our listeners. It simply means that we are to use wisdom, being led by the Spirit of God. For example, you should not give your car keys to a ten-year-old and tell them it is alright to drive the family car. It is not wrong for you to desire for them to learn how to drive, but the timing is not right. They are not ready for obvious reasons. Let us be good stewards of the…

MYSTERIES OF GOD!

December 21

AVOIDING DEBATES

There are times when debating over doctrine and scripture is profitable, but for the most part it is not. Proverbs 26:21 states…As coals are to burning coals, and wood to fire; so is a contentious man to kindle strife…The word "contentious" means: one who creates disagreement or is argumentative. The Bible teaches us to avoid these types of people and situations. 2nd Timothy 2:23

states…But foolish and unlearned questions avoid, knowing that they do gender strifes…Titus 3:9 states…But avoid foolish questions, and genealogies, and contentions, and strivings about the law; for they are unprofitable and vain…1st Corinthians 3:3 states…For you are yet carnal: for whereas there is among you envying, and strife, and divisions, are you not carnal, and walk as men?…2nd Corinthians 12:20 states…For I fear, lest, when I come, I shall not find you such as I would, and that I shall be found unto you such as you would not: lest there be debates, envyings, wraths, strifes, backbitings, whisperings, swellings, tumults…

Unfortunately, there are people who love to debate. Their very purpose is to go about causing strife. The sad part is that they actually think they are doing something good for the Kingdom of God. This type of debating is not profitable, for it causes divisions (denominations). If the goal of your debating is to prove that you are right, then your debating is in vain. IT IS BASED ON A WRONG MOTIVE! Someone might ask the question, who is right? The answer is…NO ONE! GOD ALONE IS RIGHT! ALL WE CAN DO IS DISCOVER (OR HAVE REVEALED TO US) THAT WHICH IS RIGHT. When we approach our conversations with others with this type of attitude (humility), we will be much more effective in bringing across whatever aspect of the Kingdom of God that we are talking about.

This is not to say that it is wrong to debate or passionately discuss the scriptures, but it must be centered around a quest for truth. Those who constantly debate just to prove to others that they are right are NOT BEING LED BY THE LOVE OF GOD! People who have a contentious spirit do much more damage with their words than they do good. A contentious person also muddies the waters for those who are truly sincere in their efforts to rightly divide the Word of truth. It is much harder to convince people of the goodness and love of God after they have been turned off to it by IMMATURE Christians who use the sword of the Spirit (the Word of God) to chop people to pieces. LET US GROW UP IN GOD! Before people care what you know, they want to…

KNOW THAT YOU CARE!

December 22

TEN REASONS NOT TO BELIEVE THE TEACHING OF ETERNAL TORTURE

#1 - IT IS NOT TRUE

The Bible clearly teaches us to study to show ourselves approved (2nd Timothy 2:15). Unfortunately, VERY FEW actually take this advice to heart. Not only do most Christians not study the Bible, THEY DO NOT EVEN READ THE BIBLE! As a matter of fact, most would have a hard time trying to find Genesis 1:1. Most believers in Christ base their belief system off of what everyone else believes. In other words, THEY ARE GOING TO GO WITH THE FLOW! Since they do not study or even read the Bible, they are trapped into having to believe what others (pastors) tell them about God. Most that do study and read the Bible, study and read with their minds already made up, having been deceived by their embracing of the traditions and doctrines of men. Christians, for the most part, are INTOXICATED with going to church, having church, and playing church. They are more concerned about what outfit they will wear, how big and pretty the building is that they are going to, how many members are in the church, how many degrees the pastor has, how good the singing is, if there is a children's program, how well the pastor preaches (performs), and where they are going to eat lunch afterwards. This cycle is repeated over and over again, causing Christians to remain in a trance, not being able to understand the truth about God.

When a person hears the voice of God and is awakened from the trance of organized religion, then, and only then, can he begin to discern for himself what is true and what is tradition. The Spirit of God then leads that person to study the scriptures. After that, the spirit of wisdom and revelation in the knowledge of God begins to flood that person's spirit, soul, and body, leading and guiding them into all truth.

The teaching of eternal torture is a lie! IT IS THE GREATEST LIE EVER TOLD!!! For those who are still under the trance of playing church, they will surely be offended by these statements, but those with ears to hear will follow up on what is being said in this teaching. IT WILL TAKE SOME COURAGE TO SEEK TO BE SET FREE FROM ORGANIZED RELIGION! AS WELL, **YOU WILL BE PERSECUTED (BY CHRISTIANS)!** It will take many hours of study, prayer, and being honest with yourself and God. God will bring you to the place where you begin to pray for truth. He will have you to pray, asking Him to show you not what you want to see, but what is true. As you ask, seek, and knock, your Heavenly Father will give you what you ask for. He will give you...

THE TRUTH!

December 23

TEN REASONS NOT TO BELIEVE THE TEACHING OF ETERNAL TORTURE

#2 - THE BIBLE DOES NOT TEACH IT

It is not the goal of our Creator to torture any of His created beings forever. This will become clear as one reads and studies the Bible from Genesis to Revelation. The "hell" that is taught by Evangelical Christianity IS NOT THE "HELL" OF THE BIBLE. The words "Sheol", "Hades", "Gehenna", and "Tartaroo" (the four words translated as "hell" in the King James Version) DO NOT in any way denote a physical location where God plans to quarantine people for the purpose of torturing them forever in literal fire. They do however speak of the grave, the fiery correction of God (spiritually speaking), and the corrective judgments of God, BUT THEY DEFINITELY DO NOT SPEAK OF A PHYSICAL LOCATION THAT IS PREPARED FOR THE PURPOSE OF TORTURING PEOPLE FOREVER!

In addition to this, the Bible teaches that man's torment (period of severe trial and testing) and God's judgments are age-lasting ("aionios"...of the ages), and that they are for the purpose of

CORRECTION. They are not eternal or everlasting. The King James translators did a very poor job in their translation of the words "olam", "aion", and "aionios", which refer to the AGES OF TIME, but not eternity. These words ("olam", "aion", and "aionios") speak of things that take place within the ages of time (God's purpose of the ages), but they certainly do not mean or refer to eternity. **The strongest meaning that they can possibly have is one of belonging to eternity, but not lasting through it.** We must also understand that there is a difference between eternity and time. "Eternity" is not time that goes on forever, but it is TIMELESSNESS. Something that is eternal has no beginning and no end, such as God Himself. The Bible, when speaking of God, mainly refers to Him as the God of the ages ("aionios"). This in no way negates the fact that He is eternal, for He is the GOD OF THE AGES AND THE GOD OF ETERNITY. HE IS BOTH! HE BELONGS TO THE REALM OF TIME AND ETERNITY.

After studying what the Bible actually teaches about "hell" and the "ages", a person will be well on their way to seeing right through the false teaching of eternal torture. The reason that most people do not know that this teaching (eternal torture) is false stems from: The negative power of the traditions and doctrines of men, the ability of the organized church to instill the fear of eternal torture in people, and that people (for the most part) do not read and study the Bible for themselves. In fact, most Christians are absolutely CLUELESS as to what the Bible actually teaches on many subjects.

It will take some courage to begin the journey of seeking to know the God of the Bible for yourself. You will most certainly be persecuted (especially by Christians) for this courageous effort, BUT FEAR NOT, for your reward is the assurance that...

GOD IS THE SAVIOR OF <u>ALL</u> MEN!

December 24

TEN REASONS NOT TO BELIEVE THE TEACHING OF ETERNAL TORTURE

#3 - IT GOES AGAINST THE CHARACTER AND NATURE OF GOD

According to J. Preston Eby: "When we speak of God's attributes we may say, and many do, that God is a Spirit, infinite, eternal and unchangeable in His being, wisdom, power, holiness, justice, goodness and truth. This is a very beautiful definition; but it largely defines only God's attributes, whereas the text, "God is Love," tells us WHAT HE HIMSELF IS. This text reveals His nature, His state of being. For instance, in speaking of justice, we know that God has justice as one of His attributes, but He is not justice; God IS love. This fact gives us a revelation of GOD'S VERY NATURE. This brings us face to face with the great central message of the Bible which is a message of love. We need to remember that the Personage about whom the Bible is written IS LOVE - a Being Whose very nature is love." (<u>God Is Love</u>, J. Preston Eby)

The teaching of eternal torture goes against the character and nature of God. If God is love, then how can we so confidently teach that he is going to torture billions forever? How could we not call Him a hypocrite for doing such a thing? JESUS TOLD US TO LOVE OUR ENEMIES, BUT HE IS GOING TO TORTURE HIS FOREVER??? He taught us that we must learn to forgive, yet He will never forgive anyone who has rejected Him in this life???

According to J. Preston Eby: "Even the hardest, cruelest, most brutal men cannot *torture* their fellow men for more than two or three hours without growing weak, faint, and sick (see Fox Book of Martyrs). However, Christian leaders teach that our Lord will *torture* His victims through endless ages. The scripture reveals that Christ Jesus is the *kindest, the most tender-hearted and merciful Person* this world has ever known. His mercy endures forever, or to all generations of time. The doctrine of eternal torment pictures Him to be the *most horrible monster, the most beastly, brutal, cruel, vicious Person this world has ever known.* The governments of this world, ruled by unregenerated men, put their rebels in prisons, and the very worst offenders they put to death. But our Lord Jesus Christ, the Creator and Redeemer of the world, will mercilessly *torture* those who offend Him to the most hideous and incomprehensible degree. Surely, this pagan and Romish doctrine of eternal torture does NOT glorify HIM!" (The Law Of Circularity, J. Preston Eby)

As you begin to meditate on the love of God, you will see in your heart that the TEACHING OF ETERNAL TORTURE IS NOT TRUE! **IF IT WERE TRUE, THEN JESUS IS A MILLION TIMES MORE VICIOUS AND VINDICTIVE THAN HITLER!** It is impossible for God to torture someone forever, for it goes against His character and nature. It is contrary to Who He is, for…

GOD IS LOVE!

December 25

TEN REASONS NOT TO BELIEVE THE TEACHING OF ETERNAL TORTURE

#4 - IT DECLARES THE CROSS OF JESUS CHRIST AS AN ABSOLUTE FAILURE

According to J. Preston Eby: "It is estimated that about one hundred and sixty billions of human beings have lived on the earth in the six thousand years since Adam departed from Eden. Of these, the very broadest estimate that could be made with reason would be that less than five billion were saints of God. This broad estimate would leave the immense aggregate of one hundred and fifty-five billions (155,000,000,000) who went down into death without faith and hope in the only name given under heaven or among men whereby we must be saved. Indeed, the vast majority of these never knew or heard of Jesus, and could not believe in Him of Whom they had not heard. What, I ask, has become of this vast multitude, of which figures give a wholly inadequate idea? What is, and is to be, their condition? Did God make no provision for these, whose condition and circumstances He must have foreseen? Or did He, from the foundation of the world, make a wretched and merciless provision for their hopeless, eternal torment, as many of His children claim?" (The Law Of Circularity, J. Preston Eby)

If what Evangelical Christianity teaches about eternal torture is true, then that means that almost every person (well over 95%) who has ever lived will be tortured forever. What does it say about God if 155,000,000,000 of the 160,000,000,000 people who have ever lived will be tortured forever? Could we call this a victory? Could we still call God all-powerful? Could we still say that God is love? Could we still call Jesus the Savior of the world? NO! NO! NO! NO!

THE HORRIBLE TEACHING OF ETERNAL TORTURE IS A SLAP IN THE FACE OF THE LOVE AND POWER OF GOD! This teaching would cause us to come to the conclusion that the saving effort of the Lord Jesus Christ (His death, burial, and resurrection) WAS AN ABSOLUTE FAILURE! We know that Satan was able to deceive Eve, causing Adam to fall, bringing down the entire human race. If the Lord Jesus Christ was only able to save about 3% of the human race, then who would be declared as the winner? Well…SATAN OF COURSE! Most people have never thought about what was just said. They just keep on believing something (eternal torture) that does not glorify God and is not scriptural. BUT THANK GOD THAT THIS HORRIFIC TEACHING IS NOT TRUE!

The scriptures declare to us in 1st Corinthians 15:22-28…that in Adam ALL DIE, even so in Christ shall ALL BE MADE ALIVE. **BUT EVERY MAN IN HIS OWN ORDER…THAT GOD MAY BE ALL IN ALL!!!** The power of God's love is eternal! Its glory is supernal! HIS LOVE GOES BEYOND THE HIGHEST STAR…

AND REACHES TO THE LOWEST HELL!

December 26

TEN REASONS NOT TO BELIEVE THE TEACHING OF ETERNAL TORTURE

#5 - THE MAJORITY OF THE EARLY CHURCH FATHERS DID NOT TEACH IT

(The following is an excerpt from: The Power Of Life And Death In A Greek Four Letter Word-- Aion, Gary Amirault)

According to Gary Amirault: "Many orthodox Christian historians acknowledge that the majority of the early church did not teach eternal torment. A couple of examples: Geisler- "The belief in the inalienable capability of improvement of all rational beings, and the limited duration of future punishment was so general in the West, and among the opponents of Origen, that it seems entirely independent of his system." (Eccles. Hist., 1-212). (Origen has been accused of bringing into the church the heresy of the salvation of all. Geisler points out the belief was prevalent even apart from Origen's influence.) The German theologian and historian Johann Christoph Doerderlin writes: "In proportion as any man was eminent in learning in Christian antiquity, the more he cherished and defended the hope of the termination of future torments." Professor and historian Henry Oxenham informs us that the, "Doctrine of endless punishment was not believed at all by some of the holiest and wisest of the Fathers, and was not taught as an integral part of the Christian faith by any, even of those who believed it as an opinion." Historian Pfaff says:

"The ultimate restoration of the lost was an opinion held by very many Jewish teachers, and some of the Fathers." Dietelmaier: "Universalism in the fourth century drove its roots down deeply, alike in the East and West, and had very many defenders." Reuss: "The doctrine of a general restoration of all rational creatures has been recommended by very many of the greatest thinkers of the ancient church, and of modern times." (Hist. De la Theol. Apost.). **Prior to Augustine in the 5th century, the vast majority of Christians, including the leadership, believed in the Salvation Of All Mankind through Jesus Christ.** St. Basil the Great (c. 329-379) in his De Asceticis wrote: "The mass of men (Christians) say that there is to be an end of punishment to those who are punished." St. Jerome (342-420): "I know that most understand the story of Nineveh and its King, the ultimate forgiveness of the devil and all rational creatures." The Christian leader most instrumental in bringing in the damnable heresy of eternal torment, Augustine, admits himself that "There are very many (imo quam plurimi, which can be translated majority) who though not denying the Holy Scriptures do not believe in endless torments." (Enchiria, ad Laurent. c.29) Imagine, the champion of the doctrine of eternal torment admitting out of his own mouth that as late as the 5th century many or the majority of believers did not believe in eternal torment and he said they did not deny the scriptures in believing so. **Of the six theological schools known to the early church, 4 taught the Salvation Of All, one taught annihilation, and only one taught eternal torment.** The Greek word *aion* was not used to mean eternal in the early church writings. The President of the Second Ecumenical Council of Constantinople in 381, St. Gregory of Nazianzus, was an outspoken Universalist, that is, he believed in the Salvation Of All Mankind Through Jesus Christ. Would the church designate a heretic as its head at such an important meeting? When Emperor Justinian finally declared the teaching of the Salvation Of All as heresy, he used the word "ateleutetos" to describe "eternal punishment," not *aionion* which is the Biblical term. If *aionion* meant "eternal" why didn't he use it? He didn't because it didn't mean eternal! Many writings are still preserved from the early Christian bishops which clearly show they did not teach eternal torment. To mention just a few: Clement Alexandrinus, Gregory Thaumaturgus, Ambrose, Titus of Bostra, Diodore of Tarsus, Isidore of Alexandria, Origen, Theodore of Mopsuestia, St. Gregory of Nazianzus, etc. When studying the lives of the early leaders, **those embracing the Salvation Of All clearly showed much more love and fruit in their lives than those who taught eternal torment.** Compare Origen and St. Gregory of Nyssa with Tertullian and Cyprian. If the doctrine of the Salvation Of All was heresy, why didn't the church declare it as such until the church entered the dark ages? **Could it be that when the pagan doctrine of eternal torment entered the church, this very doctrine brought about the gross darkness which the church plunged into?** It was not until the church left the Greek text and went to the Latin Vulgate Text that large numbers began to believe in eternal torment. That was because Jerome mistranslated those very words we have just been talking about. The Latin Vulgate perpetuated the error. As long as the church primarily used the Greek Text, it taught the Salvation Of All Mankind. As late as the 16th century lexicographers such as Phavorinus knew that *aion* was just a time word. But he also noted where the idea of changing the meaning came from. He writes, "*Aion*, time also life, also habit, or way of life. *Aion* is also the eternal and endless as it seems to the theologian." **Here we see where the deception came from, the theologian!**" (Gary Amirault)

So…If you believe in the Salvation Of All Mankind through Jesus Christ…

YOU ARE IN GOOD COMPANY!

December 27

TEN REASONS NOT TO BELIEVE THE TEACHING OF ETERNAL TORTURE

#6 - THE SCRIPTURES TEACH THE SALVATION OF ALL MEN

The Bible is the story of the fall and rise of the human race. It depicts all as going into Adam. As well, it depicts all as going into Christ in the dispensation of the fullness of times. Many are not aware that the Bible teaches that the same ALL that went into Adam will eventually go into Christ. As you approach the Bible with this mindset you will begin to see this theme from Genesis to Revelation. The teaching of the salvation of all men (through the Lord Jesus Christ) will literally jump off the pages of the Book (the Bible). It has always been there, but many are not able to see it due to the fact that their consciences have been seared with a hot iron by the teaching of eternal torture. It is difficult to see the truth when we approach the Bible with our minds already made up.

According to Hannah Whitall Smith: Hannah Whitall Smith testified in her book (The Christian's Secret Of A Happy Life) how that she came to understand this great truth… "Immediately the whole Book seemed to be illuminated. On every page the truth concerning the "times of restitution of all things," of which the apostle Peter says "God has spoken by the mouth of all His holy prophets since the world began," shone forth and no room was left for questioning. I turned greedily from page to page of my Bible, fairly laughing aloud for joy at the blaze of light that illuminated it all. It became a new Book. Another skin seemed to have been peeled off every text, and my Bible fairly shone with new meaning. I do not say with a different meaning, for in no sense did the new meaning contradict the old, but a deeper meaning, the true meaning hidden behind the outward form of words. The words did not need to be changed; they only needed to be understood; and now at last I began to understand them." (Hannah Whitall Smith)

There are actually hundreds of scriptures that testify of THIS GREAT TRUTH. Here are a few to consider:

Genesis 12:3 / Genesis 18:18 / Psalm 22:27-29 / Psalm 65:2 / Psalm 66:3,4 / Psalm 72:8-11 / Isaiah 25:7,8 / Isaiah 45:22-25 / Luke 2:10 / John 12:32 / Acts 3:21 / Romans chapter 5 / Romans 11:26-36 / 1st Corinthians 15:22-28 / 2nd Corinthians 5:18-21 / Ephesians 1:9-11 / Philippians 2:10,11 / Colossians 1:16-20…

KEEP DIGGING!

YOU WILL FIND HUNDREDS MORE!

❖

December 28

TEN REASONS NOT TO BELIEVE THE TEACHING OF ETERNAL TORTURE

#7 - IT POINTS TO A VICTORIOUS DEVIL, AND TO SIN AS FINALLY TRIUMPHANT OVER GOD

According to Thomas Allin: "THE question of Universalism is usually argued on a basis altogether misleading, i.e., as though the point involved was chiefly, or wholly, man's endless suffering. Odious and repulsive to every moral instinct, as is that dogma, it is not the turning point of this controversy. **The vital question is this, that the popular creed by teaching the perpetuity of evil, points to a victorious Devil, and to sin as finally triumphant over God.** It makes the corrupt, nay, the bestial in our fallen nature to be eternal. It represents what is foulest and most loathsome in man, i.e., the most obstinate sin as being enduring as God Himself. It confers the dignity of immortal life on what is morally abominable. It teaches perpetual Anarchy, and a final Chaos. It enthrones Pandemonium as an eternal fact side by side with Paradise; and, gazing over its fetid and obscene abysses, is not afraid to call this the triumph of Jesus Christ, this the realization of the promise that God shall be "All in All"." (<u>Christ Triumphant</u>, Thomas Allin)

Could we come to any other possible conclusion than this? How could it be said that God is victorious over the Devil, sin, death, hell, and evil if the majority of all the people ever born will never be delivered from these vices? How can these things co-exist as long as God Himself in light of the plain declaration of scripture that declares that **God shall be all in all (everything to everyone)**? We would be left with no other conclusion than to declare evil as victorious over good. THE POWERS OF DARKNESS WOULD BE ABLE TO FOREVER GLOAT DUE TO THEIR VICTORY! They would be able to claim that they were able to take over 97% of God's creation, bringing them into an eternal nightmare of torture.

SEARCH YOUR HEART! SEARCH THE SCRIPTURES! If you are honest with yourself and the scriptures you will surely begin to see the ABSOLUTE STUPIDITY of the teaching of eternal torture. THERE IS NO WAY TO DECLARE THAT GOD IS BOTH ALL IN ALL AND THE GOD OF ETERNAL TORTURE AS WELL. These two thoughts drastically oppose one another. It is not possible for both of these statements to be true. Either the apostle Paul was lying when he said that God would be all in all (1st Corinthians 15:28), or Evangelical Christianity is lying in declaring that the vast majority of the human race will be tortured forever. I would rather believe the inspired words of the apostle Paul than to side with the lie of Evangelical Christianity. If this teaching (eternal torture) is a lie, which it is, then we should reject it no matter how many people believe it.

THAT SETTLES IT!

December 29

TEN REASONS NOT TO BELIEVE THE TEACHING OF ETERNAL TORTURE

#8 - ETERNAL TORTURE IS UNJUST!
THE PUNISHMENT DOES NOT FIT THE CRIME!

According to George Hawtin: The following words by George Hawtin are most challenging: "The established visible church has preached its multiplied sermons seeking to prove its tradition that the vast majority of God's human creation will be LOST, finally, irrevocably, and eternally, and not only will they be lost to God forever and ever, but they will be given up to the most sadistic, inhuman, ungodly torments that could be devised only by the vilest fiends. According to the tradition of the church this hellish torment is to fall upon all who do not believe. It matters not a whit whether they had opportunity to believe or not. It matters not at all if they were born in the darkest jungles of Africa, the swamps of Borneo, or the deserts of India or China. The fact that they never heard there was a God will be no excuse whatever. The fact that they never heard that God had a Son will not impede their dreadful destruction. Heathen who never heard that God had a Son are, according to this teaching, faced with the same dreadful doom as men who heard the gospel from their birth and yet rejected it. To add to the stupidity of their teaching they make pitiful attempts to prove that this is the justice of God and that God is manifesting His love in the punishment of sin. The doctrine of eternal punishment is based on a literal interpretation of some of the metaphors of scripture, to the complete neglect of many other scriptures. No doctrine has ever been propounded with more confidence and greater bitterness nor with a grossness and coarseness more hideous and repugnant, and, in the face of the love and kindness of God, more inconceivable and incredible." -end quote (<u>According To The Purpose</u>, George Hawtin)

To eternally punish a person for 70, 80, or even 100 years of crimes (sins) is an UNJUST PUNISHMENT. Not only is it unjust, but it is INSANE! Not only is it unjust and insane, but it is also a punishment that WOULD NEVER SERVE ANY PURPOSE other than to be **vindictive, spiteful, and barbaric in nature**.

The scriptures teach that THE JUSTICE OF GOD IS FOR THE SINNER, INSURING HIS SALVATION, NOT AGAINST HIM, DEMANDING HIS CONDEMNATION. Exodus 22:5 states...If a man shall cause a field or vineyard to be eaten, and shall put in his beast, and shall feed in another man's field; of the best of his own field, and of the best of his own vineyard, shall he make restitution...This law, when applied spiritually to the entire creation, makes God responsible to make a restitution of all things, FOR GOD MADE THE BEAST (THE SERPENT OF GENESIS 3:1), setting him in the field (the Garden of Eden, the world, or the beast nature that is in man) to feed (devour). This is why God was responsible to send the best of His own vineyard (His only begotten Son) to make a restitution of all things (Acts 3:21).

IT WOULD BE UNJUST FOR GOD TO ETERNALLY TORTURE THE VERY HUMAN BEINGS THAT HE CREATED! IT WOULD BE UNJUST ACCORDING TO HIS OWN LAW (Exodus 22:5)! It would especially be unjust due to the fact that God created all things (good and evil) and subjected the creation to vanity (**not willingly**). As a result of this we are all born with a nature (the sin nature) that is contrary to the nature of God. This does not mean that man is not accountable to God for his actions, but it surely does mean that it would be extremely unjust for God to torture him (man) forever.

THANK GOD FOR HIS JUSTICE!

December 30

TEN REASONS NOT TO BELIEVE THE TEACHING OF ETERNAL TORTURE

#9 - IT PRODUCES IMMATURE CONVERTS WHO ARE MOTIVATED TO SERVE GOD OUT OF FEAR RATHER THAN LOVE

The false teaching of eternal torture is a message of fear. IT IS NOT ONE OF LOVE! Not only is that teaching a message of fear, but it breeds fear in the lives of all who embrace it. In other words, it causes a person to continually live in fear of eternal torture at all times. I guess you could call it…"the good news of fear"…It is ironic, but nevertheless, Christianity refers to their message as good news. How could it be good news to tell someone…You better get right or God is going to torture you forever??? HOW IS THAT GOOD NEWS? WELL…IT'S NOT! IT IS BAD NEWS! IT IS VERY BAD NEWS! **IT IS NOT THE GOSPEL OF JESUS CHRIST! IT MAY BE THE GOSPEL OF CHRISTIANITY, BUT ONCE AGAIN, IT IS NOT THE GOSPEL OF JESUS CHRIST!**

The Bible does speak of the "fear of the Lord", but this "fear" pertains to a reverence and awe for God, not a fear of being tortured forever. 2nd Timothy speaks of the fear that Evangelical Christianity promotes. It is referred to as "the spirit of fear". 2nd Timothy 1:7 states…For God has not given us the spirit of fear; but of power, and of love, and of a sound mind…Does the teaching of eternal torture produce power, love, and a sound mind? NO! IT PRODUCES WEAKNESS, HATE, AND CONFUSION. Modern day Christianity could be characterized as weak, hateful, and confusing. It is unfortunate to have to say these things, but nevertheless, they are true.

Now…Are you ready for some GOOD NEWS? 1st John 4:18,19 states…There is no fear in love; but perfect love casts out fear: because fear has torment. He that fears is not made perfect in love. We love Him, because He first loved us…THIS IS THE GOSPEL OF JESUS CHRIST! Jesus did not come to destroy men's lives, but to save them. He did not come to bring condemnation, but to bring redemption. He did not come to bring hate, but love. He is not the author of eternal torture, but of eternal salvation.

Man must understand that he was born (placed) into vanity, a perished condition, and death (the carnal mind). When the scriptures declare that God is not willing that any should perish, it is this that is being spoken of. He is not willing that any should remain in their fallen condition. IT IS THIS CONDITION THAT HE CAME TO SAVE US OUT OF. As we come to understand this, we should not serve Him because we are afraid of eternal torture, BUT BECAUSE HE FIRST LOVED US, SAVED US, FORGAVE US, AND DELIVERED US FROM…

THE WAGES OF SIN!

December 31

TEN REASONS NOT TO BELIEVE THE TEACHING OF ETERNAL TORTURE

#10 - THE WAGES OF SIN IS DEATH, NOT ETERNAL TORTURE!

It is AMAZING that the majority of Christians continue to teach eternal torture. This is done despite what the Bible teaches about the **love** of God. Romans 6:23 states…For the wages of sin is death; but the gift of God is eternal life through Jesus Christ our Lord…I thought that the wages of sin was eternal torture? Well…Isn't it? That is what Evangelical Christianity teaches…doesn't it?

Preachers have gotten so comfortable with teaching eternal torture that they do not even use the scriptures to do so. When they do use the scriptures, they quote a scripture and then teach something else that does not line up with the scripture that they just quoted. For example, how many times have you heard someone use Romans 6:23 (the wages of sin is death) to support their belief in eternal torture. This scripture has nothing to do with being tortured in a literal hell or flying off to a mansion in the sky after you die. People have become masters at TWISTING SCRIPTURES TO MAKE THEM FIT THEIR DOCTRINAL BELIEFS. Someone who is interested in rightly dividing the Word of truth will not do that. The correct approach is to use the Holy Scriptures as the guideline for forming correct and proper doctrinal beliefs, not trying to make the scriptures fit your doctrinal beliefs.

If the wages of sin is eternal torture, then Jesus would have to be eternally tortured to pay the price for the sin of the world. THIS ONE THOUGHT IN AND OF ITSELF IS PROOF THAT THE TEACHING OF ETERNAL TORTURE IS A LIE! If the wages of sin is death, then Jesus did pay the price for the sin of the world in being made flesh, overcoming all things, dying on the cross, and being raised again on the third day. He experienced the spiritual aspect of death (the carnal mind) and the physical aspect of death (His crucifixion).

Thank God that the wages of sin is not eternal torture, for if it were then our Lord Himself would need to be tortured forever in order to deliver the human race. Can you begin to see how ridiculous that teaching (eternal torture) is?

In conclusion, let us summarize the reasons that the teaching of eternal torture is to be discarded as false…It is not true…/ The Bible does not teach it…/ It goes against the character and nature of God…/ It declares the cross of Jesus Christ as a failure…/ The majority of the early church did not teach it…/ The scriptures teach the salvation of all men…/ It points to a victorious Devil, and to sin as triumphant over God…/ It is unjust…/ It produces immature converts who are motivated to serve God out of fear rather than love…/ The wages of sin is death, not eternal torture…

It has been my privilege to serve all who have taken the time to read this daily devotional. May the Father give you the spirit of wisdom and revelation in the knowledge of Him! Remember…GOD IS LOVE! HE LOVES ALL! GOD IS ALL-POWERFUL! HE CANNOT FAIL! HE WILL NOT FAIL! HE IS…

THE SAVIOR OF THE WORLD!

Thomas Kissinger

The following people are quoted in this daily devotional. The days on which they are quoted are listed after their name. If the quote came from a specific book, article, or work it is listed after the quote.

Abbott, Louis: April 2, September 3, November 27

Adams, A. P.: January 15, March 17, 19, April 2, September 9, 10, 23, October 2, November 28

Addair, George: February 21, September 24, October 3

Allen, Dr.: August 5

Allin, Thomas: January 2, 12, December 28

Amirault, Gary: January 20, 22, February 6, March 21, April 15, June 10, August 4, 7, 22, 23, 24, 25, 26, November 29, December 6, 26

Ayto, John: June 10

Barclay, William: January 21, February 17

Beecham, Robert: June 18, 21

Bonacorso, Randy: September 4, 13, November 14

Britton, Bill: January 16, February 1, 26, March 16, May 14, September 5, October 17, 18, 25, 27, 28, 29, November 1, 2, 3

Bullinger, Dr. E. W.: March 10, 11, July 2, 5

Burgess, Robert: July 21

Burrows, Millar: June 11

Calder, Derek: June 8

Campbell, Dr.: August 6

Chapman, Dr.: August 5

Clarke, Dr. Adam: August 3

Clement of Alexandria: January 2

Coverdale, Miles: March 25, June 11

Eby, J. Preston: January 14, February 2, 22, April 7, 22, May 27, 29, 30, 31, June 1, 3, 4, 5, July 22, August 8, 10, 14, 17, 18, 19, September 7, 15, 16, 17, 19, 21, November 30, December 1, 8, 11, 24, 25

Eckerty, Ken: April 16

Ellefson, Lloyd: December 10

Evely, Bob: July 28

Farrar, Canon: August 11

Firbairn, Dr.: August 5

Fox, Emmet: May 20

Gavazzoni, John: April 10, September 29, November 10

Gregory of Nyssa: January 2, 8

Hanson, J. W.: March 9, August 2, 3, 5, 6, 9, 10, 11

Hawtin, George: March 22, June 24, 30, September 6, 7, December 29

Hurley, Dr. Loyal: February 10, March 7

Jones, Dr. Stephen: February 25, March 14, April 5, 12, 21, June 2, 17, July 13, 14, 15, 16, 17, 18, 19,

October 1, 14, 15, 16, November 18, December 9, 14, 15, 16, 17

Kirk, Joseph E.: May 24, August 21

Knight, Ray: February 13, March 28, April 29, June 22, September 14, 18, 20, November 24

Knoch, A. E.: May 24

Le Clere: August 6

Lehman, Frederick: June 20, April 9

Leigh, Edward: August 5

Lincoln, Abraham: February 12

Lovelace, Dr. Harold: January 7, February 20, March 3, 12, 15, April 8, May 18, June 23, July 11, 20, October 1, November 8, December 7

MacDonald, George: June 12

Martin, Ernest L.: August 24, 25, 26

Milan, S. Ambrose: January 6

Newman, Keith: June 22

Origen: January 2, March 9

Pope, Alexander: April 12

Pridgeon, Charles: June 16

Prinzing, Ray: March 1, 2, June 25, 26, 27, 28, 29, July 1, 2, 3, 4, 5, 6, 7, 8, 9, 10

Reid, C. Gary: August 24, 25, 26

Roach, Elwin: May 21

Rotherham, Joseph: April 28

Rutz, Jim: July 20

Scarlett, Nathaniel: January 13, August 20

Skinner, Otis: December 10

Slagle, Charles: November 4, 6, 7

Smith, Hannah Whitall: March 30, December 27

Smith, L. Ray: August 27

Stuart, Prof.: August 5

Telford, Andrew: September 27, 28

Thayer, Dr.: August 5

Thayer, Thomas B.: November 5

Universalist Christian's Association: June 19

Vanderburg, Judy: April 20

Varner, Kelley: May 31

Weymouth, Dr. R. F.: August 23

Whitby, Rev. Dr.: August 5

Zender, Martin: September 22

ORDER FORM FOR

THE GLORY OF GOD
& THE HONOR OF KINGS

Send this form, a photocopy of this form or a letter containing the information requested below to:

Straightway Publishing Company
P.O. Box 45212 #261
Baton Rouge, LA. 70895

Enclose a check or money order for $19.95 + $5.50 for shipping and handling (total invoice amount is **$25.45**), payable to Straightway Publishing Company.

Fill in name and address where the book is to be shipped:

Name:_____

Address:_____

City:_____ State:_____ Zip:_____

In case of questions concerning your order, please give your phone number and Email address:

Telephone:_____

Email address:_____

If you have any questions, Straightway Publishing Company can be reached by calling (225) 766-0896.
If this book is unsatisfactory for any reason you may return it for a full refund.

❖   **www.hearingthetruthofgod.com**   ❖

Lightning Source UK Ltd.
Milton Keynes UK
UKOW05f1543260116

267147UK00003B/146/P